§ *William Penn and the Founding of Pennsylvania 1680–1684*

EDITOR

# Jean R. Soderlund

GENERAL EDITORS

## Richard S. Dunn

## Mary Maples Dunn

ASSOCIATE EDITORS

## Richard A. Ryerson

## Scott M. Wilds

Philadelphia 1983
UNIVERSITY OF PENNSYLVANIA PRESS
HISTORICAL SOCIETY OF PENNSYLVANIA

# William Penn
# and the Founding
# of Pennsylvania

## 1680-1684

## A Documentary History

Copyright © 1983 by the University of Pennsylvania Press
All rights reserved

Library of Congress Cataloging in Publication Data
Main entry under title:
William Penn and the founding of Pennsylvania, 1680-
    1684.
    Bibliography: p.
    Includes index.
    1. Penn, William, 1644-1718. 2. Pennsylvania— History
— Colonial period, ca. 1600-1775— Sources. I. Soder-
lund, Jean R., 1947-
F152.2.W53      1983      974.8'02      82-60306
ISBN 0-8122-7862-3

Printed in the United States of America


Designed by Adrianne Onderdonk Dudden

Maps by Quentin Fiore

The weather vane reproduced on the title page and part title pages stood on top of the first grist mill on Chester Creek, which was built by WP, Samuel Carpenter, and Caleb Pusey. Though it dates from WP's second visit to Pennsylvania in 1699, it evokes two themes already apparent during the founding years. The crown and scepter symbolize WP's proprietary power, while the initials of Carpenter and Pusey are reminders that many colonists cooperated in making Pennsylvania an economic success. Historical Society of Pennsylvania.

*To Pennsylvanians of All Centuries*

Preparation and publication of this tercentenary edition was made possible by a major grant from the Pew Memorial Trust.

Distribution of this volume to libraries throughout the Commonwealth of Pennsylvania was supervised by the Pennsylvania Department of Education.

# Acknowledgments

The editors are deeply grateful to the following for permitting us to publish documents from their collections: the American Philosophical Society, Philadelphia; the Bedfordshire Record Office, Bedford, England; the Bodleian Library, Oxford University; the Office of the Register of Deeds, Bucks County Court House, Doylestown, Pennsylvania; the Chester County Historical Society, West Chester, Pennsylvania; the Research Center of the Colonial Williamsburg Foundation, Williamsburg, Virginia; the Darlington Memorial Library, University of Pittsburgh, Pittsburgh, Pennsylvania; the Hall of Records, Dover, Delaware; the Historical Society of Delaware, Wilmington; the Historical Society of Pennsylvania, Philadelphia; the Library Company of Philadelphia; the Library of Congress, Washington, D.C.; the Library of the Religious Society of Friends, London; the Maryland Historical Society, Baltimore, Maryland; the Pierpont Morgan Library, New York City; the Philadelphia Monthly Meeting of the Religious Society of Friends; the Bureau of Archives and History, Pennsylvania Historical and Museum Commission, Harrisburg; the Public Record Office, London; the Rosenbach Museum and Library of Philadelphia; the Tulane University Library, New Orleans, Louisiana; and Owen Wynne, Warwickshire, England.

We are equally grateful to the following for permitting us to illustrate this volume with portraits, manuscripts, artifacts, and maps from their collections: the Enoch Pratt Free Library, Baltimore, Maryland; the Quaker Collection, Haverford College Library, Haverford, Pennsylvania; the Historical Society of Pennsylvania; the Library Company of Philadelphia; the National Portrait Gallery, London; the Bureau of Archives and History, Pennsylvania Historical and Museum Commission, Harrisburg; the Philadelphia City Archives; the Philadelphia Museum of Art; and Owen Wynne, Warwickshire, England.

We are particularly indebted to Mrs. Ginny Thornburgh for the interest she has shown in this volume. Sharing our belief that William Penn's papers belong in the hands of the people of Pennsylvania, she encouraged us to prepare this collection of documents on the founding of our state. We publish this volume to commemorate Pennsylvania's three-hundredth birthday. We are also deeply grateful to the Pew Memorial Trust for its generous and public-spirited grant which has supported the preparation and publication of this book and its distribution to high school, college, and public libraries throughout the Commonwealth of Pennsylvania.

This tercentenary volume is part of a larger series, *The Papers of William Penn,* sponsored by Bryn Mawr College, Haverford College, the Historical Society of Pennsylvania, and the University of Pennsylvania—all participants in the Philadelphia Center for Early American Studies. In preparing this tercentenary volume we have drawn most of our documents from Volume Two of our scholarly edition, but we have edited these documents in a decidedly different style (see the Editorial Method). We are very appreciative to the following for their generous grants to *The Papers of William Penn:* the National Endowment for the Humanities, the National Historical Publications and Records Commission, the American Philosophical Society, the Atlantic Richfield Foundation, the Barra Foundation, the Historical Foundation of Pennsylvania, the McLean Contributionship, the Philadelphia Yearly Meeting of the Religious Society of Friends, the PQ Corporation, Adolph G. Rosengarten, Jr., and the Yarway Foundation.

A special word of thanks is due to James E. Mooney, Director of the Historical Society of Pennsylvania, and to the members of the Society staff. They provided the editors with attractive working space and congenial company, free access to the Society's manuscript and book collections, and expert help whenever needed. We also wish to thank Marianne S. Wokeck, the newest Associate Editor of *The Papers of William Penn,* and Lucy Kerman, a fellow of the Philadelphia Center for Early American Studies, for their editorial assistance in annotating the documents. Joseph Casino, also a fellow of the Philadelphia Center for Early American Studies, and Marjorie George helped with modernizing the texts. Patricia Wells did the index, and Janet Greenwood did the copy editing. Adrianne Onderdonk Dudden designed the book, and Quentin Fiore designed the maps. Clyde M. McGeary, Chief of the Division of Arts and Humanities, Pennsylvania Department of Education, has supervised the distribution of this volume to libraries throughout the state. A final note of thanks goes to Walter Heppenstall and Barton L. Craig at the Winchell Company, and to Maurice English, Malcolm Call, Ingalill Hjelm, Carl Gross, and their colleagues at the University of Pennsylvania Press for their close cooperation in producing this volume.

# Contents

# Illustrations and Maps

§ *William Penn and the Founding of Pennsylvania 1680–1684*

*William Penn in Armor, Artist Unknown, HSP. This portrait is a late-eighteenth-century copy from a lost original. The date on the background, 14 October 1666, was WP's twenty-second birthday. He became a Quaker the following year.*

# Introduction

ON 5 March 1681, one day after receiving his royal charter for Pennsylvania, William Penn wrote that he believed God would make his colony "the seed of a nation." Penn certainly did not envision a nation resembling the present-day United States. The world he knew was a small-scale, preindustrial one: in 1681 England, his native country, had only one-third the population of modern Pennsylvania. WP (as he will be referred to from this point on) could never have anticipated the industrial revolution that brought steel mills and factories to the state he founded, nor could he have imagined the continental expansion that carried the American people from one ocean to another. WP had a different, but no less extraordinary, objective in mind. He wanted his Pennsylvania to be a land where people of differing languages and customs could live together, where men and women could worship as they pleased, where free men could participate fully in their government. Such a land, WP believed, would indeed be blessed by God. He proceeded toward his objective with great boldness and vigor, as we will see in many of the documents that follow.

WP was thirty-five years old in May 1680, when he petitioned Charles II, King of England, for a grant of land in America. Though there is little explicit evidence in his papers to suggest why he became interested in planting a colony in the New World, WP's efforts to reform the society in which he lived, Restoration England, began early in his life. WP was the son of a prominent English admiral, Sir William Penn, who served in the navy of Charles II and worked closely with the king's brother, James, Duke of York. In the 1640s and 1650s Admiral Penn had served the Commonwealth government (which overturned the English monarchy in the civil war of the 1640s), but he changed sides and supported the restoration of Charles II in 1660. Penn expected WP to prepare for a position suitable for the son of an admiral. In 1660 he therefore sent WP to Christ Church College at Oxford University. Less than two years later, however, WP was expelled for publicly criticizing the ceremonies of the established Church of England. After the king's restoration, this Anglican church was the only church to which English men and women could legally belong. Thus in his late teens, WP was already questioning the authority of the church in which he grew up and in doing so was challenging the right of his government to tell him what to believe and how to worship. Admiral Penn reacted to WP's expulsion from Oxford University in a way that we might expect of an upper-class, seventeenth-century Englishman: he sent his son to France in the hope that he would come to his senses and prepare to live, work, and worship within the established social order. Admiral Penn's strategy apparently met with some success, for according to the gossipy diarist Samuel Pepys, WP returned to London in 1664 dressed in French garb and having an "affected manner of speech and gait." In 1665 WP began to study law at Lincoln's Inn. Still, he had not yet given up his search for a life of sober, quiet Christianity, for in 1667, while he was in Ireland on business for his father, he became a Quaker.

Joining the Society of Friends was a daring move. Most English men and women of the time thought it was outrageous for anyone, let alone the son of an admiral, to take up with the despised followers of George Fox. The early Quakers were extreme radicals, in a social as well as a religious sense. They believed that God communicates directly with each individual, who receives the Inner Light or Truth, and they attempted to live as Christ taught by practicing equality, simplicity, and peace. The Quakers considered most aspects of the Christian tradition irrelevant: they had no need for ritual, for the sacraments, for an ordained clergy; and while they venerated the Bible, they believed that the Scriptures were not infallible. The Quakers also challenged many social traditions: they refused to fight wars or swear oaths or recognize social superiors; hence they did not bow or curtsy, they kept their hats on before kings and magistrates, and they addressed all persons as "thee" or "thou." And the Quaker style of silent, spontaneous worship totally repudiated the customs and beliefs of the established Church of England. WP's convincement to Quakerism was therefore a bold step indeed. From 1667 on, his life changed dramatically. Soon after he joined the Friends, he was arrested in Ireland, was turned out of the house by his father, and was jailed three more times in England during the next four years.

WP's conversion quickly propelled him into public life as a controversialist, religious leader, writer, and lobbyist. From 1668 he was regularly in the public eye. When he and a fellow Quaker, William Mead, were brought to trial in 1670, the case became a landmark in English legal history because the jury refused to reach the verdict directed by the judge and found them innocent. During the 1670s, WP wrote numerous religious tracts, traveled through England, Holland, and Germany on missionary journeys, and defended the Quakers against critics of many religious stripes. He became part of the inner circle of the Society of Friends, and with George Fox, George Whitehead, Alexander Parker, and other Quaker leaders, repeatedly petitioned Parliament for religious toleration. WP's first experience with colonization came in the mid-1670s when he helped promote Quaker settlement in West New Jersey.

WP never explained why he asked the king for a province in America. His correspondence and writings from the late 1670s give no hint that he was headed in that direction. However, a number of the documents included in this volume give us some ideas about his objectives in founding Pennsylvania. WP effectively summed up his intentions in a letter he wrote to two English officials shortly after he arrived in Pennsylvania in 1682, saying "the service of God first, the honor and advantage of the king, with our own profit, shall I hope be [the result of] all our endeavors" (doc. 48).

Of his three stated purposes, WP's efforts to serve God and to turn a profit for himself come through most clearly in the documents that follow. On 25 August 1681, WP wrote to James Harrison that he was founding Pennsylvania as "a holy experiment" (doc. 19). He wanted to establish a tolerant, moral society in which no one would be persecuted for his or her beliefs and in which the inhabitants would be free to make their own laws and to live as "sober and industrious people" (doc. 13). But just as clearly, WP expected to earn enough money from selling land in Pennsylvania to get himself out of debt and to secure his financial future. Though the Society of Friends preached simplicity as one of its spiritual goals, WP never abandoned his upper-class status, and he always appreciated the "good life." WP's financial accounts from the 1670s show that he lived well beyond his means. He ordered oysters and scallops by the barrel and enjoyed other delicacies such as salmon, sturgeon, partridges, larks, saffron, and chocolate. He bought three coaches in the years 1672-1674, and in 1676 he acquired at considerable cost his large estate at Warminghurst, Sussex, which required numerous servants to maintain. WP sold over a thousand acres of his wife Gulielma's land in an attempt to cover his debts, but in the late 1670s he continued to spend more money than he collected in rents from his English and Irish lands. Thus when he decided to petition the king for land in America, WP was badly in need of a fresh source of income. But the acquisition of Pennsylvania proved to be a serious disappointment for him in this respect. Though he sold over 700,000 acres of Pennsylvania land between 1681 and 1685, and collected over £9000 (in modern currency, more than a million dollars), these land sales did not bail him out of debt (see in particular doc. 41, below). Indeed his financial condition worsened as he absorbed many of the administrative costs of governing the province and had little success in collecting his quitrents, or annual taxes, on the land he sold in Pennsylvania.

This volume is an edition of the most important documents that describe WP's founding of Pennsylvania. It begins with his petition to the king in May 1680 and ends with his departure for England in August 1684. The editors have assembled a collection of letters, orders, petitions, charters, laws, pamphlets, maps, constitutional drafts, legislative journals, newspaper articles, memoranda, deeds, and other business records designed to illustrate all aspects of our topic. We have chosen 101 documents. Eighty-eight of these have been previously published in Richard S. Dunn and Mary Maples Dunn, editors; Scott M. Wilds, Richard A. Ryerson, and Jean R. Soderlund, associate editors, *The Papers of William Penn, Volume Two, 1680-1684* (Philadelphia: University of Pennsylvania Press, 1982). In that volume, WP's letters and papers are presented in seventeenth-century form and style so as to preserve WP's eccentric spelling and punctuation, his insertions and deletions, and his slips of the pen. In this present volume, the documents are presented quite differently. Texts have been modernized and occasionally abridged to allow easier reading, and the annotation has been considerably streamlined. More than half of the documents printed in *The Papers of William Penn,* Volume Two, have been eliminated from the present volume, and thirteen new documents, specially chosen for this volume, have been added. These new documents include WP's first promotional tract advertising his colony, newspaper articles reporting WP's departure for America in 1682, the minutes of the first two-house session of the Pennsylvania General Assembly, a census of early Swedish inhabitants of Philadelphia County, and letters by emigrants from England, Wales, and Germany detailing their experiences in crossing the Atlantic and beginning life in the New World.

The 101 documents in this volume are arranged in twelve sections, designed to illustrate the principal stages through which WP passed as he planned and supervised the settlement of his province. Within each section, headnotes introduce individual documents or groups of documents, and supply a running commentary upon WP's activities and other events in early Pennsylvania. Footnotes identify the more important persons and places, and clarify obscure passages in the documents. The maps locate most places mentioned in the text. The glossary defines technical terms, and readers who want further information will find a list of suggested supplementary books and articles.

From the documents presented in this volume, we can see how WP's plans were altered as he worked to obtain his patent, conferred with fellow Quakers and associates in selling land and devising the *Frame of Government,* disputed the boundary between Maryland and Pennsylvania with Lord Baltimore, and bargained with the early settlers of Pennsylvania and Delaware in establishing the provincial government. Docs. 1-10 describe WP's negotiations with the royal government between May 1680 and March 1681 over the terms of the Pennsylvania charter (doc. 11). Many key details are missing, but the documents provide evidence that WP asked the king for large powers and that he had to lobby hard in order to get most of what he wanted. He started with an ambitious design modeled on the Maryland charter of

1632, which had given the proprietor of that colony, Lord Baltimore, almost absolute authority. The English political climate was quite different in the early 1680s than it had been fifty years earlier, however. The crown was moving to control the American colonies more tightly, and, in fact, it would soon revoke the patents of the most independent colonies. WP therefore ended up with a patent that gave the proprietor considerably less power than he desired. But considering that the English government detested WP's religion and his political principles, the Pennsylvania charter was a remarkable achievement.

⚹Once WP obtained title to 45,000 square miles of American real estate, he spent the next year and a half, from March 1681 to August 1682, advertising his colony, recruiting settlers, selling land, planning the government, and preparing for his own departure for Pennsylvania. All of these activities are illustrated in this volume. WP's correspondence with Robert Turner, James Harrison, and Robert Barclay (docs. 12, 16, 19, 25) exhibits his techniques for selling land and recruiting colonists. His first promotional pamphlet, *Some Account of the Province of Pennsylvania* (doc. 15) reveals his talents as an advertiser. By the summer of 1682 he had sold half a million acres, and had persuaded several hundred First Purchasers to join him in America. Docs. 17, 22, and 24 present WP's blueprint for distributing lands and for staking out his capital city of Philadelphia.

WP's most important activity during the year and a half before he departed for Pennsylvania was to prepare his colony's constitution. He and his associates wrote an extraordinary series of draft constitutions (and critiques of constitutions); docs. 26, 27, and 29 are the most important and representative of these drafts. WP started out with a very liberal plan, the Fundamental Constitutions of Pennsylvania, in which the people not only elected their delegates to the Assembly but also gave them specific instructions. The legislature, in turn, was empowered to instruct the governor and Council. WP scrapped this plan, however, and began drafting a completely new constitution. The ultimate *Frame of Government* (doc. 30) that WP published in May 1682 still called for a popularly elected legislature and reserved surprisingly little power to the governor. But the people lost the right to instruct their representatives, and the popular Assembly lost power to the smaller Council. A number of WP's associates, including Algernon Sidney (doc. 28), Benjamin Furly (doc. 31), and Jasper Batt (doc. 54), criticized WP for abandoning his original plan. When WP convened his first two assemblies in Pennsylvania, the colonial legislators insisted on revising the *Frame;* nevertheless the second *Frame,* passed by the Assembly in April 1683, preserved the basic character of WP's constitution (doc. 63).

During the spring and summer of 1682, about two thousand settlers left the British Isles for Pennsylvania (docs. 38, 42). In August 1682 (docs. 39-41, 43), WP himself boarded ship. The focus of our story now shifts from

England to America. Docs. 45-53 report WP's arrival in Pennsylvania and supply much information about his initial organization of local and provincial government. Doc. 56 discusses the founding of Philadelphia; doc. 81 marks the surveying of Germantown. Docs. 37 and 68 illustrate WP's early Indian treaties. In his correspondence with officials in England, WP reported enthusiastically on the rapid growth of Pennsylvania (see docs. 48 and 71). In 1683 WP wrote his fullest and liveliest description of the new colony: his *Letter to the Free Society of Traders* (doc. 76). Another two thousand settlers arrived in 1683. The choicest land along the Delaware and Schuylkill rivers was now all taken up, and WP began to plan for expansion westward along the Susquehanna River (see docs. 72, 78, and 82).

All of this cheerful progress was undermined, however, by a destructive quarrel between WP and his neighbor to the south, Lord Baltimore, over the Pennsylvania-Maryland boundary line. In 1681 WP had supposed that the 40th degree of latitude, the southern boundary specified in his charter, lay as far south as the present site of Baltimore, Maryland. His original scheme of settlement, illustrated by his promotional *Map of Pennsylvania* (p. 80), was to draw settlers into the upper Chesapeake Bay as well as up the Delaware River, and so he wrote to the planters of northern Maryland (doc. 20), welcoming them to his jurisdiction. Lord Baltimore was understandably angered by this tactic, especially when he discovered that the 40th degree actually runs forty miles further north than WP supposed, through the Frankford section of present-day Philadelphia. The two proprietors had several fruitless meetings in 1682-1683 (docs. 64 and 67), and when Baltimore could not persuade WP to join him in taking a joint observation of the 40th degree, he laid claim to what is now the state of Delaware (docs. 67, 69, and 75). WP had obtained title to the so-called lower counties (now Delaware) from the king's brother, James, Duke of York, in 1682, but the duke's own right to this territory was uncertain, and the area was included within the Maryland patent. If Baltimore made good his challenge, WP would lose control of the Delaware River, and his new colony would be crippled, if not ruined.

The boundary dispute had two profound effects on WP's plans: it obligated him to integrate relatively large numbers of non-Quakers into his government and to make the changes in his policies that they demanded; and it required him to return to England in August 1684 to appeal to the crown against Lord Baltimore, leaving the colony without his personal leadership. From the moment he arrived on the *Welcome* at New Castle on 28 October 1682, WP worked to obtain and keep the allegiance of the lower county residents. Unlike the Quaker settlers to whom he had sold land in Pennsylvania, these people had no commitment to WP or his "holy experiment." WP sought the Delawareans' loyalty by confirming their titles to occupied lands and by offering them full participation in his government. He convened an Assembly at Chester in December 1682 in which representatives from Delaware met with representatives from the three new counties in Pennsylvania. This Chester Assembly, which was almost evenly divided between Quakers and non-Quakers, passed an Act of Union between Delaware and Pennsylvania and an Act of Naturalization which extended the rights of Englishmen to all foreigners who took an oath of allegiance to the king of England and to WP (see docs. 50 and 53).

During March and April 1683, WP had to work hard to conciliate the councilors and assemblymen from Delaware and Pennsylvania who met in his first two-house legislative session (see doc. 62). He accepted a revised *Frame of Government* (doc. 63) which reduced the number of representatives to the Provincial Council and Assembly, protected the right of foreigners to own land, and extended fishing and hunting privileges. The Assembly, or lower house, also tried, but failed, to gain the power to initiate legislation. Meanwhile WP made a crucial mistake by charging the residents of Delaware higher quitrents than he demanded from people in Pennsylvania. Lord Baltimore took advantage of the discontent created by this policy by offering lower taxes to Delaware residents who would transfer their allegiance from WP. By the spring of 1684 Kent County, Delaware, was in revolt. By sending in an expeditionary force that built a fort at Christiana Bridge in central New Castle County (docs. 87, 93-94), the Maryland proprietor instigated an outright border war. WP now had no choice but to return to England and appeal against Lord Baltimore. And as he prepared to leave, his Quaker colleagues within Pennsylvania began to murmur against him. In particular, they criticized his allocation of land. By the summer of 1684, some of the leading citizens of Philadelphia were lodging formal protests with the proprietor (doc. 96).

WP's departure in 1684 (docs. 97-101) and his prolonged absence from Pennsylvania severely damaged his effort to guide the colony. Under his personal supervision, the old and new settlers had come together under one government, and WP had been able to integrate their desired changes with most of the important elements of his first *Frame of Government* to create a new, workable constitution. WP's return to England to settle the Maryland-Pennsylvania border, however, left his young colony without proper leadership and vulnerable to factions and strife. Within ten years after WP's departure, the colony was rocked by a religious schism and fierce political rivalries; a decade later the lower counties separated from Pennsylvania and established their own Assembly.

WP, then, was the architect of Pennsylvania, but not its sole builder. He contributed the vision of a model society that would guarantee religious liberty, extend governmental privileges to all freemen, and preserve the Quaker ideals of consensual harmony and strict morality. He instilled the drive to make the colony a commercial success. But WP had to work with others, first to acquire Pennsylvania and then to nurture its growth. In drawing up WP's patent, English officials guarded the interests of the king. First Purchasers bargained for better terms in buying land, and associates debated with him over the principles on which his *Frame of Government* should be based. In America, the non-Quakers from Delaware made WP's province less of a Quaker commonwealth than he had expected. And settlers like William and Jane Yardley, Edward Jones, James Claypoole, and Francis Daniel Pastorius contributed their own hard work and ingenuity toward building the colony (docs. 38, 42, 44, 58, 85, and 89).

We cannot be sure whether WP was pleased with his province by the time he left it in the summer of 1684. His early letters of 1682–1683 abound with vibrant descriptions of the land and its people. To Governor Thomas Culpeper of Virginia he wrote, "I like it so well that a plentiful estate and a great acquaintance on the other side have no charms to remove, my family being once fixed with me; and if no other thing occur, I am like to be an adopted American" (doc. 55). WP was concerned that non-Quakers would gain too much power in Pennsylvania, but as he told his critic Jasper Batt, he could not prevent them from participating in government (doc. 54). He was willing to yield more on issues of politics than of property. When the First Purchasers challenged his method of distributing land, he insisted on retaining his policies (doc. 96).

It is impossible to know if WP would approve of present-day Pennsylvania and the nation to which it belongs. Certainly he would be pleased that several of his principles have endured, in theory if not always in practice. From its inception, Pennsylvania incorporated people of many different nationalities, allowed freedom of worship, offered wide participation in government, and fostered decent relations between Europeans and Indians (and somewhat later in the colonial period, Afro-Americans). Nevertheless, WP had hoped for more: he wanted a society in which the inhabitants would live in peace with one another and with people in neighboring colonies, would work toward common goals without conflict, and would avoid immorality and vice. By the time he departed for England in August 1684, WP knew that this utopia would never be.

# Editorial Method

THE editors of this volume have modernized the texts of the seventeenth-century documents, in order to make them understandable for twentieth-century readers. In the 1680s, when WP and his colleagues composed these documents, word choice, spelling, capitalization, and punctuation were far different from current standards. The authors of these texts often marked them up heavily or crossed out what they wrote; for examples of how several of our texts look in their manuscript form, see the illustrations on pp. 38, 70, and 94. Readers who wish to study these documents in their original form and style, including blemishes and errors, will find 88 of our 101 documents in *The Papers of William Penn* (*PWP*), Volume Two. For an example of a document presented in this literal style, see WP's draft letter to Charles II (doc. 74A, below). In the present volume, we have removed deletions and errors, modernized spelling and capitalization, and changed punctuation whenever necessary to clarify meaning. Provenance notes at the end of each document provide information on the manuscript or printed source, and give page references for those documents published in *PWP*, Volume Two.

Our editorial rules for this volume may be summarized as follows:

1. Most documents selected for publication in *William Penn and the Founding of Pennsylvania, 1680-1684* are printed in full. When the text is abridged, this fact is mentioned in the headnote and ellipses ( . . . ) are used in the text to indicate where material is missing.

2. Each document is numbered, for convenient cross-reference, and is supplied with a short title.

3. The format of each document (including the salutation and complimentary closure in letters) is presented as in the original text, with the following two exceptions. Addresses, endorsements, and docketing have been omitted; the reader should consult *PWP*, Volume Two, for this information. If a document is undated, an initial date line is supplied [within square brackets]. If a document is dated at the close but not at the opening, an initial date line is supplied, and the closing date line removed.

4. The dating of documents poses a further editorial problem. English men and women in WP's lifetime employed the Julian, or Old Style, calendar, which was ten days behind the Gregorian, or New Style, calendar used by most continental Europeans — and adopted by the English and Americans in 1752. Seventeenth-century English men and women started the new year officially on 25 March, but since 1 January also had currency as New Year's Day, some writers double-dated for the period 1 January to 24 March. In addition, the Quakers employed their own designations for months and days. They numbered the months, with March being the first month and February the twelfth. They also numbered the days of the week, with Sunday being the first day and Saturday the seventh.

In this edition, we have standardized the dating of each document. When a document is dated in Quaker form, a "heathen" translation of the month is supplied. When a document written between 1 January and 24 March is dated according to the previous year, a "modern" translation of the year is supplied. Thus a letter that WP dated "25th 6mo 81" (doc. 19) is rendered 25 August 1681, and a minute of the Philadelphia Monthly Meeting dated "the 9th day of the 11th month being the 3d day of the week in the year 1682" (doc. 52) is given the date line 9 January 1683. Otherwise, the Old Style calendar is retained. For example, in doc. 11, the date of the Pennsylvania charter, 4 March 1681, is not changed to 14 March, the Gregorian, or New Style, date for the charter.

5. The text of each document is presented as follows:

a. Spelling is modernized and Americanized; capitalization is standardized.

b. Punctuation and paragraphing are changed whenever necessary to enhance understanding; texts have not, however, been made to conform to modern standards of punctuation.

c. Words or phrases deleted from the text by the author of the document are omitted.

d. Contractions and abbreviations are expanded. Superscript letters are lowered to the line and expanded as necessary.

e. English pounds sterling are represented by the £ sign.

f. The editors have inserted words into the text [within square brackets] to clarify meaning and to eliminate the need for numerous footnotes. Thus a reference to "G. F." is rendered as "G[eorge] F[ox]," and "the bay" is changed to "the [Chesapeake] Bay."

g. Blanks in the manuscript, missing words, tears, and illegible words are rendered as [blank] or [missing word] or [torn] or [illegible word]. If a missing word can be supplied, it is inserted in the text. If the supplied word is conjectural, it is inserted [within square brackets] followed by a question mark.

6. Immediately following each document, a provenance note supplies the following information:

      a. A symbol indicating the nature of the document: such as ALS or Draft. See the Abbreviations, p. 399, for the explanation of these symbols.

      b. A reference to the source of the document: such as the library or archive where the original is located, or the book where the best surviving transcript is located. See the Abbreviations, p. 399, for the symbols used to identify the chief depositories.

      c. A page reference to *The Papers of William Penn,* Volume Two, is given as (*PWP,* 2:   ).

# A William Penn Chronology, 1680–1684

&

1680 *c. May.* Petitions Charles II for a colony in America.
   *June.* Crown officials begin their consideration of WP's petition.

1681 *January-February.* Crown officials draft the charter for WP's colony.
   *4 March.* Receives his charter to Pennsylvania.
   *14 March.* Son William Penn, Jr. (1681-1720) is born.
   *April.* Appoints William Markham as deputy-governor of Pennsylvania.
   Writes *Some Account of Pennsylvania,* his first advertising pamphlet.
   *Spring-summer.* Begins work on his constitution for Pennsylvania.
   *June.* Begins lobbying to secure the lower counties (Delaware) from the duke of York.
   *July.* Announces his plan of land distribution in Pennsylvania.
   *July-August.* Publishes a *Map of Pennsylvania.*
   Takes his first land selling trip to Bristol.
   *August.* His deputy-governor arrives in Pennsylvania.
   *16 September.* Writes to planters in Maryland, claiming the northern quarter of that colony.
   *September-October.* Sees his first settlers and land commissioners off to Pennsylvania.
   *October.* Writes a letter of friendship to the chiefs of the Delaware Indians.

1682 *January-April.* WP and Thomas Rudyard complete the first constitution and laws for Pennsylvania.
   *February-March.* The Free Society of Traders founded.
   *c. 1 March.* His mother, Lady Margaret Penn, dies.
   *25 April-5 May.* Publishes his *Frame of Government* and *Laws Agreed upon in England.*
   *15 July.* His agents conclude their first deed with the Delaware Indians.
   *24 August.* Receives the deeds to the lower counties (Delaware) from the duke of York.
   *30 August.* Sails for America on the *Welcome.*
   *28 October.* Lands at New Castle, Delaware.
   *29 October.* Visits Chester, Pennsylvania.
   *October-November.* Visits the site of Philadelphia.
   *November.* Visits New York and East New Jersey.

*December.* His first Assembly convenes at Chester.

Meets with Lord Baltimore concerning the Maryland-Pennsylvania boundary dispute.

Twenty-three ships arrive in 1681-1682; the colony grows rapidly.

1683  *January.* Quakers begin meeting in Philadelphia; the Philadelphia County Court is established.

*March.* Visits East New Jersey; begins distributing large numbers of Philadelphia lots.

*10 March-3 April.* His second Assembly approves a revised *Frame of Government.*

*29 May.* Meets with Lord Baltimore at New Castle.

*Spring-summer.* Acquires his country manor Pennsbury, in Bucks County.

*August.* Writes *Letter to the Free Society of Traders.* Francis Daniel Pastorius and Thomas Lloyd arrive in Pennsylvania.

*August-September.* Tries to buy Susquehanna Valley lands from the Iroquois, but is blocked by New York's Governor Thomas Dongan.

*September.* Sends William Markham to England to defend Pennsylvania's boundary with Maryland.

*September-November.* Many ships arrive; both Philadelphia and Pennsylvania continue to expand.

*October.* Germantown surveyed.

*November.* Attempts to collect his quitrents.

1684  *March.* The Welsh Tract surveyed.

*April-May.* Decides to return to England to defend his boundary against Lord Baltimore.

*May.* Lord Baltimore leaves for England.

The Assembly passes an excise tax, which WP suspends.

*July.* Philadelphia's waterfront residents protest WP's city land distribution policy.

*August.* Prepares to leave for England; appoints Thomas Lloyd president of the Provincial Council.

*18 August.* Sails for England from Lewes, Delaware.

*3 October.* Lands in Sussex, England.

# Part I

NEGOTIATING THE CHARTER
FOR PENNSYLVANIA §
MAY 1680 – MARCH 1681

DUM · CLAVUM · TENEAM

William Penn Esq. Proprietor
of Pensylvania. 1703

*WP's Bookplate with Coat of Arms, 1703, HSP.*

IN May 1680 WP was thirty-five years old. He and his wife Gulielma lived with their three young children, Springett, Laetitia, and William, Jr., in a large country house, Warminghurst Place, in Sussex, England. WP was a wealthy man, with estates in England and Ireland worth £2000 per annum —the equivalent of several hundred thousand dollars today—but he was far from being a typical country squire. Following his convincement to the Society of Friends in 1667, he had devoted his time and talent to Quaker causes. He had published fifty Quaker books, pamphlets, and broadsides, and had staged public debates with opponents of every religious persuasion. He had suffered imprisonment and abuse, had taken frequent missionary journeys, and had lobbied with the king, Parliament, and local officials to stop their persecution of Friends. In 1680, although WP was still engaged in these pursuits, he had become occupied with a new objective: the creation of his own Quaker colony in America.

WP had a variety of reasons for wishing to start his own province in America. After a dozen years of strenuous effort, he had failed to bring about what he most wanted in England, a policy of religious toleration. WP had participated in founding the Quaker colony of West New Jersey, and he could draw upon his widespread connections among Friends to recruit colonists from England, Ireland, Wales, and Scotland, and even from Holland and Germany where he had made missionary journeys. WP needed a fresh source of income in 1680. He had contracted over £10,000 in loans during the 1670s, and his Irish and English tenants were defaulting on their rents. By obtaining the proprietorship to an American colony he would be able to expand vastly his service to Quakerism and to the cause of religious and political liberty while enlarging his own property holdings.

When WP applied to the king for his charter, eleven of the thirteen original English colonies had already been founded. Some of them, such as Maryland, were proprietary colonies in which the king had granted hereditary ownership of the land and powers of government to a lord proprietor or a group of proprietors. Others, such as Massachusetts, were corporate colonies in which the king had granted powers of self-government to a company or community of settlers. Only Virginia was a royal colony, administered directly by the king. Between 1675 and 1680 Charles II's ministers had been trying to tighten royal control over the American colonies. They wanted to limit or revoke the independent powers of the proprietary and corporate colonies, to regulate the colonial assemblies, and to appoint royal governors who would strengthen the colonists' military defenses against their hostile French and Indian neighbors. Why then did the royal authorities create a new proprietary colony in Pennsylvania, headed by a pacifist Quaker of liberal political beliefs?

The documents below indicate that WP's personal connections were stronger than the government's imperial policy. WP persuaded the king and the duke to endorse his grant, and at crucial points during the negotiating process, he secured the support of powerful ministers. It is possible that Charles and James endorsed the charter as a way of getting rid of WP and the Quakers; however, it is more likely that the royal brothers saw the Pennsylvania grant as a cheap way of paying off a long-standing debt to WP's father, and an easy way of honoring the memory of Admiral Penn.

The documents printed below take us step by step through the negotiations for a new colony. The major tasks were, first, to determine whether the king was favorably inclined; next, to set the boundaries and rights to territory; and finally, to establish the extent and limits of WP's political authority as proprietor. The land WP asked for was, of course, almost entirely undeveloped from a European point of view, and its potential was only dimly perceived, but ownership of land was the primary source of wealth and status for seventeenth-century Englishmen. The government officials who negotiated with WP clearly understood that issues of sovereignty, power, and empire were at stake.

Because it involved matters of such importance, the process by which WP's charter was negotiated was from the beginning both formal and legal. It is also in a general way easily recognizable today. WP presented a request; it was referred to a committee; the committee asked for the views of those who would be Pennsylvania's neighbors and who were therefore most likely to be affected; and then it asked for expert opinion. Finally, the request was allowed and it received the stamp of approval, or in seventeenth-century terms, it passed the Great Seal. By any standard, the business was accomplished quickly. From the time WP presented his first petition to the day the charter passed the Great Seal, only ten months elapsed, and WP emerged with full title to 45,000 square miles of American real estate, and with governmental powers that permitted the practice of political and religious liberty in Pennsylvania: a remarkable achievement in the English political climate of 1680-1681.

THE first four documents take us through the first stage. Time has not been kind to WP's official petition (doc. 1) for a colony in America—as early as 1735 it was reported that half of it had "worn away." By drawing on what is known about WP's circumstances in 1680 and on specific data in other documents, the editors have attempted to restore the missing portion of WP's text. Version A, below, is the fragment; version B is our conjectural reconstruction. The original fragment makes it clear that WP built his case on the grounds that the crown was indebted to Admiral Penn (for victualing, or providing food supplies for, the navy in 1667, as WP wrote later). A few of Admiral Penn's accounts do exist for the period 1661-1667, but the record is so scanty that little can be said with certainty about the debt that WP parlayed into a province.

We can infer the king's sympathy for WP's petition from the fact that he referred it to his Privy Council, which in turn sent it to the Committee of Trade and Plantations made up of selected members of the Privy Council and usually known as the Lords of Trade (doc. 2). This committee, formed in 1675, supervised the English colonies and was responsible for the preparation of WP's charter for approval by the king and Privy Council.

The first step of the Lords of Trade, good landowning Englishmen, was to consider boundaries. They requested evaluations of WP's proposed boundaries from the agents of Charles Calvert, Lord Baltimore (1637-1715), the proprietor of Maryland. Baltimore was living in Maryland and was thus not available for consultation. His agents tried to protect his interests, but in general were cooperative. Unfortunately, at this time the precise location of the 40th degree of latitude—the northern limit of Maryland—had not been accurately determined. Thus the boundary between Maryland and Pennsylvania became the subject of a bitter dispute that went on for eighty years.

WP's other "neighbor" was James, Duke of York, whose province of New York governed the west bank of the Delaware River. His secretary, Sir John Werden (1640-1716), was anxious to protect his employer's interests (doc. 4), and was not initially cooperative. But James, who liked WP and had little interest in the Delaware Valley, soon agreed that WP could have all territory west of the Delaware twelve miles north of the town of New Castle. Eventually, in 1682, the duke transferred his rights to the rest of the Delaware colony to WP. This was of primary importance to the success of Pennsylvania, because WP could now establish a port city wherever he liked on the west bank of the Delaware and thus lay the foundations for a profitable trade.

# 1 §

## Petition to Charles II

[May? 1680]

A

For the

The Humble Ad

Son to Sir W

Showeth,

That having

in *Ireland* by the oppression of the Lord

decease (though most of it remitted by

to borrow every penny of it, by reason

*England* was under the Stop of the Ex

with the growing interest of it, and 9 ye

for the relief of his own and his mother's

ruin.

He humbly prays that

that princely respect he of

his compassion to the afflicte

*America,* lying *north* of M

River, on the west, limit

extend as far as plantable,

he doubts not by his intere

profitable plantation to the

to raise that speedy and sufficient

encumbrances, that he may

debt of at least £11,000 and be

and time as shall be most

And

Printed transcript. HSP. (*PWP,* 2:30-33).

For the King's Majesty
The Humble Ad dress of William Penn
Son to Sir W illiam Penn,[1] deceased,
Showeth,
That having sought payment for debts due to his father
in *Ireland* by the oppression of the Lord Treasurer, this account was not settled at his father's
decease (though most of it remitted by order of the Ordnance Office), he was forced
to borrow every penny of it, by reason that since the year 1672, His Majesty's Treasury of
*England* was under the Stop of the Ex chequer,[2] so that the debt now amounts to £16,000[3]
with the growing interest of it, and 9 ye ars having passed, the petitioner humbly prays
for the relief of his own and his mother's[4] great debts and otherwise certain
ruin.

He humbly prays that the King's Majesty, out of his Royal Grace and
that princely respect he of old has shown to the petitioner's father, and from
his compassion to the afflicte d, will grant him letters patent for a tract of land in
*America,* lying *north* of M *aryland,* on the east bounded with Delaware
River, on the west, limit ed as Maryland is, and northward to
extend as far as plantable, which is altogether Indian. And
he doubts not by his intere st that he will undertake to render it a
profitable plantation to the crown. And the petitioner further promises
to raise that speedy and sufficient sum of money from this grant to satisfy his
encumbrances, that he may settle his accounts and extinguish his
debt of at least £11,000 and be of such service to His Majesty in this place
and time as shall be most beneficial to the Kingdom.
And he in duty prays, etc.

1. Sir William Penn (1621-1670), admiral, was the son of Giles Penn, a Bristol merchant and mariner, and Joan Gilbert. He joined the Parliamentary Navy during the English Civil War and rose rapidly to become one of the country's most important admirals. In 1660 he supported the restoration of Charles II to the throne and became a close friend of the king's brother, James, Duke of York.

2. In 1672 the king suspended payment of orders from the Exchequer totaling £1,200,000. WP was victimized by this royal bankruptcy because he had apparently secured an order for the settlement of his father's victualing account.

3. WP mentioned this figure years later. An original debt of £11,000 could well have advanced, with interest added, to £16,000 within nine years.

4. Margaret Jasper Vanderschuren Penn (1610?-1682), WP's mother, was the daughter of a Rotterdam merchant. She first married Nicholas Vanderschuren, a Dutch merchant living in Ireland, and after his death married William Penn. Under Admiral Penn's will, she received a life interest in his personal and household goods, and she continued to live on their estate in Essex, paying WP rent for its use.

# 2 §

## Minute of the Committee of Trade

At the Committee of Trade and Plantations
In the Council Chamber at Whitehall[1]
Monday the 14th of June 1680.
Present

Lord President[2]               Bishop of London[4]
Duke of Albemarle[3]            Mr. Secretary Jenkins[5]
                Sir Thomas Chicheley

The petition of William Penn referred by an order from the earl of Sunderland[6] of the first instant[7] is read, praying, in consideration of debts due to him or his father from the crown, to grant him letters patents for a tract of land in America lying north of Maryland, on the east bounded with Delaware River, on the west limited as Maryland, and northward to extend as far as plantable. Whereupon Mr. Penn is called in and being asked what extent of land he will be contented with northerly, declares himself satisfied with three degrees to the northwards;[8] and that he is willing in lieu of such a grant to remit his debt due to him from His Majesty or some part of it, and to stay for the remainder till His Majesty shall be in a better condition to satisfy it.

Upon the whole matter it is ordered that copies of his petition be sent unto Sir John Werden in behalf of his Royal Highness [the duke of York], and unto the agents of the Lord Baltimore; to the end they may report how far the pretensions of Mr. Penn may consist with the boundaries of Maryland or the duke's propriety of New York and his possessions in those parts.

MBE. PRO. (*PWP*, 2:35-36).

1. This palace on the bank of the Thames River at Westminster was the chief royal residence from 1529 until its destruction by fire in 1698.

2. John Robartes (1606-1685), Earl of Radnor and Lord President of the Privy Council, had met WP in Ireland in 1669 and, like WP, had supported toleration of religious groups other than the Church of England as early as the 1660s.

3. Christopher Monck (1653-1688), second Duke of Albemarle. In 1687 he became governor of Jamaica.

4. Henry Compton (1632-1713), Bishop of London. A fierce anti-Catholic, he was relatively tolerant of Protestant dissenters such as the Quakers.

5. Sir Leoline Jenkins (1623-1685), who had just been appointed a principal secretary of state in Apr. 1680.

6. Robert Spencer (1641-1702), second Earl of Sunderland, was the king's other principal secretary of state at this time. He was an old friend of WP and undoubtedly helped to steer WP's petition through the Lords of Trade, but shortly before WP received his charter, Sunderland was dismissed from his post for trying to prevent the duke of York from succeeding his brother as king. Sunderland regained his office in 1683 and served until 1688, when he fled to Holland just before the Glorious Revolution.

7. 1 June 1680.

8. See doc. 75, below, for WP's statement that he originally requested the 45th degree of latitude as his northern border. The grant of three degrees gave him much of what is now New York State. The present Pennsylvania-New York boundary at the 42d degree of latitude was negotiated in the eighteenth century.

# 3 §

## Lord Baltimore's Agents to William Blathwayt

23 June 1680

Sir[1]

In answer to yours in reference to Mr. Penn's petition, some things are thought proper to be offered in respect to the particular concern of my Lord Baltimore, [and] something in reference to the public on his Lordship's behalf.

It is desired that if the grant pass unto Mr. Penn of the land petitioned for by him in America, that it may be expressed to be of land that shall lie north of Susquehanna Fort, and north of all lands in a direct line between the said fort and Delaware River, and also north of all lands upon a direct line westward from the said fort, for that fort is the boundary of Maryland northward.[2] It is further desired that there may be contained general words of restriction as to any interest granted to the Lord Baltimore and saving to him all rights granted. It is also prayed that my Lord's counsel may have a sight of the grant before it pass. On the public account, it is offered that some due caution be provided that no arms, powder, shot, or other ammunition be sold by any that shall settle in this new plantation to the Indians or natives, for thereby a common mischief may happen unto all His Majesty's neighboring plantations. This, with our thanks on my Lord Baltimore's behalf for your care on him, is all at present from

Sir,<br>
Your humble servants,<br>
Barnaby Dunch<br>
Richard Burke[3]

LS. PRO. (*PWP,* 2:36-37).

1. William Blathwayt (c. 1649-1717) was secretary to the Lords of Trade, or manager of the colonial home office, and in this place became one of the most influential men in the English government. His primary accomplishment was to centralize control of the colonies under the Lords of Trade.

2. The northern limit of Maryland was not as clearly defined as Baltimore's agents suggest, and Susquehanna Fort was not the official landmark for the boundary. The Maryland charter of 1632 placed the colony between Watkin's Point on the south and the point at which the 40th degree of latitude intersected Delaware Bay on the north. The chief problem in setting the Pennsylvania-Maryland boundary — which would lead to extended wrangling between the two colonies — was that before 1682 no one knew the actual location of the 40th degree of latitude.

3. Barnaby Dunch was a London merchant who engaged in the tobacco trade with Maryland; he died c. 1681. Richard Burke remained Lord Baltimore's agent as late as Dec. 1683; see doc. 86, below.

# 4 §

## Sir John Werden to William Blathwayt

St. James's,[1] 23 June 1680

Sir

I had answered your letter of the 14th instant sooner, but that my going to Windsor,[2] just when I received it, hindered me then, and also made me think it proper to acquaint the duke [of York] with the contents of it first. What I have now to say is this:

That by all which I can observe of the boundaries mentioned in Mr. Penn's petition, they agree well enough with that colony or plantation which has been hitherto (ever since the conquest of New York by Col. [Richard] Nicolls) held as an appendix and part of the government of New York, by the name of Delaware Colony, or more particularly New Castle Colony (that being the name of a principal place in it, the whole being planted promiscuously by Swedes, Finlanders, Dutch, and English), all which has been actually under the government of His Royal Highness's lieutenant at New York hitherto.[3] But what are its proper boundaries (those of latitude and longitude being so very little known, or so ill observed, as experience tells us, in all the West Indies), I am not able to say. If this be what Mr. Penn would have, I presume the Right Honorable the Lords of the Committee for Trade and Plantations will not encourage his pretensions to it, because of what is above mentioned, which shows plainly the duke's right preferable to all others (under His Majesty's good liking), though it should not prove to be strictly with[in] the limits of the duke's patent. But if it be any other parcel of land, unimproved in those parts, which is without all other patents, and not interfering with the possessions of His Majesty's subjects already settled there, I humbly submit to their Lordships how far they may think convenient (under fitting restrictions and qualifications, whereby to tie up the government of such [a] new colony as near as may be to the laws of England), to recommend the petitioner's request to His Majesty?

Then I think I have, as far as I am able at present, fully answered your letter upon this subject; and so I remain

Sir,

Your most affectionate friend and servant,

Mr. Blathwayt              John Werden

ALS. PRO. (*PWP*, 2:37-38).

1. St. James's Palace, London, was the residence of the duke of York.
2. Windsor, Berks., on the Thames, twenty miles west of London, was the site of Windsor Castle, one of the king's residences.
3. In August 1664 the Dutch government under Director-General Peter Stuyvesant surrendered New Amsterdam and the other Dutch possessions between Connecticut and Maryland to Col. Richard Nicolls (1624-1672), an agent of James, Duke of York. Nicolls became governor of the new English province, whose territorial limits stretched as far south as the Dutch settlement at Lewes on Delaware Bay.

*James II, by Sir Godfrey Kneller, 1685, National Portrait Gallery, London. The artist completed this painting before Charles II's death in February 1685 and, in its original state, showed James as Duke of York. Someone, not necessarily Kneller, added the crown, scepter, and orb after James's accession to the throne.*

# 5 §

## *John Darnall's Outline for the Charter of Pennsylvania*

W P not only needed the consent of the duke of York and of Lord Baltimore to his plan for a colony on the west bank of the Delaware, he
also needed to establish the terms under which he would govern his new
province. By 8 November 1680 he submitted a draft for a charter to the
Committee of Trade which was then distributed to various officials and was
altered by them. Unfortunately, WP's draft has been lost. In drawing up his
charter, WP apparently consulted John Darnall (c. 1645-1706), a prominent
lawyer from whom he sought advice on several other occasions. The outline
that Darnall drew up for WP is the earliest surviving plan for a patent for
Pennsylvania; Lord North's memorandum on WP's draft (doc. 9) follows
Darnall's outline and some details from it can be seen in the final charter (see
doc. 11). Darnall used earlier charters of other colonies, especially that of
Maryland, as a guide in sketching out this chart.

The outline that follows deals separately with the two great issues of
land and power. First, in a Greek alphabetical outline, Darnall listed all of
the assets of the land over which he believed WP should have control. WP's
lawyer wanted to secure to WP everything which, according to English law,
belonged to the king, rights which the king could grant to others. These
included the control of inland waterways, some ports and harbors, mines of
precious metals, forests, wild game, fish and fowl (the royal beast was the
deer, the royal fish were whales and sturgeon), and revenue from ship-
wrecks. In most respects, Darnall was asking for no more than what many
great landowners and colonial proprietors enjoyed, but his outline is more
detailed than the Maryland charter of 1632. In the charter of Pennsylvania,
the king did not bother to enumerate hunting (although both woods and
underwoods appear), but he definitely reserved to the crown a right to one-
fifth of any gold or silver found.

Darnall's most significant request here comes in the center paragraph.
Here he proposes that WP be granted the same privileges as the bishop of
Durham, who had *jura regalia,* i.e., within the county of Durham in northern
England, the bishop had the rights of the king in his palace. The bishop
could pardon treason and murder, appoint judges, and issue writs in his own
name rather than the king's. The sketch for a government (the list with items
numbered from 1 to 10) which follows this "Bishop of Durham clause"
would give WP extensive powers over church and state: he could set up an
assembly, courts, counties, towns, churches, and markets, and he could confer titles. Darnall added the final statement to prevent other colonies from
trying to encroach on the rights of Pennsylvania. WP knew, for example,

that New York had recently tried to collect customs duties in West New Jersey.

We do not know whether WP in fact included all of the powers listed by Darnall in the draft charter that he submitted to the Lords of Trade. If he did, the Lords believed he was asking for too much. In the final charter to Pennsylvania, WP's powers were not reinforced by a "Bishop of Durham clause" and his right to pardon crimes excluded treason and murder. In addition, he gained no authority to establish Anglican churches, had no jurisdiction over the Admiralty courts, and was not allowed to grant honors or titles. At this time the English government was much less permissive toward colonial proprietors than when Lord Baltimore received his patent in 1632; the Maryland charter did include the powerful "Bishop of Durham clause" and allowed the proprietor to confer titles. In the early 1680s, when the charters of all corporate and proprietary colonies were under close scrutiny, it is not surprising that the Lords of Trade gave WP less than absolute control.

[July? 1680]

*All that tract of land, etc.*

α. Waters, rivers, ponds, pools. Watercourses, fishing streams. All manner of royal and other fish whatsoever.

α Lakes, rivulets, streams.

β Islands.

β. Isles, marshes, swamps.

γ Havens, ports, harbors, creeks, ways.

γ. Bays, inlets, coves.

δ Woods, underwoods, timber, and trees, and all manner of royal and other beasts and fowls of what nature or kind soever.

ε Mines of gold, silver, lead, tin, iron, and copper; quarries of stone and coal, open or found, or at any time to be found.

ε. Veins, precious stone.

ξ All manner of royalties of hunting, hawking, fowling, and fishing, whatsoever.

Wrecks, etc.

To have, exercise, use, and enjoy as large and ample royalties, prerogatives, jurisdictions, privileges, liberties, and franchises, as well upon the water as the land, within the limits aforesaid and every of them as any bishop of within his bishopric or county palatine of Durham in our Kingdom of England ever had, held, used, or enjoyed, or ought or of right might have had, held, used, or enjoyed.

1. Erect it into a seigniory.[1]

2. To divide the country into
   and to erect

{ counties,
hundreds, etc.,
cities,
boroughs, castles, forts,
ports, harbors, creeks, havens, quays,
churches, advowsons, chapels,
chap[lains], oratories,[2]

And all manner of courts,    civil,                    Admiralty,
                             criminal,
                                and
                             military.

3. To make laws in Parliament
   or Assembly.
4. And under his hand and seal
   to publish them.

                             civil,
5. To constitute all officers,   criminal,    both by sea and land.
                                    and
                             military,

6. To punish
       and
7. pardon.
8. To incorporate.
9. To grant markets, fairs, tolls.
10. To confer honors.

That it shall not depend upon, or be subject to, any other colony or prince,
    but only and immediately to England's.

Draft. HSP. (*PWP,* 2:40-43).

1. A seigniory is a feudal lordship, and specifies the relationship between lord and
tenant.
2. The charters of Maryland and Carolina gave their proprietors advowsons, or
patronages, of churches and chapels; the charter of Pennsylvania gave the bishop of London the right to send Anglican priests to the colony.

THE next two documents show WP's final negotiations with the duke of
York for a determination of the border between the present states of
Delaware and Pennsylvania. The duke's secretary, Sir John Werden, was no
friend of WP (see doc. 4), but WP obviously overcame Werden's objections
by personally applying to James. Perhaps the duke was willing to be kind to

Admiral Penn's son and wanted to settle the royal debt. At this time, James had more urgent problems of his own to worry about, for Parliament was about to debate his exclusion from the royal succession. On 15 October the Privy Council advised the king to send him into exile, and on 20 October he left for Scotland. WP saw the duke just before he departed.

Werden continued to create difficulties for WP by insisting to William Blathwayt on 20 November (in a letter not printed here) that the boundary be drawn as far as thirty miles north of New Castle. Indeed, Werden pinpointed the location of the 40th degree of latitude almost exactly, but if this border had been established, WP would have controlled very little of the navigable part of the Delaware River and would not have had a decent port. In fact, the site of Philadelphia would have been in Delaware. WP gained the duke's agreement for a boundary twelve miles north of New Castle, and almost two years later, in August 1682, James deeded the rest of the Delaware colony to WP, thus giving him firmer control over Delaware River and Bay.

# 6 §

## Sir John Werden to William Blathwayt

Whitehall, 16 October 1680

Sir

You heretofore wrote to me touching Mr. William Penn's petition, then before the Right Honorable the Lords Commissioners for Trade and Foreign Plantations; to which I answered you, as at that time I was obliged to do. Since then, Mr. Penn has represented to the duke [of York] his case and circumstances (in relation to the reasons he has to expect favor from His Majesty touching that request of his) to be such, as that His Royal Highness commands me to let you know (in order to your informing their Lordships of it) that he is very willing Mr. Penn's request may meet with success. That is, that he may have a grant of that tract of land which lies on the north of New Castle Colony (part of Delaware) and on the west side of Delaware River, beginning about the latitude of 40 degrees and extending northwards and westwards as far as His Majesty pleases, under such regulations as their Lordships shall think fit. I am,

Sir,
Your very humble servant,
John Werden

ALS. PRO. (*PWP*, 2:44).

# 7 §

## Sir John Werden to William Blathwayt

St. James's, 23 November 1680

Sir

Mr. Penn having fallen into discourse with me of his concerns in America since I wrote to you on Saturday, I have told him the substance of what I wrote;[1] and he seems to fear that if his south limits be strictly set at twenty or thirty miles north from New Castle town, he shall have so little of the river left, as very much to prevent the hopes he has of improving the rest within his patent. But on the other side, he is willing that twelve English miles north of New Castle be his boundary, and believes that that distance will fall under the beginning of the 40th degree of latitude.[2] I have already signified to you all I know of the duke [of York]'s mind herein, which is in general to keep some convenient distance from New Castle northwards for a boundary to that colony. But I confess I do not understand why it is precisely necessary to insist on just such a number of miles, more or less, in a country of which we know so little, and where all the benefits are intended to this patentee that others enjoy. So as I submit this point to their Lordships' consideration, and do not think it material for me to add more at present, from

Sir,
Your very affectionate friend and servant,
Mr. Blathwayt          John Werden

ALS. PRO. (*PWP,* 2:49).

1. In the letter of 20 Nov. 1680 to William Blathwayt.
2. The 40th degree runs just north of the site WP chose for Philadelphia, through the Frankford section of the modern city.

O N 15 January 1681, the Lords of Trade set the southern boundary for WP's colony twelve miles north and west of New Castle. Their next step was to decide what powers WP should have as proprietor. They asked Chief Justice Lord North to review WP's draft charter, which is now lost but evidently followed John Darnall's outline (doc. 5) quite closely. The Lords wanted to make sure that WP's patent would conform to the king's interest and encourage emigrants to settle (doc. 8).

In accord with the English government's policy of tightening control over the colonies, Lord North wished to impose a number of severe restrictions on WP's patent (doc. 9). He would not allow WP to pardon traitors and murderers, he wanted all Pennsylvania laws submitted to the crown for review, and he required strict adherence to the Acts of Navigation, passed by the English Parliament to regulate overseas commerce. Most important, perhaps, is North's proposed clause which states that "matters both ecclesiastical, civil, and military within the said province and premises shall be subordinate and subject to the power and regulation of the Lords of the Privy Council, of us [i.e., the king], our heirs and successors, or of our or their commissioners, for the affairs relating to foreign plantations." In effect, this clause would have made WP a puppet of the Privy Council and the Committee of Trade. Fortunately for WP, it was not included in the final charter.

# 8 §

## Minute of the Committee of Trade

At the Committee of Trade and Plantations
in the Council Chamber at Whitehall
Saturday, the 22d of January 1681
Present

| Lord Privy Seal[1] | Lord Chief Justice North[4] |
| Earl of Clarendon[2] | Mr. [Edward] Seymour |
| Mr. Hyde[3] | Mr. Secretary [Leoline] Jenkins. |

Upon reading the draft of a patent for Mr. Penn, constituting him absolute proprietary of a tract of land in America northerly of Maryland, the Lords of the Committee desire my Lord Chief Justice North to take the said patent into his consideration and to provide, by fit clauses therein, that all acts of sovereignty as to peace and war be reserved unto the king, and that all acts of Parliament concerning trade and navigation and His Majesty's customs be duly observed, and in general that the patent be so drawn that it may consist with the king's interest and service and give sufficient encouragement to planters to settle under it.

A paper being also read wherein my Lord Bishop of London desires that Mr. Penn be obliged by his patent to admit a chaplain of his Lordship's appointment upon the request of any number of planters, the same is also referred to my Lord Chief Justice North.

MBE. PRO. (*PWP*, 2:57-58).

1. Arthur Annesley (1614-1686), Earl of Annesley. His presence at this meeting of the Committee of Trade is interesting because he was one of the commissioners executing the Restoration settlement in Ireland who awarded 12,000 acres to Admiral Penn, and he was also treasurer of the navy in 1667-1668, at the time when the crown became indebted to Admiral Penn for £11,000 in victualing expenses.

2. Henry Hyde (1638-1709), second Earl of Clarendon, was the brother-in-law of the duke of York.

3. Laurence Hyde (1641-1711), later Earl of Rochester, was apparently helpful to WP in negotiating the charter. WP wrote to him from Pennsylvania on 5 Feb. 1683 and thanked him for "the many favors I am indebted to thee."

4. Francis North (1637-1685), Lord North, served as chief justice of the Court of Common Pleas from 1675 to 1682, when he was named lord keeper of the privy seal.

# 9 §

## Chief Justice North's Memorandum on William Penn's Draft Charter

[c. January 1681]

The grant to erect the lands within the bounds into a province and seigniory with all franchises, etc., by name.[1]

A grant of all the lands in fee simple[2] to him, his heirs and assigns.

Of power to grant or enfeoff other persons in fee simple to hold of the said seigniory.

That his feoffees may by his license erect manors and grant in fee to undertenants to hold of the said manors,[3] but no further tenures to be; but all further alienations to be held of the same lord of whom the alienor holds.[4]

To divide the country into towns, hundreds, and counties.

To erect courts of justice, and constitute officers of justice, and officers relating to the keeping [of] the peace, according to the laws of England.

To pardon all offenses except treason. All offenses committed within the limits of this province, treason and murder excepted.

To make corporations and borough towns, fairs and markets, seaports, havens, and quays.

To appoint a Council: put Lord Baltimore's.[5]

To call Assemblies, and by their consent to make law and raise money for public uses.

To transmit all such laws to the Privy Council or Commissioners for the Plantations as soon as conveniently may be or at least within six months after the passing them; and that unless His Majesty shall within two years after they are received declare them null, they shall be and remain in force until repealed by the same authority that passed them.[6]

A strict provision to be inserted for observing the Acts of Navigation[7] and for receiving such officers or their deputies as His Majesty's commissioners of the customs shall appoint. And the proprietor to be enjoined to take care hereof or else a *scire facias* to lie against the patent for any misdemeanor in this case.[8]

They are not to trade with any prince or state or country in Christendom that is in war with the king, nor make war with any that is in amity with the king. But they may make peace or war with the Indians as they shall think fit, except His Majesty shall otherwise and especially direct.[9]

Appeals to be reserved to the king.

If any inhabitants to the number of          shall be desirous to have a minister or ministers of God's word to reside among them for their instruction, and shall apply themselves for the same to the Bishop of London for the time being, that such minister as he shall approve shall have liberty to be and remain there without molestation.[10]

The laws of property both for the descent and enjoyment of lands, and for the enjoyment and succession of goods, to be the same as in England; and the course of justice for property to be the same.

Felonies and treasons to be the same as by the common laws, and trials to be in the same manner.

The grantee to have the probate of wills and granting administration and all admiral jurisdiction. Admiral jurisdiction belongs to the duke of York and cannot be granted by the king. Nor is it proper to be granted in all its extent.

This further clause is submitted: "Provided also, and our will and pleasure is, that all and singular the powers and authorities hereby given unto the said William Penn, his heirs and assigns, for and concerning matters both ecclesiastical, civil, and military within the said province and premises shall be subordinate and subject to the power and regulation of the Lords of the Privy Council, of us, our heirs and successors, or of our or their commissioners, for the affairs relating to foreign plantations for the time being. But for all or whatsoever does, shall, or may concern the propriety of the province, or any part thereof, or any ownership or interest in any lands, tenements, or other hereditaments, goods, or chattels, the same is left wholly to the said William Penn, his heirs or assigns, according to the true intent and meaning of these presents."[11]

D. PRO. (*PWP*, 2:58-60).

1. Lord North is here following the language of the Maryland charter of 1632, which is reproduced word for word in WP's charter; it gives the proprietor the power to sell or assign land to others.

2. The most advantageous form of English land ownership, with no restrictions and with unlimited power to transfer the property to others.

3. Here again Lord North is following the language of the Maryland charter, which is reproduced verbatim in WP's charter. It allows the proprietor to create manors—territorial units of aristocratic character, in which the manor lord enjoys special authority over his land and tenants who inhabit it, and holds courts-baron, which hear civil cases arising from within the manor.

4. This restrictive clause appears in WP's charter but not in Lord Baltimore's. Only the proprietor of Pennsylvania can create manors, and WP's manor lords cannot subdivide their holdings into smaller manors. Both the Lords of Trade and WP were hostile to the establishment of a titled nobility in Pennsylvania, and while WP did set up several manors, they had little economic or social importance.

5. The Maryland charter contains no reference to councils or councilors; North's meaning therefore is not clear.

6. In the final charter, the colony was given five years to submit laws, and the crown only six months to consider them, a vastly better arrangement for Pennsylvania.

7. English laws regulating colonial trade, whose primary objective was to guarantee that colonial produce would be shipped in English vessels, that valuable American commodities like sugar and tobacco would be sent to English markets, and that England had a monopoly in furnishing the colonies with necessary supplies. In short, the Navigation Acts created a closed system of trade.

8. A *scire facias* is a legal writ which allows the king to revoke a patent or charter because certain of its provisions have not been observed.

9. This clause permitting WP to make war with the Indians was altered in the final charter. Like Lord Baltimore, WP received the powers of a captain-general, to raise troops to fight enemies, pirates, and thieves. See doc. 11, sect. 16.

10. This clause was suggested by the bishop of London, who wanted to protect the

rights of Anglicans (members of the established Church of England) in Quaker Pennsylvania. In the final version the number of Anglican inhabitants is set at twenty.

11. WP must have protested this clause, which does not appear in the final version of the charter. It would have made WP subservient to the Privy Council and Lords of Trade in all matters pertaining to the government of the colony, while reserving to WP only rights in the land.

# 10 ∫
## Warrant to the Privy Seal Office

AFTER receiving expert opinion from Chief Justice Lord North and others, the Committee of Trade asked their secretary, William Blathwayt, to draw up a new draft of WP's charter. Blathwayt prepared it for their meeting of 24 February 1681, where the Lords approved the text and agreed to send a copy to the king in council. On 25 February, the king also approved the text and named the colony "Pensilvania." The complicated process of preparing the document for the Great Seal then began. First, the secretary of state ordered the attorney-general to have a copy made for the king's signature; Charles II signed what is called the king's bill on 28 February and issued a warrant (doc. 10) for the final charter. The king's bill went first to the privy signet office where another copy was prepared. The king's signet (or seal) was attached to this new document, called the signet bill, which then went to the privy seal office. Here yet another copy was written out, folded in an unusual manner, circled by a ribbon of parchment, and sealed with the privy seal. Lord Chancellor Heneage Finch received this copy on 4 March 1681, when he broke open the privy seal and ordered the final patent to be engrossed in legal script on parchment. This last document, authenticated and made legally binding with the Great Seal of England, was the charter WP received.

28 February 1681

His Majesty is pleased to grant unto William Penn, Esquire, his heirs and assigns forever, a certain tract of land in America, to be erected into a province and to be called by the name of PENNSYLVANIA. And also to make the said William Penn, his heirs and assigns, chief governor thereof, with diverse privileges, powers, and authorities granted to the said William Penn, his heirs and assigns, in order to the good government of the said province. Subscribed by Mr. Solicitor General,[1] by Warrant, etc., supra.

MBE. PRO. (*PWP,* 2:77-78).

1. Heneage Finch (c. 1647-1719), son of the lord chancellor, Sir Heneage Finch, was made solicitor-general in 1679.

# Part II

THE CHARTER OF
PENNSYLVANIA §
4 MARCH 1681

The Charter of Pennsylvania, 4 March 1681, Bureau of Archives and History, Pennsylvania Historical and Museum Commission, Harrisburg. Detail of the first of four pages. This photograph of the original charter was taken in the late nineteenth century, before the document was torn and water stained. The damage, which began sometime before 1900, obliterates substantial portions of the text. There are several extant copies in good condition, including one made in 1876 that is also located in Harrisburg.

WP'S charter was the capstone of months of negotiations with the Lords of Trade. WP had begun with a text, modeled on Lord Baltimore's charter for Maryland, which made him virtually absolute ruler of his colony (see doc. 5). A number of officials, including Chief Justice Lord North (doc. 9), criticized WP's draft and called for substantial changes. Thus, the charter which passed the Great Seal on 4 March 1681 conferred more limited powers. WP could not build forts or confer honors or titles, his pardoning power did not extend to treason or murder, and he could grant to manor lords only certain rights. As proprietor, WP was specifically required to enforce the Acts of Navigation and to admit customs inspectors to the province, two provisos not required of Lord Baltimore. The rights of Pennsylvanians were also restricted: they were not automatically given English citizenship and they could not trade with Ireland, their laws were subject to review by the king in council, and Parliament could impose customs duties without their consent. Lord North had proposed going further than this, making WP's government a puppet of the Privy Council and Lords of Trade (see p. 32). North's proposed clause was not adopted in the final charter, but WP's powers in government were strictly limited and made subject to the home government. WP did, however, retain virtually absolute rights to the land. Another important change in WP's draft, made by William Blathwayt, secretary to the Lords of Trade, was the elimination of a clause guaranteeing religious liberty. However, the charter did not require Pennsylvanians to attend Anglican services, though the bishop of London could appoint an Anglican preacher if requested by twenty inhabitants.

The Pennsylvania charter is a long and complicated document; its text is divided into twenty-three sections. The following outline briefly summarizes the contents of each section:

The Preamble explains why the king has granted the charter.

Sect. 1 specifies the boundaries of Pennsylvania.

Sect. 2 describes the land, water, and mineral rights that are included in the grant.

Sect. 3 establishes the "true and absolute" proprietary authority of WP and his successors over the "province and seigniory" of Pennsylvania.

Sect. 4 empowers the proprietor to make laws, with the advice and consent of an Assembly of freemen or their representatives.

Sect. 5 empowers the proprietor to appoint officials, establish courts, and decide all judicial cases except treason and murder, with the reservation that Pennsylvania laws must be agreeable to English law, and that Pennsylvania judgments may be appealed to the king.

Sect. 6 empowers the proprietor to enact ordinances in emergencies without the consent of the Assembly.

Sect. 7 requires that laws be sent for review within five years of passage to the king in council.

Sect. 8 permits the king's subjects to immigrate to Pennsylvania.

Sect. 9 permits the export of goods and provisions from England as long as customs laws are obeyed.

Sect. 10 empowers the proprietor to create towns, hundreds, counties; incorporate boroughs and cities; set up fairs and markets.

Sect. 11 requires all Pennsylvania exports to be shipped to England, and then re-exported to other countries if desired after payment of duties.

Sect. 12 empowers the proprietor to create ports; requires admission of English customs officials and inspectors.

Sect. 13 empowers the Pennsylvania government to collect customs duties.

Sect. 14 requires the proprietor to appoint an agent residing in or near London to answer for any violation of the Acts of Navigation; allows the king to seize the government of Pennsylvania for nonpayment of any money due under the acts.

Sect. 15 forbids the proprietor from doing business with any nation at war with the king of England and from making war with any nation at peace with the king of England.

Sect. 16 empowers the proprietor to raise a militia, giving him all of the powers of a captain-general except that of proclaiming martial law.

Sect. 17 empowers the proprietor to sell or rent his land in Pennsylvania to purchasers and tenants.

Sect. 18 empowers purchasers of land from WP to hold or dispose of their Pennsylvania property by any method agreeable to the proprietor.

Sect. 19 permits the proprietor to create manors of himself only, thus limiting the development of a manorial system in Pennsylvania.

Sect. 20 pledges that the king shall levy no taxes or customs upon the inhabitants of Pennsylvania without the consent of the proprietor or Assembly, or by act of Parliament in England.

Sect. 21 directs the king's officials to abide by the provisions of this charter.

Sect. 22 permits twenty Anglican inhabitants to request that a preacher be sent to Pennsylvania by the bishop of London.

Sect. 23 specifies procedures to be followed if questions arise concerning the wording of the charter.

# 11 §

## The Charter of Pennsylvania

4 March 1681

Charles the Second, by the grace of God, king of England, Scotland, France, and Ireland, Defender of the Faith, etc., To all to whom these presents shall come, Greeting:

Whereas our trusty and well-beloved subject, William Penn, esquire, son and heir of Sir William Penn, deceased (out of a commendable desire to enlarge our English empire, and promote such useful commodities as may be of benefit to us and our dominions, as also to reduce the savage natives, by gentle and just manners, to the love of civil society and Christian religion), has humbly besought leave of us to transport an ample colony unto a certain country hereinafter described, in the parts of America not yet cultivated and planted, and has likewise so humbly besought Our Royal Majesty to give, grant, and confirm all the said country, with certain privileges and jurisdictions, requisite for the good government and safety of the said country and colony, to him and his heirs forever.

I. Know ye, therefore, that we (favoring the petition and good purpose of the said William Penn, and having regard to the memory and merits of his late father, in diverse services, and particularly to his conduct, courage, and discretion, under our dearest brother James, Duke of York, in that signal battle and victory fought and obtained against the Dutch fleet commanded by the Heer van Obdam, in the year 1665),[1] in consideration thereof, of our special grace, certain knowledge, and mere motion, have given and granted, and by this our present charter, for us, our heirs and successors, do give and grant unto the said William Penn, his heirs and assigns, all that tract or part of land in America, with the islands therein contained, as the same is bounded on the east by Delaware River, from twelve miles distance northward of New Castle Town, unto the three and fortieth degree of northern latitude, if the said river doth extend so far northward; but if the said river shall not extend so far northward, then by the said river so far as it doth extend; and from the head of the said river, the eastern bounds are to be determined by a meridian line, to be drawn from the head of the said river, unto the said forty-third degree. The said land to extend westward five degrees in longitude, to be computed from the said eastern bounds, and the said lands to be bounded on the north by the beginning of the three and fortieth degree of northern latitude, and on the south by a circle drawn at twelve miles distance from New Castle, northward and westward unto the beginning of the fortieth degree of northern latitude, and then by a straight line westward to the limits of longitude above mentioned.

II.   We do also give and grant unto the said William Penn, his heirs and assigns, the free and undisturbed use, and continuance in, and passage unto and out of all and singular ports, harbors, bays, waters, rivers, isles, and inlets, belonging unto, or leading to and from the country or islands aforesaid, and all the soils, lands, fields, woods, underwoods, mountains, hills, fenns, isles, lakes, rivers, waters, rivulets, bays, and inlets, situated, or being within, or belonging to the limits or bounds aforesaid, together with the fishing of all sorts of fish, whales, sturgeon, and all royal and other fishes, in the seas, bays, inlets, waters, or rivers within the premises, and all the fish therein taken; and also all veins, mines, minerals and quarries, as well discovered as not discovered, of gold, silver, gems, and precious stones, and all other whatsoever, be it stones, metals, or any other thing or matter whatsoever, found, or to be found, within the country, isles, or limits aforesaid.

III.   And him, the said William Penn, his heirs and assigns, we do by this, our royal charter, for us, our heirs and successors, make, create, and constitute the true and absolute proprietary of the country aforesaid, and of all other the premises; saving always to us, our heirs and successors, the faith and allegiance of the said William Penn, his heirs and assigns, and of all other proprietaries, tenants, and inhabitants that are, or shall be, within the territories and precincts aforesaid; and saving also unto us, our heirs and successors, the sovereignty of the aforesaid country, to have, hold, possess, and enjoy the said tract of land, country, isles, inlets, and other the premises, unto the said William Penn, his heirs and assigns, to the only proper use and behoof of the said William Penn, his heirs and assigns, forever, to be holden of us, our heirs and successors, kings of England, as of our Castle of Windsor, in our County of Berks, in free and common socage,[2] by fealty only, for all services, and not *in capite,* or by knights-service,[3] yielding and paying therefore to us, our heirs and successors, two beaver skins, to be delivered at our Castle of Windsor, on the first day of January in every year; and also the fifth part of all gold and silver ore which shall, from time to time, happen to be found within the limits aforesaid, clear of all charges. And of our further grace, certain knowledge, and mere motion, we have thought fit to erect, and we do hereby erect the aforesaid country and islands into a province and seigniory, and do call it Pennsylvania, and so from henceforth will have it called.

IV.   And forasmuch as we have hereby made and ordained the aforesaid William Penn, his heirs and assigns, the true and absolute proprietaries of all the lands and dominions aforesaid, know ye therefore, that we (reposing special trust and confidence in the fidelity, wisdom, justice, and provident circumspection of the said William Penn), for us, our heirs and successors, do grant free, full, and absolute power (by virtue of these presents) to him and his heirs, to his and their deputies and lieutenants, for the good and happy government of the said country, to ordain, make, and enact, and under his and their seals, to publish any laws whatsoever, for the raising of money for public uses of the said province, or for any other end, appertaining either unto the public state, peace, or safety of the said country, or unto the private utility of particular persons, according unto their best discretion, by and with the advice, assent, and approbation of the freemen of the said country, or the greater part of them, or of their delegates or deputies, whom, for the enacting of the said laws, when and as often as need shall require, we will that the said William Penn, and his heirs, shall assemble, in such sort and form as to him and them shall seem best, and the same laws duly to execute unto and upon all people within the said country and limits thereof.

V.   And we do likewise give and grant unto the said William Penn, and to his heirs, and to his and their deputies and lieutenants, full power and authority to appoint and establish any judges and justices, magistrates, and other officers whatsoever, for what causes soever (for the probates of wills, and for the granting of administrations within the precincts aforesaid), and with what power soever, and in such form, as to the said William Penn, or his heirs, shall seem most convenient; also to remit, release, pardon, and abolish (whether before judgment or after) all crimes and offenses whatsoever committed within the said country, against the said laws (treason, and willful and malicious murder, only excepted, and in those cases to grant reprieves, until our pleasure may be known therein), and to do all and every other thing and things which unto the complete establishment of justice, unto courts and tribunals, forms of judicature, and manner of proceedings do belong, although, in these presents, express mention be not made thereof; and by judges, by them delegated, to award process, hold pleas, and determine, in all the said courts and tribunals, all actions, suits, and causes whatsoever, as well criminal as civil, personal, real, and mixed; which laws, so as aforesaid to be published, our pleasure is, and so we enjoin, require, and command, shall be most absolute and available in law, and that all the liege people and subjects of us, our heirs and successors, do observe and keep the same inviolable in those parts, so far as they concern them, under the pain therein expressed, or to be expressed. Provided nevertheless, that the same laws be consonant to reason, and be not repugnant or contrary, but (as near as conveniently may be) agreeable to the laws and statutes, and rights of this our kingdom of England; and saving and reserving to us, our heirs and successors, the receiving, hearing, and determining of the appeal and appeals of all or any person or persons of, in, or belonging to the territories aforesaid, or touching any judgment to be there made or given.

VI.   And forasmuch as, in the government of so great a country, sudden accidents do often happen, whereunto it will be necessary to apply remedy, before the freeholders of the said province, or their delegates or deputies can be assembled to the making of laws; neither will it be convenient that instantly, upon every such emergent occasion, so great a multitude should be called together; therefore (for the better government of the said country), we will and ordain, and by these presents, for us, our heirs and successors, do grant unto the said William Penn and his heirs, by themselves, or by their magistrates and officers, in that behalf duly to be ordained as aforesaid, to make and constitute fit and wholesome ordinances, from time to time, within the said country to be kept and observed, as well for the preservation of the peace, as for the better government of the people there inhabiting, and publicly to notify the same to all persons whom the same do, or may anywise concern. Which ordinances our will and pleasure is shall be observed inviolably within the said province, under the pains therein to be expressed, so as the said ordinances be consonant to reason, and be not repugnant nor contrary, but (so far as conveniently may be) agreeable with the laws of our kingdom of England, and so as the said ordinances be not extended, in any sort, to bind, change, or take away the right or interest of any person or persons, for, or in their life, members, freehold, goods, or chattels. And our further will and pleasure is, that the laws for regulating and governing of property within the said province, as well for the descent and enjoyment of lands, as likewise for the enjoyment and succession of goods and chattels, and likewise as to felonies, shall be and continue the same as they shall be, for the time being, by the general course of the law in our kingdom of England, until the said laws shall be altered by the said William Penn, his heirs or assigns, and by the freemen of the said province, their delegates or deputies, or the greatest part of them.

VII. And to the end that the said William Penn, or his heirs, or other the planters, owners, or inhabitants of the said province may not, at any time hereafter (by misconstruction of the power aforesaid) through inadvertency or design, depart from that faith and due allegiance which, by the laws of this our realm of England, they and all our subjects in our dominions and territories always owe to us, our heirs and successors, by color of any extent, or largeness of powers hereby given, or pretended to be given, or by force or color of any laws hereafter to be made in the said province, by virtue of any such powers. Our further will and pleasure is, that a transcript or duplicate of all laws which shall be so as aforesaid made and published within the said province, shall, within five years after the making thereof, be transmitted and delivered to the Privy Council for the time being, of us, our heirs and successors; and if any of the said laws, within the space of six months after that they shall be so transmitted and delivered, be declared by us, our heirs and successors, in our or their Privy Council, inconsistent with the sovereignty or lawful prerogative of us, our heirs or successors, or contrary to the faith and allegiance due to the legal government of this realm from the said William Penn or his heirs, or of the planters and inhabitants of the said province, and that thereupon any of the said laws shall be adjudged and declared to be void by us, our heirs and successors, under our or their privy seal, that then and from thenceforth, such laws, concerning which such judgment and declaration shall be made, shall become void; otherwise the said laws, so transmitted, shall remain and stand in full force, according to the true intent and meaning thereof.[4]

VIII. Furthermore, that this new colony may the more happily increase by the multitude of people resorting thither, therefore we, for us, our heirs and successors, do give and grant, by these presents, power, license, and liberty unto all the liege people and subjects, both present and future, of us, our heirs and successors (excepting those who shall be especially forbidden), to transport themselves and families unto the said country, with such convenient shipping as by the laws of this our kingdom of England they ought to use,[5] and with fitting provision, paying only the customs therefore due, and there to settle themselves, dwell and inhabit, and plant, for the public and their own private advantage.

IX.  And furthermore, that our subjects may be the rather encouraged to undertake this expedition with ready and cheerful minds, know ye, that we, of our special grace, certain knowledge, and mere motion, do give and grant, by virtue of these presents, as well unto the said William Penn and his heirs, as to all others who shall from time to time repair unto the said country with a purpose to inhabit or trade with the natives of the said country, full license to lade and freight in any ports whatsoever of us, our heirs and successors, according to the laws made, or to be made, within our kingdom of England, and unto the said country, by them, their servants or assigns, to transport all and singular their goods, wares, and merchandises, as likewise all sorts of grain whatsoever, and all other things whatsoever necessary for food or clothing, not prohibited by the laws and statutes of our kingdom and dominions to be carried out of the said kingdom, without any let or molestation of us, our heirs or successors or of any of the officers of us our heirs and successors; saving always to us, our heirs and successors, the legal impositions, customs, or other duties and payments for the said wares and merchandises, by any law or statute due, or to be due, to us, our heirs and successors.[6]

X.  And we do further, for us, our heirs and successors, give and grant unto the said William Penn, his heirs and assigns, free and absolute power to divide the said country and islands into towns, hundreds, and counties, and to erect and incorporate towns into boroughs, and boroughs into cities, and to make and constitute fairs and markets therein, with all other convenient privileges and immunities, according to the merits of the inhabitants, and the fitness of the places, and to do all and every other thing and things touching the premises, which to him or them shall seem meet and requisite, albeit they be such as of their own nature might otherwise require a more special commandment and warrant than, in these presents, is expressed.[7]

XI.  We will also, and by these presents, for us, our heirs and successors, we do give and grant license, by this our charter, unto the said William Penn, his heirs and assigns, and to all the inhabitants and dwellers in the province aforesaid both present and to come, to import or unlade, by themselves or their servants, factors, or assigns, all merchandises and goods whatsoever, that shall arise of the fruits and commodities of the said province, either by land or sea, into any of the ports of us, our heirs or successors, in our kingdom of England, and not into any other country whatsoever. And we give him full power to dispose of the said goods, in the said ports, and if need be, within one year next after the unlading of the same, to lade the said merchandise and goods again into the same, or other ships, and to transport the same into any other countries, either of our dominions or foreign, according to law; provided always, that they pay such customs and impositions, subsidies, and duties for the same, to us, our heirs and successors, as the rest of our subjects of our kingdom of England, for the time being shall be bound to pay, and do observe the Acts of Navigation and other laws in that behalf made.[8]

XII. And furthermore, of our ample and special grace, certain knowledge, and mere motion, we do, for us, our heirs and successors, grant unto the said William Penn, his heirs and assigns, full and absolute power and authority to make, erect, and constitute within the said province and the isles and inlets aforesaid, such and so many seaports, harbors, creeks, havens, quays, and other places for discharging and unlading of goods and merchandises out of the ships, boats, and other vessels, and lading them unto such and so many places, and with such rights, jurisdictions, liberties, and privileges unto the said ports belonging, as to him and them shall seem most expedient; and that all and singular the ships, boats, and other vessels which shall come for merchandise and trade into the said province, or out of the same, shall be laden or unladen only at such ports as shall be created and constituted by the said William Penn, his heirs or assigns (any use, custom, or other thing to the contrary notwithstanding). Provided, that the said William Penn, and his heirs, and the lieutenants and governors for the time being, shall admit and receive in and about all such havens, ports, creeks, and quays, all officers and their deputies, who shall from time to time be appointed for that purpose by the farmers or commissioners of our customs for the time being.

XIII. And we do further appoint and ordain, and by these presents, for us, our heirs and successors, we do grant unto the said William Penn, his heirs and assigns, that he the said William Penn his heirs and assigns may, from time to time, forever, have and enjoy the customs and subsidies in the ports, harbors, and other creeks and places aforesaid, within the province aforesaid, payable or due for merchandise and wares there to be laded and unladed, the said customs and subsidies to be reasonably assessed upon any occasion by themselves and the people there, as aforesaid to be assembled, to whom we give power by these presents, for us, our heirs and successors, upon just cause and in a due proportion, to assess and impose the same; saving unto us, our heirs and successors, such impositions and customs as by act of Parliament are and shall be appointed.

XIV. And it is our further will and pleasure, that the said William Penn, his heirs and assigns, shall from time to time constitute and appoint an attorney or agent to reside in or near our City of London, who shall make known the place where he shall dwell, or may be found, unto the clerks of our Privy Council, for the time being, or one of them, and shall be ready to appear in any of our courts at Westminster, to answer for any misdemeanor that shall be committed, or by any willful default or neglect permitted by the said William Penn, his heirs or assigns, against the Laws of Trade and Navigation; and after it shall be ascertained, in any of our said courts, what damages we, or our heirs or successors, shall have sustained by such default or neglect, the said William Penn, his heirs or assigns, shall pay the same within one year after such taxation, and demand thereof from such attorney, or in case there shall be no such attorney by the space of one year, or such attorney shall not make payment of such damages within the space of a year, and answer such other forfeitures and penalties within the said time, as by the acts of Parliament in England are and shall be provided, according to the true intent and meaning of these presents, then it shall be lawful for us, our heirs and successors, to seize and resume the government of the said province or country, and the same to retain until payment shall be made thereof; but notwithstanding any such seizure, or resumption of the government, nothing concerning the propriety or ownership of any lands, tenements, or other hereditaments, or goods or chattels of any of the adventurers, planters, or owners, other than the respective offenders there, shall anywise be affected or molested thereby.

XV.   Provided always, and our will and pleasure is, that neither the said William Penn, nor his heirs, nor any other the inhabitants of the said province, shall at any time hereafter have or maintain any correspondence with any other king, prince, or state, or with any of their subjects, who shall then be in war against us, our heirs and successors; nor shall the said William Penn or his heirs, or any other inhabitants of the said province, make war or do any act of hostility against any other king, prince, or state, or any of their subjects, who shall then be in league or amity with us, our heirs and successors.

XVI.   And because, in so remote a country and situate near many barbarous nations, the incursions as well of the savages themselves as of other enemies, pirates, and robbers may probably be feared, therefore we have given, and for us, our heirs and successors, do give power, by these presents, to the said William Penn, his heirs and assigns, by themselves or their captains or other their officers, to levy, muster, and train all sorts of men, of what condition soever or wheresoever born, in the said province of Pennsylvania, for the time being, and to make war, and to pursue the enemies and robbers aforesaid, as well by sea as by land, even without the limits of the said province, and by God's assistance, to vanquish and take them; and being taken, to put them to death by the law of war or to save them, at their pleasure, and to do all and every other thing which unto the charge and office of a captain-general of an army belongs, or has accustomed to belong, as fully and freely as any captain-general of an army has ever had the same.[9]

XVII.   And furthermore, of our special grace, and of our certain knowledge, and mere motion, we have given and granted, and by these presents, for us, our heirs and successors, do give and grant unto the said William Penn, his heirs and assigns, full and absolute power, license, and authority that he, the said William Penn, his heirs and assigns, from time to time hereafter, forever, at his or their own will and pleasure, may assign, alien, grant, demise, or enfeoff of the premises, so many and such parts and parcels to him or them that shall be willing to purchase the same, as they shall think fit, to have and to hold to them, the said person or persons willing to take and purchase, their heirs and assigns, in fee-simple, or fee-tail, or for the term of life, lives, or years, to be held of the said William Penn, his heirs and assigns, as of the said seigniory of Windsor, by such services, customs, or rents as shall seem meet to the said William Penn, his heirs and assigns, and not immediately of us, our heirs or successors.

XVIII.   And to the same person or persons, and to all and every of them, we do give and grant, by these presents, for us, our heirs and successors, license, authority, and power that such person or persons may take the premises, or any parcel thereof, of the aforesaid William Penn, his heirs or assigns, and the same hold to themselves, their heirs and assigns, in what estate of inheritance soever, in fee-simple, or in fee-tail, or otherwise, as to him, the said William Penn, his heirs or assigns, shall seem expedient; the statute made in the Parliament of Edward, son of King Henry, late king of England, our predecessor (commonly called the statute *quia emptores terrarum,* lately published in our kingdom of England),[10] in anywise notwithstanding.

XIX.   And by these presents, we give and grant license unto the said William Penn and his heirs, and likewise to all and every such person or persons to whom the said William Penn or his heirs shall at any time hereafter grant any estate or inheritance as aforesaid, to erect any parcels of land within the province aforesaid into manors, by and with the license to be first had and obtained for that purpose, under the hand and seal of the said William Penn or his heirs, and in every of the said manors, to have and to hold a court-baron, with all things whatsoever which to a court-baron do belong, and to have and to hold view of frankpledge for the conservation of the peace and the better government of those parts, by themselves, or their stewards, or by the lords, for the time being, of the manors to be deputed, when they shall be erected, and in the same to use all things belonging to the view of frankpledge.[11] And we do further grant license and authority that every such person or persons who shall erect any such manor or manors, as aforesaid, shall or may grant all or any part of his said land to any person or persons, in fee-simple or any other estate of inheritance, to be held of the said manors respectively, so as no further tenure shall be created, but that upon all further or other alienations thereafter to be made, the said lands so aliened shall be held of the same lord and his heirs, of whom the alienor did then before hold, and by the like rents and services which were before due and accustomed.[12]

XX.   And further, our pleasure is, and by these presents, for us, our heirs and successors, we do covenant and grant to and with the said William Penn, his heirs and assigns, that we, our heirs and successors, shall at no time hereafter set or make, or cause to be set or made, any imposition, custom, or other taxation, rate, or contribution whatsoever, in and upon the dwellers and inhabitants of the aforesaid province, for their lands, tenements, goods, or chattels within the said province, or in and upon any goods and merchandizes within the province or to be laden or unladen within the ports or harbors of the said province, unless the same be with the consent of the proprietary or chief governor or Assembly, or by act of Parliament in England.

XXI.   And our pleasure is, and for us, our heirs and successors, we charge and command that this, our declaration, shall from henceforth from time to time be received and allowed in all our courts, and before all the judges of us, our heirs and successors, for a sufficient lawful discharge, payment, and acquittance, commanding all the officers and ministers of us, our heirs and successors, and enjoining them, upon pain of our highest displeasure, that they do not presume at any time to attempt anything to the contrary of the premises, or that they do, in any sort, withstand the same, but that they be at all times, aiding and assisting, as is fitting, to the said William Penn and his heirs, and unto the inhabitants and merchants of the province aforesaid, their servants, ministers, factors, and assigns, in the full use and fruition of the benefit of this our charter.

XXII. And our further pleasure is, and we do hereby, for us, our heirs and successors, charge and require that if any of the inhabitants of the said province, to the number of twenty, shall at any time hereafter be desirous, and shall, by any writing or by any person deputed by them, signify such their desire to the Bishop of London, for the time being, that any preacher or preachers, to be approved of by the said bishop, may be sent unto them for their instruction, that then such preacher or preachers shall and may reside within the said province without any denial or molestation whatsoever.[13]

XXIII. And if perchance hereafter any doubt or question should arise concerning the true sense and meaning of any word, clause, or sentence contained in this our present charter, we will, ordain, and command that at all times, and in all things, such interpretation be made thereof and allowed, in any of our courts whatsoever, as shall be adjudged most advantageous and favorable unto the said William Penn, his heirs and assigns: provided always, that no interpretation be admitted thereof, by which the allegiance due unto us, our heirs and successors, may suffer any prejudice or diminution; although express mention be not made, in these presents, of the true yearly value, or certainty of the premises, or any part thereof, or of other gifts and grants made by us and our progenitors or predecessors, unto the said William Penn, any statute, act, ordinance, provision, proclamation, or restraint heretofore had, made, published, ordained, or provided, or any other thing, cause, or matter whatsoever, to the contrary thereof in anywise notwithstanding. In witness whereof, we have caused these our letters to be made patent: witness ourself, at Westminster, the 4th day of March, in the three and thirtieth year of our reign, *annoque Domini,* one thousand six hundred and eighty-one.

By writ of privy seal,
Pigott[14]

Printed transcript. *Votes and Proceedings of the Province of Pennsylvania* (Philadelphia, 1752), 1:18-24. See *PWP,* 2:61-77, for William Blathwayt's draft of the Pennsylvania charter.

1. On 3 June 1665, the English under James, Duke of York, as lord high admiral and Sir William Penn as captain, routed the Dutch fleet at the Battle of Lowestoft. They sank the ship of the Dutch commander, Jacob, Baron van Wassenaer, Heer van Obdam en Zuidwijk (1610-1665), and killed him. Admiral Penn commanded the duke's flagship, the *Royal Charles.*

2. That is, the form of land tenure in which annual payments to the lord, or quitrents, were set at an established rate.

3. The military service that a knight was bound to render as a condition of holding his lands.

4. This clause, while providing for the review of laws passed in Pennsylvania by the

king in council, is considerably weaker than Lord North's proposal for legislative review; see doc. 9.

5. According to the navigation laws of 1660, 1663, and 1673, only English shipping could be used in the American colonies.

6. This clause is identical with sect. 11 of the Maryland charter.

7. This clause is adapted from sect. 14 of the Maryland charter, which also gave Baltimore the power to confer honors and titles. John Darnall had proposed this power for WP; see doc. 5.

8. This clause is adapted from sect. 15 of the Maryland charter. The final phrase "and do observe the Acts of Navigation and other laws in that behalf made" is not found in the Maryland charter. See doc. 9, n. 7.

9. This clause was taken verbatim from sect. 12 of the Maryland charter; not included, however, is sect. 13 of the Maryland charter, which gave Baltimore the power of a captain-general to impose martial law.

10. This clause waives the statute *quia emptores terrarum* and other laws which forbade the creation of new manors. Thus, land in Pennsylvania could be held of the proprietor, and did not have to be held of the king directly.

11. Views of frankpledge, or courts-leet, were yearly assemblies of freemen within a manor or lordship. Originally the frankpledges, or freemen, came together to pledge their collective good behavior, but these assemblies evolved into courts at which juries made presentments and petty misdemeanors were punished. A court-baron was an essential element of every manor. It handled property disputes within the manor, and cases of small debt, misdemeanors, and trespass.

12. This clause stating that all manors must be held directly of the proprietor is not found in the Maryland charter; see doc. 9, n. 4.

13. This is the clause requested by the bishop of London and drafted by Lord North; see doc. 9.

14. Sir Richard Pigott (d. 1699) of London and Woodford, Essex, was the clerk of the patents.

# Part III

PROMOTING THE NEW COLONY §
MARCH 1681–JUNE 1681

S O M E

# ACCOUNT

OF THE

# PROVINCE

OF

# PENNSILVANIA

IN

# AMERICA;

Lately Granted under the Great Seal

OF

# ENGLAND

TO

# William Penn, &c.

Together with Priviledges and Powers necef-
fary to the well-governing thereof.

Made publick for the Information of fuch as are or may be
difpofed to Tranfport themfelves or Servants
into thofe Parts.

---

LONDON: Printed, and Sold by Benjamin Clark
Bookfeller in George-Yard Lombard-ftreet, 1681.

Title Page of Some Account, 1681, Quaker Collection, Haverford College Library.
For the text of this pamphlet, which was WP's first promotional tract for Pennsylvania,
see doc. 15.

ON 5 March 1681, WP wrote to his Irish friend Robert Turner, "This day my country was confirmed to me under the Great Seal of England with large powers and privileges, by the name of Pennsylvania." He asked Turner to circulate word of his charter among fellow Quakers, and added that he would soon be advertising his plans for the new colony (doc. 12). Obtaining his charter was only the first step in founding the colony, and WP plunged into the work of promoting settlement in Pennsylvania with tremendous energy and zeal. Setting up a successful new colony in late-seventeenth-century America was a difficult task. Since job opportunities and wage levels were improving in Britain in the 1680s, the thousands of young people who had felt forced to immigrate to the colonies in the 1660s and 1670s were staying at home. WP would have to offer especially attractive terms of settlement in Pennsylvania, and he would have to publicize his colony aggressively. Again this would not be easy, for there were no newspapers and magazines with mass circulation.

WP did have one important advantage as a colonial promoter: he was personally acquainted with most of the leading Quakers, such as Robert Turner, throughout the British Isles, and he could draw upon this Quaker network in trying to sell Pennsylvania. Because they were savagely persecuted in Britain, and because most of them were hard-working, ambitious people who wanted to improve their living conditions, Quakers made excellent potential recruits for immigration to America. Still, some believed that it was wicked to flee from persecution, and those who were attracted to America had other choices besides Pennsylvania; the colonies of East and West New Jersey were also Quaker settlements. In any case, WP wanted to establish a community in Pennsylvania in which people of diverse religious persuasions could live in harmony. Thus in his promotional campaign, he deliberately tried to recruit colonists from outside as well as inside the Society of Friends.

In his first letters announcing the new colony, WP revealed an enormous confidence, born of his conviction that both God and Charles II favored his venture. WP believed God would bless Pennsylvania and "make it the seed of a nation" (doc. 12). He promised the Dutch, Swedish, and English inhabitants already living on the Delaware that he would treat them fairly and that they would be governed by laws of their own making (doc. 13). And to Lord Baltimore he offered friendship and proposed a speedy settlement of the Pennsylvania-Maryland boundary (doc. 14).

WP then set to work writing his first promotional pamphlet, *Some Account of the Province of Pennsylvania* (doc. 15), in which he described the colony and issued a call for investors and settlers. He published hundreds of copies of this ten-page pamphlet at his own expense, and also produced a shorter version, the two-page broadside *A Brief Account of the Province of Pennsylvania;* he distributed copies of both pieces to Quakers throughout the British Isles. He supplemented these publications with letters to friends and acquaintances, asking them to help him recruit buyers of Pennsylvania land. In all of this correspondence, WP stressed his hope that the new colony would serve the world as an example of just government and virtuous society. But WP was also careful to announce terms for selling or renting land which would lure as many investors and settlers as possible. For he viewed Pennsylvania as a business venture that would get him out of debt.

WP's letter to Turner, which follows, is particularly interesting because in it he describes how Pennsylvania obtained its name.

## 12 §
### To Robert Turner

5 March 1681

Dear Friend[1]

My true love in the Lord salutes thee and dear Friends that love the Lord's precious truth in those parts. Thine I have[2] and for my business here, know that after many waitings, watchings, solicitings, and disputes in [the Privy] Council, this day my country was confirmed to me under the Great Seal of England with large powers and privileges, by the name of Pennsylvania, a name the king would give it in honor to my father. I chose New-Wales, being as this [is] a pretty hilly country, but Penn being Welsh for a head, as Penmaenmawr in Wales and Penrith in Cumberland and Penn in Buckinghamshire, the highest land in England,[3] called this Pennsylvania which is the high or head woodlands. For I proposed, when the secretary, a Welshman,[4] refused to have it called New-Wales, Sylvania, and they added Penn to it; and though I much opposed it and went to the king to have it struck out and altered, he said it was passed and he would take it upon him.[5] Nor could twenty guineas move the undersecretaries[6] to vary the name, for I feared lest it should be looked on as a vanity in me and not as a respect in the king, as it truly was, to my father whom he often mentions with praise. Thou may communicate my grant to Friends, and expect shortly my proposals. It is a clear and just thing, and my God that has given it me through many difficulties will I believe bless and make it the seed of a nation. I shall have a tender care to the government that it be well laid at first. No more now, but dear love in the truth.

Thy true friend,
W Penn

Transcript. HSP. (*PWP*, 2:83-84).

1. Robert Turner (1635-1700) was a Quaker cloth merchant of Dublin who bought land in both New Jersey and Pennsylvania, and recruited Irish purchasers of Pennsylvania land for WP.

2. This letter has not been found.

3. Penmaenmawr is a mountain on the northern coast of Wales; its precipitous cliffs drop from great height into the sea. Penrith is a market town in southeastern Cumberland. Penn, Bucks., is located in the Chiltern Hills at an altitude of about 500 feet; it is by no means the highest point in England.

4. Probably Sir Leoline Jenkins, a secretary of state, who was born in Wales.

5. WP means that the king would take responsibility for choosing the name of Pennsylvania.

6. The two undersecretaries of state who could not be bribed were John Cooke and Francis Gwyn.


# 13 §

## To the Inhabitants of Pennsylvania

London, 8 April 1681

My Friends[1]

I wish you all happiness, here and hereafter. These are to let you know that it has pleased God in His providence to cast you within my lot and care. It is a business, that though I never undertook before, yet God has given me an understanding of my duty and an honest mind to do it uprightly. I hope you will not be troubled at your change and the king's choice, for you are now fixed, at the mercy of no governor that comes to make his fortune great; you shall be governed by laws of your own making, and live a free and, if you will, a sober and industrious people. I shall not usurp the right of any, or oppress his person. God has furnished me with a better resolution, and has given me His grace to keep it. In short, whatever sober and free men can reasonably desire for the security and improvement of their own happiness I shall heartily comply with, and in five months resolve, if it please God, to see you.[2] In the meantime, pray submit to the commands of my deputy[3] so far as they are consistent with the law, and pay him those dues[4] (that formerly you paid to the order of the governor of New York)[5] for my use and benefit. And so I beseech God to direct you in the way of righteousness, and therein prosper you and your children after you. I am

Your true friend,
Wm Penn

*Fairmount and Schuylkill River, by William Groombridge, 1800, HSP. Though painted 119 years after WP obtained his charter, this picture by an English immigrant of the 1790s provides some idea of the early Philadelphia landscape.*

ALS. HSP. (*PWP*, 2:84-85).

1. WP was addressing the English, Swedish, Finnish, and Dutch residents of the territory on the west bank of the Delaware, in what is now the states of Delaware and Pennsylvania. Small numbers of Europeans had been living in this area since 1638; in 1681 the total white population was less than two thousand. From 1664 to 1681 these people had been subject to the government of New York.

2. WP originally planned to depart for Pennsylvania in the late summer of 1681, but by Aug. he had decided to wait until the following spring and he did not actually leave until Aug. 1682.

3. William Markham (c. 1635-1704) was probably the son of one of Admiral Penn's sisters. WP commissioned him as deputy-governor on 10 Apr. 1681, he reached Pennsylvania in the summer of 1681, and served until WP's arrival in 1682.

4. Rents and taxes.

5. Sir Edmund Andros (1637-1714) was governor of New York from 1674 to 1681, but had been recalled to London in late 1680. He left Lt. Anthony Brockholls in charge as his deputy.

# 14 §

## To Lord Baltimore

Westminster,[1] 10 April 1681

It having graciously pleased the king upon diverse good considerations to make me a neighbor to Maryland, I thought it necessary to make some offer of friendship, and give a fit rise for a future good correspondence. I omit the particulars of my pretensions; they are so kindly and amply expressed in the king's letter,[2] and to a man of good sense, it is enough to be once told of the matter.

The bearer is a gentleman and my kinsman,[3] to whom I have left the manage of my affairs. As his integrity will insist upon my right, his prudence and experience will always guide him from any indecent thing. I only beg one thing: it is short, but the text of all that can be said, do to me as thou would be done to. I am a stranger in the affairs of the country, he can have little light from me. I do so much depend upon the influence and prevalence [that] the king's goodness will have upon thee that I omit to be any further solicitous, believing that a great and prudent man will always act with caution and obedience to the mind of his prince; so that this letter was rather to be civil, than to pass so ill a compliment upon the Lord Baltimore, or the king's letter, as to think it could give any aid to the one, or light to the other.

I shall conclude with this request, that it would please thee to give my cousin and deputy all the dispatch possible in the business of the bounds,[4] that observing our just limits in that and all other things we may begin and maintain a just and friendly intercourse, which I do here promise to endeavor and observe on my part with all the truth and care imaginable; and whatever favors he receives, I shall place to my account. And perhaps there are many ways by which I may discharge them, which may give the Lord Baltimore reason to believe I do not undeserve usage and quality of his

Very true friend,

My respects to thy lady.[5]        Wm Penn

My kinsman's name is William Markham.

ALS. Maryland Historical Society, Baltimore. (*PWP*, 2:87-88).

1. Westminster, Middlx., now a part of London, where Whitehall Palace and other governmental buildings were located.
2. Charles II wrote to Lord Baltimore on 2 Apr. 1681, informing the proprietor of Maryland that he had granted Pennsylvania to WP "from regard to the merits and services of his father Sir William Penn." The king's letter described the boundaries, asked Baltimore to assist WP's deputies and officers, and told him to assign persons to meet with WP's agents to define the boundaries of Maryland and Pennsylvania in accordance with the charter.
3. William Markham delivered this letter to Baltimore in Maryland in late Aug. 1681.
4. For discussion of the Maryland-Pennsylvania boundary controversy, see the headnote to doc. 35.
5. Baltimore's second wife, Jane, whom he married in 1666. She died in 1701.

# 15 ∫

## Some Account of the Province of Pennsylvania

L IKE real estate developers today, WP was eager to advertise the advantages of moving to his new property. He wrote eight promotional tracts "to give some public notice" of Pennsylvania "to the world." If he were trying to sell land today, he would have produced a flashy brochure filled with many pictures, but WP's promotional tracts were very different—sober and restrained in tone. He had no real need to exaggerate or oversell, for the printed word had enormous impact upon seventeenth-century readers.

*Some Account of the Province of Pennsylvania* was the first promotional tract WP wrote after obtaining his charter in March 1681. Since he was already widely known as a Quaker leader, he made no mention of his religion or of his plans for a holy experiment in this pamphlet. Clearly WP was hoping to appeal to a wider, non-Quaker audience, but he also sent the tract to Friends throughout England, Ireland, Scotland, and Wales, and it was quickly translated into Dutch and German.

Since WP had not yet been to Pennsylvania when he wrote *Some Account,* his description of his new land was necessarily brief, and his tips for packing and preparing for the journey rather vague. He concentrated instead on a lively defense of colonization, and stressed the advantages of leaving the Old World for the New, where land, material profits, improved family life, and good government awaited the industrious adventurer. The contrast he painted between the decadence of the Old World and the hard-working innocence of the New World would become a regular fixture in American literature.

SOME ACCOUNT OF THE PROVINCE OF PENNSYLVANIA
IN AMERICA;
Lately Granted under the Great Seal of ENGLAND
to William Penn, etc.
Together with Privileges and Powers
necessary to the well-governing thereof.
Made public for the Information of such as are or may be
disposed to Transport themselves or Servants into those Parts.

---

LONDON: Printed and Sold by *Benjamin Clark*[1]
Bookseller in *George Yard Lombard Street,* 1681.

Since (by the good providence of God) a country in *America* is fallen to my lot, I thought it not less my duty than my honest interest to give some public notice of it to the world, that those of our own, or other nations, that are inclined to transport themselves or families beyond the seas, may find another country added to their choice; that if they shall happen to like the *place, conditions* and *constitutions* (so far as the present infancy of things will allow us any prospect), they may, if they please, fix with me in the *province* hereafter described. But before I come to treat of my particular concernment, I shall take leave to say something of the benefit of *plantations* or *colonies* in general, to obviate a common objection.

*Colonies,* then, are the seeds of nations begun and nourished by the care of wise and populous countries, as conceiving them best for the increase of human stock, and beneficial for commerce.

Some of the wisest men in history have justly taken their fame from this design and service. We read of the reputation given on this account to *Moses, Joshua* and *Caleb*[2] in Scripture records; and what renown the *Greek* story yields to *Lycurgus, Theseus,* and those *Greeks* that planted many parts of *Asia.* Nor is the *Roman* account wanting of instances to the credit of that people. They had a *Romulus,* a *Numa Pompilius;*[3] and not only reduced, but moralized the manners of the nations they subjected, so that they may have been rather said to conquer their barbarity than them.

Nor did any of these ever dream it was the way of decreasing their people or wealth. For the cause of the decay of any of those states or empires was not their *plantations,* but their *luxury and corruption of manners.* For when they grew to neglect their ancient discipline that maintained and rewarded virtue and industry, and addicted themselves to *pleasure* and *effeminacy,* they debased their spirits and debauched their morals, from whence ruin did never fail to follow to any people. With justice, therefore, I deny the vulgar opinion against *plantations, that they weaken* England. They have manifestly enriched and so strengthened her, which I briefly evidence thus:

*1st.* Those that go into a foreign *plantation,* their industry there is worth more than if they stayed at home, the product of their labor being in commodities of a superior nature to those of this *country.* For instance, what is an improved acre in *Jamaica* or *Barbados*[4] worth to an improved acre in *England?* We know it is three times the value, and the product of it comes for *England,* and is usually paid for in *English growth* and *manufacture.* Nay, *Virginia* shows that an ordinary industry in one man produces three thousand pound weight of tobacco and twenty barrels of corn yearly. He feeds himself, and brings as much of commodity into *England* besides as being returned in the growth and workmanship of this country, is much more than he could have spent here. Let it also be remembered, that the three thousand weight of tobacco brings in three thousand twopences by way of custom to the king, which makes £25—an extraordinary profit.

*2dly.* More being produced and imported than we can spend here, we export it to other countries in *Europe,* which brings in money or the growth of those countries, which is the same thing. And this is [to] the advantage of the *English* merchants and seamen.

*3dly.* Such as could not only not *marry* here, but hardly live and allow themselves clothes, do marry there, and bestow thrice more in all necessaries and conveniencies (and not a little in ornamental things, too) for themselves, their wives, and children, both as to apparel and household stuff, which coming out of *England, I say it is impossible that* England *should not be a considerable gainer.*

*4thly.* But let it be considered *that the plantations employ many hundreds of shipping and many thousands of seamen,* which must be in diverse respects an advantage to *England,* being an island, and by nature fitted for navigation above any country in *Europe.* This is followed by other depending trades, as *shipwrights, carpenters, sawyers, hewers, trunnel-makers, joiners, slopsellers, drysalters,*[5] *iron-workers,* the *Eastland merchants, timber-sellers,* and *victualers,*[6] with many more trades which hang upon *navigation.* So that we may easily see the objection (*that colonies or plantations hurt* England) is at least of no strength, especially if we consider how many thousand *blacks* and *Indians* are also accommodated with *clothes* and many sorts of *tools* and *utensils* from *England,* and that their *labor* is mostly brought hither, which adds *wealth* and *people* to the *English Dominions.* But it is further said: *They injure* England, *in that they draw away too many of the people; for we are not so populous in the countries as formerly.*[7] I say there are other reasons for that.

*1st. Country people* are so extremely addicted to put their children into gentlemen's service, or send them to towns to learn trades, that *husbandry is neglected;* and after a soft and delicate usage there, they are forever unfitted for the labor of a *farming* life.

*2dly.* The *pride* of the age in its *attendance* and *retinue* is so gross and universal, that where a man of £1000 a year formerly kept but four or five servants, he now keeps more than twice the number. He must have a *gentleman* to wait upon him in his chambers, a *coachman,* a *groom* or two, a *butler,* a *man cook,* a *gardener,* two or three *lackies,* it may be an *huntsman* and a *falconer;* the wife, a *gentlewoman,* and *maids accordingly.* This was not known by our *ancestors* of like quality. This hinders the *plow* and the *dairy,* from whence they are taken, and instead of keeping people to manly labor, they are effeminated by a lazy and luxurious living. But which is worse, these people *rarely marry,* though many of them do worse; but if they do, it is when they are in age. And the reason is clear: because their usual *keeping* at their master's is too great and costly for them with a family at their own charge, and they scarcely know how to live lower; so that too many of them choose rather to vend their lusts at an *evil ordinary* than honestly marry and work, *the excess and sloth of the age not allowing of marriage and the charge that follows;* all which hinders the increase of our people. If men, they often turn either *soldiers,* or *gamesters,* or *highwaymen.* If women, they too frequently *dress themselves for a bad market,* rather than know the *dairy* again or honestly return to *labor,* whereby it happens that both the stock of the nation decays and the issue is corrupted.

*3dly.* Of old time, the *nobility* and *gentry* spent their estates in the country, and that kept the people in it; and their servants married and sat at easy rents under their master's favor, which peopled the place. Now the great men (too much loving the town and resorting to *London*) draw many people thither to attend them, who either don't marry, or if they do, they pine away their small gains in some petty shop; for there are so many, they prey upon one another.

*4thly.* The country being thus neglected, *and no due balance kept between trade and husbandry, city, and country,* the poor country man takes double toil, and cannot (for want of hands) dress and manure his land to the advantage it formerly yielded him. Yet must he pay the old rents, which occasions servants, and such children as go not to trades, to continue single, at least *all their youthful time,* which also obstructs the increase of our people.

*5thly.* The decay of some country manufactures (where no provision is made to supply the people with a new way of living) causes the more industrious to go abroad to seek their bread in other countries, and gives the lazy an occasion to loiter and beg or do worse, by which means the land *swarms with beggars.* Formerly it was rare to find any asking *alms* but the *maimed,* or *blind,* or *very aged.* Now thousands of both sexes run up and down, both city and country, that are sound and youthful and able to work, with false pretenses and certificates. Nor is there any care taken to employ or deter such vagrants, which weakens the country as to people and labor.

To which let me add, that the great *debauchery* in this kingdom has not only rendered many unfruitful when married, but they live not out half their time, through excesses, which might be prevented by a vigorous execution of our good laws against corruption of manners. These and the like evils are the true grounds of the decay of our people in the country, to say nothing of *plague* and *wars.* Towns and cities cannot complain of the decay of people, being more replenished than ever, especially *London,*[8] which with reason helps the country man to this objection. And though some do go to the *plantations,* yet numbering the parishes in *England* and computing how many live more than die, and are born than buried, there goes not over to all the *plantations* a fourth part of the yearly increase of the people. And when they are there, *they are not* (as I said before) *lost to* England, since they furnish them with much *clothes, household stuff, tools,* and the like necessaries, and that in greater quantities than here their condition could have needed, or they could have bought, being there well to pass that were but low here, if not poor; and now masters of families, too, when here they had none, and could hardly keep themselves. And very often it happens that some of them, after their industry and success there have made them wealthy, they return and *empty* their riches into *England,* one in this capacity being able to buy out twenty of what he was when he went over.

Thus much to justify the credit and benefit of *plantations,* wherein I have not sought to speak my interest, but my judgment; and I dare venture the success of it with all sober and considering men. I shall now proceed to give some account of my own concern.

*1st. I shall say what may be necessary of the place or province.*

*2dly. Touch upon the Constitutions.*

*3dly. Lay down the conditions.*

*4thly. Give my sense what persons will be fit to go.*

*5thly. What utensils, furniture, and commodities are fit to carry with them, with the charge of the voyage, and what is first to be done and expected there for some time.*

And lastly, *I shall give an abstract of the grant by letters patents under the Great Seal of* England, *that an account may be given of the estate and power granted to me thereby.*

## I. *Something of the Place.*

The place lies 600 miles nearer the sun than *England;* for *England* begins at the 50th degree and ten minutes of north latitude, and this place begins at forty, which is about the latitude of *Naples* in *Italy,* or *Montpellier* in *France.*[9] I shall say little in its praise to excite desires in any, whatever I could truly write as to the soil, air, and water. This shall satisfy me, that by the *blessing* of God and the honesty and industry of man, it may be a good and fruitful land.

For *navigation* it is said to have two conveniencies: the one by lying nine score miles upon *Delaware* River, that is to say, about three score and ten miles before we come to the *Falls*[10] where a vessel of two hundred tons may sail (and some creeks and small harbors in that distance, where ships may come nearer than the river into the country), and above the *Falls,* for sloops and boats, as I am informed, to the extent of the patent. The other convenience is through *Chesapeake Bay.*

For timber and other wood, there is variety for the use of man.

For *fowl, fish,* and *wild deer,* they are reported to be plentiful in those parts. Our *English* provision is likewise now to be had there at reasonable rates. The commodities that the country is thought to be *capable* of, are *silk, flax, hemp, wine, cider, woad, madder, licorice, tobacco, potashes,*[11] and *iron,* and it does actually produce *hides, tallow, pipe-staves,*[12] beef, pork, sheep, wool, corn,[13] as *wheat, barley, rye,* and also *furs,* as your *peltry, minks, raccoons, martens,*[14] and such like; store of *furs* which is to be found among the *Indians,* that are profitable commodities in *Europe.*

The way of trading in those countries is thus: they send to the southern plantations *corn, beef, pork, fish,* and *pipe-staves,* and take their growth and bring for *England,* and return with *English* goods to their own country. Their *furs* they bring for *England,* and either sell them here, or carry them out again to other parts of *Europe,* where they will yield a better price. And for those that will follow *merchandise* and *navigation,* there is conveniency, and *timber sufficient for shipping.*

## II. The Constitutions.

*For the Constitution of the country, the patent shows, first,* that the people and governor have a legislative power, so that no law can be made, nor money raised, but by the people's consent.

*2dly.* That the rights and freedoms of *England* (*the best and largest in Europe*) shall be in force there.

*3dly.* That making no law against allegiance (*which should we, it were by the law of* England, *void of itself that moment*) we may enact what laws we please for the good prosperity and security of the said province.[15]

*4thly.* That so soon as any are engaged with me, we shall begin a *scheme* or *draft* together, such as shall give ample testimony of my sincere inclinations to encourage planters, and settle a free, just, and industrious *colony* there.

## III. The Conditions.

My conditions will relate to three sorts of people: *1st,* those that will buy; *2dly,* those that take up land upon *rent; 3dly,* servants. To the first, the shares I sell shall be certain as to number of acres; that is to say, every one shall contain five thousand acres, free from any *Indian* encumbrance, the price £100, and for the quitrent but one *English* shilling or the value of it yearly for a hundred acres; and the said quitrent not to begin to be paid till *1684.* To the second sort, that take up land upon rent, they shall have liberty so to do, paying yearly *one penny* per acre, not exceeding two hundred acres. To the third sort, to wit, *servants* that are carried over, fifty acres shall be allowed to the master for every head, and fifty acres to every servant when their time is expired.[16] And because some engage with me that may not be disposed to go, it were very advisable for every three adventurers to send an overseer with their servants, which would well pay the cost.

The *divident*[17] may be thus: if the persons concerned please, a tract of land shall be surveyed, say *fifty thousand acres to a hundred adventurers,* in which some of the best shall be set out for towns or cities; and there shall be so much ground allotted to each in those towns as may maintain some cattle and produce some corn. Then the remainder of the fifty thousand acres shall be shared among the said *adventurers* (casting up the barren for commons, and allowing for the same) whereby every *adventurer* will have a considerable quantity of land together, likewise every one a proportion by a navigable river, and then backward into the country. The manner of divident I shall not be strict in; we can but speak roughly of the matter here; but let men skillful in *plantations* be consulted, and I shall leave it to the majority of votes among the *adventurers* when it shall please God we come there, how to fix it to their own content.

IV. These persons that Providence seems to have most fitted
for plantations are,

*1st.* Industrious *husbandmen* and *day laborers,* that are hardly able (with extreme labor) to maintain their families and portion their children.

*2dly.* Laborious *handicrafts,* especially *carpenters, masons, smiths, weavers, tailors, tanners, shoemakers, shipwrights,* etc.,[18] where they may be spared or are low in the world. And as they shall want no encouragement, so their labor is worth more there than here, and there provision cheaper.

*3dly.* A plantation seems a fit place for those *ingenious spirits* that being low in the world, are much clogged and oppressed about a livelihood. For the means of subsisting being easy there, they may have time and opportunity to gratify their inclinations, and thereby improve science and help nurseries of people.

*4thly.* A fourth sort of men to whom a *plantation* would be proper, takes in those that are *younger brothers* of small inheritances; yet because they would live in sight of their kindred in some proportion to their quality, and can't do it without a labor that looks like *farming,* their condition is too strait for them; and if married, their children are often too numerous for the estate, and are frequently bred up to no trades, but are a kind of *hangers on or retainers to the elder brothers' table and charity;* which is a mischief, as in itself to be lamented, so here to be remedied. For land they have for next to nothing, which with moderate labor produces plenty of all things necessary for life, and such an increase as by traffic may supply them with all conveniencies.

*Lastly,* there are another sort of persons, not only fit for, but necessary in *plantations,* and that is, *men of universal spirits* that have an eye to the good of posterity, and that both understand and delight to promote good discipline and just government among a plain and well intending people. Such persons may find *room in colonies for their good counsel and contrivance,* who are shut out from being of much use or service to great nations under settled customs. These men deserve much esteem, and would be hearkened to. Doubtless it was this (*as I observed before*) that put some of the famous *Greeks* and *Romans* upon transplanting and regulating *colonies* of people in diverse parts of the world, whose names, for giving so great proof of their wisdom, virtue, labor and constancy, are with justice honorably delivered down by story to the praise of our own times; though the world, after all its higher pretenses of religion, barbarously errs from their excellent example.

V. The Journey and its Appurtenances, and what is to be
done there at first coming.

Next let us see, *what is fit for the journey and place when there, and also what may be the charge of the voyage, and what is to be expected and done there at first,* that such as incline to go, may not be to seek here, or brought under any disappointments there. The *goods* fit to take with them for use, or sell for profit, are all sorts of apparel and utensils for husbandry and building and household stuff. And because I know how much people are apt to fancy things beyond what they are, and that imaginations are great flatterers of the minds of men, to the end that none may delude themselves with an expectation of an immediate amendment of their conditions so soon as it shall please God they arrive there, I would have them understand *that they must look for a winter before a summer comes;* and they must be willing to be two or three years without some of the conveniences they enjoy at home. And yet I must needs say that *America* is another thing than it was at the first plantation of *Virginia* and *New England,*[19] for there is better accommodation, and *English* provisions are to be had at easier rates. However, I am inclined to set down particulars as near as those inform me that know the place, and have been planters both in that and in the neighboring *colonies.*

*1st.* The passage will come for masters and mistresses at most to £6 a head, for servants £5 a head, and for children under seven years of age, fifty shillings, except they suck, then nothing.

Next being, by the mercy of God, safely arrived in *September* or *October,* two men may clear as much ground by spring (when they set the corn of that country) as will bring in that time, twelve month, forty barrels, which amounts to two hundred bushels, which makes twenty-five quarters of corn. So that the first year they must buy corn, which is usually very plentiful. They may, so soon as they come, buy *cows,* more or less, as they want or are able, which are to be had at easy rates. For *swine,* they are plentiful and cheap; these will quickly increase to a stock. So that after the first year, what with the poorer sort sometimes laboring to others, and the more able *fishing, fowl-*

*ing,* and sometimes buying, they may do very well, till their own stocks are sufficient to supply them and their families, which will quickly be, and to spare, if they follow the *English husbandry* as they do in *New England,* and *New York,* and get winter fodder for their stock.

    VI. And Lastly, an Abstract of the Patent granted by the King
to William Penn, etc., the Fourth of *March,* 1681. . . .
[There follows an outline of WP's charter, similar to the one provided in the headnote to doc. 11, above.]

    To conclude, I desire all my dear country folks, who may be inclined to go into those parts, to consider seriously the premises, *as well the present inconveniences as future ease and plenty,* that so none may move rashly or from a fickle but solid mind, *having above all things, as eye to the providence of God, in the disposal of themselves.* And I would further advise all such at least, to have the permission, if not the good liking of their near relations, for that is both natural, and a duty incumbent upon all; and by this means will natural affection be preserved, and a friendly and profitable correspondence be maintained between them. In all which *I beseech Almighty God to direct us, that His blessing may attend our honest endeavor, and then the consequence of all our undertaking will turn to the glory of His great name, and the true happiness of us and our posterity.* Amen.

WILLIAM PENN

POSTSCRIPT.

    Whoever are desirous to be concerned with me in this *province,* they may be treated with and further satisfied, at *Philip Ford's*[20] in *Bow Lane* in *Cheapside,* and at *Thomas Rudyard's*[21] or *Benjamin Clark's* in *George Yard* in *Lombard Street.*

THE END.

Printed tract. Not published in *PWP,* Vol. Two.

    1. Benjamin Clark was a London Quaker printer who published several of WP's promotional tracts.
    2. These three Hebrew leaders were regarded as colonizers by WP because they headed the exodus out of Egypt that led to the birth of Israel.
    3. Lycurgus was the legendary law-giver of Sparta; Theseus was the legendary king of Athens who unified the communities of Attica into the city-state of Athens; Romulus was the legendary founder of Rome and of the first Roman colony; and Numa Pompilius was Rome's second king and law-giver. These four figures are the first characters in Plutarch's *Lives,* which WP knew; thus WP is subtly comparing himself with these classical heroes who created powerful new nations.
    4. Jamaica and Barbados, the chief sugar islands in the British West Indies, were known for their rich soil.
    5. Hewers were wood- and stone-cutters. Trunnel-makers made wooden pegs (trunnels) used in shipbuilding. Joiners were carpenters. Slopsellers sold cheap clothing, especially sailor's clothes. Drysalters dealt in drugs and dyes, many of which were imported from America.
    6. The Eastland merchants engaged in the Baltic trade. Victualers were suppliers of food and provisions.

7. It was believed (probably correctly) that England's rural population was declining during the late seventeenth century.

8. Despite its terrible disease environment and high mortality rate, London doubled in population during the seventeenth century. In 1681 roughly 500,000 people (one-tenth of the total population of England) lived in or around the city.

9. The latitude of Naples, Italy, is 40 degrees 52 minutes north. Montpellier, in southern France, is considerably north of Pennsylvania, at almost 44 degrees.

10. The Falls of the Delaware, at present-day Trenton, New Jersey.

11. Woad is a plant whose leaves give a blue dye. Madder is a plant whose root is used in making red dye. Potash is a crude form of potassium, obtained by washing and then evaporating wood ashes in large iron pots; it was used in making soap and glass.

12. Pipe-staves were strips of wood used for making large casks to hold liquids.

13. Cereal crops, excluding Indian corn which the English called maize.

14. Martens, or sables, are small animals with soft, dark fur.

15. Up to this point, the editors have followed the original printer's use of italics. Beginning here and continuing to Part VI, however, the printer placed most of the text in italic type and used roman for words he wanted to emphasize. The editors have reversed this usage here so that this section conforms to the rest of the text; hence, words needing emphasis are printed throughout in italics.

16. For a discussion of WP's land policy, see the headnote to doc. 17.

17. The method of distributing or dividing. WP expects that groups of purchasers will receive large blocks of land collectively from the proprietor, and then share out individual holdings among themselves.

18. WP was particularly successful in recruiting craft workers of this sort for Pennsylvania. Of the 352 purchasers of land in 1681-1685 who can be identified by occupation, 48 percent were craftsmen. Only 23 percent were husbandmen, or farmers.

19. When Virginia was first settled in 1607, and New England in 1620, the colonists experienced a "starving time." As WP correctly predicted, there was no such disaster in Pennsylvania in the 1680s.

20. Philip Ford (c. 1631-1702) was a London Quaker shopkeeper whom WP employed as his principal business manager from 1669 to the 1690s, when the two men disagreed over money that WP owed Ford. After Ford's death, his widow, Bridget, sued WP for a large debt and won her case.

21. Thomas Rudyard (d. 1692), a Quaker lawyer of London, was one of WP's chief land agents and helped him draft the *Frame of Government* (see doc. 29, below). He served briefly as deputy-governor of East Jersey in 1682-1684, and fell out with WP over the privileges of First Purchasers in Philadelphia in 1684 (see doc. 96, below).

# 16 ∫

## To Robert Turner, Anthony Sharp, and Roger Roberts

WP addressed the following letter to three prominent Friends in Dublin whom he had known and worked with on Quaker causes for more than a decade. The letter provides a good illustration of how WP advertised his new colony among Quakers throughout England, Ireland, Scotland, Wales, and Holland.

Friends Robert Turner, Anthony Sharp, and Roger Roberts

My love salutes you in the abiding Truth of our God that is precious in all lands; the Lord God of righteousness keep us in it, and then shall we be the daily witnesses of the comforts and refreshments that come from it to His praise, that is the fountain of all good. Having published a paper with relation to my province in America (at least, what I thought advisable to publish), I here inclose one,[1] that you may know and inform others of it. I have been these 13 years the servant of Truth and Friends,[2] and for my testimony sake lost much, not only by the greatness and preferments of this world, but £16,000 of my estate, that had I not been what I am I had long ago obtained.[3] But I murmur not, the Lord is good to me, and the interest His Truth with His people may more than repair it. For many are drawn forth to be concerned with me, and perhaps this way of satisfaction has more of the hand of God in it than a downright payment.

This I can say, that I had an opening of joy as to these parts in the year 1661 at Oxford, 20 years since;[4] and as my understanding and inclinations have been much directed to observe and reprove mischiefs in government, so it is now put into my power to settle one. For the matters of liberty and privilege, I purpose that which is extraordinary, and to leave myself and successors no power of doing mischief, that the will of one man may not hinder the good of a whole country; but to publish those things now and here, as matters stand, would not be wise,[5] and I was advised to reserve that till I came there. Your ancient love to me makes me believe you will have a brotherly eye to my honest concern, and what Truth makes you free to do, you will, and more I expect not. It is a clear, untangled, and I may say, honorable bottom. No more, but let Friends know it, as you are free. With my [fervent] love in that which no waters can quench, nor time make wax old, nor distance wear out.

Your friend and brother,<br>Wm Penn

The enclosed was first read to traders, planters, and shipmasters that know those parts, and finally to the most eminent of Friends hereaway, and so comes forth. I have forborn pains[6] and allurement, and with Truth,

W. P.

There are several inhabitants on the place already able to yield accommodation to such as at first go, and care is taken already for to look out [for] a convenient tract of land for a first settlement.

Transcript. APS. (*PWP*, 2:88–90).

1. A copy of *Some Account*. See doc. 15.
2. WP became a Quaker in late 1667 while he was in Ireland overseeing his father's estates. He was converted after hearing Thomas Loe, a traveling minister, speak in Cork.
3. In his petition to Charles II (doc. 1), WP described his debt of "at least £11,000;" with interest, this sum could have totaled £16,000 by 1681. In addressing the king, WP blamed the Stop of the Exchequer for his financial problems, but here he presents himself to fellow Quakers as a victim of religious persecution.

4. WP entered Christ Church College, Oxford, in Oct. 1660, and was expelled a little over a year later for religious nonconformity.

5. Having received his charter through the benevolence of Charles and James, WP did not wish to alienate his court supporters by advertising plans for a government far more liberal in character than the Stuart administration in England.

6. Perhaps a copyist's mistake for "gains."

# Part IV

SELLING LAND TO THE
FIRST PURCHASERS §
JULY 1681–DECEMBER 1681

*WP's Land Sale to Philip Ford, 14 July 1681, Bedfordshire Record Office, England. WP's first sale of land in Pennsylvania; see doc. 18.*

IN July 1681, after he had advertised his new colony for four months, WP began to sell shares of Pennsylvania land to investors who became known as the First Purchasers. This was a step of crucial importance. WP needed to collect as much money as possible from land sales in order to pay off his debts and cover his colonizing expenses, which were substantial. He also had to recruit investors who would migrate to Pennsylvania, or who would at least send over servants and tenants, to supply the manpower needed by the new settlement. WP's buyers needed to meet further requirements. Some, for example, had to be prosperous people, with enough capital of their own to spend on Pennsylvania agriculture and commerce. They should bring with them a variety of occupational skills. And whether or not they were Quakers, the First Purchasers had to be men and women who shared some of WP's ideals, and who could take active part in shaping his holy experiment.

Between March and July 1681, WP revised his land policy considerably, and his plans reached final form when he pledged himself to a series of "Conditions and Concessions" (doc. 17) at a meeting in London on 11 July, attended by his chief prospective buyers. WP had wanted to sell 5000-acre "proprietary shares" for £100 each, but when he discovered that few buyers were willing or able to invest so much in the Pennsylvania wilderness, he agreed to sell 500 acres for £10, and he eventually sold tracts as small as 125 acres. He also required all purchasers to pay him an annual quitrent or tax of one shilling per hundred acres. Settlers who could not afford to buy land were invited to become WP's tenants and rent up to 200 acres from him at the higher rate of one penny per acre. Each settler who brought over a servant would receive a bonus, known as headright, of fifty acres, and each servant would also receive fifty acres from WP upon the expiration of his service. For this free land the ex-servant had to pay an annual quitrent of two shillings, and the master had to pay four shillings: much higher taxes than WP charged for purchased land (see doc. 19). To encourage quick and orderly development of the larger tracts in Pennsylvania, WP stated that he would lay out no more than 1000 acres in any one location unless the purchaser established a family upon each 1000-acre section of his grant within three years. Finally, WP pledged to give bonus lots to early purchasers in "a large town or city" (the future Philadelphia) at the rate of one acre in the city for every fifty purchased. This promise proved particularly tempting, and in 1682-1684 the First Purchasers snapped up their city lots in Philadelphia.

WP's land sales now proceeded briskly. Between July and October 1681, he sold over 300,000 acres to nearly 300 First Purchasers. Appropriately, the first deed of sale (doc. 18) was for a 5000-acre share to Philip Ford, who was WP's business agent in London and one of his principal salesmen for land in Pennsylvania. During the first four years after WP obtained his charter, about 600 First Purchasers bought more than 700,000 acres of Pennsylvania land. They paid WP approximately £9000, which was less than he had hoped for, but in every other respect his salesmanship proved to be highly successful. The First Purchasers were primarily Quaker merchants, craftsmen, shop-keepers, and farmers. Some of them came from Ireland, Wales, Scotland, Holland, France, Germany, the West Indies, and North America, but the great majority lived in the country districts of southern and western England, and in the cities of London and Bristol. About half of them actually migrated to Pennsylvania, bringing their families as well as many servants, and making possible the rapid development of the new colony.


# 17 §

## Conditions or Concessions to the First Purchasers

Certain Conditions or Concessions agreed upon by William Penn,
Proprietary and Governor of the Province of Pennsylvania, and those
who are the Adventurers and Purchasers in the same Province.
The 11th of July 1681.[1]

1st.   That so soon as it pleases God that the abovesaid persons arrive there, a certain quantity of land or ground plot shall be laid out for a large town or city in the most convenient place upon the river for health and navigation, and every purchaser and adventurer shall by lot have so much land therein, as will answer to the proportion he has bought or taken up upon rent.[2] But it is to be noted that the surveyors shall consider what roads or highways will be necessary to the cities, towns, or through the lands. Great roads from city to city, not to contain less than forty feet in breadth, shall be first laid out and declared to be for highways, before the dividend of acres be laid out for the purchaser; and the like observation to be had for streets in the towns and cities, that there may be convenient roads and streets preserved not to be encroached upon by any planter or builder, and that none may build irregularly to the damage of another, in this custom guide.

2dly.   That the land in the town be laid out together after the proportion of 10,000 acres of the whole country: that is, 200 acres if the place will bear it. However, that the proportion be by lot and entire, so as those that desire to be together, especially those that are by the catalogue laid together, may be so laid together both in the town and country.[3]

3dly. That when the country lots are laid out, every purchaser from 1000 to 10[000 acres?], or more, not to have above 1000 acres together unless in 3 years they plant a [family?] upon every 1000 acres; but that all such as purchase together lie together, and if as many as comply with this condition, that the whole be laid out together.

4thly. That where any number of purchasers more or less, whose number of acres amounts to five or ten thousand acres, desire to sit together in a lot or township, they shall have their lot or township cast together in such places as have convenient h[arbors or ?] navigable rivers attending it, if such can be found. And in case any one or more purchasers plant not according to agreement in this concession to the prejudice of others [of the same ?] township, upon complaint thereof made to the governor or his deputy with [assistance?], they may award (if they see cause) that the complaining purchaser may, paying the survey money and the purchase money and interest thereof, etc., [be] entitled, enrolled, and lawfully invested in the lands so not seated.

5thly. That the proportion of lands that shall be laid out in [the] first great town or city for every purchaser shall be after the proportion of ten acres for every five hundred acres purchased, if the place will allow it.

6thly. That notwithstanding there be no mention made in the several deeds made to the purchasers, yet the said William Penn does accord and declare that all rivers, rivulets, woods and underwoods, waters, watercourses, quarries, mines, and minerals (except mines royal[4]) shall be freely and fully enjoyed and wholly by the purchasers into whose lot they fall.

7thly. That for every 50 acres that shall be allotted to a servant at the end of his service, his quitrent shall be two shillings per annum; and the master or owner of the servant when he shall take up the other 50 acres, his quitrent shall be four shillings by the year. Or if the master of the servant (by reason in the indenture he is so obliged to do) allot out to the servant 50 acres in his own division, [the?] said master shall have on demand allotted him from the governor, the one hundred acres at the chief rent of six shillings per annum.[5]

8thly. And for the encouragement of such as are ingenious and willing to search out gold and silver mines in this province, it is hereby agreed that they have liberty to bore and dig in any man's property, fully paying the damage done; and in case a discovery should be made, that the discoverer have one-fifth, the owner of the soil (if not the discoverer) a tenth part, the governor two-fifths, and the rest to the public treasury, saving to the king the share reserved by patent.[6]

9thly. In every hundred thousand acres, the governor and proprietary by lot reserves ten to himself which shall lie but in one place.[7]

10thly. That every man shall be bound to plant or man so much of his share, or land, as shall be set out and surveyed within three years after it is so set out and surveyed, or else it shall be lawful for newcomers to be settled thereupon, paying to them their survey money, and they going on higher[8] for their shares.

11thly. There shall be no buying and selling, be it with the Indians or one among another, of any goods to be exported, but what shall be performed in public market when such places shall be set apart or erected, where they shall pass the public stamp or mark. If bad ware and prized as good, and deceitful in proportion or weights, to forfeit the value as if good and in full in weight and proportion to the public treasury of the province, whether it be the merchandise of the Indian or that of the planters.[9]

12thly. And forasmuch as it is usual with the planters to overreach the poor natives of the country in trade, by goods not being good of the kind or debased with mixtures, with which they are sensibly aggrieved, it is agreed whatever is sold to the Indians in consideration of their furs shall be sold in the marketplace, and there suffer the test whether good or bad; if good to pass; if not good, not to be sold for good, that the natives may not be abused nor provoked.

13thly. That no man shall, by any ways or means in word or deed, affront or wrong any Indian, but he shall incur the same penalty of the law as if he had committed it against his fellow planter. And if any Indian shall abuse in word or deed any planter of this province, that he shall not be his own judge upon the Indian, but he shall make his complaint to the governor of the province, or his lieutenant or deputy, or some inferior magistrate near him, who shall to the utmost of his power take care with the king of the said Indian, that all reasonable satisfaction be made to the said injured planter.

14thly. That all differences between the planters and the natives shall also be ended by twelve men, that is, by six planters and six natives; that so we may live friendly together and, as much as in us lies, prevent all occasions of heart burnings and mischiefs.

15thly. That the Indians shall have liberty to do all things relating to the improvement of their ground and providing sustenance for their families, that any of the planters shall enjoy.

16thly. That the laws, as to slanders, drunkenness, swearing, cursing, pride in apparel, trespasses, distresses, replevins, weights and measures, shall be the same as in England till altered by law in this province.[10]

17thly. That all shall mark their hogs, sheep, and other cattle, and what are not marked within three months after it is in their possession, be it young or old, it shall be forfeited to the governor; that so people may be compelled to avoid the occasion of much strife between planters.

18thly. That in clearing the ground, care be taken to leave one acre of trees for every five acres cleared, especially to preserve oak and mulberries for silk and shipping.

19thly. That all shipmasters shall give an account of their countries, names, ships, owners' freights, and passengers to an officer to be appointed for that purpose, which shall be registered within two days after their arrival; and if they shall refuse so to do, that then none presume to trade with them, upon forfeiture thereof, and that such masters be looked upon as having an evil intention to the province.

20thly. That no person leave the province without publication being made thereof in the marketplace three weeks before, and a certificate from some justice of the peace of his clearness with his neighbors and those he has dealt withal, so far as such an assurance can be attained and given. And if any master of a ship shall contrary hereunto receive and carry away any person that has not given that public notice, the said master shall be liable to all debts owing by the said person, so secretly transported from that province.

Lastly, that these are to be added to, or corrected by and with the [consent?] of the parties hereunto subscribed.

Wm Penn

Sealed and delivered in
the presence of

William Boelham,
Herbert Springett,
Thomas Rudyard.

Sealed and delivered in the
presence of all the proprietors, who have hereunto
subscribed, except Thomas
Farneborough and John
Goodson, in presence of

Hugh Chamberlain,
R. Murray,
Herbert Springett,
Humphrey South,
Thomas Barker,
Samuel Jobson,
John [and] Joseph Moore,
William Powel,
Richard Davies,
Griffith Jones,
Hugh Lamb,
Thomas Farneborough,
John Goodson.[11]

Copy. HSP. (*PWP*, 2:96-102).

1. As of 11 July, WP had apparently sold no land; the first surviving deed is dated 14 July, to Philip Ford (doc. 18, below). The "Adventurers and Purchasers" who signed doc. 17 were stating their intention to buy land.

2. WP was here pledging that every purchaser would be given bonus land in the new capital city.

3. This clause sets the ratio (1:50) of town to country acreage; in 1682, WP discovered that he had promised to give more bonus town land than he could deliver. The "catalogue" is probably a list of First Purchasers which WP sent to America with his commissioners in Oct. 1681; this list arranged 259 purchasers into thirty-two 10,000-acre sections.

4. Gold or silver mines.

5. The quitrents on land that masters received by headright and that servants earned through their service were much higher than those paid on purchased land, for which WP charged only one shilling per one hundred acres. Clearly WP wanted some long term income from this land, which he was giving away rather than selling.

6. WP's charter to Pennsylvania (doc. 11, sect. 3, above) reserved one-fifth of all gold and silver found in the colony for the crown.

7. In his charter WP was given the right to create proprietary manors; this is his first reference to their establishment.

8. Farther inland, on higher ground.

9. This clause attempts to establish a public standard for the price and quality of

Pennsylvania exports, partly to prevent cheating, and partly to protect the colony's commercial reputation.

10. According to the legal code of seventeenth-century England, people were liable to prosecution for slander, drunkenness, and trespass, and in addition they could be prosecuted for blasphemy or for wearing showy or "proud" clothing beyond their social station. Distresses were legal actions to seize property in payment of debts. Replevins were legal actions to recover property illegally taken.

11. Boelham, Springett, and Rudyard signed this document as witnesses. The other signers except "R. Murray" (perhaps a copyist's mistake for H[enry] Murrey, a minor First Purchaser), were all major First Purchasers of Pennsylvania land, and Boelham could be the purchaser William Bowman. All of these purchasers, except the Welshman Richard Davies, were residents of greater London.


# 18 §
## Land Sale to Philip Ford

14 July 1681

Know all men by these presents, that I, William Penn of Warminghurst[1] in the County of Sussex, Esquire, have had and received of and from Philip Ford of London, merchant, the sum of one hundred pounds of lawful English money, which said one hundred pounds is the consideration money for the purchase of five thousand acres of land in PENNSYLVANIA mentioned and expressed in one pair of indentures of bargain, sale, and release thereof, bearing even date herewith and made, or mentioned to be made, between me the said William Penn of the one part and Philip Ford of the other part; of and from which said one hundred pounds I, the said William Penn, do hereby for myself, my heirs, and assigns, remise[2] and release and quit claim the said Philip Ford, his heirs, executors, administrators, and assigns, and every of them, by these presents. Witness my hand this fourteenth day of July, *anno Domini* one thousand six hundred eighty and one, *annoque regni regis Carolus Secundi xxxiii*[3]

Wm Penn

Sealed and delivered in the presence of
Herbert Springett
Thomas Coxe
Isaac Swinton

DS. Bedfordshire Record Office, England. (*PWP,* 2:102).

1. In 1676 WP bought the manor house at Warminghurst, 45 miles south of London, with about 300 acres of land. He and his family lived there until 1697. WP and his son, William Penn, Jr., sold the estate in 1707.
2. Surrender.
3. "And in the year of the reign of King Charles II the thirty-third."

# 19 §

## To James Harrison

WP depended on a number of friends throughout the British Isles and in Europe to sell Pennsylvania land and to give him advice on setting up his colonial government. One man who helped promote WP's province and who later joined his inner circle of advisors in Pennsylvania was James Harrison (c. 1628-1687), a Quaker minister of Bolton, Lancs., in northern England. In this letter, WP commissions Harrison as one of his land agents, and explains his rent and quitrent policy for settlers and servants. He also delivers his most memorable description of his new colony as a "holy experiment," an example to the wicked world of service to God's truth. Harrison does not seem to have been an effective salesman, for few people in Lancashire bought land from WP. Harrison did buy 5000 acres himself, and apparently sold part of his tract to others (see doc. 65, below). He sailed to the new colony in 1682 and soon became the steward of WP's country estate, Pennsbury Manor in Bucks County.

25 August 1681

Dear J. Harrison:

In the fellowship of the Gospel of love, life, and peace, which God our Father that has brought with Jesus from the dead, do I tenderly salute thee, owning thy love and kindness to me, of which thine of the 5th month[1] gave me a sense and fresh remembrance which met me at London on my return from the west,[2] where the Lord prospered me beyond words, blessed be His honored name.

As to my voyage, it is not like to be so quick as I hoped; for the people upon whose going both my resolutions and service in going depended, though they buy and most send servants to clear and sow a [piece?] of land against they come, not one-[fifth?] can now get rid of their concerns here till spring. When they go, I go, [but?] my going with servants will not s[ettle?] a government, the great end of my going.[3] [Besides?], many flock in to be concerned with me. I am like to have many from France, some from Holland, and I hear some Scots will go.[4] For my country, [I eyed ?] the Lord in the obtaining of it; and more was I drawn inward to look to Him, and to o[we it ?] to His hand and power, than to any ot[her way ?]. I have so obtained it and desire that I may not be unworthy of His love, but do that which may answer His kind providence and serve His truth and people; that an example may be set up to the nations. There may be room there, though not here, for such a holy experiment.

Now dear James, for the 50 acres a servant to the master, and 50 to the servant, this is done for their sakes that can't buy, for I must either be paid by purchase or rent. That is, those that can't buy, may take up: if a master of a family, 200 acres at a penny an acre; afterwards, 50 acres per head for every man and maid servant but still at the same rent, else none would buy or rent, and so I should make nothing of my country. However, to encourage poor servants to go and be laborious, I have abated the 1d. to ½d. per acre when they are out of their time.[5] Now, if any about thee will engage and buy, there may be 10, yea, twenty to one share, which will be but £5 apiece, for which each will have 250 acres.[6] For those that can't pay their passage, let me know their names, and numbers, and ages; they must pay double rent to them that help them over; but this know, [that this rent is?] never to be raised and they are so to enjoy it forever. For the acre, it is the common statute acre as by our law allowed.[7] So dear James, thou may let me hear of thee and how things incline. I shall persuade none; it is a good country. With a good conscience it will do well. I am satisfied in it and leave it with the Lord. And in the love and fellowship of the Truth, I end

Thy friend and brother,

Wm Penn

My love to thy family and honest Friends. I here sign thee an authority to sell, about thee, to any that will buy. A ship goes with commissioners suddenly in 5 weeks,[8] to lay out the first and best land to the first adventurers. If any deal, let me know. I clear the king's and Indians' title.[9] The purchaser pays the scrivener and surveyor. I sign the deeds at Thomas Rudyard's when I know who and what.

Dear James Harrison, I do hereby nominate and appoint thee my lawful agent in my name and to my behoof, to bargain and sell (according to printed instructions)[10] any parcel of land in Pennsylvania (not below 250 acres to any one person) from time to time, and I shall ratify by deed under my hand all such sales. Witness my hand this 25th 6th month, 1681.

Wm Penn

ALS. HSP. (*PWP*, 2:107-9).

1. July.

2. WP had traveled to Bristol to sell land; he returned to London by 21 Aug.

3. When he wrote this letter, WP had already begun work on a constitution for his colony, but he did not complete his *Frame of Government* until Apr. 1682 (see docs. 26-30, below).

4. In fact, of the 531 First Purchasers whose geographical origins have been traced, only two came from France, one from the Netherlands, and two from Scotland.

5. Whereas WP charged the master of a servant an annual quitrent of four shillings on his fifty-acre headright, or a tax of approximately a penny per acre, he charged the ex-servant only two shillings for his fifty acres, or approximately a halfpenny per acre.

6. In June 1681, in his *Brief Account of Pennsylvania,* WP had said that ten persons could join together to purchase a 5000-acre share. Now he is willing to double the number in order to encourage small investors.

7. WP's English statute acre was 4840 sq. yds., or the modern measure. Harrison had perhaps inquired whether WP was using the Irish or Scottish acre, both of which were larger than the English.

8. See docs. 22 and 24, below.

9. See docs. 23, 36, and 37, below, for WP's clearing of titles with the Indians between 18 Oct. 1681 and 15 July 1682, before he left for Pennsylvania.

10. WP sent a package with this letter that probably included copies of his advertising pamphlets, *Some Account* and *Brief Account.*

## 20 §

## To Planters in Maryland

WP addressed the following letter to six planters who lived along the northern shore of Chesapeake Bay. It was delivered to Augustine Herrman, who lived at Bohemia Manor in Cecil County, Maryland. In this letter WP claimed jurisdiction over all people who inhabited what is now the northern quarter of Maryland. He did not know the precise location of the southern boundary granted in his charter, the 40th degree of latitude, and in the summer of 1681 he distributed a map of Pennsylvania that placed the 40th degree of latitude forty miles too far south. A section of this map is reproduced on p. 80. It shows the Pennsylvania border at the latitude of the present city of Baltimore. WP was certainly unwise in claiming so much Maryland territory before his agents had even taken an observation of the latitude at the head of Chesapeake Bay or discussed the boundary with Lord Baltimore, the proprietor of Maryland. WP's letter created a stir among the Maryland planters and triggered a bitter quarrel with Lord Baltimore, which soon consumed much of WP's time and energy, and diverted him from his central objectives in Pennsylvania.

London, 16 September 1681

My Friends[1]

I hope I do not improperly call you so, because in being so you will extremely befriend yourselves, as well as perform an act of duty to the king and justice to me.

I am equally a stranger to you all, but your being represented men of substance and reputation in that part of the [Chesapeake] Bay, which I presume falls within my patent, I choose to take this opportunity to begin our acquaintance, and by you with the rest of the people on your side of my country. And [I] do assure you and them, that I will be so far from taking any advantage to draw great profits to myself, that you shall find me and my government easy, free, and just; and as you shall study to be fair and respectful to me and my just interests, I will not be short of giving you all reasonable assurances on my part, that I will live kindly and well with you and for this you have my word under my hand.

I think fit to caution you (if within my bounds, as I am ready to believe, but I desire no more than my own) that none of you pay any more taxes or assessments by any order or law of Maryland;[2] for if you do it will be greatly to your own wrong as well as my prejudice; though I am not conscious to myself of such an insufficiency of power here with my superiors, as not to be able to weather that difficulty if you should. But the opinion I have of the Lord Baltimore's prudence as well as justice, and of your regard to your own interests and future good of your posterity, makes me to waive all ob-

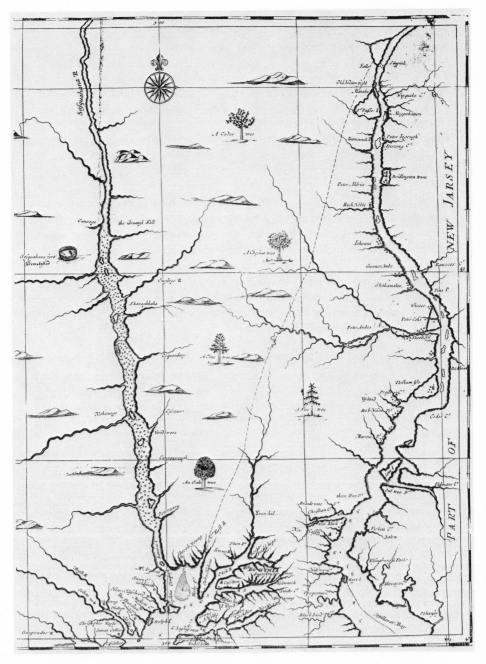

*John Thornton and John Seller.* A Map of Some of the South and Eastbounds of Pennsylvania in America. *London, 1681. HSP. (Detail)*

jections of that nature, and to hope we shall all do the thing that is just and honest (which is always wise) and according to our respective stations. I have no more to add, but my good wishes for all your happiness, and that by the help of Almighty God, next spring, you shall have some testimony of my best endeavors to contribute towards it, as becomes my duty to God, to the king, and to their people. I am

Your real friend,<br>Wm Penn

Pray salute me to all your neighbors.

ALS. Maryland Historical Society, Baltimore. (*PWP*, 2:111-14).

1. WP did not know personally the six men to whom he sent this letter, but all were prominent in local government, serving as members of the Maryland legislature, or as clerks of court or justices of the peace. The best known was Augustine Herrman (c. 1623-1686), who was born in Prague, grew up in Holland, immigrated to New Amsterdam, and then went to Maryland where he received Bohemia Manor in return for drawing his famous map *Virginia and Maryland as it is Planted and Inhabited this present Year 1670.*

2. WP's letter created considerable turmoil, as some residents of northern Maryland took his advice and refused to pay their taxes. Lord Baltimore was understandably alarmed; he pressed Deputy-Governor William Markham repeatedly for a meeting to determine the boundaries (see doc. 35, below), and sent a copy of this letter to William Blathwayt, secretary to the Lords of Trade in England.

# 21 ∫
## *News of William Markham's Arrival in Pennsylvania*

SOON after WP appointed William Markham as his deputy-governor on 10 April 1681, Markham left for America. He arrived in New York around 15 June. New York's acting governor, Anthony Brockholls, promptly conveyed the government of Pennsylvania to Markham with a proclamation instructing the inhabitants to transfer their allegiance from the duke of York to WP. Markham then traveled to the Delaware, arriving at Upland (later renamed Chester) by 3 August 1681. The newspaper report below appeared in London six weeks later. English newspapers at this date were skimpy sheets that contained little news. The un-Quakerly reception described in the article probably occurred at either New Castle in present Delaware or at Upland in Pennsylvania, both of which had numerous Swedish and Dutch residents.

London, 17 September 1681

From Pennsylvania we are advised that the deputy-governor is arrived there, and at his landing was received by a troop of horse and a company of foot, with drums beating and colors flying, having silk ensigns. Both the horse and the foot (excepting two persons) being English, Dutch, and Swedes, born in the country and understanding the language and customs of the Indians, so that there is great hopes it will in time prove as flourishing as the best of our plantations.

Newspaper item. *The Loyal Protestant, and True Domestick Intelligence, or News both from City and Country*, # 56; published in *PMHB*, 75:150. Not published in *PWP*, Vol. Two.


## 22 §
### Initial Plans for Philadelphia

HAVING promised, in July 1681, to lay out "a large town or city" in Pennsylvania (see doc. 17), WP drew up his specifications for this town in doc. 22. He named his cousin, William Crispin (1627-1681?), and Nathaniel Allen (d. 1692) and John Bezar (d. 1684), two Quakers from the western part of England, as his commissioners, and instructed them to set aside 10,000 acres on the best site for a port along the Delaware. WP did not want to build a traditional compact town, but rather a "green country town" made up of a long row of widely separated houses stretching some fifteen miles along the river. Each full shareholder among the First Purchasers was to have over 800 feet of river frontage, providing ample space for gardens, orchards, and fields surrounding his home. WP's own house would stand at the center of the town, near the principal wharf and business buildings. After receiving these instructions, Allen and Bezar sailed for America. A month later, WP issued additional instructions (doc. 24) that were carried over by Crispin (who died en route to Pennsylvania) and William Haige (1646-1688), a London Friend whom WP had just appointed as his fourth commissioner. In these further instructions, WP revealed his name for his "great town"—Philadelphia.

WP's commissioners, however, were not able to acquire enough land to carry out many of these plans because the Swedish, Dutch, and English inhabitants had already taken up most of the river frontage along the west bank of the Delaware from New Castle to the Falls opposite present-day Trenton, New Jersey. The commissioners concluded that the best site for WP's town was a few miles north of the mouth of the Schuylkill River on land patented by the Swanson family, and in the spring of 1682 they obtained 300 acres of river frontage from the Swansons—only 3 percent of what WP had hoped for—in which to lay out his capital city. See doc. 56, below, on the founding of Philadelphia, and the map on p. 214.

Instructions given by me, William Penn, Proprietor and
Governor of Pennsylvania
To
My trusty and loving friends, William Crispin, John Bezar,
and Nathaniel Allen, my commissioners for the settling of the
present colony this year transported into the said province.

First. That so soon as it shall please Almighty God to bring you well there, you take a special care of the people that shall embark with you, that they may be accommodated with conveniences as to food, lodging, and safe places for their goods, concerning which my cousin William Markham, my deputy, and now on the spot, will in a good measure be able to direct; that so none may be injured in their healths or estate in which if you find the Dutch, Swedes, or English of my side hard or griping, [and] taking an advantage of your circumstances, give them to know that they will hurt themselves thereby, for you can for a time be supplied on the other side,[1] which may awe them to moderate prices.

Second. That having taken what care you can for the people's good in the respects abovesaid, let the rivers and creeks be sounded on my side of Delaware River, especially Upland,[2] in order to settle a great town. And be sure to make your choice where it is most navigable, high, dry, and healthy; that is, where most ships may best ride, of deepest draft of water, if possible to load or unload at the bank or quayside without boating and lightering[3] of it. It would do well if the river coming into the creek be navigable, at least for boats up into the country, and that the situation be high, at least dry and sound, and not swampy, which is best known by digging up two or three earths and seeing the bottom.

3dly. Such a place being found out for navigation, healthy situation, and good soil for provision lay out ten thousand acres contiguous to it in the best manner you can as the bounds and extent of the liberties of the said town.

4thly. The proportion in the said town is to be thus: every share or five thousand acres shall have a hundred acres of land out of that ten thousand acres. If more than one be concerned in the share, as it may easily fall out, then they [are] to agree of the dividing the same as they shall think fit, still keeping to proportion as if £100 will have a hundred acres, £5 will have five acres.[4]

5thly. That no more land be surveyed or set out till this be first fixed and the people upon it, which is best both for comfort, safety, and traffic. In the next season, the Lord willing, I shall be with you; and then I shall proceed to larger lot. This was the resolution of a great part of the purchasers at London the fifteenth day of September 1681, and I find it generally approved.

6thly. If it should happen that the most convenient place for this great town should be already taken up in greater quantity of land than is consisting with the town plot, and that land not already improved, you must use your utmost skill to persuade them to part with so much as will be necessary, that so necessary and good a design be not spoiled. That is, where they have ten acres by the waterside, to abate five, and to take five more backward, and so proportionally, because that by the settlement of this town, the remaining five in two or three years' time will be worth twice as much as those ten before. Yea, what they take backward for their waterside land will in a little more time be really more valuable than all their ten forward was before. Urging my regard to them if they will not break this great and good contrivance, and in my name promise them what gratuity or privilege you think fit, as having a new grant at their old rent; nay, half their quitrent abated. Yea, make them as free as purchasers, rather than disappoint my mind in this township. Though herein be as sparing as ever you can, and urge the weak bottom of their grant, the duke of York having never had a grant from the king, etc.[5] Be impartially just and courteous to all; that is both pleasing to the Lord and wise in itself.

7thly. If you gain your point in this respect (of which be very careful), fall to dividing as before according to shares; then subdivide, in which observe that you must narrower spread by the waterside, and run backwards more or less according to the compass you have by the waterside, to bring in the hundred shares[6] for their proportion in the said ten thousand acres.

8thly. But if you cannot find land enough by the waterside to allow a hundred acres to five thousand acres, get what you can and proportionally divide it, though it were but fifty acres for a share.

9thly. Be tender of offending the Indians, and hearken by honest spies. If you can hear that anybody inveighs the Indians not to sell, or to stand off and raise the value upon you. You cannot want those that will inform you. But to soften them to me and the people, let them know that you are come to sit down lovingly among them. Let my letter and conditions with my purchasers[7] about just dealing with them be read in their tongue, that they may see we have their good in our eye, equal with our own interest. And after reading my letter and the said conditions, then present their kings with what I send them, and make a friendship and league with them according to those conditions, which carefully observe, and get them to comply with you. Be grave; they love not to be smiled on.[8]

10thly. From time to time in my name, and for my use, buy land of them where any justly pretend, for they will sell one another's if you be not careful, that so such as buy and come after these adventurers may have land ready. But by no means sell any land till I come. Allow no old patents; they have forfeited them by not planting according to the law of the place and it cost me too dear to allow such old stories.[9] Rather than fail, offer them the patent charge, and where surveyed, the survey money; but this understood only of unplanted places only.

11thly. Let no islands be disposed of to anybody, but all things remain as they were in that respect till I come.

12thly. Be sure to settle the figure of the town so as that the streets hereafter may be uniform down to the water from the country bounds. Let the place for the storehouse be on the middle of the quay, which will yet serve for market and state houses, too. This may be ordered when I come; only let the houses built be in a line, or upon a line as much as may be.

13thly. Pitch upon the very middle of the plot where the town or line of houses is to be laid or run, facing the harbor and great river, for the situation of my house; and let it be not the tenth part of the town as the conditions say, viz., that out of every hundred thousand acres shall be reserved to me ten.[10] But I shall be contented with less than a thirtieth part, to wit, three hundred acres; whereas several will have two [hundred acres] by purchasing two shares, that is ten thousand acres, and it may be fitting for me to exceed a little.

14thly. The distance of each house from the creek or harbor should be, in my judgment, a measured quarter of a mile, at least two hundred paces,[11] because of building hereafter streets downwards to the harbor.

15thly. Let every house be placed, if the person pleases, in the middle of its plot as to the breadth way of it, that so there may be ground on each side for gardens or orchards or fields, that it may be a green country town, which will never be burnt and always be wholesome.[12]

16thly. I judge that you must be guided in your breadth of land by what you can get that is unplanted and will not be parted with; but so far as I can guess at this distance methinks in a city, each share to have fifty poles[13] upon the front to the river, and the rest backward will be sufficient. But perhaps you may have more, and perhaps you will not have so much space to allow. Herein follow your land and situation, being always just to proportion.

17thly. Lastly, be sure to keep the conditions hereunto affixed, and see that no vice or evil conversation go uncomplained or punished in any, that God be not provoked to wrath against the country.

In witness hereof I do hereunto the 30th 7ber 1681 set to my hand and seal

Wm Penn

Present as witnesses:
Richard Vickris  Thomas Callowhill
Charles Jones Jr.[14]  Philip Theodore Lehnmann[15]
Ralph Withers[16]

DS. HSP. (*PWP*, 2:118-23).

1. From West New Jersey.
2. Upland had been founded about 1644 by the Swedish immigrant Jören Kyn (c. 1620-c. 1690). It was renamed Chester, Pennsylvania, by WP in Nov. 1682.
3. Transporting from ship to shore using a barge or lighter.
4. £100 purchased 5000 acres of country land and a bonus of 100 acres in town; £5 purchased 250 acres of country land (the smallest amount that WP wished to sell) and 5 acres in town.
5. In 1664 Charles II granted James, Duke of York, the provinces of New York and New Jersey, but not the western bank of the Delaware River, which James ruled without a patent after his agents conquered it from the Dutch. James formally deeded over all his interest in the lower counties (now Delaware) to WP on 24 Aug. 1682.
6. Only those purchasers who bought the first 500,000 acres in Pennsylvania were entitled to city lots. WP grouped these investors into 100 proprietory shares of 5000 acres

apiece, and the purchasers of each share were to receive 100 acres of town land, totaling 10,000 acres in all.

7. The "letter" is probably doc. 23. Sects. 11-15 of doc. 17 instruct purchasers on how to deal with the Indians.

8. See WP's full description of the Delaware Indians in doc. 76, below.

9. WP is here instructing his commissioners to ignore all patents to undeveloped land held by the "old" settlers who came to Pennsylvania before WP received his charter.

10. For his manors; see doc. 17, sect. 9, above.

11. Two hundred paces would set each house 1000 feet back from the river; a quarter of a mile would set dwellings back 1320 feet.

12. WP probably had in mind here the great plague of 1665 in London, and the great fire of 1666, the first of which he had experienced. His open town plan was designed to prevent such disasters in Philadelphia.

13. 825 feet.

14. Richard Vickris (1650?-1700), Thomas Callowhill (c. 1640-1712), and Charles Jones, Jr., (d. 1701) were all Bristol Quaker merchants who bought land in Pennsylvania but did not go to the colony. Callowhill's daughter Hannah became WP's second wife in 1696. Jones's daughter Mary married WP's son William in 1699.

15. Philip Theodore Lehnmann (d. 1687), whom WP sometimes called "Philip the German," had been WP's secretary since about 1673. He accompanied WP to America in 1682.

16. Ralph Withers (1631-c. 1683) was a Quaker First Purchaser from Wiltshire who immigrated to Pennsylvania and became deputy-treasurer of the Free Society of Traders and a provincial councilor.


# 23 §
## To the Kings of the Indians

ON the eve of European colonization, the Lenni Lenape (or Delaware) Indians inhabited the region from northern Maryland into New York, from the Atlantic Ocean to the western edge of the Delaware River watershed. Their language was Algonkian, and the name of their tribe meant "Original People." The Lenni Lenape lived a seminomadic village existence and raised crops of corn, beans, and squash. In the wintertime they left their small villages of six to eight houses to hunt. In the spring they returned to their villages to plant their crops. By 1680 the Lenni Lenape had been in contact with Europeans for nearly eighty years, and the use of European cloth, kettles, blankets, guns, liquor, hatchets, and other tools had become common among them. European contact also brought new diseases, such as smallpox, tuberculosis, and measles, against which the Lenni Lenape had no immunity; thus the native population was sparse. Before the arrival of the Quakers, the Swedish and Dutch colonists had fortified their settlements against Indian attack. WP intended to dispense with fortifications and live in peace with the Indians, but he also intended to purchase large tracts of land from them before allowing his settlers to come. In doc. 22, WP instructed his agents to deal fairly with the Indians. Doc. 23, WP's first letter to the Lenni Lenape, outlines more directly his ideas for Indian-white relations.

*Tishcohan, by Gustavus Hesselius, 1735, HSP. This portrait of an eighteenth-century Lenni Lenape leader was probably commissioned by WP's son, John Penn.*

London, 18 October 1681

My Friends

There is one great God and power that has made the world and all things therein, to whom you and I and all people owe their being and well-being, and to whom you and I must one day give an account for all that we do in this world. This great God has written his law in our hearts, by which we are taught and commanded to love and help and do good to one another, and not to do harm and mischief one unto another. Now this great God has been pleased to make me concerned in your parts of the world, and the king of the country where I live has given unto me a great province therein, but I desire to enjoy it with your love and consent, that we may always live together as neighbors and friends, else what would the great God say to us, who has made us not to devour and destroy one another, but live soberly and kindly together in the world.

Now I would have you well observe, that I am very sensible of the unkindness and injustice that has been too much exercised towards you by the people of these parts of the world, who have sought themselves, and to make great advantages by you, rather than be examples of justice and goodness unto you; which I hear has been matter of trouble to you and caused great grudgings and animosities, sometimes to the shedding of blood, which has made the great God angry. But I am not such a man, as is well known in my own country. I have great love and regard toward you, and I desire to win and gain your love and friendship by a kind, just, and peaceable life; and the people I send are of the same mind, and shall in all things behave themselves accordingly. And if in anything any shall offend you or your people, you shall have a full and speedy satisfaction for the same by an equal number of honest men on both sides,[1] that by no means you may have just occasion of being offended against them.

I shall shortly come to you myself, at what time we may more largely and freely confer and discourse of these matters. In the meantime, I have sent my commissioners to treat with you about land and a firm league of peace. Let me desire you to be kind to them and the people, and receive these presents and tokens which I have sent to you as a testimony of my good will to you and my resolution to live justly, peaceably, and friendly with you. I am your friend.

Wm Penn

LS. HSP. (*PWP*, 2:127-29).

1. Similar provisions for juries of Indians and whites were included in the West New Jersey Concessions of 1676, which WP may have played a role in drafting, and in WP's "Conditions or Concessions to the First Purchasers" (see doc. 17, sect. 14, above).

# Additional Instructions to William Markham

London, 28 October 1681

Memorandum of Additional Instructions to
William Markham and William Crispin and John Bezar

First, to act all in my name as proprietary and governor.[1]

Secondly, to buy land of the true owners, which I think is the Susquehanna people.[2]

Thirdly, to treat speedily with the Indians for land before they are furnished by others with things that please them. Take advice in this.

Fourthly, that all evidence or engagements be without oaths, thus: "I, A.B., do promise in the sight of God and them that hear me, to speak the truth, the whole truth, and nothing but the whole truth. A.B."[3]

Fifthly, I do call the city to be laid out by the name of Philadelphia,[4] and so I will have it called.

Given under my hand and seal, 28  8th month 1681 at London.

Wm Penn

Sealed and delivered in the presence of
George Fox,[5] Richard Davies,[6] Christopher Taylor,[7] Thomas Rudyard.

Transcript. Chester County Historical Society. (*PWP*, 2:129-30).

1. WP intended that Crispin be Gov. Markham's first assistant. On 25 Oct. 1681 WP had appointed Crispin, Bezar, William Haige, and Nathaniel Allen as commissioners to distribute land to the First Purchasers.

2. It was difficult to determine the "true owners" of the west bank of the Delaware River in 1681. The area had long been occupied by the Delaware (Lenni Lenape) Indians, but the Susquehannocks had moved from the Susquehanna River (near present-day Lancaster) to settle among the Delaware in the 1670s. The Delaware had a better claim and had not been conquered by the Susquehannocks, but WP, like some others in his day and since, may have thought they had been.

3. WP, like all Quakers, believed that the swearing of oaths was blasphemy against God, and he had been sent to prison in 1671 for refusing to swear a loyalty oath. In Pennsylvania, the colonists were to pledge their honor by affirmation, not oaths.

4. WP undoubtedly chose this Greek name for its meaning: city of brotherly love. The ancient city of Philadelphia, one of the major Christian cities in Asia Minor (now Turkey), was praised in Revelation 2-3 for its faithfulness and was promised protection "from the hour of temptation." WP may also have been thinking of the Philadelphians, an English pietist group, many of whose members became Quakers.

5. George Fox (1624-1691), founder of the Society of Friends, and a close friend and colleague of WP from 1669.

6. Richard Davies was a Welsh Quaker and a First Purchaser of 5000 acres; he signed WP's "Concessions" of 11 July 1681 (doc. 17, above). His son, David, came to Pennsylvania and settled in Bucks Co.

7. Christopher Taylor (d. 1686) was a Quaker preacher and schoolmaster from Yorks. He was a First Purchaser of 5000 acres who immigrated to Pennsylvania, where he served in the Assembly and on the Provincial Council.

# 25 §

## From Robert Barclay

W P wanted to sell Pennsylvania land in Scotland; thus he enlisted the
aid of Robert Barclay (1648-1690), the leading Scottish Friend and
author of the *Apology,* the most influential statement of Quaker beliefs. Barclay talked to a number of wealthy Scots about colonization and advised WP
on the terms his countrymen would find attractive. As the letter below indicates, Barclay thought WP's prices were too high, especially since the
principal Quaker proprietor of West New Jersey, Edward Byllynge (c. 1623-
1687), was offering much better terms. Barclay ended up selling no land in
Pennsylvania. By December 1681 he learned that several Scottish Presbyterians were interested in investing in America, and in 1682 he became the
absentee governor of East New Jersey. During the next half-dozen years,
Barclay worked vigorously to recruit Scottish investors and colonists for
East Jersey, not Pennsylvania.

Edinburgh, 19 November 1681

Dear WP

I have been endeavoring since I came to this place vigorously to advance
thy plantation, and have begot in many an inclination that way. This day I
had a meeting with the Earl of Perth and his brother,[1] the Lord Tarbat, now
Lord Register,[2] and several other persons who seem willing to engage and
are able to send over many people, beside a prospect we have to get many
Presbyterians to go over. But there are two things thou must lay account
for, else it will hardly work. The one is they will never pay so great a quitrent
as thou proposes, and that above 5 shillings for the 5000 acres they will
hardly go.[3] The next is they will never pay the money until they hear from
the factor[4] they send over [that] it is measured out to them, but will give me
their obligations to pay it when an account comes that is done; so if thou
expect any advance here, let me have thy answer to this per first [post], as
also by post, 20 or 30 more of thy papers.[5] [Thou] can deal there with the
post and pay for them, as E[dward] B[yllynge] did for his,[6] else the postmas-
ter here may extort. The noise that a propriety in New Jersey will be 30,000
acres and is sold for £300 makes thine seem dear. We would also know if for
servants sent over we may not be allowed 50 acres per head over and above
our proprieties.[7] Thou has land enough, so need not be a churl[8] if thou
intend to advance thy plantation. We are to have another meeting next week
and expect several others to come in, but little can be done until there be an
answer of this. Which is all at present. Desiring a speedy return to

Thy friend and brother in the Truth,

For William Penn          RB

B[enjamin] C[lark],

If WP be in town [thou] can deliver this speedily to him. If not, either thou thyself must send a bearer a purpose or get Philip Ford to do it, for it requires haste and WP will willingly pay the charge.

This with my love is all at present from thy friend,

RB

ALS. HSP. (*PWP*, 2:132-33).

1. James Drummond (1648-1716), fourth Earl of Perth, was a member of the Scottish Privy Council. He was a distant cousin but fairly close friend of Barclay, and in 1682, along with his brother, John Drummond (1649-1714), joined Barclay as a proprietor of East New Jersey. The meeting described here may perhaps be considered the beginning of Scottish efforts to colonize in that area.

2. George Mackenzie (1630-1740), Lord Tarbat, became lord clerk register, the custodian of all official records in Scotland, on 1 Oct. 1681. Tarbat later bought part of Perth's share of East New Jersey and strongly supported Scottish settlement in that colony.

3. In his *Some Account* (doc. 15), WP had set the quitrent, or tax paid annually to the proprietor by purchasers of land, at 50s. for 5000 acres.

4. An agent.

5. One or more of WP's propaganda pieces for Pennsylvania, such as *Some Account* or *Map of Pennsylvania* (see p. 80).

6. Edward Byllynge had recently sent his advertising pamphlet, *The Present State of the Colony of West-Jersey, in America,* to Scotland.

7. WP's basic price for 5000 acres was £100, double the price that Barclay quotes for large tracts of West New Jersey land. On the matter of headrights, WP was already granting what Barclay asked for—an additional 50 acres of land for every servant brought to America. But the quitrent he set for that headright—4s. for 50 acres—probably struck Scotsmen as astronomical.

8. A miser.

# Part V

## THE FRAME OF GOVERNMENT
## OF PENNSYLVANIA

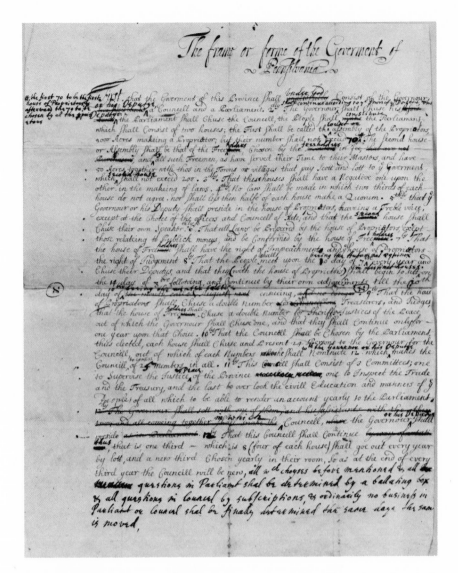

*The First Draft of the Frame of Government, c. 1681, HSP. This earliest of ten drafts for WP's* Frame of Government *covers only a single page. The text was written by one of WP's clerks and then revised by someone else, probably not WP. See doc. 27.*

A S soon as WP received his charter to Pennsylvania, he told Robert Turner: "I shall have a tender care to the government that it be well laid at first" (doc. 12, above). His plan was to draft and publish a constitution, with a set of fundamental laws, as the basis for virtuous and just government in the colony. WP was consciously trying to improve upon the unwritten English constitution and the English system of common law, and to devise a government that would establish the colonists' fundamental rights and promote their good conduct. Between March 1681 and April 1682, he spent much time composing his constitution and laws. He asked for and received advice from several men with sharply differing approaches toward government, including the radical republican Algernon Sidney (see doc. 28); the Quaker lawyer Thomas Rudyard (see doc. 29); and the Quaker merchant-scholar Benjamin Furly (see doc. 31). The end result of these labors was a pamphlet, probably published in May 1682, entitled *The Frame of the Government of the Province of Pennsylvania in America: Together with certain Laws Agreed upon in England by the Governor and Divers Freemen of the aforesaid Province* (doc. 30).

In preparing this constitution, WP and his advisors composed numerous drafts, critiques, and charts or outlines of the proposed government. Twenty of these drafts have survived, in the manuscript collections of the HSP. They reveal a great deal about WP's political ideas and his efforts to apply these ideas in Pennsylvania. Three of the most important drafts for the constitution, along with the published *Frame* and a critique of the *Frame* by Benjamin Furly, are printed below.

WP changed his mind considerably in the course of drafting his constitution. His initial intention seems to have been to transmit as much political power to the colonists as possible, "and to leave myself and [my] successors no power of doing mischief" (doc. 16). In the "Fundamental Constitutions" (doc. 26), the colonists were empowered to instruct their representatives in the assembly as to what laws should be passed, and the assembly was empowered to instruct the governor and council. When this style of government was challenged by WP's advisors, WP abandoned his plan for direct popular sovereignty. The final *Frame of Government* (doc. 30) granted considerably less authority to the people and to the lower house of the legislature than did the "Fundamental Constitutions," and gave far more independence to the Provincial Council. It also established the proprietor as a powerful, yet carefully controlled executive. Benjamin Furly immediately criticized the *Frame* (see doc. 31), and in 1682-1683 Pennsylvania's assemblymen insisted on making certain changes in it before they would accept it as their constitution (see docs. 62-63, below). Over the next twenty years, the colony's leaders would thoroughly revise WP's *Frame of Government*.

# 26 §

## *The Fundamental Constitutions*

PROBABLY the earliest plan of government composed by WP and his advisors in 1681-1682 was the "Fundamental Constitutions of Pennsylvania." This scheme, consisting of twenty-four articles or "constitutions," may have been drafted by WP himself. It is the most liberal of the early plans of government for Pennsylvania. Its opening section declares religious liberty for all inhabitants. Other clauses provide for trial by jury, curtail the common practice of imprisoning debtors, and abolish capital punishment for theft. At the same time, however, WP provided for the close regulation of his settlers' morals so that they would not, through drinking, dancing, gambling, or sport, fall into "idleness and looseness." The legislature was to be the dominant branch of government, and the voters were to retain substantial control over its operations. The assembly was to be composed of representatives elected annually, who brought signed instructions from their constituents to each legislative session and were required to follow these instructions exactly. The power of the governor and his council was quite limited. The assembly was to choose the council from among its own members, and the governor and his council were given the authority merely to advise the assembly and delay legislation. They had no veto power. One feature that was not liberal, however, was the absence of any provision for amending the constitution.

The ample powers given to the voters and their representatives by the "Fundamental Constitutions" firmly root this plan in the political tradition of the radical Whigs, or Commonwealthmen, who began to devise plans for popularly elected republican government during and after the English Civil War, in the 1640s and 1650s. WP probably borrowed several details— notably the number of councilors, the division of the council into four committees, and the periods and proportions of their staggered terms in office— from a famous republican tract of 1656, James Harrington's *Oceana*. Another likely source for the document is the West New Jersey Concessions of 1676, which also provided for a powerful legislative assembly and strictly limited executive powers; WP may have helped to write this constitution when he was supervising Quaker settlement in West New Jersey. However, for reasons that remain unclear, in 1681-1682 WP abandoned this liberal plan of government and turned instead to an alternative "Frame of Government" (doc. 27). Despite the opening statement in its title, the "Fundamental Constitutions" was probably never signed by any prospective settlers, nor ever published in WP's lifetime.

[summer 1681?]

The
Fundamental Constitutions
of
Pennsylvania
as
they were drawn up, settled, and signed by William Penn,
Proprietary and Governor, and consented to and subscribed by all
the first adventurers and freeholders of that province,
as the ground and rule of all future government.

The Preamble or Introduction[1]

When it pleased Almighty God, the creator and upholder of all things, to make man His great governor of the world, He did not only endue him with excellent knowledge but an upright mind, so that his power over the creation was balanced by an inward uprightness, that he might use it justly. Then was the law of light and truth writ in his heart, and that was the guide and keeper of his innocence; there was not need of any external precepts to direct or terrify him. But when he leant his ear to another voice, and followed his lust, and did the thing he was forbidden of God, the law was added. That is, the external law came to awe and terrify such as would not do the thing that was just according to the righteous law within themselves. Thus transgression introduced and occasioned the outward law, and that [introduced] government, and both [introduced] magistracy, [so] that those that would not answer the righteous law within, might be compelled by an impartial execution of the righteous law without. Wherefore the apostle made it the end of magistracy, to be a terror to evildoers, and a praise to them that do well.

Good government, then, is a constitution of just laws, wisely set together for the well ordering of men in society, to prevent all corruption or justly to correct it.

Wherein it is most evident that the governors and governed have but one interest by the constitution: to wit, preserving of right to all and punishing corruption in all, which is the end of government and consequently of governors. So that if any governors shall set up another interest to themselves than that which tends to preserving right to all and punishing evil in all, they contradict the constitution; and instead of serving government, make government only serve to their avarice or ambition. This is that corruption in mankind which government is by consent of all established to prevent. If then government itself be subservient to a higher end, to wit the general good, much more is it reasonable to believe that all instruments and forms of government are to be subjected to that end, to which government itself is but a means.

This duly weighed leads me to consider what is that manner or frame of government that shall preserve magistracy in reverence with the people and best keep it from being hurtful to them. This is a matter of great weight, but once to be well done, and that is by the founders of governments. An error here is a successive mischief to the governed in every age; and what troubles have followed in ancient and present governments from this unskillfulness are rather to be lamented and avoided than in the least doubted.[2] I know not any greater helps from example in a business of this moment, than an exact consideration of the government God established among the Jews, [or?] what His providence and the wisdom of our ancestors have settled among us English. Yet I shall not refuse the assistance that may be yielded from the wisdom of other governments, whether ancient or modern, since the main thing in hand is to lay such a foundation as may be most agreeable with right reason and conducive to the end of government: to wit, the virtue, peace, and prosperity of the people, to which all form and customs ought to yield. For it were a most condemnable superstition to perpetuate anything for being ancient or domestic that were not otherwise useful to this great end; much less should [we] follow those copies if time has proved them hurtful instead of being beneficial to societies.

Upon the whole matter [in] this draft of constitutions I, [William Penn, the said proprietary and Governor], do for me and mine, in honor to God and love to mankind, give, fix, and confirm so far forth as I, by my authorities granted to me in the king's letters and patents, am enabled to do.

### I Constitution

Considering that it is impossible that any people or government should ever prosper where men render not unto God that which is God's, as well as to Cæsar that which is Cæsar's; and also perceiving the disorders and mischiefs that attend those places where [there is] force in matters of faith and worship; and seriously reflecting upon the tenure of the new and spiritual government, and that both Christ did not use force and that He did expressly forbid it in His holy religion, as also that the testimony of His blessed messengers was that the weapons of the Christian warfare were not carnal but spiritual; and further weighing that this unpeopled country can never be planted if there be not due encouragement given to sober people of all sorts to plant, and that they will not esteem anything a sufficient encouragement where they are not assured, but that after all the hazards of the sea and the troubles of a wilderness, the labor of their hands and sweat of their brows may be made the forfeit of their conscience, and they and their wives and children ruined because they worship God in some different way from that which may be more generally owned. Therefore, in reverence to God the Father of lights and spirits, the author as well as object of all divine knowledge, faith, and worship, I do hereby declare for me and mine and establish it for the First Fundamental of the government of my country, that every person that does or shall reside therein shall have and enjoy the free possession of his or her faith and exercise of worship towards God, in such way and manner as every person shall in conscience believe is most acceptable to God, and so long as every such person uses not this Christian liberty to licentiousness (that is to say, to speak loosely and profanely of God, Christ, or religion, or to commit any evil in their conversation), he or she shall be protected in the enjoyment of the aforesaid Christian liberty by the civil magistrate. Very good.[3]

## II Constitution

Because corruption of manners and remissness in magistrates to punish evildoers, by which means virtue often falls in the streets, have ever provoked God's heavy displeasure against both governors and people, and that I cannot hope it should prosper better with me and mine and the people that do or shall inhabit this country if an effectual care be not taken to prevent or appease the wrath of God by an impartial execution of justice upon every evildoer according to the law provided in such cases; therefore I do for me and mine declare and establish for the Second Fundamental of the government of this country, that all those laws which relate to prevention or correction of vice and injustice be impartially and vigorously executed; and that those magistrates that do not in their respective charges vigilantly and impartially execute all such laws to the terror of evildoers and praise of those that do well, *shall be reputed and marked as breakers of the Fundamental Constitutions of the country, and therein as well public enemies to God as the people, and never to bear office till they have given good testimony of their repentance.*

## III Constitution

And since it has been the judgment of the wisest men and practice of the most famous governments in all ages, as well as that it is most natural, reasonable, and prudent in itself, that the people of any country should be consenting to the laws they are to be governed by, therefore I do for me and mine hereby declare and establish for the 3d Fundamental Constitution of the government of this province, that there shall be held once every year, that is to say on the first day of the first month called March, an Assembly shall be duly chosen by the freeholders of this country to serve as their deputies to consult, debate, and resolve, and in their names to consent to the enacting or abolishing of laws, *and whatever is the privilege of an English House of Commons.* And lest this excellent and necessary constitution should be [in] any ways abused or obstructed, it is hereby declared that the aforesaid freeholders shall of themselves meet on the first day of every twelfth month called February, in their respective places, and there choose their deputies to serve for them as aforesaid, without any writs or mandates to be issued forth by the Governor or his deputy, or any else in authority whatever for that purpose. And being so chosen and assembled, they shall not sit less than two months, unless it be their own choice or desire, but longer if public business require it. And this shall be called the Assembly of the province, of which not less than two-thirds of the whole shall make a quorum.

## IV Constitution

But because this Assembly cannot be so large at first as hereafter, when the place is peopled, and yet some care must be taken both to have one now and to limit it, that the number do not exceed what may be convenient and proportionable to the province, I do hereby for me and mine declare and establish for the Fourth Fundamental of the government of this country that the country shall be cast into 24 counties, each county into 4 hundreds, and each hundred into two tribes. And each tribe shall choose two of their own tribe in best repute with them for virtue, wisdom, and integrity, to serve in Assembly for the peace and the prosperity of the province, which comes to 384 persons for the whole country. And till such time as the said counties are peopled, let the number be chosen equally out [of] the county or counties that are in any respect planted and able to send them.

## V Constitution

To the end that it may not be in the power of any member or deputy in the Assembly to betray his trust, I do hereby for me and mine, declare and establish it for the Fifth Fundamental Constitution of the government of this province, that every such deputy shall bring his instructions signed under the hands of the electors, and his own hand as accepting of them. And that a copy be kept thereof and registered in every respective tribe, and if it shall so happen that he shall act contrary to the same, that then he never more presume to stand, unless the people, sensible of his repentance, shall forgive and choose him.

## VI Constitution

And that all those mischiefs may be avoided which attend hasty resolutions, I do for me and mine hereby declare and establish this for the Sixth Fundamental Constitution in the government of this province, that during the time of any Assembly, no law shall be made or abrogated, or money raised, by the deputies of the tribes without first consulting the mind of their principals or tribes that depute them; that they may always remember they are but deputies and men intrusted to the good of others and responsible for that trust.

## VII Constitution

For the better completing of the frame of this government, and to the end that the Assembly and Governor may have all possible help in the knowledge and dispatch of affairs, I do for me and mine hereby declare and establish for the 7th Fundamental of the government of this province, that there shall be a Council of 48 persons, thus chosen, continued, and altered: that is to say, the Assembly shall choose out of the members serving for each county two persons of best repute for their understanding and faith and fullness. There being 24 counties, the Council will consist of 48 persons; the places of these persons so chosen, to be filled up by a new election of such of the tribes as they related to. This Council is to continue entire for one year; then a third part, that is to say 16, to go out (4 of each committee as expressed hereafter), and so many of the next Assembly to be chosen in their stead; so that in 3 years the Council is new. They go out by lot; this Council is to sit with the Governor.

Apart from the Assembly, their share in the government is this: first to receive all proposals from the Assembly, be they to make or abrogate laws or what they shall concern, and to consult of what may be most beneficial to the public in all respects; and after they have fully considered the matter before them, to propose their deliberations, by the way of conferences, to the Assembly. And if upon due consideration they are by them agreed to, then and not otherwise, to be engrossed and presented to the Governor or his lieutenant or deputy for his confirmation in order to a law, and the yearly meeting of Governor, Council, and Assembly shall be called the General Assembly of the province. The Council is to continue in the intervals of the Assembly, to advise and assist the Governor or his lieutenant or deputy in the business of the government. The Council shall be divided into several committees, or commissions, and each of them shall have a proportion assigned by the Governor or his lieutenant or deputy in the government; that is to say, to divide the whole into 4 committees, which makes 12 in each committee.

The first committee is to supervise the justice of the province, as to judges, courts, justices, inferior officers of justice, registers, etc., in the discharge of their duty; and these shall be called the commissioners of justice.

The second committee shall have the charge of trade, and shall be called the commissioners of trade; which will take in all foreign correspondence, merchandise, manufactures, the advancement of the country growth, provision against begging by the employment of the poor, and prevention of corruption and fraud in dealing.

The third committee is to inspect and manage the public treasury of the country on all occasions, and to be accountable to the General Assembly of all monies intrusted with them, that the people may be satisfied in the employment of their contributions to the public; and this committee shall be called the commissioners of the treasury.

The 4th and last committee will be the commissioners of education, who shall inspect the breeding of youth, as to schools, masters, books, and the way and method of cultivating and improving of science truly so called which may be useful and laudable among good men. That so youth may be grounded in the way of virtue and wisdom, and the successive generations secured against declension and corruption of manners, which draws after it slavery and beggary and, which is worse, the wrath of God, too.

But because it may in divers respects so fall out that the whole Council may not be able to yield a constant attendance, therefore in the interval of the General Assembly, any twelve of them consisting of 3 of each committee or commission shall be sufficient to dispatch any business belonging to the whole, except some extraordinary business happens. And in all such cases, that the rest, upon the Governor's summons or his lieutenant's or deputy's, shall forthwith repair to give their attendance for the service of the public.

## VIII Constitution

And because the end of governors is the good of government and the end of the government [is] the good of the governed, and that the Governor's right and share in the government and propriety of the province *is not in danger, he does not in wisdom think fit to leave himself* [open to] *the jealousies of the people when he may safely to himself and his heirs remove or prevent them.* Therefore I do for me and mine, etc., establish for the 8th Fundamental of the government of this province, that all bills agreed upon by the Council and Assembly that do not infringe the right of the Governor and his heirs and assigns, either as to his share in the government or in the propriety of the province, which are hereby all along intended to be acknowledged and confirmed, and are hereby acknowledged and confirmed, shall in fourteen days after their presentment to the Governor or his lieutenant or deputy for his assent, [and] not by him assented, stand good and available in law as [if] assented unto by the Governor, or his lieutenant or deputy.

## IX Constitution

That the people of this province may love and obey the government of it from the share they have in it, I do for me and mine declare and establish for the 9th Fundamental in the government thereof, that all towns and cities where magistrates of any degree are thought necessary, whether they be mayors, bailiffs, provosts, sheriffs, constables, etc., or by any other name styled, they shall be chosen by the inhabitants thereof that are housekeepers, [and] that receive no alms to their maintenance. And in all counties, the freemen of every tribe shall present to the Governor, or his lieutenant or deputy, two [candidates] for justices of the peace; and the county at their county court, two for sheriffs. And if the Governor, or his lieutenant or deputy, shall not within 20 days after the said presentation choose one of the two for sheriff for that county, and the one of the two for a justice of peace for that tribe, that then the first set down for the county for sheriff and by the tribe for justice shall stand and serve for the ensuing year as legally as if he were elected by the Governor, or his lieutenant or deputy.

## X Constitution

To prevent that corruption which men not guided by a just principle are subject to, for fear or favor, and that much of the mischief which attends the decision of controversies by voices in great assemblies, I do for me and mine hereby declare and establish for the 10th Fundamental of the government of this province, that at the election of deputies to serve in Assembly, and in the Assembly itself upon all questions, the decision shall be by balloting as in Venice. Only in the Council it shall be by subscription, which the numbers of the other two will not permit without great delay to business.[4]

## XI Constitution

And because great inconveniences do oftener arise from hasty than deliberate councils, I do for me and mine declare and establish it for the Eleventh Fundamental of the government of this province, that unless it be in a case of such imminent and immediate danger as will not give a day to consider, no business of state in Assembly or Council shall be resolved the day it is proposed; to the end, time may be given to learn all that may be known or said about the matter in hand, in order to a clear and safe determination.

### XII Constitution

That this government may appear equal in itself, and agreeable to the wisdom God gave unto Moses and the practice of our best ancestors, and that we may avoid heart burnings in families and the foundation of much misery and beggary or worse, I do for me and mine hereby declare and establish for the 12th Fundamental of the government of this province, that what estate every person dying has in it (though he or she die elsewhere), having children, shall be equally shared, after such person's decease, among the children of the said person, saving only that the eldest if the first born shall have (according to the law of God by Moses given to the Jews) a double portion for his inheritance and not otherwise.[5]

### XIII Constitution

And that lawsuits and animosities among people may be prevented, which have so lamentably consumed the estates of many families in divers nations, as well as sown and fixed perpetual hatred between neighbors and near kindred, I do for me and mine declare and establish for the 13th Fundamental of the government of this province, that there shall be a register of all deeds, mortgages, settlements, conveniencies,[6] trusts, sales, bonds, bills, receipts, etc., that from time [to] time shall be transacted in this province, both in the capital town of every county and also in the chief city of the province; that so all may be secured from those frauds and abuses which the want of it has brought to other countries and those perplexing and expensive suits that follow thereupon.

### XIV Constitution

It is so sad a thing to behold the jails of nations filled with prisoners for debts that they can never pay, and so their confinement can only be the effect of an unprofitable revenge, that I do for me and mine hereby declare and establish it a Fundamental in the government of this province, that no man shall be imprisoned for any debt that is not above the sum of £10, nor yet for any debt at all if he will subscribe such a declaration to be recorded as shall be presented to him, that he is not worth £10 in the world, and he can get two sufficient creditable persons to sign a declaration that they believe he is not worth £10 in the world. But if it should afterwards appear that such a person was then worth more than £10 and purposely concealed it, that then the said estate so concealed shall go to the satisfaction of his creditors, and he become their bondsman during their pleasure, to work only to their behoof.

### XV Constitution

Since the due proportion of rewards and punishments is the wisdom and justice of government, and that the example be of God's law as well as the reason of the thing, [this] guides all men to believe that to shed man's blood and take away his life for worldly goods is a very hard thing, especially considering the tenderness of the holy merciful Christian law. And considering the little reformation this severity brings, and that it tempts the thief to be a murderer when the punishment is the same, to kill whom he robs that so he may not discover or prosecute him that robs him, which instead of making thieves afraid may constrain them to destroy good men; therefore I do for me and mine hereby declare and establish for the 15th Fundamental of the government of this province, that no person committing felony within the limits thereof shall die for the same. But for the first offense, if a single man and able, he shall make satisfaction. For the second offense, he shall if able make double satisfaction; [and] if not, be kept in a workhouse till he have wrought out such a satisfaction. And for the 3d offense, he shall if able pay a 3-fold satisfaction; if not able, be a perpetual bondsman. If married and has children, then, unless the thing stolen be found upon him or amongst his goods, he shall not be put to make satisfaction to the prejudice of his children that were innocent of the fact, and which would only serve to increase the poor and so the public charge; but that he shall for the first offense work out a satisfaction, for the second offense a double satisfaction, and for the 3d offense he shall be a perpetual bondsman to the behoof of those he has wronged whether by work or sale, which is more terrible to idle and high-minded persons than death itself, and therefore better to prevent the evil.

## XVI

That justice may be speedily as well as impartially done, and that to prevent tedious and expensive pilgrimages to obtain it, I do for me and mine hereby declare and establish for the Sixteenth Fundamental in the government of this province, that monthly sessions shall be held in every county in which all sorts of causes belonging to that county shall be heard and finally determined, whether relating to civil or criminal acts. And the parties [be] obliged to submit to that determination upon bonds beforehand to be taken on that account to prevent the renewal of suits out of a litigious mind, and that every person may freely plead his own cause or bring his friend to do it for him. And the judges are hereby obliged to inform him or her what they can to his or her assistance in the matter before them, that none be prejudiced through ignorance in their own business; which judges shall be of the same county, but last not longer than one year in office.

## XVII Constitution

And that we may, in whatever we can, resemble the ancient constitution of England, I do for me and mine hereby declare and establish for the Seventeenth Fundamental of the government of this province, that all trials and determinations of causes, and concerning life, liberty, good name, or estate, shall [be] by the verdict and judgment of twelve of the neighborhood to the party or parties concerned, and near as may be of the same degree that they may be equals, lest being poorer they be awed with fear or drawn by rewards to a corrupt judgment, or by being richer and greater, be careless of their verdict upon an inferior person whose low condition are not or is not able to call them to question. And these twelve men shall sit with the judges, six on a side, or on a bench on purpose at another side of the court, but that no verdict be given without their withdrawing to consult the matter. No person to be admitted to them nor any note or letter to be delivered to any of them from the time they withdraw till they return to the bench, and then publicly delivered. The charge given the 12 men or verdictors by the judges to be [given] audibly in open court before the party concerned, the judges and the 12 men to speak only to one another what the court and party concerned shall hear. The verdict being given, the judges in a grave and sober manner to pronounce sentence accordingly.

## XVIII Constitution

To avoid all delays or denials of justice and all briberies to injustice in officers of justice or persons chosen to serve in Assembly or Council, I do for me and mine hereby declare and establish for the Eighteenth Fundamental of the government of this province, that all such officers of justice as delay or deny justice, being convicted thereof, shall pay or make good the wrong or prejudice the party aggrieved seeks redress from, and satisfaction for such delay or denial beside; or if they or those that serve in Assembly shall at any time in any case take any bribe or secret reward from any person to favor him or her, or his or her cause or business, being proved by sufficient witnesses, that every such person shall be immediately discharged from all employment forever, and pay to the public treasury threefold. Very good.[7]

## XIX Constitution

Because all may be useful and beneficial in evidence to the public after the example of those countries that comply with the tenderness of their consciences that can't take any oath, and yet are often the only persons [able] to prove either theft, murder, titles of land, wills, etc.; and having reflected on the reverent [laws enforced by] many courts [against][8] swearing, and that shutting out oaths there would be the best way to shut all loose and vain swearing out of the country, I do for me and mine hereby declare and establish for the Nineteenth Fundamental of the government of this province that all evidence shall be by subscription upon record after this form: "I, A. B., do from the very bottom of my heart hereby engage and promise in the presence of God and the court to declare the whole truth, and nothing but the truth, in the matter I am to be inquired upon. Witness my hand this ____ of _____ in the year _____. A. B."

And if it shall afterwards appear that any person has declared and subscribed that which is false, that then he sustain the same injury he by false evidence brings to the person or estate of any person wronged thereby, and be exposed in the tribe where he lives as a false man, never to be received in any evidence anymore, much less employed in any office in the province.

## XX Constitution

And forasmuch as divers inconveniencies may arise by undue imprisonments of persons upon mere surmises, and that in several [respects] to prevent which a law of habeas corpus was lately made in the kingdom of England[9] to secure the people from any such disadvantages, I do for me and mine hereby declare and establish for the 20th Fundamental of the government of this province, that no man shall be imprisoned for any case but on good evidence, and that the same law of habeas corpus shall be in full force in this province, and that all persons imprisoned, whether innocent or guilty, shall not be obliged to pay any fees to the keeper of the prison, but the said keeper be maintained at the charge as an officer belonging to state.

## XXI

And as government can not well subsist and prosper where virtue and industry are not carefully promoted, and that it is impossible to do if the lets[10] to both are not [prevented] or removed, I do therefore for me and mine hereby declare and establish for 21st Fundamental of the government of this province that there shall be no taverns nor alehouses endured in the same, nor any playhouses, nor morris dances,[11] nor games as dice, cards, board tables, lotteries, bowling greens, horse races, bear baitings, bull baitings, and such like sports, which only tend to idleness and looseness; and that all those that go about to erect or use any of these things, be fined to the government and put into the next common workhouse and kept by the space of 6 months to hard daily labor as if he were some petty felon.

## XXII Constitution

And to the end that none may be destitute of subsistence in case of any calamities or afflictions that may fall upon their parents or them in their estates, from which no sort or degree of men are free, and that all may labor as well as eat and be useful and not as [idle, and to][12] prevent the many inconveniencies that follow idleness, I do for me and mine hereby declare and establish as the Two-and-Twentieth Fundamental of the government of this province, that every child that is of the age of 12 years shall be taught some trade or skill by which to exercise their minds and bodies in honest [suitable] labor, and that of all degrees and qualities without respect to persons, as well females as males. This will give the country and people wealth and reputation and keep out idleness, the mother of many mischiefs.

## XXIII

And to the end whatever relates to the property, liberty, trials by twelve equals of the neighborhood, equal and proportionable fines and amercements[13] for faults committed, [and] not delaying, denying, or selling of justice, contained in the great English charter with the like civil privileges, and all those acts of Parliament confirmatory of the same, more especially that called the Petition of Right in the 3d year of Charles the First, I do hereby declare and establish, for the 23d Fundamental of the government of this province, that all the said privileges of the great charter before expressed, and the laws confirmatory of the same, especially that called the Petition of Right in the 17th year of Charles the First, be and remain in full force as an effectual part of the government of this province.[14]

## XXIIII Constitution

And because it may so fall out that the Governor, or his lieutenant or deputy, may by the evil insinuations and pernicious councils of some in power or esteem with him, or from his mistaking the true extent of his authority, or possibly by the instigations of his own ambition, command or require the officers or magistrates in this province, or any of them, to do a thing that is contrary to these Fundamentals or any law that may be hereafter made for the well ordering of this province, I do for me and mine hereby declare and establish, for the last Fundamental of the government of this province, that though any desire, order, precept, or command should come from the Governor, or his lieutenant or deputy, to any officer or magistrate as before said, to do any act or thing that is contrary to these Fundamentals or the law of the land, whether it be to commit injustice or to omit and delay justice in the cause of any person or [in] other ways, be it signified by word of mouth, by letter, or any little or great seal,[15] every such officer or magistrate shall be surely obliged to reject the same and follow the tenure of these Fundamentals and the express law of the province. And if he shall offer or dare to waive and desert his duty by law to answer any such mistake or illegal passion in the Governor, or his lieutenant or deputy, that for so doing he shall be accountable to the next General Assembly of the province, in whose power it shall be to proportion his satisfaction and disgrace to the [nature] and degree of his lie or offense. More[over], if any of them, or any members of either Assembly or Council, or any not in office or trust, for private and corrupt ends of their own, having the temptation of such an illegal desire or command from a superior, shall oppose, betray, [or in any] respect by word or deed deviate or derogate from these Fundamental Constitutions, shall they lie under the examination and sentence of the next General Assembly, who have hereby power to proportion the satisfaction and disgrace of the offending [person] to the nature and degree of the offense. And I do further desire and establish that a copy thereof may be hung up in the places where the Assembly and Council sit, and that they be all read in the presence of the Governor, or his lieutenant or deputy, and the Council and Assembly as the first thing at the opening of every General Assembly in the province, and that the testimony of their acknowledgment of them shall be signified by the standing up of the Governor, or his lieutenant or deputy, and the Council and Assembly, and lifting up of their right hands after they are all audibly read; which done, their so acknowledging of them as the rule of their laws and government shall be recorded in the journal book of both the Council and Assembly, that if possible they may not be forgotten, or in anywise contradicted.

These four and twenty articles are the Fundamental Constitutions of the province of Pennsylvania in America, by me drawn up, settled, and confirmed so far as in me lies, for an abiding ground and rule to all future laws and government. And I do hereby desire, charge, and command all my children and their and my posterity whose lot it may be to be concerned in this province to remember, love, and preserve with all care and faithfulness [these] Fundamental Constitutions, being the establishment of me, their father and ancestor, as the discharge of my conscience to God, the giver of this country unto me and them, and as they hope to keep it and His blessing upon it.

We whose names are here underwritten and subscribed, being freeholders of the province of Pennsylvania in America, do with much clearness and satisfaction hereby testify [and] declare our consent and agreement with William Penn, proprietary and Governor of the said province, in the above written Fundamental Constitutions as the ground and rule of all future laws and government in that country. And we do hereby promise everyone for himself, that by God's assistance we will remember, love, and preserve to the utmost of our power the aforesaid Fundamentals inviolably, and do hereby desire and charge our posterity to do the same as they hope to enjoy what we leave them and the blessing of God with it.

Draft. HSP. (*PWP*, 2:140-56).

1. It is interesting to compare this preamble with the preface to *The Frame of Government* (doc. 30). Both pursue some of the same arguments about the need for government, but in the "Fundamental Constitutions" WP is far more optimistic about his ability to devise a plan for preserving liberty and punishing evil. The extended months of constitution-making in 1681-1682 made WP far more aware of the difficulties of constructing a government that would be satisfactory to a wide range of people.

2. Many seventeenth-century English political writers believed that any new government was best devised by a single wise man. This was an ancient Greek idea that was popularized by the Renaissance Italian political thinker Niccolo Machiavelli (d. 1527) and gained currency in England with the publication of James Harrington's *Oceana* (1656).

3. The phrase "very good" was a marginal comment, possibly by WP.

4. Voting by secret ballot, developed in medieval and Renaissance Venice, was popularized in England in the 1650s by James Harrington and other radical political thinkers; WP and his colleagues had already incorporated it into the West New Jersey Concessions in 1676. Voting "by subscription" probably meant by signing a roll; thus the Council would have an open roll-call vote.

5. For the Mosaic Law on inheritance, see Deuteronomy 21:15-17.

6. Probably the copyist meant "conveyances," documents that transfer property from one person to another.

7. This marginal comment is possibly in WP's handwriting.

8. The manuscript text is garbled at this point; the interpolated words convey WP's probable meaning.

9. The Habeas Corpus Act of 1679 established the right of any Englishman who was imprisoned without being formally charged with a crime to obtain an order that required his jailer to state the cause of imprisonment, and to bring him to court, where he could have a bail hearing or a trial.

10. Obstacles.

11. Folk dances in costume, or mummers' dances, often depicting characters from the Robin Hood legends. The term probably derives from "Moorish dance."

12. The manuscript text is garbled at this point; the interpolated words convey WP's probable meaning.

13. Arbitrary fines or other punishments.

14. The "great English charter" is the Great Charter of 1225. This document replaced the more famous Magna Carta of 1215, which it closely resembled, and it was regarded as the fundamental pledge by the English crown to respect the basic legal rights of its subjects, especially the right to a fair trial by jury. The Petition of Right of 1628, presented by Parliament to Charles I in the third (not the seventeenth) year of his reign, reaffirmed the trial rights guaranteed in the Great Charter and the principle of no taxation without representation established in the fourteenth century.

15. An order from the governor, stamped with his seal of office.

# 27 §

## First Draft of the Frame of Government

THE document below is the earliest of ten surviving drafts for WP's *Frame of Government*. The text covers a single page and includes only the first twelve frames or articles of this constitution (see p. 94, for a photograph of the original manuscript). The new constitutional plan, even in this abbreviated early draft, is a sweeping rejection of WP's more liberal "Fundamental Constitutions." Gone is the large, powerful lower house of 384 legislators, chosen by all male inhabitants, possessed of all of the rights of the English House of Commons, and limited only by the instructions given them by their constituents. In its place is a strong upper house composed of and chosen by major landowners only, and a weaker lower house composed of and chosen by owners of small farms and taxpaying city dwellers. Only the upper house could propose bills to become law. Each house nominated lists of candidates for executive and judicial office, and for a small governor's council, with the governor making all final selections. Under this new Frame, the lower house lost its right to initiate legislation, the people lost their right to elect local officials and to nominate justices to the governor, and the governor, although he still had no formal veto power, gained a treble vote in the powerful upper house.

### The Frame or Form of the Government of Pennsylvania.

First. That the government of this province shall under God consist of the Governor or his deputy, a Council, and a Parliament.

2dly. The Governor shall continue according to the powers of the patent,[1] and he shall choose his deputy. The Parliament shall choose the Council, [and] the people shall constitute the Parliament, which shall consist of two houses. The first shall be called the Court or Assembly of the Proprietors, 5000 acres making a proprietor; but their number shall not exceed 70, the first 70 [proprietors] to be the first House of Proprietors,[2] and afterward the 70 to be chosen by all the proprietors. The second house or Assembly shall be that of the freeholders, chosen by the freeholders in fee, and by all such freemen as have served their time to their masters and have 50 acres, together with those in the towns or villages that pay scot and lot to the government;[3] which second house shall not exceed 200.

3dly. That these houses shall have a negative, one upon the other, in the making of laws.

4thly. No law shall be made in which two-thirds of each house do not agree, nor shall less than half of each house make a quorum.

5thly. That the Governor, or his deputy, shall preside in the House of

Proprietors, having a treble voice, except at the choice of the officers and Council of State; and that the second house shall choose their own Speaker.

6thly. That all laws be prepared by the House of Proprietors, except those relating to public money, and be confirmed by the House of Freeholders.[4]

7thly. That the House of Freeholders shall have the right of impeachment; and the House of Proprietors, the right of judgment.[5]

8thly. That the people shall meet upon the 10th day of September (being the autumnal equinox)[6] every year, and choose their deputies, and that they (with the House of Proprietors) shall begin to sit in distinct houses on the 14th day of October following, and continue by their own adjournments till the 10th day of December (being the winter solstice) ensuing.

9thly. That the House of Proprietors shall choose a double number for treasurers and judges, [and] that the House of Freeholders shall choose a double number for sheriffs and justices of the peace, out of which the Governor shall choose one; and that they shall continue only for one year upon that choice.

10thly. That the Council shall be chosen by the Parliament, thus elected: each house shall choose and present 24 persons to the Governor for the Council, out of which of each numbers he shall nominate 12, which with the Governor or his deputy makes the Council to consist of 25 members in all.

11thly. This Council shall consist of 3 committees: one to supervise the justice and peace of the province, one to inspect the trade and the treasury, and the last to overlook the civil education and manners of the people; of all which to be able to render an account yearly to the Parliament.[7] In which Council, the Governor or his deputy shall preside.

12thly. That this Council shall continue thus: that is, one-third—which is 8 (four of each House)—shall go out every year by lot, and a new third chosen yearly in their room, so as at the end of every third year the Council will be new. All which choices before mentioned and all questions in Parliament shall be determined by a balloting box, and all questions in Council by subscriptions,[8] and ordinarily no business in Parliament or Council shall be finally determined the same day the same is moved.

Draft. HSP. (*PWP*, 2:163–66).

1. WP's royal charter for Pennsylvania (doc. 11, above).
2. That is, the first seventy men to purchase a 5000-acre proprietary share in Pennsylvania from WP. They would sit in the first legislature only; thereafter, the members of the House of Proprietors would be elected from and by all proprietary shareholders.
3. Freeholders "in fee" were landholders whose property was subject only to nominal feudal obligations to the crown or to another landowner; they could freely will it to heirs or sell it. This was the most secure kind of land ownership in England and the English colonies. "Scot and lot" was a graduated tax, levied by many English cities, and paid by inhabitants who owned property in a city or town. It usually carried with it the right to vote for officeholders.
4. This principle, that all laws should originate in the upper house of the legislature,

was central to James Harrington's *Oceana*. WP defended it tenaciously for twenty years against the protests of his colonists before abandoning it.

5. That is, the right to determine whether an official who was impeached or indicted for misconduct in office should be convicted. The United States Constitution provides for the same system of impeachment of federal officials by the House of Representatives, and conviction by the Senate.

6. England was still using the Julian calendar in 1681, and would continue to use it until 1752. By the seventeenth century this calendar had fallen ten days behind the solar seasons, and so the autumnal equinox was about 10 Sept. by English reckoning. Today, of course, we use the Gregorian calendar, which now places the autumnal equinox on about 21 Sept.

7. This provision follows the plan in the "Fundamental Constitutions" (doc. 26, article 7), combining the second and third committees of the Council, on trade and treasury, into one.

8. Probably by answering a roll call, or even by signing a book, making the Council voting open rather than secret.

# 28 §
## To Algernon Sidney

IN drafting his constitution, WP consulted a number of lawyers and political theorists; among the latter was his old friend, the zealous republican Algernon Sidney (1622-1683). Sidney had fought for Parliament in England's Civil War of the 1640s, had served in some of the republican governments of the 1650s, and had gone into exile when the monarchy was restored in 1660. Returning to England in 1677, he ran for Parliament, with WP's enthusiastic support, but was defeated. WP's letter indicates that Sidney wrote a draft for WP's constitution in 1681, but this draft has been lost. Sidney's chief political work, the *Discourses Concerning Government,* written about 1680 but not published until 1698, justified several ideas that could scarcely have been congenial to WP. These included violent rebellion against any form of oppression, constant change in government, and warfare as the test of freedom. WP, for his part, was clearly deeply wounded by Sidney's jibes against his idealistic constitution-making. Two years after the two men quarreled, Sidney was arrested for joining the Rye House Plot against Charles II and was executed, becoming England's most celebrated Whig martyr.

13 October 1681

There are many things [that] make a man's life uneasy in the world which are great abatements to the pleasure of living; but scarcely one equal to that of the unkindness or injustice of friends.

I have been asked by several since I came last to town if Col. Sidney[1] and I were fallen out; and when I denied it, and laughed at it, they told me I was mistaken. And to convince me, [they] told me that he had used me very ill to several persons, if not companies, saying I had a good country but the basest laws in the world, not to be endured or lived under, and that the Turk[2] was not more absolute than I. This made me remember the discourse we had at my house about my drawing constitutions, not as proposals but as if fixed to the hand, and that as my act, to which the rest were to comply if they would be concerned with me.[3] But withal I could not but call to mind that thy objections were presently complied with, both by my verbal denial of all such construction as the words might bear as if they were imposed, and not yet free for debate, and also that I took my pen and immediately altered the terms so as they corresponded (and truly I thought more properly) with thy objection and sense. Upon this thou did draw a draft as to the frame of the government, gave it [to] me to read, and we discoursed [about] it with a considerable agreement. It was afterwards called for back by thee, to finish and polish. I suspended proceeding in the business of the government ever since (that being to be done after other matters), instead of any further conference about it.

I meet with this sort of language in the mouths of several. I shall not yet believe it, it were not well in me to an enemy, less so to a friend; but if it be true, I shall be sorry we were ever so well acquainted, or that I have given so much occasion to them that hate us, to laugh at me for more true friendship and steady kindness than I have been guilty of to any man I know living. It becomes not my pretenses to the things of another life to be much in pain about the uncertainties of this; but be it as it will, I am yet worth a line. I would pray one of the truth of the fact, for the injury it has done me already is nothing to the trouble it will give me if I have deserved it; and if I have not, of losing a friend upon a mistake, not that I meanly creep for a friendship that is denied me. I were unfit for it then. I can be but where I was before, not less in myself nor my own peace, which a steady virtue will make a sufficient comfort and sanctuary.

Thy real friend,
Wm Penn

Transcript. HSP. (*PWP*, 2:124-25).

1. WP may possibly have addressed this letter to Algernon Sidney's brother Henry (1641-1704); both brothers held the title "colonel." Henry Sidney had more conventional political opinions than Algernon, however, and was much less likely to denounce WP's constitutional plan as Turkish despotism.

2. The sultan, or emperor of the Turkish empire, was the most common model of absolute tyranny for seventeenth- and eighteenth-century Englishmen.

3. Sidney's complaint here is that WP imposes his constitution on the colonists with no mechanism for popular consultation, ratification, or amendment.

# 29 §

## Thomas Rudyard's Commentary on the Frame of Government

WP'S chief advisor in writing his constitution was Thomas Rudyard, the London Quaker lawyer who assisted WP's defense at the Penn-Mead trial in 1670, a landmark case in the growth of freedom of speech and of trial by jury in England. Rudyard was among the most active members of the Quaker colonization movement, and would serve from 1682 to 1684 as deputy-governor of East New Jersey. In January 1682, he criticized the early drafts of WP's Frame of Government in the commentary printed below, and proposed several major revisions. From January to March 1682, Rudyard and WP worked as close partners in composing and revising the final six drafts of the Pennsylvania constitution.

Rudyard's commentary on the Frame of Government, written as a cryptic series of notes to WP, is difficult to understand but worth the effort. Somewhat like James Madison, in his famous tenth essay of *The Federalist* a century later, Rudyard discusses the economic causes of factionalism in a representative system of government and proposes a method to curb class conflict. Rudyard objects to the earlier drafts of the Frame of Government for two principal reasons. First, he wants WP to change the system of legislative representation as the colony grows, with one system for the first seven years, and another for the period after 1690 when Pennsylvania will be better populated. Second, Rudyard wants WP to guard against the "clamor, insolence, [and] ambition" produced by a legislature divided into an upper house, chosen by the wealthy proprietors, and a lower house, chosen by the poor small farmers. He argues that the Pennsylvania legislature cannot imitate the British Parliament, for Pennsylvania has no hereditary aristocracy such as the membership of the House of Lords, and if the colony's upper house is reserved for wealthy landowners, then the small freeholders, many of them former servants, will elect men of their own inferior status to serve in the lower house — a far cry from the English House of Commons, with its wealthy and distinguished membership. Rudyard's solution is to create a one-house legislature; he supposes that the Pennsylvania voters will then follow the practice of English voters, and choose representatives of high status, education, and talent.

Rudyard did not persuade WP to adopt a two-stage plan of government, but his advice may have prompted WP, once he reached Pennsylvania, to summon a small assembly in December 1682 with only 42 elected representatives and no council (see doc. 50). And as Rudyard and WP jointly composed the final six drafts of the Frame of Government, they ended up with a constitutional plan quite different from the first draft of the Frame (doc. 27). They made the upper house decidedly more powerful than before; it was now called the Provincial Council and had a combination of legislative and executive powers, in effect pooling the functions of two bodies—the upper legislative house and the executive council—in the first draft. And they made the lower house, or Assembly, less powerful than before; it was now reduced to the watchdog role of vetoing undesirable legislation and impeaching misbehaving officials. Thus the published *Frame* (doc. 30) came close to Rudyard's goal of a one-house legislature.

WP's reasons for agreeing to these changes are unclear. It has been argued that Rudyard persuaded him to advance the interests of the wealthy Quaker elite, the major purchasers of Pennsylvania land and the natural candidates for election to the Provincial Council. But WP may have been moved by other considerations as well. He wanted, as Rudyard also did, to promote a Quaker-meeting spirit of loving harmony in Pennsylvania politics, and if he concluded that this could best be accomplished by consigning most political authority to the upper house, he also provided that all Pennsylvania voters, rich or poor, should join in voting for representatives to both houses. Thus Rudyard and WP tried to reduce class conflict between Pennsylvania's large landowners and its small farmers, renters, and former servants.

13 January 1682

As for the Parliament or grand Assembly,
these things rest on my mind.
I. In the infancy of the province.
II. In time of its further growth.

I. In the infancy—for 7 years or till anno 1690.

It's proposed[1] that every proprietor or purchaser of 5000 acres residing in the province be a member of the grand Assembly or Parliament.
For these reasons:

1. The proprietors resident in the province, in respect of the purchasers of future proprieties, may in probability (in the time prefixed) be but few of them there, and not too numerous for a grand Assembly.

2. Such who have a part or a small parcel of a propriety (if not all resident) cannot elect, because [they are] not all there.

3. The freeholders' representatives — [such] as servants, etc. — cannot be elected in the infancy, because there's no freeholders.[2] Nor very requisite they should have any, before such time they have such improvements as are in some measure meriting a representative.

4. But to allow in general, hereafter, 5000 acres to send a representative (if the province be peopled); in some time they must, after that rate, send thousands of representatives.

5. And if otherwise, it must be distinguished what 5000 [acres] must

have a representative and what 5000 no representatives. For every 5000 to have one, will be too numerous.

And until counties, towns corporate, and cities are settled, and they are to send their respective numbers of representatives (as it may be provided for), it's questioned how it shall be practicable to have any other grand Assembly than the first proprietors—which seems most practicable and not in the least offensive in the infancy of government.

Yet allowing if all the purchasers of any 5000 acres be all resident in the province, and do send any of themselves as their representative, [then] such to be a member of the grand Assembly.

This only for the first 7 years or
till anno Domini 1690.

As for the Parliament or grand Assembly
after the year 1690:
As to their election—and as to their session,
after and forever.

1. It's proposed that in the Constitutions provision be made, and that therein be determined and affixed, what number or quantity of acres, fit for cultivation, taken up, set out (besides barrows[3] left for commons, etc.), shall be a county or shire.

2. That until the year     , how many representatives each county or shire shall send to parliament? and from and after that year — how many forever?

3. That a town corporate or city—what or how many inhabitants paying scot and lot shall make one? What representatives from and after the year 1690 — until the year     ? And after that how many representatives or burgesses shall they send forever? This seems reasonable to be settled by the Concessions or Fundamental Constitutions.[4]

To have any other election than by counties, cities, towns corporate, etc., after 1690 seems not only troublesome, but uncertain if not impracticable.

1. Each county, city, [and] town corporate know best their own freeholders, citizens, burgesses, freemen.

2. These are always together and can choose without difficulty.

3. But the quantity of 5000 or 10,000 acres, divided amongst men having only 50, 100, or 200, how shall these be laid or appropriated together, or how shall the possessors thereof come together? Each 50 or 100 acres, and the possessor thereof, being separate and dispersed through the country—as the servants' 50 acres will and must probably be.

Which please to consider.

Further as to election and session
after the year 1690.

As we have experimentally found here in England that the more considerable and valuable (in terra firma, etc.) our representatives have been, with the greater honor and safety to the nation and its reputation also have they carried on and managed affairs. — So (it's expected) it will be in Pennsylvania.

But on the same grounds, or for the same reason, that 2 houses to sit apart and to be chosen distinctly or differently are proposed, do I propose one house only. And but one kind or sort of election.

Upon these reasons and considerations following.

1. We see in England, that although in all counties from 40s. to £40 per anno freeholders[5] are 20, if not 40, times the number of men exceeding £40 per anno, yet scarce our age can give us an instance of any man between 40s. or £40 per anno was chosen by them. And rarely, if ever, less than a man of £500 or £1000 per anno. So in great probability, allowing the freemen who have been servants freedom of election—he will be content with his election and representative, and yet choose no servant.

2. Every servant or 50 acres freeholder having his freedom of choice is represented, as if he had one of his fellow servants there—but denying him choice of a proprietor, is to direct him to choose a 50 acres man.

3. To have one house of Parliament, and that of the greater number of members of men of 50 acres, of such parts, education, abilities, etc., as they will probably be — may produce clamor, insolence, [and] ambition, if not worse; such person[s] being unmeet for council and government.

4. To have 2 separate houses, an upper and lower (when all the neighboring provinces and plantations in America have but one),[6] may in all probability breed differences and emulations between the upper and lower house, hinder dispatch of business, and reflect on us[7] as a people who assert grandeur beyond our pretensions, and set up that in state polity which in our religious capacity we have struck against beyond any people whatsoever.

It is said our 2 houses of Parliament here in England were originally but one—and all sat in one house till corruption and ambition made them two.

5. If it be alleged that 2 houses in [Pennsylvania's] Parliament is like ours in England, as Lords and Commons, I answer in some sort they are, but not on the same grounds.

    1. It's alleged (as mentioned before) in our original fundamentals, or principal agreements of the people, it was not so in England, but all in one house.[8]

    2. The upper house in England is a house of honor, and those called there [are] only whom the kings of England dignify with honor, and by virtue of that, they sit. The Spiritual Lords for life. The Temporal and their heirs, forever (till they be degraded), whether they have estates in land or not.[9]

    3. This upper house proposed for Pennsylvania is not to sit for honor, but territory or land. Now we have no one in England, have he £5, £10, or £20,000 per anno, [who] can sit for his territory without choice of the freeholders who have territory.

    4. But should the king appoint, or were it so in England that every person of £500[10] or £10,000 per anno should be members or

chosen by such—and all other members chosen by all inferior freeholders and those then sat in 2 houses, it would be parallel to the two houses proposed, else I conceive not.

6. Besides the aforesaid consequences and probable conveniencies before mentioned, one house and so chosen bears a parallel with all our assemblies and meetings in affairs religious and civil in which the God of heaven has blessed us in our men's meetings and women's meetings, our monthly and quarterly meetings, which as the Lord set up in His power we must yet have to His glory. In which (as we are worthy) are we members of one body, etc.

All which I freely submit to consideration, not putting so much estimate upon what came upon my mind to differ with any about it.

Draft. HSP. (*PWP*, 2:184-89).

1. Rudyard is here presenting his plan as a substitute for a plan proposed by John Darnall, that the upper House of Proprietors in Pennsylvania have a limited membership, while the lower House of Freeholders have a representative for every 5000 acres. Darnall was the lawyer who had proposed an outline for the Pennsylvania charter in 1680 (doc. 5). He wrote several plans of government for the new colony, and WP evidently showed them to Rudyard.

2. In the early years of the colony there would be too few inhabitants to make the election of representatives possible. Rudyard, however, anticipated that Pennsylvania would grow more slowly than it actually did.

3. Hills.

4. Rudyard means that this question should be settled in whatever constitution is devised for Pennsylvania.

5. Property holders whose land is valued, in rental terms, at 40s. to £40 per year. These small property holders were eligible to vote in English parliamentary elections, but only the large property holders, with land valued well above £40, actually stood for election.

6. Rudyard was incorrect here; several American colonies — Massachusetts Bay, East New Jersey, Maryland, and Virginia—had two-house legislatures in 1682. In East New Jersey, Maryland, and Virginia, however, the upper house was a council appointed by the governor that had limited legislative powers, not a powerful elective body.

7. The Quakers.

8. Here Rudyard may to be referring to the contention of England's radically democratic Levellers, in their various Agreements of the People (1647-1649), that Parliament was originally a democratic body and not a baronial assembly. He may also be referring to some lost draft constitution for Pennsylvania.

9. England's "Spiritual Lords" were the two archbishops and approximately two dozen bishops of the Church of England. The "Temporal" lords were the nation's dukes, marquises, earls, viscounts, and barons. All sat together in England's House of Lords.

10. This may be an error for £5000.

# The Frame of Government *and* Laws Agreed Upon in England

WHEN WP had revised his constitution to his satisfaction, he published it in a pamphlet issued in London, probably in May 1682. The *Frame* is dated 25 April; the *Laws,* 5 May. In his preface to the two documents, WP remarked that he was uneasy about publishing his constitution and exposing it to public censure; but he wanted the Pennsylvania colonists to know his political intentions, and he hoped to persuade them to accept the *Frame* and *Laws* without alteration. Once WP arrived in Pennsylvania, however, he quickly agreed to the colonists' demands for substantial changes in his constitution. On 2 April 1683, the Provincial Council and General Assembly approved the revised or second *Frame of Government* (doc. 63, below); this became Pennsylvania's constitution for the next decade.

The major provisions of the first *Frame of Government* are as follows:

The Preface gives WP's personal philosophy of government, stressing its religious foundations and its moral goals.

Article 1 states that the colony is to be administered by a governor and a two-house legislature, consisting of a Provincial Council and a General Assembly.

Articles 2-4 describe elections to the Council, providing for the election of one-third of the seventy-two councilors each year, and require that each councilor retire for at least a year before seeking reelection.

Articles 5-13 explain the powers, responsibilities, and procedures of the governor and Council: they have the sole right to prepare laws for passage, to execute all laws, to appoint most provincial officials and judges, and to manage the public treasury. The governor has three votes in all of their decisions. To carry out its duties, the Council is divided into four committees: on land development, on justice, on trade and the treasury, and on education and morals.

Articles 14-16 establish a General Assembly, of up to 200 members, which must approve all Council bills before they can become law.

Articles 17-18 specify that some officials are to be nominated by the Council, and others by the Assembly, and grant WP the right to make all initial nominations in the colony.

Articles 19-20 explain the powers of the General Assembly, including impeachment; set the length of Assembly sessions; and require that all elections be by secret ballot.

Article 21 gives the rules for guardianship should the proprietorship pass to a child who had no guardian appointed by his father.

Article 22 prohibits government business on Sunday.

Article 23 requires the consent of the governor and six-sevenths of the legislators to make any amendments to the *Frame of Government.*

Article 24 gives WP's pledge that he and his heirs will observe the provisions of the *Frame of Government* forever.

In addition to his constitution, WP published a set of forty fundamental laws that he hoped the Council and Assembly would speedily confirm in Pennsylvania. The major provisions of these *Laws Agreed Upon in England* are as follows:

Law 1 declares the *Frame of Government* to be the fundamental law of Pennsylvania forever.

Laws 2-3 define the electoral system in Pennsylvania; the franchise is open to all men who own one hundred acres, rent and improve one hundred acres, or earn fifty acres through bond servitude and improve them, or who pay municipal taxes.

Law 4 prohibits taxation without representation.

Laws 5-13, 17-18, 24-26, and 30 establish and regulate the court system, guaranteeing both traditional English rights and several new ones. Persons of all religious faiths can appear in court, and all courts use jury trials, assess moderate court fees, and guarantee accused persons bail except in cases of murder or treason. Witnesses are not required to swear oaths, but can be punished for making false statements. Slander and bribery are severely punished, but thieves are liable to forced labor rather than capital punishment; and all prison costs are paid by the state rather than the prisoner.

Laws 14-16, 19-23, and 33 regulate the inheritance of estates, the possession of land, the performance of marriages, and the transaction of business.

Law 27 forbids the holding of more than one public office at one time.

Laws 28-29 provide for the education of youth and protect the rights of indentured servants.

Law 31 confirms the powers granted by WP to the Free Society of Traders (see docs. 34 and 76, below).

Law 32 is left blank (see n. 15, below).

Law 34 requires that all voters and officeholders be professing Christians, but, unlike laws in England and in most English colonies, does not discriminate against Roman Catholics.

Law 35 guarantees religious freedom to all inhabitants who believe in one God.

Laws 36-37 prohibit work on Sunday, and a wide range of immoral behavior: swearing, all sexual activity outside of marriage, all violence, stage plays, gambling, dancing, and most entertaining sports, especially cock-fighting and bull- and bear-baiting.

Law 38 requires the annual reading and public display of the *Laws Agreed Upon in England* in the Council and in all provincial courts.

Law 39 requires the consent of the governor and six-sevenths of the legislators to make any alterations in the *Laws Agreed Upon in England*.

Law 40 delegates all further issues to the governor and the legislature.

The FRAME of the
GOVERNMENT
of the
**Province** of **Pennsylvania**
in
AMERICA:
Together with certain
LAWS
Agreed upon in England
by the
GOVERNOR
and
Divers FREEMEN of the aforesaid
PROVINCE.

To be further Explained and Confirmed there by the first
**Provincial Council** and **General Assembly** that shall be held,
if they see meet.

---

Printed in the Year MDCLXXXII.


The
PREFACE.

When the great and wise God had made the world, of all His creatures it pleased Him to choose man [as] His deputy to rule it. And to fit him for so great a charge and trust, He did not only qualify him with skill and power, but with integrity to use them justly. This native goodness was equally his honor and his happiness; and while he stood here, all went well. There was no need of coercive or compulsive means; the precept of divine love and truth in his own bosom was the guide and keeper of his innocence. But lust prevailing against duty made a lamentable breach upon it; and the law, that before had no power over him, took place upon him and his disobedient posterity, that such as would not live conformable to the holy law within, should fall under the reproof and correction of the just law without in a judicial administration.

This the Apostle[1] teaches in divers of his epistles: the law (says he) was added because of transgression. In another place, knowing that the law was not made for the righteous man, but for the disobedient and ungodly, for sinners, for unholy and profane, for murderers, for whoremongers, for them that defile themselves with mankind, and for manstealers, for liars, for perjured persons, etc. But this is not all; he opens and carries the matter of government a little further. Let every soul be subject to the higher powers; for there is no power but of God. The powers that be, are ordained of God: whosoever therefore resists the power, resists the ordinance of God. For rulers are not a terror to good works, but to evil: will thou then not be afraid of the power, do that which is good, and thou shall have praise of the same. He is the minister of God to thee for good. Wherefore, ye must needs be subject, not only for wrath, but for conscience sake.[2] This settles the divine right of government beyond exception, and that for two ends: first, to terrify evildoers; secondly, to cherish those that do well; which gives government a life beyond corruption, and makes it as durable in the world, as good men shall be. So that government seems to me a part of religion itself, a thing sacred in its institution and end: for if it does not directly remove the cause, it crushes the effects of evil, and is as such (though a lower, yet) an emanation of the same divine power that is both author and object of pure religion; the difference lying here, that the one is more free and mental, the other, more corporal and compulsive in its operations. But that is only to evildoers; government in itself being otherwise as capable of kindness, goodness, and charity as a more private society. They weakly err that think there is no other use for government than correction, which is the coarsest part of it. Daily experience tells us that the care and regulation of many other affairs, more soft and daily necessary, make up much the greatest part of government; and which must have followed the peopling of the world had Adam never fallen, and will continue among men on earth under the highest attainments they may arrive at, by the coming of the blessed second Adam, the Lord from Heaven.[3] Thus much of government in general, as to its rise and end.

For particular frames and models, it will become me to say little; and comparatively I will say nothing. My reasons are, first, that the age is too nice[4] and difficult for it, there being nothing the wits of men are more busy and divided upon. It is true they seem to agree in the end [of government], to wit, happiness; but in the means they differ, as to divine, so to this humane felicity; and the cause is much the same, not always want of light and knowledge, but want of using them rightly. Men side with their passions against their reason; and their sinister interests have so strong a bias upon their minds, that they lean to them against the good of the things they know.

Secondly, I do not find a model in the world, that time, place, and some singular emergencies have not necessarily altered; nor is it easy to frame a civil government that shall serve all places alike.

Thirdly, I know what is said by the several admirers of monarchy, aristocracy, and democracy, which are the rule of one, a few, and many, and are the three common ideas of government, when men discourse of that subject. But I choose to solve the controversy with this small distinction, and it belongs to all three: any government is free to the people under it (whatever be the frame) where the laws rule, and the people are a party to those laws, and more than this is tyranny, oligarchy, or confusion.

But lastly, when all is said, there is hardly one frame of government in the world so ill designed by its first founders, that in good hands would not do well enough; and [hi]story tells us, the best in ill ones can do nothing that is great or good; witness the Jewish and Roman states. Governments, like clocks, go from the motion men give them; and as governments are made and moved by men, so by them are ruined too: wherefore governments rather depend upon men, than men upon governments. Let men be good, and the government can't be bad; if it be ill, they will cure it. But if men be bad, let the government be never so good; they will endeavor to warp and spoil it to their turn.

I know some say, let us have good laws, and no matter for the men that execute them. But let them consider, that though good laws do well, good men do better; for good laws may want good men, and be abolished or evaded by ill men; but good men will never want good laws nor suffer ill ones. It is true, good laws have some awe upon ill ministers, but that is where they have not power to escape or abolish them, and the people are generally wise and good. But a loose and depraved people (which is the question) love laws and an administration like themselves. That therefore which makes a good constitution must keep it, viz.: men of wisdom and virtue; qualities, that because they descend not with worldly inheritances, must be carefully propagated by a virtuous education of youth; for which after-ages will owe more to the care and prudence of founders and the successive magistracy than to their parents for their private patrimonies.

These considerations of the weight of government, and the nice and various opinions about it, made it uneasy to me to think of publishing the ensuing Frame and conditional Laws, foreseeing both the censures they will meet with from men of differing humors and engagements, and the occasion they may give of discourse beyond my design.

But next to the power of necessity (which is a solicitor that will take no denial), this induced me to a compliance, that we have (with reverence to God and good conscience to men) to the best of our skill contrived and composed the Frame and Laws of this government to the great end of all government, viz.: to support power in reverence with the people, and to secure the people from the abuse of power; that they may be free by their just obedience, and the magistrates honorable for their just administration. For liberty without obedience is confusion, and obedience without liberty is slavery. To carry this evenness is partly owing to the constitution, and partly to the magistracy; where either of these fail, government will be subject to convulsions; but where both are wanting, it must be totally subverted. Then where both meet, the government is like to endure, which I humbly pray and hope, God will please to make the lot of this of Pennsylvania. Amen.
William Penn.

The
FRAME
of the
**Government of Pennsylvania**
in
AMERICA, etc.

**To all people,** *to whom these presents shall come:*

WHEREAS King Charles the Second, by his letters patents under the Great Seal of England, for the considerations therein mentioned, has been graciously pleased to give and grant unto me, William Penn (by the name of William Penn, Esquire, son and heir of Sir William Penn, deceased), and to my heirs and assigns forever, all that tract of land or province called Pennsylvania, in America, with divers great powers, pre-eminencies, royalties, jurisdictions, and authorities necessary for the well-being and government thereof.

Now know ye, that for the well-being and government of the said province, and for the encouragement of all the freemen and planters that may be therein concerned, in pursuance of the powers aforementioned, I, the said William Penn, have declared, granted, and confirmed, and by these presents for me, my heirs, and assigns, do declare, grant, and confirm unto all the freemen, planters, and adventurers of, in, and to the said province, these liberties, franchises, and properties to be held, enjoyed, and kept by the freemen, planters, and inhabitants of and in the said province of Pennsylvania forever.

*Imprimis,*[5] that the government of this province shall, according to the powers of the patent,[6] consist of the Governor and freemen of the said province, in the form of a Provincial Council and General Assembly, by whom all laws shall be made, officers chosen, and public affairs transacted, as is hereafter respectively declared; that is to say,

II. That the freemen of the said province shall on the twentieth day of the twelfth month, which shall be in this present year one thousand six hundred eighty and two,[7] meet and assemble in some fit place, of which timely notice shall be beforehand given by the Governor or his deputy, and then and there shall choose out of themselves seventy-two persons of most note for their wisdom, virtue, and ability, who shall meet on the tenth day of the first month next ensuing, and always be called and act as the Provincial Council of the said province.

III. That at the first choice of such Provincial Council, one-third part of the said Provincial Council shall be chosen to serve for three years then next ensuing, one-third part for two years then next ensuing, and one-third part for one year then next following such election, and no longer; and that the said third part shall go out accordingly. And on the twentieth day of the twelfth month, as aforesaid, yearly, forever afterward, the freemen of the said province shall in like manner meet and assemble together, and then choose twenty-four persons, being one-third of the said number, to serve in Provincial Council for three years, it being intended that one-third of the whole Provincial Council (always consisting and to consist of seventy-two persons, as aforesaid) falling off yearly, it shall be yearly supplied by such new yearly elections as aforesaid. And that no one person shall continue therein longer than three years. And in case any member shall decease before the last election, during his time, that then, at the next election ensuing his decease, another shall be chosen to supply his place for the remaining time he was to have served, and no longer.

IV. That after the first seven years, every one of the said third parts that goes yearly off, shall be incapable of being chosen again for one whole year following: that so all may be fitted for government, and have experience of the care and burden of it.

V. That the Provincial Council in all cases and matters of moment, as their arguing upon bills to be passed into laws, erecting courts of justice, giving judgment upon criminals impeached, and choice of officers in such manner as is herein after mentioned, not less than two-thirds of the whole Provincial Council shall make a quorum; and that the consent and approbation of two-thirds of such quorum shall be had in all such cases or matters of moment. And moreover, that in all cases and matters of lesser moment, twenty-four members of the said Provincial Council shall make a quorum, the majority of which twenty-four shall and may always determine in such cases and causes of lesser moment.

VI. That in this Provincial Council the Governor or his deputy shall or may always preside and have a treble voice; and the said Provincial Council shall always continue and sit upon its own adjournments and committees.

VII. That the Governor and Provincial Council shall prepare and propose to the General Assembly, hereafter mentioned, all bills which they shall at any time think fit to be passed into laws within the said province; which bills shall be published and affixed to the most noted places in the inhabited parts thereof thirty days before the meeting of the General Assembly, in order to the passing of them into laws, or rejecting of them, as the General Assembly shall see meet.

VIII. That the Governor and Provincial Council shall take care, that all laws, statutes, and ordinances, which shall at any time be made within the said province, be duly and diligently executed.

IX. That the Governor and Provincial Council shall at all times have the care of the peace and safety of the province; and that nothing be by any person attempted to the subversion of this Frame of Government.

X. That the Governor and Provincial Council shall at all times settle and order the situation of all cities, ports, and market towns in every county, modeling therein all public buildings, streets, and marketplaces; and shall appoint all necessary roads and highways in the province.

XI. That the Governor and Provincial Council shall at all times have power to inspect the management of the public treasury, and punish those who shall convert any part thereof to any other use than what has been agreed upon by the Governor, Provincial Council, and General Assembly.

XII. That the Governor and Provincial Council shall erect and order all public schools, and encourage and reward the authors of useful sciences and laudable inventions in the said province.

XIII. That for the better management of the powers and trust aforesaid, the Provincial Council shall from time to time divide itself into four distinct and proper committees, for the more easy administration of the affairs of the province, which divides the seventy-two into four eighteens, every one of which eighteens shall consist of six out of each of the three orders or yearly elections, each of which shall have a distinct portion of business, as follows. First, a Committee of Plantations, to situate and settle cities, ports, market towns, and highways, and to hear and decide all suits and controversies relating to plantations. Secondly, a Committee of Justice and Safety, to secure the peace of the province and punish the maladministration of those who subvert justice to the prejudice of the public or private interest. Thirdly, a Committee of Trade and Treasury, who shall regulate all trade and commerce according to law, encourage manufacture and country growth, and defray the public charge of the province. And fourthly, a Committee of Manners, Education, and Arts, that all wicked and scandalous living may be prevented, and that youth may be successively trained up in virtue and useful knowledge and arts. The quorum of each of which committees being six, that is, two out of each of the three orders or yearly elections, as aforesaid, make a constant or standing Council of twenty-four, which will have the power of the Provincial Council, being the quorum of it, in all cases not excepted in the fifth article; and in the said committees and standing Council of the province, the Governor or his deputy shall or may preside, as aforesaid. And in the absence of the Governor or his deputy, if no one is by either of them appointed, the said committees or Council shall appoint a president for that time, and not otherwise; and what shall be resolved at such committees, shall be reported to the said Council of the province, and shall be by them resolved and confirmed before the same shall be put in execution, and that these respective committees shall not sit at one and the same time, except in cases of necessity.

XIV. And to the end that all laws prepared by the Governor and Provincial Council aforesaid may yet have the more full concurrence of the freemen of the province, it is declared, granted, and confirmed that at the time and place or places, for the choice of a Provincial Council, as aforesaid, the said freemen shall yearly choose members to serve in a General Assembly, as their representatives, not exceeding two hundred persons, who shall yearly meet on the twentieth day of the second month, which shall be in the year 1683 following, in the capital town or city of the said province, where during eight days the several members may freely confer with one another; and if any of them see meet, with a committee of the Provincial Council (consisting of three [councilors] out of each of the four committees aforesaid, being twelve in all) which shall be at that time purposely appointed to receive from any of them proposals for the alteration or amendment of any of the said proposed and promulgated bills. And on the ninth day from their so meeting, the said General Assembly, after the reading over of the proposed bills by the clerk of the Provincial Council, and the occasions and motives for them being opened by the Governor or his deputy, shall give their affirmative or negative, which to them seems best, in such manner as hereafter is expressed. But not less than two-thirds shall make a quorum in the passing of laws and choice of such officers as are by them to be chosen.

XV. That the laws so prepared and proposed as aforesaid, that are assented to by the General Assembly, shall be enrolled, as laws of the province, with this style: "By the Governor, with the assent and approbation of the freemen in Provincial Council and General Assembly."

XVI. That for the better establishment of the government and laws of this province, and to the end there may be a universal satisfaction in the laying of the fundamentals thereof, the General Assembly shall or may for the first year consist of all the freemen of and in the said province; and ever after it shall be yearly chosen, as aforesaid; which number of two hundred shall be enlarged as the country shall increase in people, so as it does not exceed five hundred at any time. The appointment and proportioning of which, as also the laying and methodizing of the choice of the Provincial Council and General Assembly in future times most equally to the division of the hundreds and counties, which the country shall hereafter be divided into, shall be in the power of the Provincial Council to propose, and the General Assembly to resolve.

XVII. That the Governor and the Provincial Council shall erect from time to time standing courts of justice in such places and number, as they shall judge convenient for the good government of the said province. And that the Provincial Council shall on the thirteenth day of the first month yearly elect and present to the Governor or his deputy a double number of persons to serve for judges, treasurers, [and] masters of rolls within the said province for the year next ensuing. And the freemen of the said province in their county courts, when they shall be erected, and till then in the General Assembly, shall on the three and twentieth day of the second month yearly elect and present to the Governor or his deputy a double number of persons to serve for sheriffs, justices of peace, and coroners for the year next ensuing. Out of which respective elections and presentments the Governor or his deputy shall nominate and commission the proper number for each office the third day after the said respective presentments, or else the first named in such presentment for each office shall stand and serve for that office the year ensuing.

XVIII. But forasmuch as the present condition of the province requires some immediate settlement and admits not of so quick a revolution of officers, and to the end the said province may with all convenient speed be well ordered and settled, I, William Penn, do therefore think fit to nominate and appoint such persons for judges, treasurers, masters of the rolls, sheriffs, justices of the peace, and coroners, as are most fitly qualified for those employments; to whom I shall make and grant commissions for the said offices, respectively to hold to them to whom the same shall be granted, for so long time as every such person shall well behave himself in the office or place to him respectively granted, and no longer. And upon the decease or displacing of any of the said officers, the succeeding officer or officers shall be chosen as aforesaid.

XIX. That the General Assembly shall continue so long as may be needful to impeach criminals fit to be there impeached, to pass bills into laws that they shall think fit to pass into laws, and till such time as the Governor and Provincial Council shall declare that they have nothing further to propose unto them for their assent and approbation. And that declaration shall be a dismissal to the General Assembly for that time; which General Assembly shall be notwithstanding capable of assembling together upon the summons of the Provincial Council at any time during that year if the said Provincial Council shall see occasion for so assembling.

XX. That all the elections of members or representatives of the people to serve in Provincial Council and General Assembly, and all questions to be determined by both or either of them that relate to passing of bills into laws, to the choice of officers, to impeachments made by the General Assembly, and judgment of criminals upon such impeachments by the Provincial Council, and to all other cases by them respectively judged of importance, shall be resolved and determined by the ballot; and unless on sudden and indispensible occasions, no business in Provincial Council or its respective committees shall be finally determined the same day that it is moved.

XXI. And that at all times, when and so often as it shall happen that the Governor shall or may be an infant under the age of one and twenty years, and no guardians or commissioners are appointed in writing by the father of the said infant, or that such guardians or commissioners shall be deceased, that during such minority the Provincial Council shall from time to time, as they shall see meet, constitute and appoint guardians or commissioners, not exceeding three, one of which three shall preside as deputy and chief guardian during such minority, and shall have and execute with the consent of the other two all the power of a Governor in all the public affairs and concerns of the said province.

XXII. That as often as any day of the month mentioned in any article of this charter shall fall upon the first day of the week, commonly called the Lord's Day, the business appointed for that day shall be deferred till the next day, unless in case of emergency.

XXIII. That no act, law, or ordinance whatsoever shall at any time hereafter be made or done by the Governor of this province, his heirs or assigns, or by the freemen in the Provincial Council, or the General Assembly, to alter, change, or diminish the form or effect of this charter, or any part or clause thereof, or contrary to the true intent and meaning thereof, without the consent of the Governor, his heirs or assigns, and six parts of seven of the said freemen in Provincial Council and General Assembly.

XXIV. And lastly, that I, the said William Penn, for myself, my heirs, and assigns, have solemnly declared, granted, and confirmed, and do hereby solemnly declare, grant, and confirm, that neither I, my heirs nor assigns shall procure or do any thing or things, whereby the liberties in this charter contained and expressed, shall be infringed or broken. And if anything be procured by any person or persons contrary to these premises, it shall be held of no force or effect. In witness whereof I, the said William Penn, have unto this present Charter of Liberties set my hand and broad seal this five and twentieth day of the second month, vulgarly called April, in the year of our Lord one thousand six hundred eighty and two.

William Penn.

**Laws agreed upon in England**
by the
GOVERNOR
And Divers of the
**Freemen of Pennsylvania,**
To be further Explained and Confirmed there by the first
*Provincial Council* and *General Assembly* that shall be held
in the said *Province,* if they see meet.

I. THAT the Charter of Liberties declared, granted, and confirmed the five and twentieth day of the second month called April, 1682, before divers witnesses by William Penn, Governor and chief proprietor of Pennsylvania, to all the freemen and planters of the said province, is hereby declared and approved, and shall be forever held for a fundamental in the government thereof, according to the limitations mentioned in the said Charter.

II. That every inhabitant in the said province that is or shall be a purchaser of one hundred acres of land or upwards, his heirs and assigns; and every person who shall have paid his passage, and taken up one hundred acres of land at one penny an acre, and have cultivated ten acres thereof;[8] and every person that has been a servant or bondsman, and is free by his service, that shall have taken up his fifty acres of land and cultivated twenty thereof; and every inhabitant, artificer, or other resident in the said province that pays scot and lot[9] to the government, shall be deemed and accounted a freeman of the said province; and every such person shall and may be capable of electing or being elected representatives of the people in Provincial Council or General Assembly in the said province.

III. That all elections of members or representatives of the people and freemen of the province of Pennsylvania, to serve in Provincial Council or General Assembly, to be held within the said province, shall be free and voluntary. And that the elector that shall receive any reward or gift in meat, drink, money, or otherwise, shall forfeit his right to elect. And such person as shall directly or indirectly give, promise, or bestow any such reward as aforesaid to be elected, shall forfeit his election, and be thereby incapable to serve, as aforesaid. And the Provincial Council and General Assembly shall be the sole judges of the regularity or irregularity of the elections of their own respective members.

IV. That no money or goods shall be raised upon or paid by any of the people of this province by way of a public tax, custom, or contribution, but by a law for that purpose made. And whosoever shall levy, collect, or pay any money or goods contrary thereunto, shall be held a public enemy to the province, and a betrayer of the liberty of the people thereof.

V. That all courts shall be open, and justice shall neither be sold, denied, nor delayed.

VI. That in courts all persons of all persuasions may freely appear in their own way, and according to their own manner, and there personally plead their own cause themselves, or if unable, by their friends. And the first process shall be the exhibition of the complaint in court fourteen days before the trial. And that the party complained against may be fitted for the same, he or she shall be summoned no less than ten days before, and a copy of the complaint delivered [to] him or her at his or her dwelling house. But before the complaint of any person be received, he shall solemnly declare in court that he believes in his conscience [that] his cause is just.

VII. That all pleadings, processes, and records in courts shall be short and in English, and in an ordinary and plain character, that they may be understood, and justice speedily administered.

VIII. That all trials shall be by twelve men and, as near as may be, peers or equals, and of the neighborhood, and men without just exception. In cases of life there shall be first twenty-four returned by the sheriff for a grand inquest, of whom twelve at least shall find the complaint to be true, and then the twelve men or peers, to be likewise returned by the sheriff, shall have the final judgment. But reasonable challenges shall be always admitted against the said twelve men, or any of them.

IX. That all fees in all cases shall be moderate and settled by the Provincial Council and General Assembly, and be hung up in a table in every respective court. And whosoever shall be convicted of taking more shall pay twofold, and be dismissed his employment, one moiety[10] of which shall go to the party wronged.

X. That all prisons shall be workhouses for felons, vagrants, and loose and idle persons, whereof one shall be in every county.

XI. That all prisoners shall be bailable by sufficient sureties, unless for capital offenses where the proof is evident, or the presumption great.

XII. That all persons wrongfully imprisoned or prosecuted at law shall have double damages against the informer or prosecutor.

XIII. That all prisons shall be free, as to fees, food, and lodging.

XIV. That all lands and goods shall be liable to pay debts, except where there be legal issue, and then all the goods, and one-third of the land only.

XV. That all wills in writing, attested by two witnesses, shall be of the same force, as to lands, as other conveyances, being legally proved within forty days, either within or without the said province.

XVI. That seven years' quiet possession [of real estate] shall give an unquestionable right, except in cases of infants, lunatics, married women, or persons beyond the sea.

XVII. That all briberies and extortions whatsoever shall be severely punished.

XVIII. That all fines shall be moderate, and saving men's contenements, merchandise, or wainage.[11]

XIX. That all marriages (not forbidden by the law of God, as to nearness of blood and affinity by marriage) shall be encouraged; but the parents or guardians shall be first consulted, and the marriage shall be published before it be solemnized, and it shall be solemnized by taking one another as husband and wife before credible witnesses. And a certificate of the whole, under the hands of parties and witnesses, shall be brought to the proper register of that county, and shall be registered in his office.

XX. And to prevent frauds and vexatious suits within the said province, that all charters, gifts, grants, and conveyances of land (except leases for a year or under), and all bills, bonds, and specialties[12] above £5 and not under three months, made in the said province, shall be enrolled or registered in the public enrollment office of the said province, within the space of two months next after the making thereof, else to be void in law. And all deeds, grants, and conveyances of land (except as aforesaid) within the said province, and made out of the said province, shall be enrolled or registered, as aforesaid, within six months next after the making thereof, and settling and constituting an enrollment office or registry within the said province, else to be void in law against all persons whatsoever.

XXI. That all defacers or corrupters of charters, gifts, grants, bonds, bills, wills, contracts, and conveyances, or that shall deface or falsify any enrollment, registry, or record within this province, shall make double satisfaction for the same; half whereof shall go to the party wronged, and they shall be dismissed of all places of trust, and be publicly disgraced, as false men.

XXII. That there shall be a register for births, marriages, burials, wills, and letters of administration distinct from the other registry.

XXIII. That there shall be a registry for all servants, where their names, time, wages, and days of payment shall be registered.

XXIV. That all lands and goods of felons shall be liable to make satisfaction to the party wronged [at] twice the value; and for want of lands or goods, the felon shall be bondsman, to work in the common prison or workhouse, or otherwise, till the party injured be satisfied.

XXV. That the estates of capital offenders, as traitors and murderers, shall go one-third to the next of kin to the sufferer, and the remainder to the next of kin to the criminal.

XXVI. That all witnesses coming or called to testify their knowledge in or to any matter or thing in any court, or before any lawful authority within the said province, shall there give or deliver in their evidence or testimony by solemnly promising to speak the truth, the whole truth, and nothing but the truth to the matter or thing in question. And in case any person, so called to evidence, shall afterwards be convicted of willful falsehood, such person shall suffer and undergo such damage or penalty as the person or persons against whom he or she bore false witness did or should undergo, and shall also make satisfaction to the party wronged, and be publicly exposed as a false witness, never to be credited in any court or before any magistrate in the said province.

XXVII. And to the end that all officers chosen to serve within this province may with more care and diligence answer the trust reposed in them, it is agreed that no such person shall enjoy more than one public office at one time.

XXVIII. That all children within this province of the age of twelve years shall be taught some useful trade or skill, to the end none may be idle, but the poor may work to live, and the rich, if they become poor, may not want.

XXIX. That servants be not kept longer than their time; and such as are careful be both justly and kindly used in their service, and put in fitting equipage[13] at the expiration thereof, according to custom.

XXX. That all scandalous and malicious reporters, backbiters, defamers, and spreaders of false news, whether against magistrates or private persons, shall be accordingly severely punished, as enemies to the peace and concord of this province.

XXXI. That for the encouragement of the planters and traders in this province who are incorporated into a society, the patent granted to them by William Penn, Governor of the said province, is hereby ratified and confirmed.[14]

XXXII. _____

_____

_____ [15]

XXXIII. That all factors or correspondents[16] in the said province wronging their employers shall make satisfaction, and one-third over, to their said employers; and in case of the death of any such factor or correspondent, the Committee of Trade shall take care to secure so much of the deceased party's estate as belongs to his said respective employers.

XXXIV. That all treasurers, judges, masters of the rolls, sheriffs, justices of the peace, and other officers or persons whatsoever relating to courts or trials of causes, or any other service in the government, and all members elected to serve in Provincial Council and General Assembly, and all that have right to elect such members, shall be such as profess faith in Jesus Christ, and that are not convicted of ill fame or unsober and dishonest conversation, and that are of one and twenty years of age at least; and that all such so qualified shall be capable of the said several employments and privileges, as aforesaid.

XXXV. That all persons living in this province who confess and acknowledge the one almighty and eternal God to be the creator, upholder, and ruler of the world, and that hold themselves obliged in conscience to live peaceably and justly in civil society, shall in no ways be molested or prejudiced for their religious persuasion or practice in matters of faith and worship, nor shall they be compelled at any time to frequent or maintain any religious worship, place, or ministry whatever.

XXXVI. That according to the good example of the primitive Christians, and for the ease of the creation,[17] every first day of the week, called the Lord's Day, people shall abstain from their common daily labor, that they may the better dispose themselves to worship God according to their understandings.

XXXVII. That as a careless and corrupt administration of justice draws the wrath of God upon magistrates, so the wildness and looseness of the people provoke the indignation of God against a country. Therefore,

That all such offenses against God, as swearing, cursing, lying, profane talking, drunkenness, drinking of healths, obscene words, incest, sodomy, rapes, whoredom, fornication, and other uncleanness (not to be repeated); all treasons, misprisions,[18] murders, duels, felonies, sedition, mayhems, forcible entries, and other violence to the persons and estates of the inhabitants within this province; all prizes, stage plays, cards, dice, May games,[19] gamesters, masques, revels, bull-baitings, cock-fightings, bear-baitings, and the like, which excite the people to rudeness, cruelty, looseness, and irreligion, shall be respectively discouraged and severely punished according to the appointment of the Governor and freemen in Provincial Council and General Assembly, as also all proceedings contrary to these laws, that are not here made expressly penal.

XXXVIII. That a copy of these laws shall be hung up in the Provincial Council and in public courts of justice, and that they shall be read yearly at the opening of every Provincial Council and General Assembly and court of justice, and their assent shall be testified by their standing up after the reading thereof.

XXXIX. That there shall be at no time any alteration of any of these laws without the consent of the Governor, his heirs or assigns, and six parts of seven of the freemen met in Provincial Council and General Assembly.

XL. That all other matters and things not herein provided for, which shall and may concern the public justice, peace, or safety of the said province, and the raising and imposing [of] taxes, customs, duties, or other charges whatsoever, shall be and are hereby referred to the order, prudence, and determination of the Governor and freemen in Provincial Council and General Assembly, to be held from time to time in the said Province.

Signed and sealed by the Governor and freemen aforesaid, this fifth day of the third month, called May, one thousand six hundred eighty and two.

Printed tract. *The Frame of the Government of the Province of Pennsilvania in America: Together with certain Laws Agreed upon in England by the Governour and Divers Free-men of the aforesaid Province* (London, [c. May] 1682). (*PWP,* 2:211-27).

1. St. Paul.
2. WP has quoted here from three of St. Paul's epistles: Galatians 3:19; 1 Timothy 1:9-10; and Romans 13:1-5.
3. Jesus Christ.
4. Fastidious, discriminative, or critical. The meaning of this word varied widely in the seventeenth century.
5. First.
6. The Pennsylvania charter (doc. 11, above).
7. 20 Feb. 1683. Note that WP uses Quaker dating throughout this constitution, with March as the first month.
8. This clause refers to renters, who paid WP one penny per acre in annual rent. Had they purchased land from WP, they would have paid nearly 5d. per acre.
9. Taxes levied on town dwellers (see doc. 27, n. 3, above). Thus, this article grants voting rights to purchasers of 100 acres, whether or not improved; to renters of 100 acres, slightly improved; to ex-servants who had improved 40 percent of their fifty-acre grants; and to taxpaying town dwellers. For more details, see doc. 17, above.
10. Half, that is, one-half of the fine.
11. "Contenement" meant either "freehold," or more generally, "property"; "wainage" usually referred to carts used in agriculture, but could also mean "profit," or "advantage."
12. A legal contract, obligation, or bond.
13. Furnishings or clothing, provided to the servant by the master.
14. This clause refers to the charter granted by WP to the Free Society of Traders. For that company's rights and privileges, see docs. 34 and 76, below.
15. Law 32 is marked as missing in all surviving manuscript versions of the *Laws,* as well as in the printed pamphlet. The editors have found no evidence to suggest what this intended law might have contained.
16. Business agents.
17. In the manuscript draft of the *Laws,* this clause reads: "for the ease of man and beast from their common daily labor."
18. Concealment of crime.
19. Games and dancing held on the first of May; more generally, merrymaking, sport, or frolic.

# 31 §
## Benjamin Furly's Criticism of The Frame of Government

ONE advisor who remained dissatisfied with WP's new constitution
was the Quaker Benjamin Furly (1636-1714), of Rotterdam in the
Netherlands. Furly sent WP two critiques of the *Frame of Government,* one
of which is printed (in abridged form) below. Furly opens his commentary
with a series of specific requests for further changes in the *Frame.* He wants
better legal protection for foreigners, such as Dutchmen and Germans, who
buy land in Pennsylvania. He wants changes in the inheritance laws, funding
for social services, revisions in the jury system, a prohibition against slavery,
and guarantees of freedom of conscience for all settlers, even those who do
not believe in observing the Sabbath. Following his numbered paragraphs,
Furly plunges into a general comparison of the "Fundamental Constitutions" (doc. 26) with the final *Frame* (doc. 30). In sharp contrast to Thomas
Rudyard in doc. 29, Furly much prefers the "Fundamental Constitutions,"
and objects in particular to those clauses in the *Frame* that increased the power
of the Provincial Council and decreased the power of the Assembly. He also
distrusts the governor's authority, especially since WP's successors might be
unworthy men. Several of Furly's criticisms sound much like those made by
Algernon Sidney (doc. 28, above), and like those made by Jasper Batt (see
doc. 54, below). His advice was not altogether ignored, for two of his sug-
gestions—the provision guaranteeing the landholding rights of non-British
settlers, and the extension of hunting and fishing rights to all inhabitants—
were taken up by the Pennsylvania Assembly and incorporated into the second *Frame of Government* of 1683 (doc. 63, below).

[1682]

For the security of foreigners who may incline to purchase land in Pennsylvania,[1] but may die before they themselves come there to inhabit:

### I

If the forfeitures of foreigners' land do there fall to the Governor, as in
England to the king, let an article be added to the Frame by which the Governor binds himself, heirs, and assigns, that in such cases he will not take any
advantage thereat, but freely and at his charge restore the said lands to the
heirs of the deceased foreigners from time to time, forever.

### Or II

If it will stand in law, let a law be made declaring every man natural[ized] by virtue of his purchase, provided he send one to inhabit there with
full power to subscribe to the fundamentals of the government. As it is in

the Carolina constitutions,[2] that everyone who does there in person subscribe shall be thereby naturalized.

One or both [of] these must be, or else persons dying after purchase before they can get over with their families to be denizened[3] or naturalized, their heirs may have their land forfeited to the king. . . .

## V

That a law be made, as in the first draft of the Governor, Art. — [4] declaring all children to have an equal share in the estates of their parents, dying without will.

## VI

That all wills be so far regulated by law, that the children may not for mere will and pleasure, and without sufficient reason, be disinherited on the one side; nor the parents deprived on the other side of a power of countenancing and rewarding virtue, obedience, and sweetness, and discountenancing vice and refractoriness in their children.

In order whereunto, let the father have the full disposal of the one-half of the children's ⅔ parts of the estate,[5] to dispose of in legacies, and to such of his children as shall have been most deserving. And the other half let be firmly established upon the children equally, as their legitimate portion. . . .

## VIII

Let a certain part of every man's gain, whether husbandman, tradesman, handicraftsman, merchant, or by whatsoever name distinguished, be set apart, and brought into a common treasury, whether $\frac{1}{10}$, $\frac{1}{15}$, or $\frac{1}{20}$th part of their gain. I say gain, that so the laborious husbandman may not (as in that oppression of tithes),[6] be compelled to pay where he reaps not sufficient to pay for his seed and labor, etc. And as the country increases let this be kept in each county where it arises.

Let this be set apart for these uses: 1. For erecting and maintaining of free schools; 2. For erecting and maintaining of hospitals, for aged and disabled men and women and orphans. . . .

Thus both rich and poor will see a moral certainty, that into what state soever they or their posterity shall come, they shall not want for being well provided for, and their children bred up to learning if capable and thereunto inclined. This fund may be employed for the transporting of poor families [to Pennsylvania] that gladly would transport themselves (but cannot for want of means), if any would but furnish them with so much as is necessary to their transportation and settlement, upon their bonds to repay them again, with a reasonable interest and allowance for their moneys and risk. . . .

## IX

Concerning Juries. Especially where life will be concerned, as in murder and treason where the Governor has no power to pardon, let God rather than men be intrusted with that affair in the first place, that all corruption in packing of juries to hurry men out of the world without just cause may be prevented.

To which purpose let the names of all the freeholders, or such as are capable of serving, be written in papers, and let 48 draw; which done, let the prisoner have his liberty still to except, giving sufficient reasons to the court, that so things may go squarely on both sides.

Only in cases that will touch life, let no man that scruples to pass upon life in any case be imposed upon. As I myself and many more, to me known, do. . . .

## XIX

The 36th law enjoining all to abstain from labor on the first day may prove a vile snare to the conscience of many in this day, who do not look upon that day as of any other than human institution, and may be pressed in spirit (whether right or wrong is not the question) sometimes to work upon that day, to testify against that superstitious conceit that it is of divine institution, and is the Christian sabbath.

Only thus far there may a service be in setting servants at liberty from the oppressions of grinding, covetous masters, etc., that it be declared that no master shall compel his servant to labor on that day because it's fit that the very body of man and beast should have some rest from their continual labor.

## XX

That no public tax be for longer than a year, which will make the Assembly always necessary. And consequently keep ministers[7] in awe. . . .

## XXII

That a form of a deed be agreed upon that's short and plain, that we be not bound to the tricks of the lawyers of England. And let possession be given and taken as in Holland, in open court, by the persons themselves or their attorneys. In Holland, the mode is thus: The seller takes his hat, and turning the crown downwards holds it by two fingers and his thumb. The buyer likewise takes hold of it, and the seller says that he thereby surrenders to him all his right and title, leaving the hat in the hand of the buyer, who afterwards gives it [to] him and there's an end.

## XXIII

Let no blacks be brought in directly. And if any come out of Virginia [and] Maryland in families that have formerly bought them elsewhere, let them be declared (as in the West Jersey constitutions)[8] free at 8 years' end. . . .

## XXIV

That the royalties (being not in the deeds expressed) be added to the frame as an article, and the liberty of hunting, fowling, [and] fishing [be] expressed in plain terms. And afterwards in the register. Things securing men's rights and properties cannot be writ too plain.[9]

That which I have now further to add is that I far prefer thy first draft[10] to this last, as being most equal, most fair, and most agreeing with the just, wise, and prudent constitutions of our ancestors. And most likely to keep us in a good and fair correspondence with the nation,[11] which, and the interest thereof will stand, when that of a few corrupt and guilty courtiers will sink, etc.

Indeed, I wonder who should put thee upon altering them for these, and as much how thou could ever yield to such a thing. Especially after thou were so much satisfied in them as to charge all thy children, and theirs, to love and preserve them, as being the establishment of thee their father and ancestor, as *the discharge of thy conscience* to God, the giver of this country to thee and them, and as *they hope to keep it and His blessing upon it.*[12]

As much do I wonder that any of the freeholders that had subscribed them with *much clearness and satisfaction* as the ground and rule of all future laws and government, promising everyone for himself *that, by God's assistance,* they would remember, love, and preserve them *to the uttermost of their power* as fundamentals, *inviolably,* charging their posterity to do the same, *as they hope to enjoy what they should leave them, and the blessing of God with it.* Who has turned you aside from these good beginnings, to establish things unsavory and unjust; as fundamentals to which all generations to come should be bound?

The 3d Constitution, which gives the Assembly the power of making and abolishing all laws, and whatsoever is the privilege of an English House of Commons, the power of determining how long within their year to sit, is more fair and equal than the 19th of the new Frame, which deprives them of both.[13]

The 5th Constitution, that provides against any deputy's betraying his trust in voting against his principals, or electors, by obliging him to bring instructions, is in the new [Frame], without ground in my judgment, left out.

The 8th Constitution, which lodges but a consultative faculty in the Council of 48 upon the bills and proposals of the Assembly, and then to propose their deliberations by way of conference to the Assembly, is much more fair and equal, in my mind, than the 5[th] and 7th of the new Frame, which take from the General Assembly the whole faculty of proposing any bills, and lodges it solely in the Provincial Council, which seems to be a divesting of the people's representatives (in time to come) of the greatest right they have; and will lay morally a certain foundation for dissension amongst our successors, and render the patronizers of this new Frame obnoxious to future parliaments.[14] For the people of England can never, by any prescription of time, be dispossessed of that natural right of propounding laws to be made, by their representatives. Let us then, in settling foundations, avoid such precipices.

And let the General Assembly be restored to those powers and privileges which thy first Constitutions do give it, and the Provincial Council, whether of 48 or 72, brought to its place there allotted to it.

And if upon conference they cannot agree, let those matters, which can never be many, be reserved to the judgment of God, by lot, or by the ⅔ of the members of the Provincial Council and General Assembly.

However, I would not be misunderstood, as if I judged it absolutely necessary that now, at the beginning, there should be an Assembly of 200, and a Council of 72. For I know not but 72 may be a very competent number of representatives for such a body of people as may be upon the place in our day. And consequently, if the people did once a year choose 72 persons as their representatives (after the first year, where all freeman may conveniently appear and vote for themselves),[15] it might be enough.

But what I speak is with reference to future ages, when the very Frame supposes it may be needful to have 500 representatives; unto which times this Frame shall be as binding as it is at this day. And whatsoever inconvenience may then [be] found in it at that day cannot be removed without the consent of the Governor, who 500 years hence may be such a man, as the present Governor, if he could help [it], would not allow the meanest office of trust in the government.

My earnest entreaty, then, is that these foundations be not laid as unalterable, as they are, but only to continue for a term of years or for the life of the present Governor; and then be alterable by ⅔ of the 2 assemblies, as above mentioned. For to have a great nation bound up to have no laws but what two-thirds of 72 men shall think fit to propound, whereof but 24 shall be yearly chosen, and sit 3 years to be corrupted by a Governor who has 3 voices, that is 1/16 of the quorum, is not consistent with the public safety, which is and always will remain the supreme law, and [will] bring to certain destruction all that go about to make it void.

I should like it much better that they[16] were chosen every 3 months by the General Assembly or by the people, that so they might not be so liable to be corrupted by an ill-minded, ambitious Governor, for such opportunities do present for mischief in 3 years that do not in 3 months, at least the designs are not so easily brought to perfection in 3 months as in 3 years.

Concerning Nomination of Judges, etc.

Let the nomination of 2 be by the General Assembly, and [the] election of one by the Provincial Council, which is the safer way than to hang the final election upon one man, which if not good and virtuous may make an ill use of it, and attract to himself bribes and flatterers, which I would never expose my posterity to.[17]

Concerning the committees.[18]

Let them all be subjected to the animadversions[19] of the General Assembly, especially those of justice and the treasury.

Finally, if this Frame be continued, I desire at least that to the 6th Article be added the word "only," and the words "no negative," to prevent that most absurd interpretation of that Article, that because the governor has not *in terminis*[20] renounced a right to a negative voice, or not said *only* a treble voice, therefore he has, to help him at a deadlift,[21] [the] right to use a negative when his treble voice will not do.

That the General Assembly have a right of proposing as well as the Provincial Council.

That to the 19th Article be added these words (instead of *as may be*): *as they shall judge* needful to impeach such criminals as they shall judge fit. That they have [the] right to adjourn or prorogue themselves; and the Provincial Council of calling them sooner, if need be.

That the 23d and 24th Articles of the Frame, and [the] 1st and 39th Laws, for ratification of them, may be expunged, because it binds our posterity forever, and gives the Governor a negative voice in these 2 grand cases of the Provincial [Council] and General Assembly (although some that have read them could not believe it). 1. And to secure liberty of conscience; 2. balloting in elections and resolutions; 3. the way of trials; 4. gavelkind[22] for succession of estates real and personal; 5. marriages; 6. the register;[23] 7. speedy justice; 8. law in English; 9. property, etc., may be established as fundamentals; [which should] be delivered to the supreme assembly to be only conservators of, and the utmost penalty upon any that at any time in any council should move for the alteration of any of them, which will be all the security we can have, or desire.

ADf. HSP. (*PWP*, 2:229-38).

1. Furly was particularly interested in this issue because, as WP's land agent in Holland, he was selling Pennsylvania land to prospective Dutch and German immigrants.

2. "The Fundamental Constitutions of Carolina" (1669), probably written by the earl of Shaftesbury and his secretary, the political philosopher John Locke. Furly became a close friend of Locke by 1686.

3. Granted all the rights of native-born citizens. The estates of deceased aliens were protected from forfeiture in the revised *Frame of Government* of 2 Apr. 1683 (doc. 63, below).

4. Furly evidently had a copy of the "Fundamental Constitutions." He is referring here to Constitution 12, in doc. 26, above.

5. The *Laws Agreed Upon in England* (see doc. 30, above) did not include an inheritance law. Furly's proposal, that widows receive one-third of the estate, that children receive one-third, and that fathers have free disposal of the remaining third, was adopted by the Pennsylvania legislature in 1683. In 1684, however, the legislature passed a law that gave to the children of every man dying without a will two-thirds of his estate, and granted his eldest son a double portion, thus agreeing with Constitution 12 of the "Fundamental Constitutions" (doc. 26, above).

6. A tax of one-tenth of one's income, traditionally levied in England and in Europe to support the established national church.

7. Public officials, called ministers of state; not religious leaders.

8. Furly is mistaken here. Neither the West New Jersey Concessions, written in 1676, nor the supplemental set of fundamental laws passed by the West Jersey Assembly in 1681 make any reference to slavery, and slavery was not limited by law in New Jersey until 1804.

9. Some of these changes were made in the revised *Frame of Government* of 2 Apr. 1683 (doc. 63, below). By the "register," Furly probably meant the register of all land and business transactions, provided for in the *Laws Agreed Upon in England,* Law 20 (doc. 30, above).

10. The "Fundamental Constitutions" (doc. 26).

11. England.

12. All italicized phrases in this and the following paragraph are from the concluding paragraphs of the "Fundamental Constitutions" (doc. 26, above).

13. The comparisons in this and the following paragraphs are between the sections of the "Fundamental Constitutions" (doc. 26), which Furly calls "Constitutions," and the sections of *The Frame of Government* (doc. 30).

14. By "parliaments," Furly means Pennsylvania legislatures.

15. WP provides for this initial mass meeting of freemen in article 16 of the *Frame of Government,* although he never convened such a meeting in Pennsylvania.

16. The councilors.

17. Furly is criticizing the provisions in doc. 30, article 17.

18. Furly is referring to the Provincial Council's four executive committees on plantations, justice, trade, and education and morals, as described in doc. 30, article 13.

19. Judicial examinations, leading to censure and punishment.

20. "In the end," rather like the expression "in the final analysis."

21. In an extremity.

22. An English custom of dividing a decedent's real property equally among his sons. This was less common in England than the practice of leaving either all or most of the real property to the eldest son.

23. The *Laws Agreed Upon in England* provided for three registers: one for property and business transactions; one for births, marriages, deaths, and wills; and one for recording the contracts of indentured servants. See doc. 30, Laws 20, 22, and 23, above. Furly probably intends the first of these registers.

# Part VI

## PREPARING TO LEAVE
## FOR PENNSYLVANIA §
## JANUARY 1682–SEPTEMBER 1682

*Deed from the Delaware Indians, 15 July 1682, HSP. See doc. 37 for the text of this first deed, negotiated by WP's agent William Markham, for land in Bucks County. At the bottom of the deed are the distinctive marks, or signatures, of the Indian leaders.*

IN the last eight months before he sailed for Pennsylvania, WP busied himself tying up loose ends. In March (doc. 34) he granted extensive privileges to the Free Society of Traders, a commercial corporation designed to trade with the Indians and to promote the business development of Philadelphia. In May he published his constitution for Pennsylvania, *The Frame of Government* (doc. 30, above). At about this time he also published a revised, enlarged version of his most famous religious tract *No Cross, No Crown.* In June he wrote to the Indians north of Pennsylvania, asking them to trade with his colony through the Free Society of Traders and to sell him land (doc. 36). In August, after eighteen months of negotiations, he secured title to New Castle and the lower counties (now Delaware) from James, Duke of York, thus gaining control of the entire west bank of the Delaware River. Meanwhile, in Pennsylvania, Deputy-Governor William Markham and WP's commissioners purchased land from the Delaware Indians (docs. 32, 37) and started negotiations for settling the Maryland-Pennsylvania boundary with Lord Baltimore (doc. 35).

While preparing for his trip to Pennsylvania, WP experienced a series of painful blows. His mother, Lady Margaret Penn, died about 1 March, and he became depressed by her death (see doc. 33). By August his mother-in-law, Mary Penington, was also dying, and his wife, Gulielma, was newly pregnant and in delicate health. This meant that WP would have to go to America without his wife and three young children. His long, emotional letter of farewell to his family (doc. 39) testifies to the pain of this separation. Furthermore, a week before he sailed, WP discovered that his financial condition was considerably worse than he had supposed. Instead of paying off his debts by selling Pennsylvania land, he was incurring new debts because of his proprietary expenses, and he found himself £2851 in debt to his steward Philip Ford. In order to cover this debt, WP granted a mortgage to Ford for 300,000 acres of Pennsylvania land (doc. 41) and a bond of £6000 as security. WP was, perhaps, too preoccupied with his upcoming voyage to recognize the seriousness of this contractual obligation, which would send him to debtor's prison in 1708. WP took leave of family and friends, and on

29 August he boarded ship at Deal (doc. 43). Two days later the *Welcome* set sail for America.

WP's ship was among twenty-three vessels that carried passengers and cargo to Pennsylvania between December 1681 and December 1682. While WP prepared to leave, hundreds of people throughout the British Isles pondered whether to pull up stakes at home and move with him to America; see doc. 33 for WP's advice to a young woman trying to make this decision. Those who resolved to go undertook a series of difficult steps. While we know all too little about the experiences of most settlers, three letters printed in this section illustrate some of the obstacles that the colonists encountered. James Claypoole's letter (doc. 44) details only a few of the maneuvers required to transfer a merchant's business from London to Pennsylvania. From William and Jane Yardley (doc. 38) we gain a glimpse of the terrors of the ocean voyage. And the Welshman Edward Jones, on arriving in Pennsylvania, found that his problems had only begun: the sea captain left his belongings at Upland, miles from his destination, and Jones had trouble getting his land surveyed (see doc. 42). Immigrants who went to Pennsylvania in the early 1680s did not go through the "starving times" that early Virginians and New Englanders had experienced. Nevertheless, migrating to Pennsylvania was a risky move. Ocean travel could be treacherous in small, disease-ridden, seventeenth-century ships, and life in undeveloped Pennsylvania was as arduous as on any newly-settled frontier.

# 32 §
## Bill for Lasse Cock's Services

SOON after WP received his charter of 4 March 1681 (doc. 11), he sent William Markham to Pennsylvania as his deputy-governor. One of Markham's primary responsibilities was to begin negotiations with the Indians for the purchase of their lands. Since Markham was unfamiliar with the language of the Lenni Lenape, he engaged a prominent local Swede, Capt. Lasse Cock (1646-1699), as his interpreter and messenger to the Indians. After Cock died in 1699, his executors submitted a bill to WP for goods and services rendered to Markham in 1682; this bill is printed below. It gives a good idea of the kinds of merchandise used in negotiating for land and shows the cost of each item in pounds, shillings, and pence. WP's expenses in Pennsylvania were beginning to accumulate even before he left England.

| 1682 | Estate of William Penn, Esq., to Estate of Laurence Cox, deceased | Debtor | | |
|---|---|---|---|---|
| | | [£] | [s] | [d] |
| | To maintaining the Indians in meat and drink when Gov. Markham and others that came with him to make first purchase of land[1] | 5 | 16 | |
| | To hiring of Indians and myself and horses to go to Susquehanna River about the Indians killing a man | 9 | 17 | 6 |
| | To journey by order of Gov. Markham to Lahhai,[2] and the presents given to the Indians: 8 lb. powder at 2/8 per, and 20 lb. of lead at 5d. per, and 6 gallons rum [at] 5 per | 4 | 4 | 4 |
| | To 12 guns paid to the Indians | 12 | | |
| | To 6 ditto paid to the Schuylkill Indians | 6 | | |
| | To 12 yds. matchcoat[3] at 4/6 per | 2 | 14 | |
| | To 12 lb. of powder | | 18 | |
| | To 2 guns paid the Fall Indians[4] | 2 | | |
| | To £8 in wampum[5] | 8 | | |
| | To paid Christiana Indians in goods for 32 bears and beavers at 12/ per | 19 | 4 | |
| Sept. 24 | To 20 lb. of lead 3d. per | | 5 | |
| Sept. 24th | To 16 stroudwater[6] coats paid the Indians | 19 | 4 | |
| | To making the coats, buttons, and thread | 2 | 8 | |
| | To left unpaid of the log house that was the prison | 6 | | |
| | To journey to [New] York by Gov. Markham's order to buy goods to pay the Indians | 4 | 10 | |
| | | £103 | | 10 |

D. HSP. (*PWP,* 2:242-43).

1. See doc. 37, below.
2. Perhaps "Lehigh." The name of the Lehigh River in present-day Northampton Co. is derived from the Indian word *Lechauweeki.*
3. A matchcoat (Algonkian *matchcore*) was a sleeveless coat or blanket of coarse woolen cloth worn draped around the shoulders.
4. Probably the Indians at the Falls of the Delaware, with whom Markham negotiated his first sale. See doc. 37, below.
5. *Wampum,* or *wampumpeag* (an Algonkian term), were cylindrical beads of shell or fishbone used as currency. In 1643 in New England, white wampum were valued at six to eight per English penny, while black wampum were worth twice as much.
6. Stroudwater cloth was blue and red woolen cloth made in England, popular with the Indians.

## 33 §
### *To Elizabeth Woodhouse*

IN this letter, WP writes to a young Quaker woman, Elizabeth Woodhouse, daughter of Dr. Christopher Woodhouse of Berkhampsted, Herts., who is trying to decide whether or not to go to Pennsylvania. Far from coaxing her to do so, WP urges her to discover through personal soul searching whether her religious mission is genuine, and so he counsels her "to sink down into the seasoning, settling gift of God" and wait for His direction. Woodhouse later decided not to emigrate. Also of interest in this letter is WP's expression of grief at his mother's death.

London, 8 March 1682

Dear Friend

Both thy letters came in few days one of the other. My sickness upon my mother's death (who was last 7th day[1] interred) permitted me not to answer thee so soon as desired. But on a serious weighing of thy inclinations, and perceiving per last thy uneasiness under my constrained silence, it is most clear to me to counsel thee to sink down into the seasoning, settling gift of God, and wait to distinguish between thy own desires and the Lord's requirings. Have a care, and be reverent towards God's holy power in all thy motions. Thou art His; and in this nation He has brought thee forth. As to thy natural and spiritual capacity, act in subjection, and rather in the cross than forwardness; and if thou has a true drawing, and are satisfied in thyself to go, go, and the Lord be with thee; else stay. But I beseech thee [to] be cool and patient and contented with God's will. What I can do in counsel or assistance shall not be wanting. I only add, have a tender regard to thy father and mother and be not hasty in the execution of what perhaps thou has a true sense and sight of, lest an offense enter. The Lord God establish and direct thee in that which may bring a lasting peace to thy immortal soul.

Thy very true friend,
Wm Penn

Transcript. Chester County Historical Society. (*PWP*, 2:245-46).

1. 4 Mar. 1682. Lady Margaret Penn had been a widow since 1670, and lived at Walthamstow, Essex. The exact date of her death is not known.

# 34 §

## Charter for the Free Society of Traders

WP intended Pennsylvania to be a commercial success as well as a holy experiment. That is why he placed so much importance in founding Philadelphia as a trading center and why he tried to obtain access to the rich Susquehanna Valley through Chesapeake Bay (see doc. 35, below). But buying ships and cargoes, and building warehouses, mills, and industrial plants, required a great deal of capital—much more than WP could afford on his own. Thus he was very pleased when a group of nine London merchants approached him with their plan to set up a company, which—if WP gave it special privileges—would undertake to stimulate industry and manage trade out of Pennsylvania. They called it the Free Society of Traders because membership was open to anyone who bought shares in the company. The merchants intended to send 200 indentured servants to work for the Free Society as farmers, fishermen, miners, tanners, millers, glassmakers, brickmakers, and cloth workers, and they hoped to recruit colonists to settle on their land. WP was more than willing to give the Free Society special consideration, and on 24 March 1682 he signed their charter.

Excerpts from this charter are printed below. WP empowered the Free Society to set up a manor of 20,000 acres, called the Manor of Frank, and his charter recites in lengthy detail the Society's manorial rights. Within its own territory, the Society could appoint officials, administer justice, and collect taxes. Of even greater consequence, the Society was permitted to place three of its officers on the Pennsylvania Provincial Council.

The Free Society of Traders seemed to start well. Nearly 225 investors bought shares in the Society, and by September 1682 these shareholders had paid in £6000—a very good sum, considering that WP himself had only received £6693 in sales for Pennsylvania land by August 1682. Between 1682 and 1684, the company set up a tannery, purchased a grist mill, initiated a whale fishery, and started to construct a glass factory, brick kilns, and a sawmill. But despite this early activity, the Free Society was soon in trouble. To begin with, much of the capital needed for such projects was used to extend credit to colonists who bought company goods, and the Free Society was never able to monopolize trade along the Delaware. Shareholders were more interested in pursuing their own private ventures than in working for the Society. And in December 1682, because other Pennsylvania residents resented the special privileges that WP had granted to the Free Society, the Assembly refused to confirm this charter (see James Claypoole's letter, doc. 58, below). This left the Society with no legal status in Pennsylvania. In the mid-1680s, the company was hit by many costly lawsuits and became practically defunct. Thus, contrary to WP's expectations, Pennsylvania developed commercially through the initiative and investment of individual businessmen, not because of the enterprise of a privileged corporation.

24 March 1682

**To all people** to whom these presents shall come—

**Whereas** King Charles the Second by his letters patents under the Great Seal of England, for the considerations therein mentioned, has been graciously pleased to give and grant unto me, William Penn (by the name of William Penn, Esquire, son and heir of Sir William Penn, deceased), and to my heirs and assigns forever, a certain province in America by the name of **Pennsylvania,** and has thereby also given me power (and to my heirs) to grant or alien[1] any part or parcel of the said province to any person or persons in fee simple, or for any other estate to be holden of me and my heirs by such rents, customs, and services as shall seem fit unto me, the said William Penn, and my heirs, with a clause of *non obstante* to the statute of *quia emptores terrarum* made in the eighteenth year of the reign of King Edward the First;[2] and also to erect into manors, any such parcels of land as I and my heirs shall have granted or aliened as aforesaid, and to enable such grantees or alienees and their heirs to have and to hold courts-baron, courts-leet, and view of frankpledge[3] within the same, and to give and grant to any other person or persons any part or parcel of the lands granted or aliened to them by me or my heirs to be holden of them and their heirs.

**And whereas** I have by my several indentures of lease bearing date the two and twentieth, and of release[4] bearing date the three and twentieth day of the first month called March in the four and thirtieth year of the said now king's reign, granted unto Nicholas More of London, medical doctor,[5] James Claypoole, merchant,[6] Philip Ford, William Shardlow of London, merchants, Edward Peirce of London, leather seller,[7] John Simcock[8] and Thomas Brassey of Cheshire, yeomen,[9] Thomas Barker of London, wine cooper, and Edward Brookes of London, grocer,[10] and their heirs, to the use of themselves and their heirs and assigns, twenty thousand acres of land, parcel of the said province of Pennsylvania, in trust nevertheless for the Free Society of Traders in Pennsylvania and their successors, as soon as the said Free Society should be by me incorporated or erected, as in and by the said indentures (relation being thereunto had) more fully does appear.

**Now know** all men by these presents, that I, the said William Penn, according to the power given by the said letters patents,[11] do erect the said twenty thousand acres into a manor and do constitute, make, and confirm the same to be henceforth a manor by the name of the **Manor of Frank**[12] to all intents and purposes, and I do hereby authorize, give power, and grant to the said Nicholas More, James Claypoole, Philip Ford, William Shardlow, Edward Peirce, John Simcock, Thomas Brassey, Thomas Barker, and Edward Brookes, and to such other persons as they shall hereafter receive into their society by the name of the Free Society of Traders in Pennsylvania and to their successors (whom I hereby erect and constitute a corporation by that name), to all intents and purposes, for the better improvement of trade, to sue and be sued, and to answer and be answered by that name; and by that name to give and grant to any person or persons such part or parcel of the said Manor of Frank, as to them shall seem meet, to be holden of them and their successors in free and common socage,[13] by such rents, customs, and services as to them and their successors shall seem meet, so as the same be consistent with the said tenure in free and common socage. . . .

**And** I do also, according to the said powers given by the said letters patents, grant unto the said Free Society of Traders in Pennsylvania and their successors, that they by themselves or by the justices and keepers of the peace hereinafter mentioned may from henceforth hold two sessions and jail deliveries yearly, at such convenient times as they shall think best, who may hear and determine all pleas and controversies, as well civil as criminal, which shall arise within the said Manor of Frank and corporation aforesaid, wherein no other justices or other officers of the said province shall intermeddle; and that they by themselves or by their steward may forever hold a court-baron within the said manor and may do and execute all such matters and things as are belonging and incident unto, or are used and accustomed to be done in, a court-baron. . . .

**And whereas** by the said letters patents, full power is granted unto the said William Penn and his heirs to appoint judges, lieutenants, justices, magistrates, and officers for what cause so ever; and with what power and in such form as to me seems convenient with liberty to import the growth and manufactory of that province into England, paying the legal duties; as also to erect ports, harbors, creeks, havens, quays, and other places for merchandise, with such jurisdictions and privileges as to me, William Penn, shall seem expedient. **Now further witness** these presents that I, William Penn, according to the power given by the said letters patents do for me and my heirs authorize and give power to the said Free Society of Traders and their successors, for the better carrying on of their trade and for the common execution of justice in the said Manor of Frank, from time to time and at all times hereafter, to appoint, to place, and to remove whom they will of themselves for president, deputy-president, treasurer, secretary, sheriff, surveyor, agents, stewards, and all other under officers and servants of the said Free Society of Traders and their successors and of the said corporation and Manor of Frank as to them shall seem meet and most convenient, and that the said officers or servants of the said Free Society or of their successors and the tenants of the said Manor of Frank and the inhabitants within the same shall not be impleaded[14] without the said manor for any plea arising within the said manor, and that none shall lodge within the houses or lands within the said manor by force, and all the freemen of the said Free Society and their goods shall be quit and free,[15] throughout the province and the ports thereof, of and from all toll passage, listage, and all other customs and payments whatsoever, excepting only such as shall be taxed by common consent of the Provincial Council and General Assembly of the said province; and also that their courts may sit once in a week, that is to say on the second day of the week called Monday, and that right be done them according to law.

**And** I do further grant them, according to that authority given me, acquittal of murder[16] **within the said** manor and that none of the said Free Society or of their successors or of the said manor be compelled to wage battle,[17] and that they may discharge themselves of the pleas belonging to the province according to what laws and customs shall be justly established in the said Free Society. . . . **Provided** nevertheless that all persons who shall inhabit in time to come within the liberties and franchises of the said manor or any of the precincts, circuits, or compass thereof and all buildings therein built and to be built, and all lands, tenements, and hereditaments[18] within the said manor from henceforth shall be forever quit and free from all taxes and other burdens of scot [and] lot, watch and ward,[19] through and within the said manor to be paid, made, sustained, or contributed, except the charges and expenses due and reasonable for the defense of the province and such like special public services and taxes by common consent of the Provincial Council and General Assembly as aforesaid, and except the charges for ways, pavements, ditches, bridges, and watercourses within the circuits, precincts, liberties, and jurisdictions of the aforesaid manor respectively to be paid.

**And** that all freemen of the Free Society aforesaid, for the time being inhabiting or who shall inhabit within the liberties and franchise of the said manor, shall be chargeable and liable to serve in all offices and charges as well of president, deputy-president, treasurer, secretary, agents, sheriff, steward, and whatsoever other office he or they shall be deemed meet for by the said Free Society.

**And furthermore** for the better and common profit of the said Free Society and for the accommodation and support of the charges and expenses of the said Free Society and their successors, I grant to the said Free Society of Traders and to their successors, that from henceforth and forever all and singular persons, though they be not free of the same Free Society, who shall hereafter be dwelling within the liberties or precincts of the said manor in all aids, tallages,[20] grants, and other contributions whatsoever that shall be taxed to the use and service of the said Free Society for the maintaining the magistracy and other public charges, as in cities or towns are to be maintained by the freemen and inhabitants of the same for the public good howsoever, shall be reasonably and proportionably taxed and assessed. . . .

**And** I do for myself and my heirs grant unto the said Free Society of Traders and their successors to choose three officers of the said Free Society to be of the said Provincial Council of the province,[21] and when by any article in the intended Frame of Government any one of the said three officers shall go out, then the said Free Society of Traders and their successors shall choose another and so successively forever.

**And** I do for myself and my heirs and assigns grant unto the said Free Society of Traders and their successors all manner of mines and metals, as well royal mines of gold and silver as other mines, which shall be found in the said twenty thousand acres or any part of them, excepting only that fifth part reserved by the king of England to himself, his heirs, and successors, and excepting also one other fifth part of all the ore which shall be found in any mines of gold and silver to me, the said William Penn, my heirs and assigns.

**And** I do for myself and my heirs and assigns grant unto the said Free Society of Traders, free fishing of whales, sturgeon, and all royal and other fishes in the main sea and bays of the said province, and in the inlets, waters, and rivers within or adjoining to the said twenty thousand acres or any part thereof, the said Free Society of Traders and their successors yielding and paying unto me, William Penn, my heirs and assigns, the sum of one shilling yearly upon the day of the vernal equinox[22] or within one and twenty days after, at my dwelling house in the capital city of Pennsylvania.

**And lastly** I do also grant for me and my heirs to the said Free Society and their successors forever all and every one of the things aforesaid, and further that no manner of person whatsoever shall inspect their books, warehouses, or houses without their own consent but shall in all respects be free to trade, build, and plant and to appoint fairs and markets at such convenient times as they shall think fit within the corporation and manor aforesaid, together with all other reasonable liberties, franchises, and immunities whatsoever which have at anytime heretofore been granted to the city of London.[23]

**In witness** whereof I have put my name and seal this four and twentieth day of the first month called March in the four and thirtieth year of the said now king's reign and in the year of our Lord according to the computation of England, one thousand six hundred eighty one/two.

Wm Penn

Copy. Bucks County Court House, Doylestown. (*PWP*, 2:246–56).

1. To transfer property to another.
2. *Non obstante* literally means "nevertheless." See sect. 18 of WP's charter (p. 48), which waived the statute "quia emptores terrarum" and other laws which forbade the creation of new manors.
3. For definitions of these terms, see doc. 11, p. 50.
4. Indentures of lease and release were used to transfer the title of property from one person to another.
5. Nicholas More (c. 1638–1687), a London Anglican and the only non-Quaker in this group, proved to be a poor leader of the Free Society. He bought 10,000 acres of land in Pennsylvania, was the Free Society's first president, and the speaker of the Assembly in 1684, among other offices. But he soon quit the Society presidency, and was expelled from the Assembly for judicial misconduct.
6. James Claypoole (1643–1687), a prominent London Quaker, was treasurer of the Free Society of Traders and became a leading member of the Provincial Council after immigrating to Pennsylvania in 1683. See docs. 44, 58, and 85, below, for letters Claypoole wrote to his brother Edward in Barbados and to WP.
7. William Shardlow (c. 1624–1704) and Edward Peirce (c. 1636–1689), both London Quakers, did not immigrate to Pennsylvania. They served on the council that managed the Free Society's affairs in England.
8. John Simcock (c. 1639–1703) became the Free Society's deputy-president for a seven-year term. A First Purchaser of 5000 acres, he arrived in Pennsylvania in Aug. 1682 and settled near Ridley Creek, Chester Co. He was a member of the first Assembly, and a provincial councilor.

9. Thomas Brassey (d. 1690) also emigrated in 1682, and became head of the Free Society's Pennsylvania committee. He purchased 5000 acres, settled in Chester, was prominent in Quaker meetings, and served as an assemblyman.

10. Thomas Barker (c. 1640-1710) and Edward Brookes (c. 1618-1698) both purchased land in Pennsylvania. Barker remained in London and sat on the Free Society's council there. Brookes immigrated to Pennsylvania in 1683 but soon returned to England.

11. WP's charter for Pennsylvania (doc. 11).

12. During the 1680s, the Free Society acquired many separate tracts of land, though it never claimed all 20,000 acres that it had purchased. The company built several mills and other enterprises on one of its first grants, about 670 acres located five miles north of Philadelphia along Frankford Creek. This tract was known as the Manor of Frank.

13. The form of land tenure in which annual payments to the lord, or quitrents, were set at an established rate.

14. Sued or prosecuted.

15. Exempt.

16. Under the terms of his charter (doc. 11), WP could not pardon persons found guilty of treason or murder. He is thus granting the Free Society the power to try persons for murder within their manor; he cannot give them the right to pardon murderers.

17. Waging battle was a medieval procedure for resolving legal cases; at this time it was still permissible, but was rarely used. It was based on the assumption that "heaven would unquestionably give the victory to the innocent or injured party."

18. A tenement was any rented property; a hereditament was any property that could be inherited.

19. Scot and lot was a tax paid in some English cities by men qualified to vote. Watch and ward was a form of guard duty, sometimes required as an obligation to a lord or a town government.

20. Aids and tallages were taxes paid to medieval lords.

21. The Free Society was here given as many votes in the Council as WP himself possessed. The Pennsylvania Assembly found this provision unacceptable and, at least partly for this reason, refused to ratify the charter.

22. About 11 Mar., Old Style.

23. In England, towns and cities could hold fairs and markets only at times established by tradition, a royal charter, or an act of Parliament. The City of London had special privileges and it alone could operate a market six days a week.

# 35 §

## Lord Baltimore to William Markham

WHEN WP sent William Markham to America in April 1681, he directed him to settle the boundary between Pennsylvania and Maryland with Lord Baltimore. The charters of both colonies set the boundary at the 40th degree of latitude, but without an exact measurement no one knew where that was. In the summer of 1681 WP thought he knew, and he published *A Map of Pennsylvania* which placed the 40th degree at the location of present-day Baltimore (see p. 80). Other maps set the boundary considerably farther north. Soon after his arrival in Pennsylvania, Markham went to visit the proprietor of Maryland; he delivered WP's conciliatory letter of 10

April 1681 (doc. 14, above) and the king's instructions of 2 April 1681 to fix the boundary. Markham and Baltimore agreed to meet in October to find the location of the 40th degree. Markham fell seriously ill, however, and postponed this meeting until the next spring. In the meantime, WP and his agents made several moves that angered Lord Baltimore and probably eliminated any possibility of settling the border amicably. WP's letter to six Maryland planters (doc. 20, above), in which he asserted that Cecil and Baltimore counties lay within his territory, arrived in January 1682. Then Commissioner William Haige made a private observation of the degree of latitude at the head of Chesapeake Bay. Having without doubt discovered that the 40th degree lay at least forty miles farther north than WP thought, he and Markham decided to delay any further meeting with Baltimore. As doc. 35 suggests, the proprietor of Maryland guessed their motive and pressed for a speedy settlement.

When Markham continued to stall, the Maryland proprietor decided to take matters into his own hands. In September 1682, he went directly to Markham's lodging in Upland (later renamed Chester) and forced WP's deputy to make an observation. Probably to neither man's surprise, they found that the 40th degree ran over ten miles north of Upland. From this point on, Baltimore demanded all the territory south of the 40th degree of latitude. If WP had given in without a fight, he would have lost his site for Philadelphia and surrendered control of most of the navigable part of the Delaware River. WP, however, was on firm ground in defending his right to the Delaware side of his province, because his charter specifically granted him all land along the western shore of the river, beginning twelve miles north of New Castle. He further strengthened his position in August 1682 by acquiring title to New Castle and the lower western shore of the Delaware from James, Duke of York.

Baltimore would continue to dispute WP's claim to the area that is now Delaware and southeastern Pennsylvania, but WP's title was strong enough to keep possession. On the Chesapeake side, however, WP's hopes were dashed. He had envisioned the Susquehanna Valley as the center of his province and hoped to establish a lucrative fur trade with the Indians of New York. But because the true location of the 40th degree was so far north, he did not have the entry to the Susquehanna from Chesapeake Bay that he needed to do this. WP met with Baltimore in Maryland on 11 December 1682 and offered to buy land at the head of Chesapeake Bay from the Maryland proprietor. He was fearful that otherwise the back of his colony would be "but a dead lump of earth." No settlement was reached at the December conference, but the two proprietors agreed to meet again in March 1683 to fix the boundary. For the next stage in the border dispute, see the headnote to doc. 64.

Sir

I have received yours of the 26th of the last month and am sorry it came no sooner to my hands, for I have dispatched some gentlemen away to meet you at the time appointed[1] and therefore am no wise willing to put off this business of the ascertaining [of] the bounds betwixt Mr. Penn and me. There are many reasons to be given by me for it, but at present shall only offer you these two: First, that by a letter from his Most Sacred Majesty procured and sent by the said Penn, I am commanded to join with Mr. Penn or his agents for the speedy settling our bounds; and then Mr. Penn's own letter, which you brought me, pressed very much the same thing. Secondly, that Mr. Penn the last shipping writ and sent in a letter to several gentlemen of note that are certainly within my province, as Mr. Augustine Herrman, Captain [Henry] Ward, Col. Wells,[2] etc., hinting to them that he was confident they would come within his government; a thing not kindly taken and, to be plain, not according to the golden rule mentioned in Mr. Penn's letter to me, *Do to thy neighbor as thou would he should do to thee.*[3] Now certainly such proceedings were not neighborlike, and when I have the happiness to see my friend, I must be plain with him as to that point. For as I desire no more than my due, so I take it very unkindly that some of the inhabitants up the [Chesapeake] Bay should be so possessed as they have been by that letter of Mr. William Penn's.

For these reasons, sir, I must beg leave to say I will not admit of any further delay. You well know that your late sickness has been the only hindrance hitherto. Let me therefore now press you to send persons qualified, and equally impowered, with those persons who on my part are already gone and will be, in all probability, with you before this will arrive at your hands. I having positively ordered them to request the same from you on the behalf of, sir,

Your faithful friend and servant,
C.B.

Copy. Maryland Historical Society, Baltimore. (*PWP,* 2:256-59).

1. Baltimore had arranged to meet Markham on 10 June 1682 at Augustine Herrman's plantation in Cecil Co., Md. Neither man actually attended, but Baltimore did send commissioners in his place. Markham sent no representatives, and so Baltimore's agents proceeded to New Castle where they made an observation and found the latitude to be 39 degrees and 40-odd minutes.

2. Probably George Wells (d. c. 1695) of Baltimore Co., a wealthy Protestant planter and member of the Maryland Assembly. Wells was not one of the six planters addressed in WP's letter of 16 Sept. 1681 (doc. 20).

3. Luke 6:31; see doc. 14, above.

*Wampum Belt, c. 1682, HSP. According to legend, the Lenni Lenape gave this belt, fashioned from oyster-shell beads and leather, to WP at Shackamaxon in November 1682. While there is no record that a treaty was negotiated at that time, the wampum belt has become a symbol of WP's policy of purchasing land from the Indians and living peacefully with them.*

IN dealing with the Indians, WP had two chief concerns: establishing trade and gaining title to Pennsylvania lands in a peaceful manner. Docs. 36 and 37 illustrate WP's handling of each. In doc. 36, he addresses an Indian mysteriously styled as the "Emperor of Canada." Who this person was we do not know—possibly a chieftain in French Canada, more likely in upper New York. It is clear that WP wanted to open commerce with Indians to the north through the Free Society of Traders (see doc. 34, above). In particular, he hoped to secure the lucrative northern fur trade with the Five Nations of the Iroquois, a trade monopolized up to this time by New Yorkers operating out of Albany. Later, in 1683, WP sent agents to Albany to negotiate for the fur trade, and also for title to land along the upper reaches of the Susque-hanna which he was granted in his charter and which the Five Nations claimed through conquest. For discussion of these negotiations, see docs. 72 and 78, below.

Doc. 37 describes WP's first purchase of land from the Lenni Lenape (or Delaware) Indians (see doc. 23, above) in southeastern Pennsylvania. Deputy-Governor William Markham negotiated this purchase in April 1682, goods were paid to the Indians at the end of June, and the formal deed (doc. 37A) was signed by twelve Indian leaders, or sachems, on 15 July 1682. Some of the land included in this purchase had already been sold to Gov. Andros of New York in 1675 by four of the same Indians. The deed to WP sets the boundaries from a point above the Falls of the Delaware westward to certain marked trees and southward to Neshaminy Creek (see the map on p. 159). This territory included the land that became WP's estate of Penns-bury Manor. Doc. 37B is an addendum to the deed signed on 1 August by three more sachems who claimed part of this territory. In this addendum they relinquished their claim and clarified some of the terms of the original settlement. Doc. 37C is a memorandum written by William Markham, in which he spelled out agreements that the English and Indians had made to maintain peaceful relations. This memorandum also itemizes the trade goods, valued at £250, that were used in the purchase (see also doc. 32, above).

## 36 §

## To the Emperor of Canada

London, 21 June 1682

To the Emperor of Canada.

The great God, that made thee and me and all the world, incline our hearts to love peace and justice that we may live friendly together as becomes the workmanship of the great God. The king of England, who is a great prince, has for divers reasons granted to me a large country in America which, however, I am willing to enjoy upon friendly terms with thee. And this I will say, that the people who come with me are a just, plain, and honest people, that neither make war upon others nor fear war from others because they will be just. I have set up a Society of Traders in my province to traffic with thee and thy people for your commodities, that you may be furnished with that which is good at reasonable rates. And that Society has ordered their president [Nicholas More] to treat with thee about a future trade, and have joined with me to send this messenger to thee with certain presents from us to testify our willingness to have a fair correspondence with thee. And what this agent shall do in our names we will agree unto. I hope thou will kindly receive him and comply with his desires on our behalf, both with respect to land and trade. The great God be with thee. Amen.

Philip Theodore Lehnmann, Secretary

Wm Penn

DS. Division of Land Records, Bureau of Archives and History, Harrisburg. (*PWP*, 2:260-61).


## 37 §

## Deed from the Delaware Indians

A

15 July 1682

This indenture made the fifteenth day of July in the year of our Lord according to English account, one thousand six hundred eighty and two, between Idquahon, Janottowe, Idquoqueywon, Sahoppe for himself and Okanickon, Merkekowen, Oreckton for Nanacussey, Shaurwawghon, Swanpisse, Nahoosey, Tomackhickon, Westkekitt, and Towhawsis, Indian sachemakers[1] of the one part, and William Penn, Esq., chief proprietor of the province of Pennsylvania of the other part. Witnesses that for and in consideration of the sums and particulars of goods, merchandise, and utensils hereinafter mentioned and expressed, that is to say: three hundred and fifty fathoms[2] of wampum, twenty white blankets, twenty fathoms of stroudwaters, sixty fathoms of duffels,[3] twenty kettles (four whereof large), twenty guns, twenty coats, forty shirts, forty pair of stockings, forty hoes, forty axes, two barrels of powder, two hundred bars of lead, two hundred knives, two hundred small glasses, twelve pair of shoes, forty copper boxes, forty tobacco tongs, two small barrels of pipes, forty pair of scissors, forty combs, twenty-four pounds of red lead, one hundred awls,[4] two handfuls of fishhooks, two handfuls of needles, forty pounds of shot, ten bundles of beads, ten small saws, twelve drawing knives,[5] four ankers[6] of tobacco, two ankers of rum, two ankers of cider, two ankers of beer, and three hundred guilders,[7] by the said William Penn, his agents or assigns, to the said Indian sachemakers for the use of them and their people, at and before sealing and delivery hereof in hand paid and delivered whereof and wherewith they, the said sachemakers, do hereby acknowledge themselves fully satisfied, contented, and paid.

The said Indian sachemakers (parties to these presents), as well for and on the behalf of themselves as for and on the behalf of their respective Indians or people for whom they are concerned, have granted, bargained, sold, and delivered, and by these presents do fully, clearly, and absolutely grant, bargain, sell, and deliver unto the said William Penn, his heirs and assigns, forever, all that or those tract or tracts of land lying and being in the province of Pennsylvania aforesaid, beginning at a certain white oak in the land now in the tenure of John Wood[8] and by him called the "Graystones" over against the Falls of Delaware River, and so from thence up by the riverside to a corner marked spruce tree with the letter "P" at the foot of a mountain, and from the said corner marked spruce tree along by the ledge or foot of the mountains west-northwest to a corner white oak marked with the letter "P" standing by the Indian path that leads to an Indian town called Playwicky,[9] and near the head of a creek called Towamensing,[10] and from thence westward to the creek called Neshaminy Creek and along by the said Neshaminy Creek unto the river Delaware, alias Makerisk Kittan.[11] And so bounded by the said main river to the said first-mentioned white oak in John Wood's land. And all those islands called or known by the several names of Matinicum Island, Sepassincks Island, and Oreckton's Island,[12] lying or being in the said river Delaware, together also with all and singular isles, islands, rivers, rivulets, creeks, waters, ponds, lakes, plains, hills, mountains, meadows, marshes, swamps, trees, woods, mines, minerals, and appurtenances whatsoever to the said tract or tracts of land belonging or in anywise appertaining. And the reversion and reversions, remainder and remainders thereof, and all the estate, right, title, interest, use, property, claim, and demand whatsoever, as well of them the said Indian sachemakers (parties to these presents) as of all and every other the Indians concerned therein or in any part or parcel thereof. To have and to hold the said tract and tracts of land, islands, and all and every other the said granted premises, with their and every of their appurtenances unto the said William Penn, his heirs and assigns, forever, to the only proper use and behoof of the said William Penn, his heirs and assigns, forevermore. And the said Indian sachemakers and their heirs and successors and every of them, the said tract or tracts of land, islands, and all and every other the said granted premises with their and every of their appurtenances, unto the said William Penn, his heirs and assigns, forever, against them the said Indian sachemakers, their heirs and successors, and against all and every Indian and Indians and their heirs and successors claiming or to claim any right, title, or estate into or out of the said granted premises or any part or parcel thereof, shall and will warrant and forever defend by these presents. In witness whereof the said parties to these present indentures interchangeably have set their hands and seals the day and year first above written, 1682.

| | |
|---|---|
| The mark of Idquahon | The mark of Shaurwawghon |
| The mark of Janottowe | The mark of Swanpisse |
| The mark of Idquoqueywon | The mark of Nahoosey |
| The mark of Sahoppe | The mark of Tomackhickon |
| The mark of Merkekowen | The mark of Westkekitt |
| The mark of Oreckton for himself and Nanacussey | The mark of Towhawsis |

Memorandum: That the day and year within written, full and peaceable possession and seisin[13] of the within granted tract and tracts of land and all other the premises with their and every of their appurtenances was had, taken, and delivered, by the within named Janottowe for and on the behalf of the within written sachemakers unto William Haige, Gent., to and for the within named William Penn to hold to him, his heirs and assigns, forever, according to the purport, true intent, and meaning of the deed within written. In the presence of

The mark of
Kowyockhicken
Lasse Cock
Silas Crispin[14]
Richard Noble[15]

B

First day of August 1682
At the house of Capt. Lasse Cock.

We whose names are here underwritten for ourselves and in name and behalf of the rest of the within mentioned sachemakers (in respect of a mistake in the first bargain betwixt us and the within named William Penn of the number of ten guns more than are mentioned in the within deed, which we should have then received) do now acknowledge the receipt of the said ten guns from the said William Penn. And whereas in the said deed there is only mention made of three hundred and fifty fathom of wampum, not expressing the quality thereof, we therefore for ourselves and in behalf as said is declare the same to be one half white wampum, and the other half black wampum. And we Kekerappamand, Pytechay, and Essepamazatto,

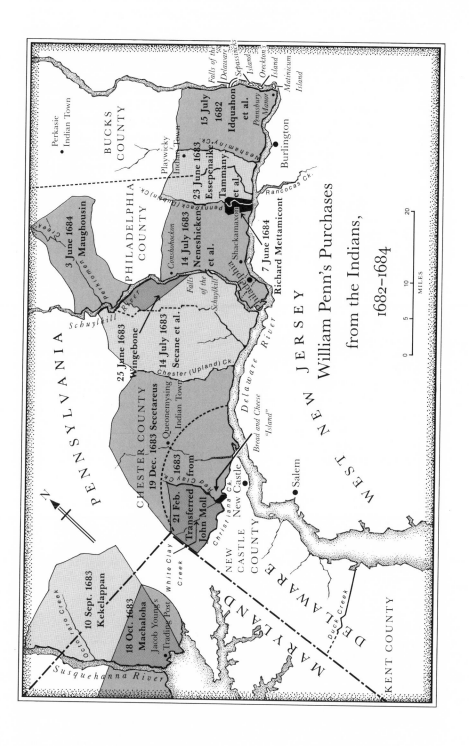

William Penn's Purchases from the Indians, 1682–1684

Indian sachemakers who were the right owners of the land called Sepassincks, and of the island of the same name, and who did not formerly sign and seal the within deed, nor were present when the same was done, do now by signing and sealing hereof ratify, approve, and confirm the within named deed and the possession of the lands therein mentioned, writ, and given on the back thereof, in all the points, clauses, and articles of the same, and do declare our now sealing hereof to be as valid, effectual, and sufficient for the conveyance of the whole lands and others within named to the said William Penn, his heirs and assigns, forevermore, as if we had then with the other within named sachemakers signed and sealed the same.

Signed, sealed, and delivered in presence of us

| Nathaniel Allen | The mark of Idquoqueywon |
| Lasse Cock | The mark of Swanpisse |
| | The mark of Kekerappamand |
| | The mark of Nannecheschan[16] |
| | The mark of Essepamazatto |
| | The mark of Pytechay |

## C

Memorandum:

### 1

That they[17] make no differences between the Quakers and English.

### 2

To take upon their delivery of the land a turf out of the ground, to bring them (upon the treaty with them) to give us notice if any other Indians have any design against us.

### 3

Remembering our neighboring colonies.

### 4

That there be a meeting once every year to read the articles over; the day to be appointed.

### 5

That we may freely pass through any of their lands, as well that which is not purchased as that which is, without molestation as they do quietly amongst us.

### 6

That if English or Indian should at any time abuse one the other, complaint might be made to their respective governor, and that satisfaction may be made according to their offense.

### 7

That if at any time an Englishman should by mistake seat himself upon land not purchased of the Indians, that the Indians shall not molest them before complaint made to the government where they shall receive satisfaction.

| | | | £ | s | d |
|---|---|---|---|---|---|
| The prices of the whole 600 fathoms of wampum, half white, half black, white at 3 guilders per fathom and black at 5 guilders per fathom is | | | 60 | 00 | 00[18] |
| Falls purchase | 40 white blankets | | 25 | 0 | 0 |
| 80 yds. | 40 fathom stroudwaters | | 27 | 0 | 0 |
| 120 | 60 fathom duffels | | 28 | 0 | 0 |
| | 40 kettles, 4 whereof large | | 25 | 0 | 0 |
| | 40 guns | | 30 | 0 | 0 |
| | 40 kersey[19] coats | | 30 | 0 | 0 |
| | 60 shirts | | 15 | 0 | 0 |
| | 40 pair stockings | | 04 | 0 | 0 |
| X | 20 mounteare[20] caps | | 5 | 0 | 0 |
| | 40 hoes | | 4 | 0 | 0 |
| | 40 axes | | 4 | 0 | 0 |
| 150 lb. | 3 half ankers powder | | 7 | 10 | 0 |
| | 300 small bars lead | | 3 | 15 | 0 |
| | 200 knives | | 2 | 10 | 0 |
| | 200 small glasses | | 3 | 6 | 8 |
| | 20 pairs shoes | | 4 | 0 | 0 |
| | 40 copper tobacco boxes | | 2 | 0 | 0 |
| | 40 tobacco tongs | | 0 | 13 | 4 |
| | a small barrel [of] pipes | | 0 | 10 | 0 |
| | 40 pair scissors | | 0 | 10 | 0 |
| | 40 combs | | 0 | 13 | 4 |
| | 12 lb. red lead | | 0 | 06 | 0 |
| | 200 awls | | 0 | 16 | 8 |
| | 15 pistols | | 7 | 10 | 0 |
| | Two handfuls fishhooks | | 1 | 0 | 0 |
| | One handful needles | | 1 | 0 | 0 |
| | 50 lb. duck shot | | 1 | 5 | 0 |
| | 10 bundles of small beads | | 10 | 15 | 0 |
| X | 20 glass bottles | | 0 | 10 | 0 |
| | 5 small saws | | 0 | 10 | 0 |
| | 6 drawing knives | | 0 | 15 | 0 |
| | 2 ankers tobacco | | 0 | 10 | 0 |
| | 2 ankers rum | | 2 | 10 | 0 |
| | 1 anker cider | | 0 | 10 | 0 |
| | 2 ankers beer | | 0 | 10 | 0 |
| | | | 240 | 16 | 0[21] |
| | | | 240 | 16 | |
| | | | 60 | 0 | |
| | | | 541 | 02 | |
| | | | 40 | | |
| | | | 21644[22] | | |

The deed of 15 July 1682 and supplement of 1 Aug. 1682 are DS, HSP. The second memorandum and list of goods are reprinted from Albert Cook Myers, *William Penn, His Own Account of the Lenni Lenape or Delaware Indians 1683* (Moylan, Pa., 1937), pp. 79-81. (*PWP*, 2:261-69).

1. Sachemakers, or sachems, were leaders, or "kings," of Indian bands or tribes. Four of these men, Idquoqueywon (d. c. 1711), Okanickon (d. 1682), Oreckton, and Nanacussey, had sold this same tract of land to representatives of Gov. Andros of New York in 1675. Most of the others are known to have sold land elsewhere in Pennsylvania and New Jersey to the English in the 1670s.

2. A fathom is six feet.

3. Stroudwater cloth was blue and red woolen cloth made in England. Duffel was a coarse woolen cloth.

4. An awl is a pointed tool used for making holes in wood or leather.

5. A blade with handles at both ends, used for shaving wood.

6. An anker is a cask or keg holding about ten U.S. gallons.

7. A Dutch coin, the *gulden* was corrupted in English to "guilder," or "gilder." See n. 18, below.

8. John Wood (d. 1692), a farmer from Sheffield, Yorks., landed at Burlington, New Jersey, in 1678 and soon moved across the Delaware, settling at the Falls. In 1679 he held 478 acres along the Delaware River and an island opposite. He was probably not a Quaker.

9. The exact location of Playwicky is disputed, though there is a marker one-half mile west of Neshaminy Creek, two and one-half miles west of Langhorne, Bucks Co. This Delaware village was the home of "King" Tammany, who sold the lands between Neshaminy and Pennypack creeks to WP on 23 June 1683.

10. Towamensing Creek (the Indian name probably means "the fording place at the Falls") was where the Indian trail crossed the Delaware.

11. Probably *Maquaas-Kittan*, meaning "the great river of the Mohawks."

12. Two islands in the Delaware were known as Matinicum or Tinicum. The one referred to here is now known as Burlington Island; the other is south of the mouth of the Schuylkill River at present-day Tinicum. Sepassincks is the name given to the island and adjoining lands at the Falls of the Delaware, just below present-day Trenton. Oreckton's Island is probably the island opposite Trenton now known as Biles Island.

13. Legal possession.

14. Silas Crispin (c. 1655-1711), son of William Crispin, was a First Purchaser and an assistant to Deputy-Governor William Markham.

15. Richard Noble, a Quaker, came to West Jersey in 1675. In 1679 he was made surveyor of the west side of the Delaware for the duke of York's government, and, in 1682, he became the first sheriff of Bucks Co.

16. Probably Nanacussey, who was absent when the 15 July deed was signed.

17. The Indians.

18. By this computation, there were 40 gulden per English pound. In fact, there were about 11.1 gulden per pound sterling. The author may have confused the gulden with the *schellingen*, valued at about 37 per pound sterling. In the following list, note that some items differ in quantity from the amount specified in the deed, or (especially those items marked with Xs) are not included at all in the deed.

19. Kersey, a woolen fabric, often ribbed.

20. Perhaps an error for "Monmouth" cap, a type popular with sailors and soldiers.

21. There is a mistake in the addition. The correct sum, excluding £60 for wampum, is £250.10.−.

22. This is an effort to compute the total in gulden. £240.16 + £240.16 + £60 = £541.2.0. £541.2 times 40 gulden per pound equals 21,644 gulden. Just why the sum £240.16 should be doubled is not clear. See n. 18, above.

## 38 §

# *William and Jane Yardley to James Harrison*

IN the spring of 1682 large numbers of WP's settlers boarded ships bound
for Pennsylvania. Among them were the Quakers William and Jane
Yardley who set sail from Liverpool, the major port in northwestern England, on the *Friend's Adventure*. Their letter to James Harrison offers a rare
glimpse of the conditions that seventeenth-century immigrants experienced
during their travels. Battering winds and choppy seas, unappetizing food,
and disabling seasickness were enough to make these prospective colonists
wonder if they had displeased God by leaving home. But the Yardleys believed "these things to be but accidental" and were satisfied that "the Lord's
ordering hand" was with them. Indeed, they arrived in Pennsylvania by the
end of September and staked out their Bucks County farm.

Ramsey in the Isle of Man,[1] 21 July 1682

Dear Brother[2]

Having this opportunity I could not well omit it but send thee a line or
two by which you might have a little understanding [of] how things are with
us. Upon the 14th instant in the evening we left Liverpool, then set sail,
having a very fair gale of wind. But it did not long continue but turned very
cross, so that it made the sea very rough, which caused the most of us to be
very sick. And though we had got part of the island on our right hand yet
the night following, by reason the wind proved so cross, that we were forced
to leave the south side and fall to the north, and so came along the island till
we came to this bay called Ramsey Bay, where some of us that evening went
ashore. It being the first day of the week, we met with some Friends and
were glad to see them, and after we had refreshed ourselves, we went aboard
again. Having got a little milk, we took it with us aboard, which was very
acceptable to our poor weak women and children. We stayed then at anchor
that night, and the next day we came ashore again and bought some fresh
provisions and took in some fresh water. So that evening the wind presented
very fair, we set sail and sailed all night very quietly, and the next morning
we got sight of Ireland and was in hopes to have gained the Irish shore. But
the wind turning westerly proved very boisterous and being so cross that it
made the sea very turbulent, that caused us to be many of us very sick, and
that night it was very stormy so that it made the sea very turbulent that we
were forced to go round the island and come to this bay again where we are
at anchor at this present. Randolph Blackshaw, his maid[3] came ashore with
our maid to wash some linen and is stolen away and we are in doubt we shall
lose her. We are both of us very weak in body yet very fervent in mind, for
we look upon these things to be but accidental, although we are satisfied the
Lord's ordering hand is with us, and we can say that it is good, and we hope

that in His own due time He will bring us safe to our desirable place. So with our unchangeable love to thee, thy dear wife and cousins with the rest of your families, we rest thy dear brother and sister,

William and Jane Yardley

Our children are aboard and are pretty well and can eat the ship's fare wonderfully. Dear Elinor Pownall has a bad stomach; so have we. She and her husband's[4] dear love is to you all,

W. Y.

ALS. HSP. Not published in *PWP*, Vol. Two.

1. Ramsey is on the northeast coast of the Isle of Man, which is located in the Irish Sea off northwestern England.

2. James Harrison (see doc. 19, above) sailed for Pennsylvania from Liverpool on the *Submission* on 6 Sept. 1682. He probably received this letter before he left home.

3. That is, Randolph Blackshaw's maid, who traveled with several other servants he sent to Pennsylvania on the *Friend's Adventure*. Blackshaw, of Cheshire, sailed on the *Submission* with James Harrison.

4. Elinor and George Pownall, Quakers of Cheshire, settled in Makefield Twp., Bucks Co., on the lot next to the Yardleys. George was killed by a falling tree shortly after their arrival.

THOUGH WP wished to take his wife and children to America, he left without them in August 1682, probably because Gulielma was newly pregnant and her mother was fatally ill. WP's decision to go without his family had important consequences: as long as he was separated from them he was really only visiting his colony, not moving to Pennsylvania. The following letter of farewell is by far the best-known and best-loved of WP's letters: it is deeply felt, eloquently composed, and full of moral advice. WP conveys his heartfelt distress at parting from his delicate wife and their three young children, and he is more candid with Gulielma about his financial problems than in any other letter of this period. He advises his wife—rather pompously—to keep a regular schedule in housekeeping and "to live low and sparingly till my debts are paid." He wants his children to be educated at home, because schools are corrupting, and to be taught practical skills. And he urges his children to choose a simple country life, to obey God and their mother, and to love one another. Doc. 40 adds three very short letters to his children, seven-year-old Springett, four-year-old Laetitia, and one-year-old William, Jr.

## 39 §

## *To Gulielma Penn and Children*

Warminghurst, 4 August 1682

My dear Wife and Children.[1]

My love, that sea, nor land, nor death itself can extinguish or lessen toward you, most endearedly visits you with eternal embraces and will abide with you forever. And may the God of my life watch over you and bless you and do you good in this world and forever. Some things are upon my spirit to leave with you, in your respective capacities, as I am to one a husband, and to the rest a father, if I should never see you more in this world.

My dear wife, remember thou was the love of my youth, and much the joy of my life, the most beloved, as well as most worthy, of all my earthly comforts. And the reason of that love was more thy inward than thy outward excellences (which yet were many). God knows, and thou knows it. I can say it was a match of providence's making, and God's image in us both was the first thing and the most amiable and engaging ornament in our eyes. Now I am to leave thee, and that without knowing whether I shall ever see thee more in this world. Take my counsel into thy bosom and let it dwell with thee in my stead while thou lives.

1st. Let the fear of the Lord, and a zeal and love to His glory, dwell richly in thy heart, and thou will watch for good over thyself and thy dear children and family, that no rude, light, or bad thing be committed, else God will be offended, and He will repent Himself of the good He intends thee and thine.

2dly. Be diligent in meetings of worship and business; stir up thyself and others herein; it is thy day and place. And let meetings be kept once a day in the family to wait upon the Lord, who has given us much time for ourselves. And my dearest, to make thy family matters easy to thee, divide thy time, and be regular. It is easy and sweet. Thy retirement[2] will afford thee to do it, as in the morning to view the business of the house and fix it as thou desire, seeing all be in order, that by thy counsel all may move, and to thee render an account every evening. The time for work, for walking, for meals, may be certain, at least as near as may be. And grieve not thyself with careless servants. They will disorder thee. Rather pay them and let them go if they will not be better by admonitions. This is best, to avoid many words, which I know wound the soul and offend the Lord.

3dly. Cast up thy income and see what it daily amounts to, by which thou may be sure to have it in thy sight and power to keep within compass. And I beseech thee to live low and sparingly till my debts are paid;[3] and then enlarge as thou see it convenient. Remember thy mother's example when thy father's public-spiritedness had worsted his estate[4] (which is my case). I know thou loves plain things and are averse to the pomp of the world, a nobility natural to thee. I write not as doubtful, but to quicken thee, for my sake, to be more vigilant herein, knowing that God will bless thy care, and thy poor children and thee for it. My mind is wrapped up in a saying of thy father's, "I desire not riches, but to owe nothing." And truly that is wealth; and more than enough to live is a snare attended with many sorrows.

I need not bid thee be humble, for thou are so; nor meek and patient, for it is much of thy natural disposition. But I pray thee, be often in retirement with the Lord and guard against encroaching friendships. Keep them at arm's end; for it is giving away our power, aye, and self too, into the possession of another. And that which might seem engaging in the beginning, may prove a yoke and burden too hard and heavy in the end. Wherefore keep dominion over thyself, and let thy children, good meetings, and Friends be the pleasure of thy life.

4thly. And now, my dearest, let me recommend to thy care my dear children, abundantly beloved of me as the Lord's blessings and the sweet pledges of our mutual and endeared affection. Above all things, endeavor to breed them up in the love of virtue and that holy plain way of it which we have lived in, that the world, in no part of it, get into my family. I had rather they were homely than finely bred, as to outward behavior; yet I love sweetness mixed with gravity, and cheerfulness tempered with sobriety. Religion in the heart leads into this true civility, teaching men and women to be mild and courteous in their behavior, an accomplishment worthy indeed of praise.

5thly. Next, breed them up in a love one of another. Tell them, it is the charge I left behind me, and that it is the way to have the love and blessing of God upon them; also what his portion is who hates, or calls his brother fool.[5] Sometimes separate them, but not long; and allow them to send and give each other small things, to endear one another with once more. I say, tell them it was my counsel, they should be tender and affectionate one to another.

For their learning, be liberal. Spare no cost, for by such parsimony all is lost that is saved; but let it be useful knowledge, such as is consistent with truth and godliness, not cherishing a vain conversation or idle mind, but ingenuity mixed with industry is good for the body and mind too. I recommend the useful parts of mathematics, as building houses or ships, measuring, surveying, dialing,[6] navigation, etc.; but agriculture is especially in my eye. Let my children be husbandmen and housewives. It is industrious, healthy, honest, and of good example, like Abraham and the holy ancients who pleased God and obtained a good report. This leads to consider the works of God and nature, of things that are good and divert the mind from being taken up with the vain arts and inventions of a luxurious world. It is commendable in the princes of Germany, and [the] nobles of that empire, that they have all their children instructed in some useful occupation. Rather keep an ingenious person in the house to teach them than send them to schools, too many evil impressions being commonly received there. Be sure to observe their genius and don't cross it as to learning. Let them not dwell too long on one thing, but let their change be agreeable, and all their diversions have some little bodily labor in them.

When grown big, have most care for them; for then there are more snares both within and without. When marriageable, see that they have worthy persons in their eye, of good life and good fame for piety and understanding.

I need no wealth but sufficiency; and be sure their love be dear, fervent, and mutual, that it may be happy for them. I choose not they should be married into earthly covetous kindred. And of cities and towns of concourse[7] beware. The world is apt to stick close to those who have lived and got wealth there. A country life and estate I like best for my children. I prefer a decent mansion of a hundred pounds per annum before ten thousand pounds in London, or suchlike place, in a way of trade.[8]

In fine, my dear, endeavor to breed them dutiful to the Lord, and His blessed light, truth, and grace in their hearts, who is their Creator, and His fear will grow up with them. Teach a child (says the wise man) the way thou will have him to walk; and when he is old, he will not forget it. Next, obedience to thee their dear mother; and that not for wrath, but for conscience sake. [Be] liberal to the poor, pitiful to the miserable, humble and kind to all. And may my God make thee a blessing and give thee comfort in our dear children; and in age, gather thee to the joy and blessedness of the just (where no death shall separate us) forever.

And now, my dear children that are the gifts and mercies of the God of your tender father, hear my counsel and lay it up in your hearts. Love it more than treasure and follow it, and you shall be blessed here and happy hereafter.

In the first place, remember your Creator in the days of your youth. It was the glory of Israel in the 2d of Jeremiah: and how did God bless Josiah, because he feared him in his youth![9] And so He did Jacob, Joseph, and Moses. Oh! my dear children, remember and fear and serve Him who made you, and gave you to me and your dear mother, that you may live to Him and glorify Him in your generations. To do this, in your youthful days seek after the Lord, that you may find Him, remembering His great love in creating you; that you are not beasts, plants, or stones, but that He has kept you and given you His grace within, and substance without, and provided plentifully for you. This remember in your youth, that you may be kept from the evil of the world; for, in age, it will be harder to overcome the temptations of it.

Wherefore, my dear children, eschew the appearance of evil, and love and cleave to that in your hearts that shows you evil from good, and tells you when you do amiss, and reproves you for it. It is the light of Christ, that He has given you for your salvation. If you do this, and follow my counsel, God will bless you in this world and give you an inheritance in that which shall never have an end. For the light of Jesus is of a purifying nature; it seasons those who love it and take heed to it, and never leaves such till it has brought them to the city of God that has foundations. Oh! that ye may be seasoned with the gracious nature of it; hide it in your hearts, and flee, my dear children, from all youthful lusts, the vain sports, pastimes and pleasures of the world, redeeming the time, because the days are evil. You are now beginning to live—what would some give for your time? Oh! I could have lived better, were I as you, in the flower of youth. Therefore, love and fear the Lord, keep close to meetings; and delight to wait upon the Lord God of your father and mother, among his despised people, as we have done. And count it your honor to be members of that society, and heirs of that living fellowship, which is enjoyed among them — for the experience of which your father's soul blesses the Lord forever.

Next, be obedient to your dear mother, a woman whose virtue and good name is an honor to you; for she has been exceeded by none in her time for her plainness, integrity, industry, humanity, virtue, and good understanding, qualities not usual among women of her worldly condition and quality. Therefore, honor and obey her, my dear children, as your mother, and your father's love and delight; nay, love her too, for she loved your father with a deep and upright love, choosing him before all her many suitors.[10] And though she be of a delicate constitution and noble spirit, yet she descended to the utmost tenderness and care for you, performing in painfulness acts of service to you in your infancy, as a mother and a nurse too. I charge you before the Lord, honor and obey, love and cherish, your dear mother.

Next betake yourselves to some honest, industrious course of life; and that not of sordid covetousness, but for example and to avoid idleness. And if you change your condition and marry, choose with the knowledge and consent of your mother, if living, guardians, or those that have the charge of you. Mind neither beauty nor riches, but the fear of the Lord and a sweet and amiable disposition, such as you can love above all this world and that may make your habitations pleasant and desirable to you. And being married, be tender, affectionate, and patient, and meek. Live in the fear of the Lord, and He will bless you and your offspring. Be sure to live within compass; borrow not, neither be beholden to any.[11] Ruin not yourselves by kindness to others, for that exceeds the due bounds of friendship; neither will a true friend expect it. Small matters I heed not.

Let your industry and parsimony go no farther than for a sufficiency for life, and to make a provision for your children (and that in moderation, if the Lord gives you any). I charge you to help the poor and needy. Let the Lord have a voluntary share of your income, for the good of the poor, both in our Society and others; for we are all His creatures, remembering that he that gives to the poor, lends to the Lord. Know well your incomings, and your outgoings may be the better regulated. Love not money, nor the world. Use them only and they will serve you; but if you love them, you serve them, which will debase your spirits as well as offend the Lord. Pity the distressed, and hold out a hand of help to them; it may be your case, and as you mete[12] to others, God will mete to you again.

Be humble and gentle in your conversation; of few words, I charge you; but always pertinent when you speak, hearing out before you attempt to answer, and then speaking as if you would persuade, not impose.

Affront none, neither revenge the affronts that are done to you; but forgive, and you shall be forgiven of your Heavenly Father.

In making friends, consider well, first; and when you are fixed, be true, not wavering by reports nor deserting in affliction, for that becomes not the good and virtuous.

Watch against anger; neither speak nor act in it, for like drunkenness, it makes a man a beast and throws people into desperate inconveniences.

Avoid flatterers; for they are thieves in disguise. Their praise is costly, designing to get by those they bespeak. They are the worst of creatures; they lie to flatter and flatter to cheat, and, which is worse, if you believe them, you cheat yourselves most dangerously. But the virtuous—though poor—love, cherish, and prefer. Remember David, who asking the Lord, "Who shall abide in Thy tabernacle; who shall dwell in Thy holy hill?" answers, "He that walks uprightly, works righteousness, and speaks the truth in his heart; in whose eyes the vile person is condemned, but honors them who fears the Lord."

Next, my children, be temperate in all things: in your diet, for that is physic[13] by prevention; it keeps, nay, it makes people healthy and their generation[14] sound. This is exclusive of the spiritual advantage it brings. Be also plain in your apparel; keep out that lust which reigns too much over some. Let your virtues be your ornaments; remembering, life is more than food, and the body than raiment.[15] Let your furniture be simple and cheap. Avoid pride, avarice, and luxury. Read my *No Cross, No Crown;*[16] there is instruction. Make your conversation with the most eminent for wisdom and piety; and shun all wicked men, as you hope for the blessing of God, and the comfort of your father's living and dying prayers. Be sure you speak no evil of any; no, not of the meanest, much less of your superiors, as magistrates, guardians, tutors, teachers, and elders in Christ.

Be no busybodies; meddle not with other folks' matters but when in conscience and duly pressed, for it procures trouble, and is ill-mannered, and very unseemly to wise men.

In your families, remember Abraham, Moses, and Joshua, their integrity to the Lord; and do as [if] you have them for your examples. Let the fear and service of the living God be encouraged in your houses, and that plainness, sobriety, and moderation in all things, as becomes God's chosen people. And, as I advise you, my beloved children, do you counsel yours, if God should give you any. Yea, I counsel and command them, as my posterity, that they love and serve the Lord God with an upright heart, that He may bless you and yours, from generation to generation.

And as for you who are likely to be concerned in the government of Pennsylvania and my parts of East Jersey,[17] especially the first, I do charge you before the Lord God and his only angels that you be lowly, diligent, and tender; fearing God, loving the people, and hating covetousness. Let justice have its impartial course, and the law free passage. Though to your loss, protect no man against it, for you are not above the law, but the law above you. Live therefore the lives yourselves you would have the people live; and then you have right and boldness to punish the transgressor. Keep upon the square,[18] for God sees you; therefore do your duty; and be sure you see with your own eyes, and hear with your own ears. Entertain no lurchers;[19] cherish no informers for gain or revenge; use no tricks, fly to no devices to support or cover injustice, but let your hearts be upright before the Lord, trusting in Him above the contrivances of men, and none shall be able to hurt or supplant.

Oh! the Lord is a strong God; and He can do whatsover He pleases. And though men consider it not, it is the Lord that rules and overrules in the kingdoms of men; and He builds up and pulls down. I, your father, am the man that can say, he that trusts in the Lord shall not be confounded. But God, in due time, will make His enemies be at peace with Him.

If you thus behave yourselves, and so become a terror to evildoers and a praise to them that do well, God, my God, will be with you, in wisdom and a sound mind, and make you blessed instruments in His hand for the settlement of some of those desolate parts of the world — which my soul desires above all worldly honors and riches, both for you that go and you that stay, you that govern and you that are governed — that in the end you may be gathered with me to the rest of God.

Finally, my children, love one another with a true and endeared love, and your dear relations on both sides; and take care to preserve tender affection in your children to each other, often marrying within themselves, so [long] as it be without the bounds forbidden in God's law.[20] That so they may not, like the forgetting and unnatural world, grow out of kindred and as cold as strangers; but, as becomes a truly natural and Christian stock, you and yours after you may live in the pure and fervent love of God toward one another, as becomes brethren in the spiritual and natural relation.

So my God, that has blessed me with His abundant mercies, both of this and the other and better life, be with you all, guide you by His counsel, bless you, and bring you to His eternal glory, that you may shine, my dear children, in the firmament of God's power, with the blessed spirits of the just, that celestial family, praising and admiring Him, the God and Father of it, forever and ever. For there is no God like unto Him: the God of Abraham, of Isaac, and of Jacob; the God of the Prophets, the Apostles, and Martyrs of Jesus; in whom I live forever.

So farewell to my thrice dearly beloved wife and children. Yours, as God pleases, in that which no waters can quench, no time forget, nor distance wear away, but remains forever,

William Penn

Transcript. HSP. (*PWP*, 2:269-77).

1. Gulielma Maria Springett Penn (1644-1694) married WP in 1672. She never visited Pennsylvania. They had eight children in all, but only the three addressed here, Springett (1675-1696), Laetitia (1678-1746), and William, Jr. (1681-1720), survived infancy. Laetitia accompanied her father and his second wife, Hannah Callowhill Penn, to Pennsylvania in 1699-1701. William, Jr., eventually left the Society of Friends. He visited Pennsylvania once, in 1704, where his high living greatly disturbed his father.

2. WP assumes that his absence will be a time of seclusion for his family. Moreover, he probably knew that Gulielma was again pregnant. She would give birth in Mar. 1683 to a daughter, who would live only three weeks. See also doc. 77, below.

3. WP had been spending beyond his income ever since his marriage, and had accumulated about £10,000 in debts by 1680. At the time he wrote this letter, he may have supposed that he was clearing these debts through the sale of Pennsylvania land, but on

23 Aug. he discovered from his steward, Philip Ford, that his expenses in 1680-1682 continued to exceed his income and that he owed Ford a new debt of £2851. See doc. 41, below.

4. Gulielma's mother, Mary Proude Springett Penington (c. 1625-1682) married Gulielma's stepfather, Isaac Penington (1616-1679), in 1654. Penington became a Quaker in 1658. He was imprisoned for his faith six times and lost much property, but Mary Penington cleared these debts.

5. WP is referring here to Matthew 5:22, part of the Sermon on the Mount, in which Christ warned that any person who called his brother a fool shall be in danger of hellfire.

6. Surveying underground, as in a mine.

7. Crowded towns.

8. This was easy for WP to say, since his own decent country mansion at Warminghurst had cost £4450 and his land in England and Ireland brought him at least £700 per year.

9. Josiah became King of Israel at the age of eight and was a great religious reformer.

10. Gulielma had many suitors, but she resisted them and lived with her mother until she married WP at the relatively late age of twenty-eight.

11. This is ironic advice from WP, a habitual borrower.

12. Portion out.

13. Medicine.

14. Offspring.

15. Clothing.

16. *No Cross, No Crown* is WP's most famous book, an extended sermon in which he preaches that the good life is spiritual combat against sin, the Christian crown of eternal life. WP published the first version of this text in 1669; he revised it radically, and published a new version in 1682, probably a few months before he wrote this letter.

17. WP and eleven colleagues bought East New Jersey from Elizabeth Carteret, Sir George Carteret's widow, in Feb. 1682, but in Aug. WP sold $^{11}/_{12}$ of his share to Robert Barclay for £320, leaving himself only a small interest in the colony.

18. "Be honest and straightforward."

19. A petty thief, swindler, or rogue.

20. Here WP seems to be arguing somewhat contrary to the Quaker practice of prohibiting first-cousin and other "near kindred" marriages.


# 40 §

## To Springett Penn, Laetitia Penn, and William Penn, Jr.

19 August 1682

My Dear Springett,

Be good, learn to fear God, avoid evil, love thy book, be kind to thy brother and sister, and God will bless thee and I will exceedingly love thee. Farewell dear child,

> Thy dear father,
> Wm Penn

My love to all the family and to Friends.

Dear Laetitia,

I dearly love thee, and would have thee sober. Learn thy book, and love thy brothers. I will send thee a pretty book to learn in. The Lord bless thee and make a good woman of thee. Farewell.

Thy dear father,
Wm Penn

My love to the family.

Dear Billy,

I love thee much, therefore be sober and quiet, and learn his[1] book. I will send him one. So the Lord bless thee. Amen.

Thy dear father,
Wm Penn

My love to all the family.

ALS. HSP. (*PWP*, 2:280-81).

1. WP may shift to the third person here because "Billy" was only seventeen months old.

# 41 §

## *Mortgage to Philip Ford*

WP signed the following receipt for a mortgage on 300,000 acres of Pennsylvania land to his steward, Philip Ford, just before he set sail for America. Behind this receipt lies a complicated financial story. WP had for a long time allowed Ford to handle his business affairs. Ford received the money from WP's land sales in Pennsylvania and rental income from WP's Irish and English property. He used this money to settle WP's household bills; he paid for the costs of negotiating the Pennsylvania charter and advertising the new colony; and he sent almost £3000 worth of goods to Pennsylvania for WP. By 1682, WP was badly in debt to Ford: the Pennsylvania land sales had not offset the high cost of colonizing. On 23 August 1682, shortly before WP's departure, Ford presented WP with an account of his expenses which showed that WP owed him £2851. WP was preoccupied with his upcoming voyage and signed this account without checking it—his usual habit in dealing with Ford, since he trusted his Quaker steward completely.

During the next several days, Ford presented two contracts for WP's signature: a mortgage on 300,000 acres of Pennsylvania land and a bond of £6000 as security for WP's repayment of the £2851 debt to Ford. Doc. 41 is WP's receipt for the mortgage. These contracts formed the basis for what became a protracted financial dispute between WP and his steward. WP came to believe that Ford had falsified his bookkeeping in order to trick WP into signing over the colony. WP claimed, in retrospect, that Ford had billed him in August 1682 for £914 in goods that were actually shipped for other Pennsylvania investors. But even if we accept WP's revised calculation of this account, he still owed Ford nearly £2000. Ford had reason for concern about this debt. He might never see WP again, he had no assurance of repayment, and if the boom in Pennsylvania land sales ended, WP's debt was likely to escalate. Thus, from Ford's point of view, by obtaining this mortgage on Pennsylvania land, he was simply getting a written guarantee that WP would repay his debt. However, WP never did settle the account of August 1682, and when Ford began charging compound interest, WP's debt grew rapidly. Eventually, Ford laid claim to the proprietorship of Pennsylvania, his heirs sued WP for £20,000, and in 1708 — twenty-six years after the dispute began — they won a judgment of £7600 against him.

24 August 1682

KNOW all men by these presents that I, William Penn, of Warminghurst in the County of Sussex, Esquire, have had and received of and from Philip Ford of London, merchant, the sum of £3000 sterling, being for the purchase of 300,000 acres of land in Pennsylvania,[1] and the consideration money mentioned to be paid in and by one pair of indentures of release and confirmation[2] bearing even date[3] herewith and made between me, the said William Penn, of the one part, and the said Philip Ford of the other part, according to the purport of the same indentures of and from which said sum of £3000, I, the said William Penn, do hereby for myself, my heirs, executors, administrators, and assigns, release, quitclaim, and forever discharge the said Philip Ford, his heirs, executors, administrators, and assigns, and every of them, by these presents. Witness my hand and seal this four and twentieth day of August *anno Domini 1682 annoque regis Caroli secundi nunc Angliæ, etc., tricesimo quarto.*[4]
Sealed and delivered,

Wm Penn

In the presence of Francis Taylor,
Porten Paul
Mark Swanner

DS. Bedfordshire Record Office, England. (*PWP*, 2:290-92).

1. The "purchase" money that WP received from Ford is WP's debt of £2851. Why Ford bound WP to the higher figure of £3000 is not clear. Years later, WP protested this figure.
2. A contract used to transfer ownership of land.
3. "The same date."
4. "And in the thirty-fourth year of King Charles II now of England, etc."

# Edward Jones to John ap Thomas

THE following letter is a rare firsthand account of the sea voyage to Pennsylvania, and conditions in the new settlement shortly before WP's arrival, from the perspective of a Welsh colonist. Edward Jones (1645-1737), a Quaker surgeon of Bala, Merionethshire, sailed on the *Lyon* of Liverpool with his wife Mary (d. 1726), the daughter of Thomas Wynne (see doc. 52, below), and two children, Martha and Jonathan. Jones led a party of forty Welshmen, the first to arrive in Pennsylvania. They settled at Merion, in what is now the Main Line suburbs of Philadelphia, with the intention of establishing the Welsh Tract or "barony," where Welsh families would live together, separate from the English and Swedes. They hoped in this way to preserve their Welsh language and customs.

Jones sent this letter to his partner, John ap Thomas, with whom he had bought 5000 acres from WP. Thomas planned to follow Jones to Pennsylvania, but he fell sick and died in May 1683. His widow, Katherine (d. 1698), immigrated with her seven children and arrived in the colony in November 1683. She brought Jones' letter with her to Pennsylvania, so perhaps she followed his shrewd advice on what to pack, how to deal with the ship captain, and what to expect on arrival. Jones gives some rare information about the wages workers could command in Pennsylvania, and suggests what kinds of trading goods to import. His sensible advice to bring blue cloth rather than white reminds us that Pennsylvania in 1682 was very much a frontier—where the work was dirty and the laundry facilities poor.

Schuylkill River, 26 August 1682

My endeared friend and brother,

My heart dearly salutes thee in a measure of the everlasting Truth, dear friend, hoping that these few lines may find thee in health or no worse than I left thee. This shall let thee know that we had been aboard eleven weeks before we made the land (it was not for want of art but contrary winds) and one [week] we were in coming to Upland. The town[1] is to be built 15 or 16 miles up the river. And in all this time we wanted neither meat, drink, or water, though several hogsheads of water run out. Our ordinary allowance of beer was 3 pints a day for each whole head,[2] and a quart of water; 3 biscuits a day and sometimes more. We laid in about a half hundred[weight] of biscuits, one barrel of beer, one hogshead of water—the quantity for each whole head—and 3 barrels of beef for the whole number (40) and we had one [barrel of beef] to come ashore. A great many could eat little or no beef, though it was good. Butter and cheese eats well upon the sea. The remainder of our cheese and butter is little or no worse; butter and cheese is at 6d. per

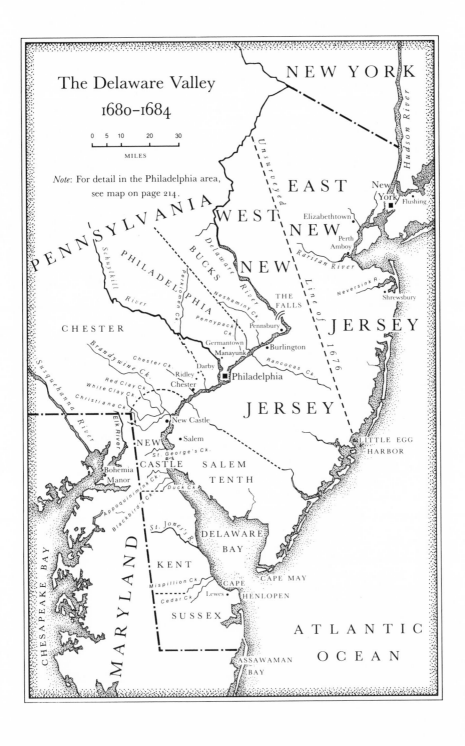

The Delaware Valley
1680–1684

0  5  10    20      30
MILES

*Note*: For detail in the Philadelphia area,
see map on page 214.

NEW YORK

PENNSYLVANIA

EAST

WEST

NEW

JERSEY

Hudson River

New York

Flushing

Elizabethtown

Perth
Amboy

Raritan River

Neversink R.

Shrewsbury

Unsurveyed

Line of 1676

Schuylkill River

PHILADELPHIA

BUCKS

Delaware River

Perkiomen Ck.

Neshaminy Ck.

Pennypack Ck.

THE
FALLS

Pennsbury

CHESTER

Brandywine Ck.

Chester Ck.

Germantown

Manayunk

Darby

Burlington

Rancocas Ck.

Red Clay Ck.

White Clay Ck.

Christiana Ck.

Ridley

Chester

Philadelphia

JERSEY

Susquehanna River

Elk River

New Castle

Salem

NEW

CASTLE

SALEM

TENTH

LITTLE EGG
HARBOR

Bohemia
Manor

St. George's Ck.

Appoquinimink Ck.

Duck Ck.

Blackbird Ck.

St. Jones's R.

DELAWARE

BAY

CHESAPEAKE BAY

MARYLAND

KENT

Mispillion Ck.

Cedar Ck.

Lewes

CAPE

HENLOPEN

CAPE MAY

SUSSEX

ASSAWAMAN
BAY

ATLANTIC

OCEAN

lb. here, if not more. We have oatmeal to spare, but it is well that we have it, for here is little or no corn[3] till they begin to sow their corn; they have plenty of it.

The passengers are all living, save one child that died of a surfeit.[4] Let no Friends tell that they are either too old or too young, for the Lord is sufficient to preserve both to the uttermost. Here is an old man about 80 years of age; he is rather better than when he set out. Likewise here are young babes doing very well considering sea diet. We had one ton of water and one of drink to pay for at Upland, but the master would fain[5] be paid for 13 or 14 hogsheads that run out by the way, but we did not. And about 3 quarters of a ton of coal we paid for; we laid in 3 ton of coal and [it] yields no profit here.

We are short of our expectation by reason that the town is not to be built at Upland; neither would the master bring us any further [than Upland], though it is navigable for ships of greater burden than ours. The name of the town lots is called now Wicaco.[6] Here is a crowd of people striving for the country land, for the town lot is not divided, and therefore we are forced to take up the country lots [first]. We had much ado to get a grant[7] of it, but it cost us 4 or 5 days' attendance, besides some score of miles we traveled before we brought it to pass. I hope it will please thee and the rest that are concerned, for it has most rare timber. I have not seen the like in all these parts. There is water enough beside. The end of each lot will be on a river as large or larger than the Dee at Bala;[8] it is called Schuylkill River. I hope the country land will within this four days [be] surveyed out. The rate for surveying 100 acres [is] twenty shillings, but I hope better orders will be taken shortly about it.[9]

We liked him, the captain,[10] well enough when eating our own victuals: but beware of his provisions, because it was only bread, salt meat, with little beer, and foul water, usually. But he made a great fuss over me and my wife and over most of those who could talk with him [in English]. There is another captain living in the same town,[11] and passengers from Carmarthenshire[12] came over with him on his provision; and they spoke well of him; but they paid him £4, 10s. each; children under twelve years of age, 52s.; and getting plenty to eat and good drink. The name of this good man is Captain [Robert] Crossman;[13] and as to the others I have not seen them. It is cheaper to furnish our own provisions than to pay £4, 10s. each; this would be more satisfactory to me.

I think most of the things will not be sold until you come over, because so many things had previously been brought here. And as to the articles to bring with you they had better be some white fustian, serge[14] to make clothes, men's hats, such as the country affords, saddles, bridles, and what belongs to them, shoes for men and women; blue flannel is most called for here; but all colors are used. Don't bring much white flannel with you; stuff dyed blue we like best.

The people generally are Swedes, which are not very well acquainted.[15] We are amongst the English, which sent us both venison and new milk, and the Indians brought venison to our door for sixpence the quarter. And as for the land, we look upon it [as] a good and fat soil, generally producing twenty, thirty, and forty fold. There are stones[16] to be had enough at the falls of the Schuylkill, that is, where we are to settle, and water enough for mills. But thou must bring millstones and the irons that belong to it, for smiths are dear.[17] Iron is about 32 or 40s. per hundred; steel about 1s. 6d. per lb. The best way is to make your pickaxes when you come over, for they cannot be made in England, for one man will work with them as much as two men with ours.

Grindstones yield good profit here. Ordinary workmen have 1s. 6d. a day. Carpenters three or four shillings a day. Here are sheep, but dear, about 20s. apiece. I cannot understand how they can be carried from England. Tailors have 5s. and 6s. a day. I would have you bring salt for the present use; here is coarse salt, sometimes two measures of salt for one of wheat, and sometimes very dear. Six penny and eight penny nails are most in use. Horseshoes are in no use. Good large shoes are dear. Lead in small bars is vendible,[18] but guns are cheap enough. They plow, but very bungerly,[19] and yet they have some good stone. They use both hooks and sickles to reap with.

Time will not permit me to write much more for we are not settled. I [send] my dear love and my wife's unto thyself and thy dear wife and the rest of my dear friends, H[ugh] Ro[berts], Rich. P., Evan Reese, J[ohn] ap Ed[ward], Elizabeth Williams, E. and J. Ed[wards], Gainor R[oberts], Ro[bert] O[we]n, Jo[hn] Humphrey, Hugh J[ohn] Tho[mas], and the rest of Friends as if named.[20]

I remain thy loyal friend and brother while I am,

Edd Jones

My wife desires thee to buy her one iron kettle 3s. or 3s. 6d.; 2 pair of shoes for Martha, and one pair for Jonathan, let them be strong and large. Be sure and put all your goods in cases; if they be dry they keep well, otherwise they will get damp and moldy.

Compel the master of the ship to come to the town of Philadelphia with your goods. I had to pay to others 30s. for hauling the things up; and be sure to pay for carrying your luggage, and everything else that you had started with, to the captain.

Transcript. *PMHB,* 4:314-17; 5:358-59; Charles H. Browning, *Welsh Settlement of Pennsylvania* (Philadelphia, 1912), pp. 65-70. Not published in *PWP,* Vol. Two.

1. Jones means Philadelphia, which was built, as he says, about sixteen miles up the river beyond Upland or Chester.
2. Each adult passenger. A child was reckoned as a "half head."
3. Grain such as wheat or rye, not Indian corn.
4. Fever.
5. Gladly.
6. The only clustered European settlement within the limits of present Philadelphia before WP laid out his town was at Wicaco, the Indian name for Southwark, in South Philadelphia, where the Swedish colonists in 1682 had a Lutheran church.
7. A grant or warrant to survey the land.
8. The Dee River flows from Bala Lake in northern Wales to the Irish Sea. Jones came from the town of Bala, which is located at the northern end of the lake.

9. Jones hopes that the charge for surveying will be lowered.

10. John Compton, captain of the ship Jones traveled on, the *Lyon*. Jones wrote this and the next paragraph, and the last paragraph of the postscript, in Welsh, because he sent his letter back to Wales with Compton and did not want the captain to know what he was saying about him.

11. Liverpool.

12. A county in southern Wales.

13. Crossman's ship, the *Friendship* of Liverpool, arrived about the same time as the *Lyon*. One passenger was John Simcock, deputy-president of the Free Society of Traders.

14. Fustian is a coarse cloth made of cotton and flax; serge is a ribbed woolen cloth.

15. With the Welsh language.

16. For houses and other buildings.

17. Expensive.

18. Salable.

19. Clumsily.

20. Most of these people eventually immigrated to Pennsylvania. Hugh Roberts (c. 1644-1702) arrived in Pennsylvania in Sept. 1683 and was active in the Quaker meeting in Merion. Gainor Roberts, his sister, emigrated in 1683 as well, as did Hugh John ap Thomas, a farmer and miller. Elizabeth Williams and Robert Owen were both active Quaker ministers. Evan Reese bought land in Pennsylvania, but never emigrated.


# 43 §

## *News of William Penn's Departure for Pennsylvania*

WP was a newsworthy character in England, thanks to his upper-class status, his association with the despised Quakers, and his new colony in America. The London newspapers of 1682 were small affairs, with little room for news, but two journals reported WP's departure for Pennsylvania from Deal, Kent, an anchorage eight miles north of Dover. WP's ship, the *Welcome,* did not sail until 31 August 1682, but its "lading," or loading, began several weeks before that date. As early as 7 July 1682, passengers arranged for the storage of their belongings; WP himself had £1449 in household goods and retail merchandise on board. Details of the *Welcome's* actual journey to America are few, but we do know that WP's ship had a much worse crossing than most of the other ships arriving in Pennsylvania during the 1680s. Thirty-one *Welcome* passengers died of smallpox on the way over.


London, 26 August 1682

This day William Penn, Esq., took his leave of his friends and departed the town, in order to his voyage to Pennsylvania, of which place he is proprietor, having taken along with him many families and others who are gone to settle themselves in that colony, it being in all probability likely to prove a most plentiful and pleasant place to live in.

Being Wednesday, the wind east-northeast, William Penn, Esq., sole proprietor and governor of Pennsylvania, went on board the *Welcome,* in order to his voyage for that province, accompanied with his wife and others to Dover Road, where they parted. There are ships from several parts preparing to go; and likewise another ship from London, on the account of the Free Society of Traders in Pennsylvania,[1] which is already fallen down to Gravesend,[2] and is to follow after the 10th instant.

Newspaper items. *The Loyal Protestant, and True Domestick Intelligence, or News both from City and Country,* # 200; *The Epitome of the Weekly News,* # 2; published in *PMHB,* 75:153. Not published in *PWP,* Vol. Two.

1. The *Jeffrey* of London carried workmen, a large amount of goods, and several officers of the Free Society of Traders, including president Nicholas More.
2. Gravesend, on the Thames, twenty-two miles east of London.

# 44 §

## *James Claypoole to Edward Claypoole*

PREPARATIONS for migrating to Pennsylvania took months, especially for a wealthy London merchant like James Claypoole, who had established a trading network that ranged as far as Ireland, Germany, and the West Indies. Many of Claypoole's letters from this period survive. They show in great detail the painstaking arrangements he had to make in order to transfer his principal base of operations to Pennsylvania, while continuing his business in England under several assistants. In the following excerpt from a letter to his older brother Edward (d. 1692), a plantation owner in Barbados, Claypoole asks his brother to keep sending his sugar to these London assistants after Claypoole leaves for Pennsylvania. He also talks about the laborers he needs for his new home. Claypoole has already sent a servant to build his house in Philadelphia, and he now wants Edward to send him four black slaves from Barbados to assist this servant and to work in his household after he arrives with his family. James Claypoole was a Quaker in good standing; his comments provide invaluable insight into the considerations that influenced a late-seventeenth-century English Quaker's decision to buy slaves. See docs. 58 and 85, below, for later letters from Claypoole to WP and brother Edward.

London, 23 September 1682

Dear Brother Edward Claypoole

. . . My purpose of going with my family to Pennsylvania is still the same as advised in my last. I purpose to be ready to go on shipboard about the end of the 1st month or beginning of the second month.[1] In the meantime I shall be looking out for servants which may be proper to take with me, as two carpenters, a bricklayer, a husbandman, and 2 laborers. I have sent by Captain Arnold[2] (who is in the Downs[3] bound for Pennsylvania) an honest man to build me a slight house, and plant an orchard and clear some ground with the help of a carpenter that is going with another friend. My man is a brickmaker but has skill in planting and husbandry, and a piece of a carpenter; he is an honest, industrious, solid man of about 47 years old and one called a Quaker.[4]

For his assistance and for my use and service, I desire thee to provide me 2 good stout Negro men, such as are like to be pliable and good-natured and ingenious. I question not but thou knows better than I do which may be fittest for me, and I hope thou will be so kind as to let me have those which are good likely men, for some I hear are so ill-natured and surly that a man had better keep a bear; and some again, so ingenious, diligent, and good-natured, that they are a great comfort and benefit to a man and his family. And my family is great and I have 3 young children[5] so that it may be very prejudicial to me to have bad Negroes.

I would also have a boy and a girl to serve in my house; I would not have either of them under 10 years or above 20. But principally observe their nature and capacity. If I have them in the 3rd or 4th month in Pennsylvania may be well,[6] but the men I would have sent by the first opportunity in spring, directed to John Goodson at Upland in Pennsylvania, surgeon to the Society of Traders,[7] or in his absence to Ralph Withers, to whom I have given a letter of attorney, to be deputy-treasurer to the Society till my arrival.

I hope thou will get in the money of [William] Lewger and send it [to] me in good sugar, if that be not too troublesome for thee, but I leave that to thee, either to send bill[8] or goods. And for buying the Negroes, I intend by John Strutt to send thee a letter of attorney, to receive my effects of Joseph Grove[9] and several others. Further, as to thy corresponding with me, I desire it may continue as it is, and I shall take all necessary care therein, even to the last day. And when I go away, [I] shall leave my letter of attorney with some diligent, honest person that may be as capable to serve thee as myself, and if I have a part of the commission, I will be security for him.

I have something of that kind under consideration with my servant,[10] who has now about 2 years and ¾ to serve. He has been very true and diligent in my business and has learned so much that I could leave all to him for a year together, if I was not to remove. Besides, there is a young man [who] proposes to be his partner; him I know very well to be diligent, honest, capable, and sufficient, that they will neither want money nor credit. So I desire thee, brother, do not promise or engage thy business to anyone, but let it continue as it is, and for the future I hope my proposals shall be as well to be accepted of as anyone's. My man is about 24 years of age and the other, 28 years; they are both solid and sober and not given to any extravagancy and are called Quakers. It's possible they may dwell in my house where I live now, if we can agree. I intend to write thee again by John Strutt, so with my true love to thyself and my sister,[11] I conclude at present.

In the ship bound for Pennsylvania in the Downs is the president of the Society[12] with about 60 or 70 servants, besides many other passengers. It is a great ship, near 500 tons and never was at sea. We reckon there may be near 1000 people gone this year. There is some probability of my brother Wingfield's[13] going with us to Pennsylvania; he is resolved upon it if he can get his concerns from Ireland. As to our coming to Barbados to stay 3 or 4 weeks, he likes that well, but I know not yet how it may be.[14] I have endeavored to get thee a servant or two, but as yet I cannot, but I doubt not to get some before I go away.

Sent copy per Strutt the 12th October.

LBC. HSP. Not published in *PWP,* Vol. Two.

1. Mar.-Apr. 1683. Claypoole did not actually leave until July 1683.
2. Capt. Thomas Arnold, master of the *Jeffrey* (see doc. 43, above).
3. A sheltered anchorage along the coast of Kent, in the English Channel.
4. Edward Cole was bound as a servant to Claypoole for four years. See doc. 85, below, for Claypoole's comments on what he accomplished in Philadelphia before Claypoole himself arrived.
5. Claypoole and his wife, Helena (d. 1688), had seven children living at home at this time. The youngest three were Nathaniel (b. 1672), George (b. 1675), and Joseph (b. 1677). His oldest son, John (1658-1700), was already in Pennsylvania. Six additional children had died.
6. According to doc. 85, Claypoole had not received the blacks he requested by Dec. 1683.
7. John Goodson (d. 1727), a Quaker surgeon, sailed to Pennsylvania in 1682. He was active both in the Philadelphia Monthly Meeting and in Pennsylvania government.
8. A bill of exchange, like a modern check, was a written order that a certain amount of money be paid to a specific person.
9. John Strutt was a Quaker shipmaster who sailed frequently to the West Indies. Joseph Grove, also a Quaker, had recently migrated to the West Indies.
10. Probably Edward Haistwell (c. 1658-1709), who had served Claypoole for almost four years at this time. Haistwell had earlier worked as George Fox's clerk.
11. Claypoole means his brother Edward's wife, Abigail.
12. Nicholas More.
13. Wingfield Claypoole, another of James's older brothers, apparently never came to Pennsylvania. As James was preparing to emigrate, Wingfield added to his difficulties by threatening to have him imprisoned for a £50 debt.
14. Many ships traveling from England to North America took a southerly route via the West Indies in order to catch the favorable trade winds.

# Part VII

FIRST MONTHS IN AMERICA §
OCTOBER 1682–MAY 1683

*The Landing of William Penn from the* Welcome *at Upland, by Arnold Anderson, 1931, HSP.*

WP sighted Delaware Bay on 24 October 1682, landed at New Castle on 28 October, and arrived at Pennsylvania the next day. His ship, the *Welcome,* was part of a fleet of twenty-three ships that carried approximately two thousand men, women, and children to Pennsylvania in 1681 and 1682. These numbers may seem small, but more people came to Pennsylvania in the early 1680s than to any new colony since the founding of Massachusetts fifty years before. Once arrived, the colonists spread into the three counties of Pennsylvania—Chester, Philadelphia, and Bucks—where they staked out their farms and town lots and formed their Quaker meetings for worship. The proprietor himself plunged into the business of organizing his government, negotiating with the Indians, supervising the distribution of land to the new colonists, laying out his city of Philadelphia, and dealing with his neighbors in Maryland, New Jersey, and New York.

WP was extremely busy during these opening months in America. He shuttled back and forth between New Castle, Chester, and Philadelphia, and also traveled to New York, New Jersey, and Maryland. He had little time to write letters, and few of those that he did write have survived. His fellow colonists likewise left disappointingly meager trace of their activities. We have no passenger list for the *Welcome* or for most of the other incoming ships. We have no record of WP's initial meeting with the Delaware (Lenni Lenape) Indians. The proprietary authorities kept inadequate record of the land warrants, surveys, and patents they issued to the new settlers in 1682-1683. The minutes of the first Pennsylvania Assembly in December 1682 are skimpy, the records of local administration in Chester, Philadelphia, and Bucks counties are incomplete, as are the records of Quaker meetings in 1682-1683.

Nevertheless, as the following seventeen documents demonstrate, many of WP's actions during his first months in America can be reconstructed in fascinating detail. In particular, we can see how WP approached the problem of administering two distinctly different territories: Quaker Pennsylvania and the non-Quaker lower counties (present Delaware). Just before he left England, WP had been given title to the lower counties by the duke of York, but since he did not have a royal charter, his claim to the region could be disputed. He needed to assert his authority over the lower counties in order to establish a base for the political development of Pennsylvania and the economic control of the Delaware River, but to do so he had to win the allegiance of the Swedish, Dutch, Finnish, and English people who had settled in this region during the previous forty years. Docs. 45–47 and 49–50 show how he met this problem and brought about a political union between Delaware and Pennsylvania in the fall of 1682.

ALTHOUGH the two eyewitness accounts we have of WP's landing on the Delaware are both rather defective, they present sharply contrasting images of the arrival ceremonies. John Moll, whose account is printed in doc. 45, was the justice of New Castle court and the chief local administrator for the duke of York; he describes the public ritual in which WP presented his credentials of ownership to Moll and then took possession as a feudal lord of the fort, the soil, and the water of New Castle. Even though Moll's account was not written until some years later, and was not recorded until 1724, his memory of the event was probably accurate. Quite different is WP's own description of his arrival, in a letter to Philip Ford, his London agent; Ford published an abstract of WP's letter (doc. 46) in order to disprove a rumor circulated by WP's enemies that the Quaker leader had died. WP's actual letter has unfortunately been lost, but the abstract dwells chiefly on his inaugural address at New Castle (not mentioned by Moll), and on the joyful greeting he received (also not mentioned by Moll) from the colonists in Delaware and Pennsylvania.

## 45 §

## John Moll's Account of the Surrender of the Three Lower Counties to William Penn

[1682][1]

THESE are to certify [to] all whom it may concern that William Penn, Esq., proprietor and governor of the province of Pennsylvania and the territories thereunto belonging, etc., at his first arrival from England by the town of New Castle upon Delaware River in the month of October anno 1682, did send then and there one messenger ashore to give notice unto the commissioners of his desire to speak with them aboard. I (being then left the first in commission by Sir Edmund Andros, governor-general under his Royal Highness, James, Duke of York and Albany, etc., of all his territories in America) did go aboard with some more of the commissioners. At which time Esquire Penn did show me two sundry indentures or deeds of enfeoffment[2] from under the hand and seal of his Royal Highness granted unto him, both bearing date the 28th day of August anno 1682:[3] the one for the County of New Castle with twelve miles distance north and south thereunto belonging; and the other beginning twelve miles below New Castle and extending south unto Cape Henlopen,[4] together with the soils and waters of the said river, bay, rivulets, and the islands thereunto belonging, etc. Underneath of both which said indentures or deeds of enfeoffment were added his Royal Highness's letters of attorney, directed unto me and Ephraim Herrman, deceased,[5] with full power and authority for to give in his Royal Highness's name unto the said William Penn, Esq., quiet and peaceable possession of all what was inserted in the said indentures as above briefly is specified. But the said Ephraim Herrman happened to be gone from home, so that he was not at that time aboard with me of the said ship. I therefore did desire from Esquire Penn four and twenty hours consideration for to communicate with the said Herrman and the rest of the commissioners about the premises. In which compass of time we did unanimously agree to comply with his Royal Highness's orders. Whereupon, by virtue of the power given unto us by the above mentioned letters of attorney, we did give and surrender in the name of his Royal Highness unto him the said William Penn, Esq., actual and peaceable possession of the fort at New Castle, by giving him the key thereof, to lock upon himself alone the door, which being opened by him again, we did deliver also unto him one turf with a twig upon it, and a porringer[6] with river water and soil, in part of all what was specified in the said indenture or deed of enfeoffment from his Royal Highness and according unto the true intent and meaning thereof. And [a] few days after that we went to the house of Captain Edmund Cantwell[7] at the south side of Appoquinimink Creek, by computation above twelve miles distance from the town of New Castle, as being part of the two lower counties here above mentioned and specified in His Royal Highness's other indenture or deed of enfeoffment; and after we had shown unto the commissioners of those counties the power and orders given unto us, as aforesaid, we asked them if they could show us any cause why and wherefore we should not proceed to act and do there as we had done at New Castle? And finding no manner of obstruction, we made then and there in his Royal Highness's name the same manner and form of delivery as we had done at New Castle. Which actings of us was fully accepted and well approved of by Anthony Brockholls,[8] then commander in chief, and his Council at New York as appears by their declaration bearing date the 21st of November anno 1682, from which jurisdiction we had our dependence all along ever since the conquest,[9] until we had made the above related delivery unto Governor William Penn by virtue of his Royal Highness's orders and commands, etc.

John Moll.

DS. HSP. (*PWP*, 2:304–8).

1. Although this narrative recounts events of 27 and 28 Oct. and of 7 Nov. 1682, it was not written until at least 1689.
2. Grants of feudal title. On 24 Aug. 1682 the duke of York had conveyed the area

that is now the state of Delaware to WP in two deeds. The first deed transferred owner-ship of New Castle and a twelve-mile circle surrounding the town, and the second deeded the territory below the twelve-mile circle, or in modern terms, Kent and Sussex counties.

3. The deeds were actually dated 24 Aug. 1682; see doc. 35, above.

4. Cape Henlopen here refers to the present southeastern boundary of Delaware, rather than to the cape (now known as Cape Henlopen) twenty-five miles north at the entrance to Delaware Bay, which was called Cape Cornelis at this time.

5. Ephraim Herrman (b. 1652), the son of Augustine Herrman (see doc. 20), died in 1689, so Moll wrote this document later than 1689.

6. A small basin from which soup or porridge is eaten.

7. Edmund Cantwell (d. 1685) was sheriff of New Castle Co. between 1668 and 1683, and a major landowner in New Castle Co., where he owned over 3000 acres by the time of his death. Cantwell's home was near modern Odessa, Del.

8. Anthony Brockholls was acting governor of New York from late 1680 to early 1683; after the arrival of Gov. Thomas Dongan (doc. 48), Brockholls continued as com-mander of the garrison at New York until 1690.

9. The conquest of New Netherlands by the English in 1664.


# 46 §
## To Philip Ford

An Abstract of [a] letter from William Penn, Proprietor of Pennsyl-vania, to P[hilip] F[ord] etc. Dated at Upland, . . . November 1, 1682, signifying his safe arrival; and that day six weeks [after] they lost sight of land in England, they saw it in America; and being about twelve leagues off from the coast, the air smelled as sweet as a garden new blown.[1] As they sailed up the river they received visits and invitations from the inhabitants, the people being joyful to see him, both Dutch, Swedes, and English com-ing up to New Castle, they received and entertained him with great expres-sions of joy, after their sort.

Next day after his arrival, he had the people summoned together to the courthouse at New Castle, where possession was legally given him. And after that he made a speech to the old magistrates and the people, signifying to them the end of his coming, the nature and end of government, and that [government] especially he came to establish, assuring them of their spiritual and temporal rights: liberty of conscience and civil freedoms. All he prayed, expected, or required, was sobriety and loving neighborhood. Then he re-newed their commissions and so left them. He went from thence to a place called Upland, where he called an Assembly and gave them as ample satis-faction as at New Castle, so they signed an acknowledgment and were very joyful. The Swedes sent one Captain Lasse Cock to acquaint him that they would serve, love, and obey him with all they had, and that it was the best day they ever saw.

Printed abstract. Philip Ford, *A Vindication of William Penn* (London, 1683). Not pub-lished in *PWP,* Vol. Two.

1. In bloom. WP had special reason for enjoying the sight and smell of land. During the voyage of the *Welcome,* thirty-one passengers had died of smallpox.

WHEN WP took possession of the three lower counties on the Delaware River—New Castle, St. Jones's (renamed Kent in 1682), and Whorekill (renamed Sussex in 1682)—he moved quickly to win the support of the colonists already living there. To keep them from wishing to return to the government of New York, or to join the government of Maryland, WP did some careful public relations work. Carrying out the promise he made in his inaugural address at New Castle (see doc. 46), he offered the colonists in the lower counties a privilege they had never enjoyed under either the Dutch or the duke of York—representation in a legislative assembly on the same terms enjoyed by the settlers in Pennsylvania. Doc. 47 is WP's directive to the sheriff of Sussex County to gather the voters so that they could choose seven representatives. The voters met twelve days later, as the sheriff reports in doc. 49, and made their choice. WP's shrewd management soon paid off. Although the representatives from the lower counties were mostly non-Quaker and non-English, when they attended the first Pennsylvania Assembly at Upland in December 1682 they petitioned to be united with Pennsylvania, in order to enjoy their neighbors' rights and privileges (see doc. 50). All seven of the Sussex representatives joined in signing this petition.

# 47 §
## Writ to John Vines to Call an Election

8 November 1682

William Penn, proprietary and governor of Pennsylvania, New Castle, St. Jones's, [and] New Deal (alias Whorekill), with their proper liberties.

These are in the king's name to require and empower thee to summon all the freeholders within the precincts of thy office to meet on the twentieth day of this instant month of November, and that there they elect, [or] choose out of themselves, seven persons of most note for wisdom, sobriety, and integrity, to serve as their deputies and representatives in General Assembly to be held at Upland in the province of Pennsylvania, the first day of December next; and then and there to consult with me for the common good of the inhabitants of that province and the adjacent counties of New Castle, St. Jones's, [and] New Deal (alias Whorekill), under my charge and jurisdiction, of which make due and just return unto me. Given under my hand and seal this eighth day of November, one thousand six hundred eighty two.

Wm Penn

To John Vines,[1] high sheriff of the County of Whorekill (alias New Deal).

MBE. HSP. (*PWP*, 2:310-11).

1. John Vines (d. 1689) was first appointed sheriff of Whorekill by Gov. Andros in 1679 and was reappointed by WP on 18 Nov. 1682.

# 48 §

## To William Blathwayt and Francis Gwyn

IN the fall of 1682 WP wrote a number of letters to his friends and family in England to announce his arrival in America. The following letter is the only one that has survived. He sent it to the two royal bureaucrats at Whitehall who had most to do with the passage of his Pennsylvania charter — Secretary Blathwayt of the Lords of Trade, and Undersecretary of State Gwyn.

New York, 21 November 1682

My Kind Friends

I wear your favors about me which will not let me forget you, though this be but a lean remembrance. I am come well hither, I thank God, and like the land, air, and food very well. I never ate better in England at Lamb's or Locket's;[1] the English [are] ingenuous[2] and well stored. I have received universal civilities and congratulations from the people of divers governments. I hope for a lasting concord among us. The service of God first, the honor and advantage of the king, with our own profit, shall I hope be [the result of] all our endeavors. There is little news from these parts; next spring may fill a letter. I am now at New York, where I last night persuaded all parties to let fall their animosities, which they promised;[3] and since the duke has named another governor,[4] to think of ways how to maintain their charge in consideration of the privileges the duke had on those terms assured them they should enjoy.[5] I must needs say that the fault I find upon Sir Edmund Andros is sometimes an over eager and too pressing an execution of his powers, where provoked, especially. I think he may deserve not wholly to be forgotten of the duke his master. I speak like a man of my profession, that loves even enemies, for I cannot think him to have been (in my American business) a friend to me.[6] I shall say no more, but pray number me among the first of your friends, and believe that you shall find me in all occasions

Your very grateful and faithful friend,
Wm Penn

ALS. The Research Center of the Colonial Williamsburg Foundation. (*PWP*, 2:311-12).

1. Patrick Lamb, a master cook to Charles II, operated a tavern within Whitehall

Palace for the entertainment of courtiers. Locket's was a very fashionable eating house at Charing Cross in London.

2. WP probably means "ingenious." He is describing the English colonists he has met so far, along the Delaware, in New Jersey, and in New York.

3. New York, under the feeble stewardship of Acting Governor Brockholls, was in a state of near anarchy in 1681-1682. Taxes could not be collected; a member of the Council was tried for treason; the English and the Dutch agitated against each other; and the Long Island towns convened illegally to lobby for a representative assembly. WP, as a visiting arbitrator, was trying to restore harmony.

4. On 30 Sept. 1682 the duke of York commissioned Thomas Dongan (1634-1715) to be governor of New York, replacing Sir Edmund Andros, but Dongan did not arrive in the colony until Aug. 1683.

5. In Mar. 1682 the duke of York told Brockholls that he would permit a representative assembly in New York, on condition that the colonists provided enough revenue to support the government.

6. As governor of New York, Andros had tried to expand his authority into New Jersey, and he had probably advised the duke of York not to surrender the west bank of the Delaware to WP. Although the duke recalled Andros from New York in 1682, when he became king he appointed Andros royal governor of the Dominion of New England, 1686-1689, and in the 1690s Andros was royal governor of Virginia.

# 49 §

## John Vines's Election Return

Whorekill alias Deal, 21 November 1682

Proprietary and Governor William Penn, Esquire, etc.

In obedience to thy warrant dated the eighth day of this instant to me directed, I did summon all the freeholders within this county to meet at this town on the twentieth instant to elect and choose out of themselves seven persons of most note for wisdom, sobriety, and integrity, to serve as their deputies and representatives in General Assembly to be held at Upland in the province of Pennsylvania the sixth day of December next. At which time the freeholders did then and there meet; and with a general vote they did elect and choose the persons whose names I here return unto thee according to thy order, and take leave to subscribe myself thy faithful friend and humble servant,

Edward Southrin,
William Clarke,
Alexander Draper,
John Rhoads,
Luke Watson,
Nathaniel Walker,
Cornelis Verhoofe.[1]

signed John Vines,
sheriff

MBE. HSP. (*PWP,* 2:312-13).

1. These seven representatives had all settled in Whorekill Co. during the 1670s or earlier. All of them had been local officeholders under the duke of York's administration,

and all of them except Nathaniel Walker continued to hold local offices under WP. William Clarke (d. 1705), a Quaker attorney, became one of WP's chief lieutenants in the lower counties; see docs. 67 and 69, below.

# 50 §
## Petition for an Act of Union

WP convened his first Assembly at Chester, formerly Upland, on 4 December 1682. There are a number of mysteries surrounding this legislative session. No membership list has survived, and whoever kept the minutes of the meeting did not make a full list of the laws passed or even indicate the name of the Speaker of the Assembly. Probably seven representatives came from each of the six counties — Sussex, Kent, New Castle, Chester, Philadelphia, and Bucks. There was as yet no Pennsylvania Council. Thus WP's first Assembly by no means conformed to his *Frame of Government* (doc. 30), which called for a Council of seventy-two members and an Assembly of two hundred members. WP seems to have called this hurried initial session as a device for bringing together the new Quaker colonists from Pennsylvania and the "old" non-Quaker colonists from the lower counties. If this was his intention, he succeeded very well.

The Assembly met for four days, during which time it established procedural rules; passed an act of naturalization for the Swedish, Finnish, and Dutch inhabitants; and approved many of the *Laws Agreed Upon in England* (doc. 30) that WP had published the previous spring. It refused, however, to confirm the charter that WP had granted to the Free Society of Traders (doc. 34). On 6 December, John Moll and Francis Whitwell, leaders of the New Castle and Kent County delegations, presented the following petition to the Assembly, asking that the three lower counties be united with the three Pennsylvania counties. The petition was signed by eighteen representatives from the lower counties; presumably, three members from Kent and New Castle were either absent or hostile to this petition. The Assembly immediately approved the petition, and the next day WP and the Assembly passed an Act of Union, by which the lower counties were annexed to Pennsylvania. This union lasted less than twenty years however. Friction gradually developed between the two regions, and in 1701 the lower counties separated from Pennsylvania and formed their own province of Delaware.

6 December 1682

To the Honorable Proprietor and Governor of Pennsylvania, etc.
The humble request of the freeholders of the three counties of New Castle, St. Jones's, and New Deal alias Whorekill,

Humbly desiring that they may be favored with an Act of Union by the Governor and Assembly, for their incorporation in and with the province of Pennsylvania, in order to their enjoyment of all the rights and privileges of the aforesaid province, and that they might be forever after esteemed and accounted as freemen of the before-named province. This being our desires and humble request in the Assembly, we have desired the President[1] and two other members of the upper county[2] part of this province to present it to your honor, and if we are so happy as to obtain our request, we will forever acknowledge it and in all faithfulness subscribe ourselves yours in all lawful obedience.

| For New Deal alias Whorekill[3] | For St. Jones's | For New Castle |
|---|---|---|
| William Clarke | Francis Whitwell | John Moll |
| Luke Watson | John Hillyard | John Cann |
| Nathaniel Walker | John Briggs | Casparus Herrman |
| John Rhoads | John Curtis | Richard Smith |
| Cornelis Verhoofe | Thomas ⊗ Heatherd his mark | John Darby |
| Edward Southrin | Daniel ⊗ Jones his mark | |
| Alexander Draper | | |

DS. HSP. (*PWP*, 2:318-20).

1. Dr. Nicholas More, president of the Free Society of Traders.
2. Christopher Taylor of Phila. Co. joined More in presenting the Assembly's bill of union to WP. The third cooperating assemblyman from the upper, or Pennsylvania, counties is unknown.
3. The seven Whorekill (Sussex) petitioners had all been elected to the Assembly on 20 Nov.; see doc. 49. Two of the St. Jones's (Kent) petitioners were illiterate, and so had to make their marks. All eighteen of the petitioners had settled in the lower counties before WP's arrival; most of them had been officeholders under the duke of York, and continued to hold local or provincial office under WP. However, Francis Whitwell and John Hillyard temporarily withdrew their allegiance from WP's government in 1684, when Lord Baltimore claimed authority over the lower counties; for this crisis, see doc. 93.

# 51 §

## To Justices of the Peace

ONCE the representatives from the lower counties had agreed with the representatives from Pennsylvania at the Chester Assembly of 4-7 December 1682 to unite in a single administration (see doc. 50, above), WP moved to standardize local government in his six counties. In late December, he sent a series of instructions to the justices of the peace, who served as the chief administrators of county business and as the judges of the county courts. In the following circular order, WP directed them to dispense justice fairly and wisely — a point of special significance in a society dedicated to virtuous conduct. He also called for a detailed census of all inhabitants and landholders in the six counties. If the justices compiled such a census, it would have given WP a clear picture of the settlement pattern in his new colony. However, only one census compiled pursuant to this order survives —a listing for part of Philadelphia County. See doc. 59, below.

New Castle, 21 December 1682

Since it has pleased God to put the government of the west side of Delaware River and Bay into my hands, I cannot but in good conscience endeavor to promote justice and righteousness among the inhabitants thereof, knowing that He who is the judge of quick[1] and dead will remember us for good, if we forget not Him, and that a government laid and begun by the line of equity and true judgment will not fail of prosperity. I therefore most earnestly recommend to you, who are the ministers of justice for the county you live in, vigilancy and fidelity, that you may neither neglect nor pervert justice, and in order thereunto, that you keep your courts with constancy and gravity; and that you have your ears open to hear all, as well the poor as the rich, and in all cases to judge according to the truth of the evidence, without fear, favor, affection, or reward, that God may bless you, and the people bless you, which seldom fails to be the reward of wise, just, and virtuous magistrates. So I bid you all heartily farewell. Given under my hand at New Castle, this 21st of 10ber 1682, being the second year of my government.

I do also think fit that an exact catalogue be returned to me of the names of all the people of your county: masters, mistresses, servants, parents, children. Also the number of acres each freeholder has, and by whom and when granted, all in distinct columns, with a mark on nonresidents that have claims.

D. Historical Society of Delaware, Wilmington. (*PWP*, 2:323).

1. Living.


# 52 ∫

## Minute of the Philadelphia Monthly Meeting

QUAKERS began meeting in Philadelphia as soon as the town was occupied. On 9 January 1683 they established the Philadelphia Men's Monthly Meeting for business, which supervised financial and disciplinary matters for several Quaker meetings for worship in the Philadelphia area. The meeting met at Christopher Taylor's house on Front Street, between

Walnut and Chestnut. The Quaker women set up their own separate meeting for business. Throughout Pennsylvania and New Jersey men and women established other local monthly meetings and, collectively, they formed the Philadelphia Yearly Meeting. The following are the first minutes of the men's meeting in Philadelphia. They give a good idea of how the Society of Friends took care of its business. The Friends appointed committees to oversee construction of a meeting house and to provide poor relief for needy members. And they started keeping records (for which Quakers are justly famous) of deaths, marriages, and the certificates that Friends were required to bring from their home meetings to show that they were good, upstanding members. Of particular interest here are the details of the marriage between Thomas Smith and Priscilla Allen, the first recorded marriage in the Philadelphia Monthly Meeting. The Friends in Pennsylvania apparently followed English Quaker marriage customs, which were very formal. The man and woman went first to the women's meeting, and then a female Friend introduced them to the men's meeting. This meeting requested the permission of both sets of parents, even if the couple were of age, and further investigated whether the couple were free of previous engagements and were good Friends. The couple returned to the men's meeting the following month, and if everything was in order, they were given permission to marry.

Philadelphia, 9 January 1683

The first meeting of Friends to treat of business occurring amongst themselves was at Philadelphia the 9th day of the 11th month being the 3rd day of the week in the year 1682, the proceedings whereof were as follows, viz.,

1. The Friends of God belonging to the meeting in Philadelphia in the province of Pennsylvania being met in the fear and power of the Lord at the present meeting place in the said city, the 9th day of the 11th month being the 3rd day of the week in the year 1682, they did take into their serious consideration the settlement of meetings therein for the affairs and service of Truth according to that Godly and comely practice and example which they had received and enjoyed with true satisfaction amongst their friends and brethren in the land of their nativity; and did then and there agree that the first 3rd day of the week in every month shall hereafter be the monthly meeting day for men and women's meetings for the affairs and service of Truth in this city and county, and every third meeting shall be the quarterly meeting of the same.

2. A fit place to build a meeting house in this city, as also the manner and form of building it being taken into the consideration of Friends, the whole was referred to the care and management of Thomas Holme,[1] John Songhurst, Thomas Wynne, and Griffith Jones[2] or any three of them; and that the charge thereof shall be borne by this meeting consisting of the Friends belonging to the said city.

3. It is agreed and concluded that necessary books be provided for the service of Truth in the said meeting, and that the persons aforesaid take care therein.

4. It is also agreed that the Friends of this meeting do bring in their certificates from the respective meetings of Friends they belonged to in other countries and that they be registered according to the time of their arrival here in this province.

5. It is agreed that the names of those Friends of this city and county that have deceased since their arrival be brought in and recorded in the monthly meeting book.

6. It is agreed, because some may through sickness, weakness, or death of relations be reduced to want or distress, that care shall be taken to administer present supplies; and John Hart and Henry Waddy[3] for the upper part of the county, and Thomas Bowman and Henry Lewis[4] for the city and lower part of the county, are appointed to visit the poor and the sick thereof, and minister what they shall judge convenient, and report the same to the next monthly meeting.

7. Thomas Smith of the County of Philadelphia, husbandman, and Priscilla Allen of the same, spinster,[5] having both appeared before a monthly meeting of Friends in this county at Shackamaxon,[6] and there declared their intentions of marriage if Friends standing in the counsel of the Lord saw good; and the said meeting having appointed Thomas Fairman on the man's part, and Ellen Cross on the woman's part,[7] to enquire of their clearness from all others. And the said Thomas Smith and Priscilla Allen appearing before this meeting and declaring their intentions of marriage as aforesaid, and Thomas Fairman and Ellen Cross having also reported the said persons are clear of all others to the best of their knowledge, and that the man's parents are deceased and the young woman's consenting, Friends are satisfied that they proceed to take each other as man and wife according to the good order and practice of Friends in the like cases.

8. It is agreed that the next meeting shall commence the first third day of the week in the next month about the 10th hour in the morning, and so consequently every public meeting to begin about the same hour of the day.

Adjourned.

MBE. Arch Street Meeting House, Philadelphia. (*PWP*, 2:333-37).

1. Thomas Holme (1624-1695), whom WP appointed surveyor-general for the colony in 1682; he held the post for life. He was elected to the first Assembly and sat on the Provincial Council. See pp. 320-21 and 337 for his famous maps, *A Portraiture of the City of Philadelphia* (1683) and *A Mapp of the Improved Part of Pensilvania in America* (1687).

2. John Songhurst (d. 1689), a carpenter originally of Chiltington, Sus., Thomas Wynne (d. 1692), a Welsh doctor and Quaker minister, and Griffith Jones (d. 1712), a prosperous glover of Bermondsey, Sur., were all First Purchasers and were prominent in the Pennsylvania government. Wynne was Speaker of the Assembly in 1683 and later served on the Supreme Court.

3. John Hart, a yeoman of Witney, Oxf., and Henry Waddy (d. c. 1694), a Middlx. milliner, were First Purchasers who immigrated in 1682. Both served in the Assembly; Waddy sat on the first grand jury of Phila. Co. in 1683.

4. Thomas Bowman, a glazier of Wandsworth, Sur., was the son of William Bowman, who purchased 5000 acres from WP. Thomas came on the *Amity* of London in Aug. 1682; in 1686 he sold his father's rights in Pennsylvania and returned to England the next year. Henry Lewis (d. 1690), a Welsh carpenter, bought 300 acres in Pennsylvania and was one of the founders of Haverford Twp. He served on the first grand jury of Phila. Co. in 1683.

5. Thomas Smith (d. 1692) owned the first brick-making business in Philadelphia, located in the Northern Liberties. Priscilla Allen was the eldest daughter of Samuel and Mary Allen, originally of Chew Magna, Somerset. She arrived with her family on the *Bristol Factor* in 1681.

6. In 1681-1682 Friends in the Philadelphia area met at Thomas Fairman's house in Shackamaxon, a short distance north of the site of Philadelphia.

7. Thomas Fairman (d. 1714), originally of Herts., had lived at Shackamaxon since 1680. He helped William Markham take soundings of the channel of the Delaware River and surveyed the site of Philadelphia. Ellen Cross has not been identified; she was perhaps the wife of Thomas Cross who sat on the first grand jury of Phila. Co. in 1683.


# 53 §

## *Naturalization of Swedish Inhabitants*

WHEN the Philadelphia County Court held its first session on 11 January 1683, seventeen Swedish settlers presented themselves and asked for the rights and privileges of citizenship. Three of these men, Swan Swanson (c. 1630-1696) and his brothers Wolle (1642-1693) and Andrew (1646-1694), held land along the Delaware on the site of Philadelphia, and WP traded with them for other land in order to obtain the river frontage he needed for his city. See the map on p. 214 for the lands held by other Swedes in this group. The Act of Naturalization passed by the Assembly in December 1682 gave landowning foreigners residing in Pennsylvania or the lower counties three months to be naturalized. They swore allegiance to the king of England and obedience to WP as governor, and paid a fee of twenty shillings sterling. By doing so, they received the same rights as their English-born neighbors.

[11 January 1683]

| | | |
|---|---|---|
| Lasse Cock | Eric Cock | Andrew Salem |
| Peter Rambo | Gunnar Rambo | John Stille |
| Swan Swanson | Peter Nilsson Laykan | Lasse Dalbo |
| Andrew Swanson | Christian Thomas | |
| Wolle Swanson | Eric Mullica | |
| Lasse Anderson | Peter Cock, Jr. | |
| Mouns Cock | John Boules | |

They whose names are above written, in obedience to a law of this

*First Swedes' Church and House of Swan Swanson, by John Fanning Watson, manuscript draft of* Annals of Philadelphia, *Vol. Two, p. 379, c. 1820-1850, HSP. In the 1670s the Swedes converted their log blockhouse at Wicaco into a church. This building was replaced in 1700 by Gloria Dei, also known as Old Swedes' Church.*

province for naturalization, appeared before this court and did there solemnly promise faith and allegiance to the king of England and his heirs and successors, and fidelity and lawful obedience to William Penn, proprietary and governor of the province of Pennsylvania and territories thereunto belonging, and his heirs and assigns, according to the letters patents and deeds aforesaid.

Copy. APS. (*PWP*, 2:337-39).

# 54 §

## To Jasper Batt

WP could write tender, loving letters, as we saw in doc. 39, above, and he could also write sharp, biting letters to people who disagreed with him. During the 1670s, when WP was passionately defending his religious ideas against opponents of many stripes, he wrote aggressive and abusive letters to those Anglicans, Catholics, Presbyterians, Baptists, and Quakers who disputed his beliefs. Now in the 1680s, he wrote in similar style to people who criticized his new colony. One example (doc. 28, above) is his bitter response to Algernon Sidney. Another is the following letter to Jasper Batt (d. 1702) of Somerset, a prominent English Quaker minister who had accused WP of grabbing too much wealth and power in the new colony. Batt also protested that the Quakers had no guarantee of political control in Pennsylvania: non-Quaker freemen might take over the government, and the proprietary Penn family might become idiots or atheists. Batt's critique clearly stung WP and he responded by pointing out the great labors, sufferings, and sacrifices he had personally experienced in becoming a Quaker, in founding a colony, and in immigrating to America. WP admitted that non-Quakers had come close to controlling the Pennsylvania Assembly of December 1682, but he remained committed to the principles of religious toleration, and to political freedom for all Pennsylvania colonists, Quakers and non-Quakers alike.

Chester, 5 February 1683

That the entailment[1] of the government of this province may be to David's stock, the tribe of Judah,[2] I close[3] with thee with all my heart. But tell me, how that shall be? It has been the earnest desire of my soul, that it might ever anchor there. Show us the way, and thou shall be the man. The power I have by patent runs thus: that I and my heirs, with the assent of the freemen or their deputies, from time to time may make laws, so [long] as they be not repugnant to the allegiance we owe to the king as sovereign.

I have given to the freemen all but a kind of tribute rather than pawn.

Three voices (which 3 servants, mark, that are out of their time will equal, that have but 50 acres apiece, while I have 3 millions perhaps[4]). Now, if these freemen and their heirs fear God, the entailment will be to David's stock; if not, how can I or mine help it? Which leads me to ask what security there is that their heirs may not be idiots and atheists as well as mine? And then what security shall my heirs have against such misusing this power to Truth's and their damage? And this only I might have answered to thy objection to me, viz., thou has provided against thy heir's being an infant, but not if an idiot or an atheist, etc.

But Jasper, I will suppose that thou intended that God's power among honest Friends should have the rule and dominion, and that is David's stock in spirit. With my whole soul, Jasper! But will thou secure [that] they or theirs shall not be corrupted as well as I or mine? Besides, tell me, what will these *Jethros, centurians, and Gamaliels*[5] think, who in outward things that belong to the spirit of a man, are rightfully interested as well as we and have wisdom as men? Shall they neither choose nor be chosen? If not, the patent is forfeited, for that right is founded upon civil and not spiritual freedom. The freemen of the province shall, etc.[6] Besides, we should look selfish, and do that which we have cried out upon others for; namely, letting nobody touch with government but those of their own way. And this has been often flung at us, viz., if you Quakers had the power, none should have a part in the government but those of your own way. On the other hand, if all that are freemen may choose or be chosen members of the Provincial Council and General Assembly, and that I and my heir have only 3 voices in 272,[7] in case they should outnumber us upon vote, we are gone; and this having been like to be done the last Assembly in choosing of a Speaker (Friends carrying it but by one voice, and that through the absence of two of the other side that were not Friends).[8] Friends have several of them lamented that I have given so much power away as I have done, at least until Truth's interest had been better settled, and [they] desire me to accept of it again, saying: that as God so signally cast it into my hand, and they believe, for a purpose of glory to His name and for the good of His people, and since the eyes and hearts of people are after me in so eminent a manner here, if I receive it not, they shall as yet be little regarded in the use of it. Come Jasper, I could speak largely of God's dealings with me in getting this thing; what an inward exercise of faith and patience it cost me in passing; the travail was mine as well as the debt and the cost. Through the envy of many, both professor, false friend, and profane, my God has given it [to] me in the face of the world and it is to hold it in true judgment as a reward of my sufferings, and that is seen here, whatever some despisers there[9] may say or think. The place God has given me, and I never felt judgment for the power I kept, but trouble for what I parted with. It is more than a worldly title and patent that has clothed me in this place. Jasper, keep in thy place; I am in mine, and have served the God of the whole earth since I have been in it. Nor am I sitting down in a greatness that I have denied, as thou suggests. I am day and night spending my life, my time, my money, and am not sixpence enriched by this greatness; costs in getting, settling, transportation, and maintenance now in a public manner at my own charge duly considered, to say nothing of my hazard and the distance I am at from a considerable estate, and which is more, my dear wife and poor children.

Well, Jasper, the Lord is a God of righteous judgment. Had I sought greatness, I had stayed at home, where the difference between what I am here, and was offered and could have been there in power and wealth, is as wide as the places are. No, I came for the Lord's sake, and therefore have I stood to this day, well and diligent and successful, blessed be His power, so that the 45 of Jeremiah and the 4-5 verse I send thee back again, and they that fear God, will rebuke thy application of it to me that know it.[10] My God has given sentence for my innocence in my own soul; nor shall I trouble myself to tell thee what I am to the people of this place in travels, watchings, spendings every way and my servants freely (not like a selfish man). I have many witnesses, but it is below me to do it, I mean in my place on God's account. I pretend to no more, nor no other in my answer to thee but as a Friend. And thy conclusion overthrows thy work. Thou says, "I desire thou may be sensible that I distinguish between property and government. *The first not questioned*, but good laws and government [are] that right which God gives to all and is not to be bought and sold."

Now Jasper, what civil right has any man in government besides property? At least without it, can a farmer, a copy holder, [or] an almsman[11] in England choose a Parliament man? Is it not men's freehold that entitles them to choose or be chosen a member to make laws about right and property? Is not this to their heirs? And is not English freehold entailed while they keep their lands; and will not Jasper allow me and my heirs as much as three 50-acre men, having in the government that have fifty hundred times more property? No, Jasper, thy conceit is neither religious, political, nor equal; and without high words, I disregard it as meddling, intruding, and presumptuous. However, in this I rejoice, that dear George Fox, Alexander Parker, George Whitehead, William Gibson, L[eonard] Fell,[12] J[ames] Claypoole, Christopher Taylor, and a hundred more honest Friends, have liked it to the present state of things, and the wise men of the world not a little admired it and valued Friends as a discreet people upon it. But all are, it seems, under thy judgment.

To conclude, it is now in Friends' hands. Through my travail and faith and patience it came (I let the cost alone). If Friends here keep to God and in the justice, mercy, equity, and fear of the Lord, their enemies will be their footstool; if not, their heirs, and my heirs too, will lose all and desolation will follow. But, blessed be the Lord, we are well and in the dear love of God and the fellowship of His tender heavenly spirit, and our faith is for ourselves and one another that the Lord will be with us a king and a counselor forever. So, Jasper, desiring thou may act more righteously than to smite the innocent behind his back, and thy suffering brother too, and that in a wrong matter and upon a false or an impossible ground, I take my leave and rest

Thy ancient though grieved Friend,
WP

ADf. HSP. (*PWP*, 2:346-49).

1. Limitation of political control or property to specified heirs.

2. The most powerful of the twelve tribes of Israel. King David, who in Hebrew tradition was the founder of the greatest Jewish dynasty, was a member of this tribe. In Christian tradition, David was the precursor or ancestor of Christ. To Batt and to WP, the Quakers were descended from the special stock, or house, of David.

3. Agree.

4. In his letter to WP (which has disappeared), Batt apparently complained that the *Frame of Government* reduced the freemen of Pennsylvania to the status of pawns or hostages of the proprietor, who had excessive personal power because of his three votes in the Provincial Council. WP denies both charges; he says that the Pennsylvania freemen enjoy complete independence except that they pay WP a quitrent or tribute, and he argues that the proprietor's treble vote is fair, considering how much more land he owns than the freemen, some of whom possess only fifty acres apiece. Actually, WP underestimated his holdings; under the 1681 charter his Pennsylvania property exceeded 25 million acres.

5. WP refers here to men who, while not of God's chosen people, behave justly, fear the Lord, and aid and defend God's people. His examples include Jethro, Moses's father-in-law; the Roman centurians who treated Christ's followers kindly; and the Jewish rabbi Gamaliel who defended Peter and the other Apostles at their trial in Jerusalem.

6. See doc. 11, sect. 4, above, which empowers the proprietor to make laws with the advice and consent of an assembly of freemen or their representatives. Freemanship in Pennsylvania is nowhere defined in religious terms in the charter of 1681.

7. Under *The Frame of Government* (doc. 30), the Council had 72 members, the Assembly had 200 members, and the proprietor, sitting with the Council, had a treble vote.

8. In the first Assembly of Dec. 1682, most legislators from the upper counties — Bucks, Chester, and Philadelphia — were probably Quaker, and most from the lower counties — Kent, New Castle, and Sussex — were non-Quaker. Complete membership lists for the first Assembly of December 1682 have not survived.

9. In England.

10. WP probably meant Jeremiah 45:4-5, which reads: "Behold, that which I have built will I break down, and that which I have planted I will pluck up, even this whole land. And seekest thou great things for thyself? seek them not: for, behold, I will bring evil upon all flesh, saith the Lord: but thy life will I give unto thee for a prey in all places whither thou goest."

11. In England, tenant farmers, long-term leaseholders (copyholders), and poor men supported by charity were all barred from voting for members of Parliament.

12. Alexander Parker (1628-1689), George Whitehead (c. 1636-1723), William Gibson (1629-1684), and Leonard Fell (1624-1699) were all leading English Quaker ministers who joined Fox in supporting WP's colony, although — unlike Claypoole and Taylor — they did not immigrate to Pennsylvania.

# 55 §

## To Lord Culpeper

WP kept in contact with the governors of neighboring colonies during his stay in America. He had special reasons for dealing with his immediate neighbor, Lord Baltimore, concerning the Maryland boundary (see doc. 64, below), and with the governor of New York concerning the Indian fur trade (see doc. 72, below). But he also wanted to win the favor of the king's chief representative in North America, Thomas, Lord Culpeper (1635-1689), the royal governor of Virginia from 1678 to 1683. In the following letter, WP urges Culpeper, who had been forced to return to Virginia against his wishes, to stay in America. Taking up his theme in *Some Account* (doc. 15, above), WP argues that the simplicity of the New World is far superior to "European cunning." Indeed, WP says he likes Pennsylvania so much that he is "like to be an adopted American." Culpeper did not agree; he soon returned to England without permission and was dismissed from his post.

Chester, 5 February 1683

My worthy Friend,

I received a letter from thee per Col. Ed[ward] Hill, recommending him in an interest he had in this province.[1] I was glad of any opportunity to express my inclinations to a good correspondence, and took the offer for a favor. How well I have acquitted myself, I cannot tell; but I am sure his credentials and his own worth deserved all the kindness [that] justice could allow, and if that be not done him (we are all mightily to blame for defects in form), he will place to the accounts of our infancy. I dare say, he will not prove an evil spy. His good nature will overrule his censure and palliate[2] our infirmities.

I was very glad to hear of thy arrival, not less that there was no need of it.[3] I mightily love that officious people should be disgraced by their over-business, as they are always sure to inherit the shame of time and inquiry. Yet in this we are beholden to them, that they have driven a man of quality and sense among us, to help to balance against the uneven weight of the other side of the world.

Pray stay, and let us be the better for thy coming. Here is more room for parts[4] with less envy, as well as more need of them. And to be happy in solitude is to live of a man's own, and to be less a debtor to the contributions of others.

I am mightily taken with this part of the world. Here is a great deal of nature, which is to be preferred to base art, and methinks simplicity with enough is gold to lacquer, compared to European cunning. I like it so well that a plentiful estate and a great acquaintance on the other side have no charms to remove, my family being once fixed with me; and if no other thing occur, I am like to be an adopted American.

Our province thrives with people; our next increase will be the fruit of their labor. Time, the maturer of things below, will give the best account of this country. Our heads are dull.[5] What fineness transplantation will give I know not; but our hearts are good and our hands strong.

I hear thou intends a progress into Maryland this summer.[6] If this place deserves a share of it, all that I can command shall bid thee welcome. I am, thou knows, an unceremonious man; but I profess myself a man of Christian decency, and besides a relation by my wife (whose great-grandmother was thy great aunt[7]), with all sincerity.

Copy. FLL. (*PWP,* 2:350-51).

1. Col. Edward Hill (1637-1700), a prominent Virginian, had visited Pennsylvania to claim a ship in which he had ⅞ ownership; the captain of this ship had sailed to Pennsylvania without his permission.
2. Excuse.
3. Culpeper had been ordered to return to Virginia to suppress the so-called Plant Cutter's Rebellion, in which Virginia tobacco growers had begun to destroy the current crop because of the low price of tobacco. However, by the time he arrived in Virginia, 17 Dec. 1682, the disturbance had already been put down.
4. For men of parts; persons of special talent, experience, or quality.
5. WP is not saying that the Pennsylvanians are stupid. Rather, he means that the future is unclear, that only time will tell what "fineness transplantation will give."
6. Culpeper met with Lord Baltimore in Maryland in May 1683.
7. Gulielma Penn's paternal great-grandmother was Susanna Partridge (d. 1603), whose mother in a second marriage had a son, Thomas Culpeper (1578-1662), the grandfather of Lord Culpeper.

# 56 §
## *Laying Out Philadelphia Lots*

ONE of WP's most important and most difficult tasks was to lay out his capital city. Originally (docs. 17, 22), he wanted to set aside 10,000 acres for Philadelphia, but since all of the choicest riverfront property along the western bank of the Delaware was already patented (see the map on p. 214), WP's commissioners had to settle for a much smaller site. In early 1682 they bought a tract, extending a mile along the Delaware River, from three Swedes, the Swanson brothers of Wicaco (see doc. 53 for their naturalization as citizens of Pennsylvania). Dissatisfied with this cramped area, WP acquired a mile of river frontage on the Schuylkill from two other Swedes, Peter Cock and Peter Rambo, parallel to his frontage on the Delaware. This gave him a rectangle of 1200 acres, stretching two miles in length from east to west between the two rivers, and one mile in width from north to south. Within this rectangle Surveyor-General Thomas Holme plotted his famous grid plan of the city, illustrated on pp. 320-21.

As laid out by Holme, Philadelphia had by far the largest acreage of any seventeenth-century North American town, but it was a much smaller place than WP had originally intended. He was thus forced to abandon his original scheme of granting one city acre for every fifty acres purchased, which would have given a 100-acre city lot to each First Purchaser of 5000 acres (see doc. 17). Instead, he apportioned lots of only one-half to one acre in his great town. First Purchasers who received less land in Philadelphia than they had been promised would be granted additional lands near the city. WP set aside about 8000 acres in what is now North and West Philadelphia as liberty lands for the use of the First Purchasers. Another change was to give land on the Schuylkill to First Purchasers who had not emigrated; in this way WP made the most desirable lots along the Delaware available for persons who were not among the First Purchasers but who were present in the province and ready to build.

Surveying on the Delaware side of town began in December 1682; by January several purchasers had cleared their land and built houses. Surveying began along the Schuylkill in April 1683, but this side of town would develop more slowly. The following exchange of letters between Holme and WP illustrates how these planners of Philadelphia worked out the survey of the city in detail.

17 March 1683

Governor:

I went yesterday with Christopher Pennock[1] to Schuylkill, and Richard Noble has not yet set out the Front Street there[2] and so is gone again today. And Christopher being concerned for his (now) own lot and Limerick Lot, as I am for Wexford Lot,[3] and Samuel Claridge [being concerned] in all 4 lots, if thou please to grant us liberty to take the 4 together where we think meet (the corner lots of the High Street [being] the promising place of advantage, we shall decline unless permitted by thee[4]), we are willing to set to work with all speed to build upon them, which may encourage others to do the like, seeing us begin. Please to favor us with thy order hereunder for this, that we may signify it to Ireland for the satisfaction of the concerned.

Thy friend to serve thee,
Thomas Holme

18 March 1683

Thomas Holme,

The side of the High Street next [to] my hill[5] and the two corners of the street answerable to thy house in that street[6] excepted, choose for the Irish lots.

William Penn

Copy. Division of Land Records, Bureau of Archives and History, Harrisburg. (*PWP*, 2:358-61).

1. Christopher Pennock (d. 1701), an Irish Quaker from Cork, bought land in Pennsylvania and was an agent for several other Irish purchasers. He represented Richard Pierce of Limerick (whose lot was probably the "Limerick Lot"), Samuel Claridge (1631-post 1714) of Dublin, and other Irish purchasers from Cork. These men had not immigrated to Pennsylvania and so received lots on the less-desirable Schuylkill side of town.

2. In Thomas Holme's original plan, the first street back from the Schuylkill (and also the first street back from the Delaware) was called Front Street. The streets then numbered in toward Center Square, beginning with Schuylkill 2nd Street and Delaware 2nd Street. Schuylkill Front Street, laid out in Mar.-Apr. 1683, was set well back from the marshy bank of the river, and became the present-day 22nd Street.

3. This lot was presumably intended for First Purchasers from Wexford, an Irish seaport.

4. Lots at the intersection of Schuylkill Front and High streets (presently 22nd and Market streets) were likely to become valuable if the Schuylkill riverfront developed commercially. Several of the Irish investors did receive their lots in this area.

5. WP probably means Fairmount, where he hoped to build a manor house for his son and heir, Springett Penn. He did not want Holme to plot the Irish investors' land north of Vine Street, the southern boundary of WP's manor land.

6. "Answerable" here probably means "corresponding to," that is, positioned as Holme's house was, on the other side of town at the corner of Mulberry (now Arch) and Delaware Front streets; this suggests that WP was reserving the intersection of Mulberry and Schuylkill Front streets for some other purpose or purchaser.

# 57 §
## Tavern Regulations

THE following document is the rough draft of an early law regulating taverns, or ordinaries as they were called. WP had initially considered prohibiting all taverns in Pennsylvania, but he changed his mind. Instead, he set out an elaborate series of regulations for the operation of the tavern— fixing prices and making other rules—as well as regulations for the behavior of the tavern's patrons. Doc. 57 illustrates the kind of social behavior WP and other Quakers considered unacceptable.

[c. 23 March 1683]

Laws and Orders for
the Keepers and Frequenters
of Ordinaries

Righteousness exalts a nation but sin is the shame of any people.[1]

Thou shall not keep an ordinary but by special license from the governor.

Thou shall not swear, the penalty 5 shillings or 5 days imprisonment at hard labor in the house of correction, and bread and water only.

Thou shall not curse, the penalty 5 shillings or 5 days imprisonment at hard labor in the house of correction, and bread and water only.

Thou shall not speak profanely, the penalty 5 shillings or 5 days imprisonment at hard labor in the house of correction, and bread and water only.

Thou shall not be drunk, the penalty 5 shillings or 5 days imprisonment at hard labor and work in the house of correction, and bread and water.

Thou shall not drink healths to provoke to drinking, the penalty 5 shillings.

Thou shall not sell strong spirits and liquors to the natives,[2] the penalty £5.

Thou shall not play at cards, dice, or suchlike vain and evil sports, the penalty 5 shillings or 5 days imprisonment at hard labor, and bread and water only.

Thou shall not speak seditiously, the penalty 20 shillings.

Thou shall not speak slightingly against any magistrate, the penalty 20s. or ten days imprisonment at hard labor in the house of correction.

Thou shall not report false news nor defame any person, the penalty that of a breaker of the peace.

Thou shall not clamor, scold, or rail, the penalty 3 days imprisonment in the house of correction at hard labor.

Thou shall not keep an ordinary without a license.

Thou shall not demand more than 6 pence for a meal of flesh meat and small beer. Thou shall not demand more than two pence for a Winchester quart[3] of strong barley malt beer. Thou shall not demand more than one penny for one Winchester quart of any molasses beer.[4]

Thou shall have stabling to hold four horses and hay for them, and ask no more than 6 pence for every night for each of them.

Thou shall have 4 beds for strangers and shall ask no more than two pence a night for one person's lodging and such only as travel on foot.

Thou shall not suffer any to stay in thy house after 8 at night, travelers and lodgers excepted.

Thou shall give an account to the next justice of the peace in the place, of the name of every stranger and traveler that comes to the house from time to time after daylight.

Thou shall not suffer any indweller of the place[5] to stay longer than one whole hour at one time in thy house, unless at a meeting of business.

Thou shall not suffer any disorder or breach of law in thy house on pain of the same punishment due to the transgressor.

AD. HSP. (*PWP*, 2:367-69).

1. Proverbs 14:34.
2. To the local Indians. Note how much larger this fine was than those for other offenses.
3. Standard measure. The official dry and liquid measures for a quart, gallon, and bushel were originally deposited at Winchester, England.
4. A light beer brewed from molasses and water.
5. Resident of the town. This regulation would prevent local residents from wasting too much time at the tavern, or mixing too familiarly with travelers who stayed at the tavern overnight.

# 58 §

## From James Claypoole

THIS letter from a Quaker merchant begins with a long passage, common in Quaker correspondence, in which James Claypoole describes his religious feelings. Notice how he is hinting that WP should take special pains to keep humble, "as low as the dust of the earth;" otherwise, he cannot carry out the Lord's service in Pennsylvania. Many of WP's Quaker friends worried that he was becoming too proud of his personal accomplishments in America. Another point of special interest in this letter is Claypoole's expression of admiration and devotion for George Fox, who had led the Society of Friends for nearly forty years and was now in somewhat frail health. But Claypoole is also much concerned with business matters. As treasurer of the Free Society of Traders, he is distressed to hear that this ambitiously designed commercial corporation (see doc. 34, above) is off to a poor start in Pennsylvania, and that the local colonists have refused to endorse its charter.

London, 1 April 1683

Dear Wm Penn

In the pure heavenly love by which we are brought nigh unto the Lord and unto one another, I salute thee, feeling as I have done oftentimes since thou went hence, the streams thereof flowing to our mutual comfort. I wrote to thee at large the 5th [of the] 11th month by Tho[mas] Singleton[1] who had a good wind for many days, so that we hope he might arrive with you above a month since. I had the sight of two letters from thee, one to G[eorge] F[ox] and one to A[lexander] P[arker] and G[eorge] W[hitehead], which were very acceptable to us, after the many wicked lying reports that were spread about concerning thee.[2] And indeed it was very comfortable to us to hear and see of the goodness of the Lord to you, and how eminently He did appear to your refreshment, and how His wisdom and authority was with thee and other Friends, so that the spirits of people, both high and low, were bowed and truth shined over all, and the name of the Lord was magnified. To Him be the praises forever, who fits His people for His service, and honors those that honor Him, and He will still keep you and prosper your ways, and increase His love and life and power and wisdom among you, as you keep low in His counsel, and have an eye to His glory above and beyond all. I know the Lord never did forsake such nor ever will, but attends them with His presence and carries them through all difficulties; but if we look out and have an eye to self, and take any part of God's honor, He will suffer us to be abased. Oh, I have found it great hindrance and hurt, when I have had precious gifts and openings, and an utterance has been given for the service of the Lord. Looking a little at self, I have been shut up and sorrow has come over me, and I have travailed in spirit and cried to the Lord many a time, that that might be removed out of the way that would exalt self, and thus hinders the work of the Lord. And truly my fervent desire still is that I may be kept in the simplicity, in tenderness, in fear and true humility, and be nothing but what the Lord will, that I may be as low as the dust of the earth as to His truth and service, and always empty unless the Lord fills me. I know it is always best with us when we are kept low, for the Lord beautifies the meek with salvation, and He teaches the humble His ways, and the high and lofty one that inhabits eternity and dwells in the highest heavens, He dwells also in the humble and contrite heart; and the beauty of humility shines most and is most amiable in persons that are set in high places. And this is a defense upon our glory which can never be stained while we keep here, so my prayers to the Lord is that thou and I and all God's people may be preserved in this tender, humble, contrite state, that we may go on in the work and service of the Lord to His praise and glory, and finish our testimony with joy, keeping always the assurance of an immortal crown of life that is laid up for us and for all the true Israel of God.

Two days since, I received thine to me and my wife[3] dated 29th 10th month, which was a great refreshment to us; and I take it very kindly that in the midst of such great concerns thou would remember us and write to us, two sides with thy own hand, for I believe thou has but little time to spare and many people to write to. Truly I value thy love and do hope I shall never lose that place I have in thine and the hearts of Friends, for it's part of my best treasure and I prize it beyond all outward things. The 20th instant, my wife and I with G[eorge] F[ox] and Bridget Ford[4] came to thy house at Warminghurst where we were very kindly entertained by thy dear wife and stayed there till the 26th, then came away, and that morning she and thy 4 children[5] were in good health. We had a comfortable time of it with George; I believe I shall never forget it, the benefit of his society is highly to be valued, that innocent, pure, heavenly, seasoning, savory life that appears always in him is as a continual meeting. Thou and the Friends in those parts are much engaged to him for his fatherly care for your good, and the good of the country, and [he] is so glad when he meets with anything of good advice that may be beneficial either inwardly or outwardly. We left him at John Rous's at Kingston,[6] where he is, I suppose, at this time. Our meetings are kept in the street still, and almost every day the informers and constables are at Friends' houses to distrain,[7] but I shall say the less because William Gibson[8] goes in this vessel (F[rancis] Richardson, master[9]) and can give thee a more full account.

I have not had one letter from Pennsylvania but thine. I wonder that neither my son John nor Edward Cole, my servant, nor Thomas Holme, John Goodson, R[alph] Withers, Dr. [Nicholas] More would not write me one line, yet I cannot tell what to think, unless some letters be miscarried or gone far about. Thou say thou has written to P[hilip] Ford about the [Free] Society [of Traders], but he tells me little but that the charter[10] was not confirmed by the Assembly, and that the president wanted assistants to carry on the affairs of the company; so that we are like to suffer, both in our stock and reputation. When it comes among the people[11] I am afraid they will say they are all cheated, for the charter or patent which thou signed was a great inducement to many to subscribe and to others to pay in their money that had subscribed, and we did not doubt but according to our desire and thy promise, the first Assembly would confirm the charter and choose assistants to manage the business. As to the president, he has no power but by a committee or court of assistants, and he and the other officers must see that their orders be performed; but if you leave him alone and will not afford him help, he may well be disgusted and let the company's concerns go to ruin, and that will greatly redound to the dishonor of Truth and the reputation of Friends both as men and Christians (thee as well as others) and be a great hurt to the country. So, dear William, I entreat thee, do not slight it, but get all things done in relation to the company to answer our engagements and the people's expectations. If the charter be uneasy, let it be mended; if it cannot be mended, lay it aside and make another, for a charter there must be, or the company cannot subsist. And then as to assistants, if some refuse, others may be chosen, and if not so many as the articles express, yet some there ought to be that may have the power and carry on the business to the people's satisfaction. I know it not, but I doubt there is some feud which the height of the president[12] possibly might occasion, but thou knows that it is meekness [which] must overcome haughtiness, and love must overcome enmity. He is a man [who] may be won and governed in love; but if he would not be persuaded, but be perverse and stubborn to the prejudice of the Society, he may by our first constitution and agreement be laid aside, and another chosen in his room. If R[alph] Withers would not act in my stead, he should not have taken it upon him, and then we should have taken another.[13] I think it is very unkindly done and I know not how he can answer it, but I do not conclude it to be so till I hear further.

I am still preparing to get away, and many have been my exercises and troubles with unreasonable men, but I have ended most of them. The greatest bar in my way at present is about £700 I have at Bremen and Hamburg, most of it in goods unsold, and my correspondent at Bremen lately dead and another there has played the knave with me, so but for that I would have been ready at this time. But I cannot well discharge all concerns here, to go away with a good repute, unless I have at least ½ that home, which I am now in good hopes of in 2 or 3 weeks, having sent a letter of attorney, etc. So I have agreed with one William Jeffries, master of the Concord, a ship of 500 tons, a brave, strong, good ship every way, and the master an experienced man that has been 7 or 8 times at Virginia. He is to be ready to set sail from Gravesend the 16th next month.[14] I am glad to hear our son John is employed in surveying, and take very kindly thy counselling of him. I hope he will reform and be a comfort to us at last.[15] I and my wife and 7 children are all in good health, and very well satisfied in our intended voyage, still believing that the Lord will bless us and carry us through to our joy and comfort. With mine and my wife's dear and sincere love to thee, I rest

Thy friend and brother in the blessed Truth

My dear love to C[hristopher] Taylor and his wife [Frances], J[ames] Harrison, R[alph] Withers, etc.

Sir T[homas] Clutterbuck[16] is dead.

I have had several letters lately from dear Robert Lodge. In one dated the 5th [of the] 12th month he writes that his wife was deceased,[17] and that the priest was so envious that he had indicted him and some other Friends at the sessions[18] for the burial, and the 21st [of the] 1st month he writes that he would gladly come to see us before we go away, but has not freedom to stir much from home, being in daily expectation to be taken to prison. He desires me in that letter to mind his dear love to thee,

J[ames] C[laypoole].

LBC. HSP. (*PWP*, 2:369-73).

1. Thomas Singleton (c. 1650-1685), the Quaker master of the *Thomas and Anne* which sailed from London for New York and Philadelphia in Jan. 1683.

2. Claypoole is probably referring to rumors that WP had converted to Catholicism. See doc. 76, n. 3.

3. Helena Mercer Claypoole (d. 1688), who married James in 1658.

4. Bridget Gosnell Ford (c. 1636-1710), who married Philip Ford in 1672.

5. Springett, Laetitia, William, Jr., and a daughter born in early Mar. 1683. See doc. 77, n. 1.

6. John Rous (d. 1696), a Barbados Friend who had returned to England. His wife, Margaret Fell (c. 1633-1706), was the daughter of Margaret Fox. Rous' house at Kingston-upon-Thames was near London.

7. When the London Friends were locked out of their two meeting houses in early 1683, they preached in the streets. The authorities then arrested and fined them, and when they refused to pay the fines, distrained or confiscated their property. Eight days after he wrote this letter, Claypoole himself was imprisoned for preaching in the street.

8. William Gibson purchased 5000 acres in Pennsylvania; if he came to the colony in 1683, his stay was short, for he died in London in 1684.

9. Francis Richardson, the Quaker captain of the *Endeavour,* which was loading cargo in London for a voyage to New York and New Jersey in Apr. 1683.

10. See doc. 34, above.

11. When the English shareholders in the Free Society of Traders learn of the Assembly's opposition.

12. Claypoole knew that Nicholas More, president of the Free Society of Traders, had an overbearing personality.

13. Claypoole was treasurer of the company; Withers, who came to Pennsylvania before Claypoole, had been appointed as his deputy, but apparently refused to serve.

14. Claypoole and his family sailed to Pennsylvania on this ship, but they did not leave until Aug. 1683, about three months later than Claypoole anticipated.

15. John Claypoole (1658-1700), eldest child of James, had gotten into trouble in Ireland before his father sent him to Pennsylvania in 1682. He served as assistant-surveyor, and later as sheriff of Phila. Co., but was eventually dismissed from the post for "lameness and misbehavior."

16. Sir Thomas Clutterbuck (d. 1683) owed a debt that Claypoole had been unsuccessfully attempting to collect for several years. At Clutterbuck's request, WP attempted to mediate the dispute, but Clutterbuck evaded several meetings before WP sailed to Pennsylvania. He had not yet paid the debt when he died.

17. Robert Lodge (1636-1690) was a Quaker butcher who bought 500 acres of Penn-

sylvania land. His wife, Esther, died on 26 Dec. 1682 and was buried two days later in a Quaker cemetery, thus depriving the local Anglican clergyman of his burial fee.

18. One of the local courts at which justices of the peace heard cases.


# 59 §

## Early Census of Philadelphia County Inhabitants

ON 21 December 1682 WP directed justices of the peace in each county to compile a census of all inhabitants and landholders (see doc. 51, above). This order was apparently not carried out. On 14 April 1683, in a follow-up to WP's directive, the justices for Philadelphia County ordered all freeholders to report their landholdings within three weeks or be fined twenty shillings each. Once again, this order seems to have been ignored by the newly arrived English colonists, but the Swedes who occupied the southern and western perimeter of WP's new capital city did make a return. The two lists printed below, compiled by Lawrence Dalbo for the Kingsessing district in present Southwest Philadelphia and by John Cock for the Passyunk district in present South Philadelphia, form the earliest census we have of residents in Pennsylvania.

Unfortunately, the census-takers did not follow WP's original instructions. They omitted women and children from their lists, and identified only males between the ages of sixteen and sixty, perhaps because men in this age bracket customarily paid a poll tax (head tax) and were enrolled in the militia —an institution which, of course, was nonexistent in Quaker Pennsylvania. Dalbo's and Cock's lists reveal that this group of Swedes, many of whom had settled within the limits of Pennsylvania a generation or more before WP founded his colony, were very simple wilderness farmers. They had considerable manpower at their disposal; about half of them had adult sons, brothers, servants, or black slaves in their households. The holdings of these Swedish farmers may look impressive when shown on the map on p. 214, but the landholders identified here owned about 250 acres apiece, of which a mere 12 acres were actually under cultivation. Thus when WP arrived, very little Pennsylvania acreage had been developed. This left much land for him to distribute to the new immigrants.

[post 14 April 1683]

By virtue of a warrant received from Benjamin Chambers,[1] I have taken a true account of all the male inhabitants from Peter Cock's Island to Anders Boon's and Carkoens Hook and along the Mill Creek to Peter Yocum's and Kingsessing to Cinnaminson[2] that are above 16 years of age to the age of 60 years and the quantity of land they hold and how much of the said land is clear.

By me
Lawrence Dalbo,[3]
Collector

| | years old | the quantity of land | whereof is cleared acres |
|---|---|---|---|
| Peter Cock[4] | 72 | 200 | 30 |
| Gabriel Cock | about 20 | | |
| Mats Handrix | about 21 | | |
| William Shute | 40 | | |
| Thomas Shute[5] | 17 | | |
| Anders Swanson Boon[6] | 63 | 750 | 60 |
| Swan Boon | about 22 | | |
| Peter Boon | about 19 | | |
| Andris Homan | 62 | 160 | 10 |
| Lawrence Homan | 20 | | |
| Banke Johnson | 50 | | |
| Hance Peterson | 35 | | |
| Luck Hank | 50 | | |
| Peter Ellitt | 40 | | |
| Lawrence Dalbo | 26 | 120 | 10 |
| William Dalbo | 23 | | |
| Andris Peterson | 26 | 150 | 10 |
| Jonas Nilsson | 63 | 200 | 8 |
| Mouns Nilsson | 20 | | |
| Renner Peterson | 25 | 50 | 8 |
| Mouns Justis | 25 | 250 | 10 |
| Charles Justis | 23 | | |
| Hance Justis | 21 | | |
| Justa Justison | 28 | 50 | 6 |
| Thomas Paschall | 46 | 500 | 4 |
| William Paschall | 18 | | |
| Thomas Rogers | 22 | | |
| Henry Love | 30 | | |
| Obadiah Hyerson | 17 | | |
| Neils Johnson | | 200 | 6 |
| Peter Yocum | 30 | 400 | 10 |
| John Minsterman | 36 | 100 | |

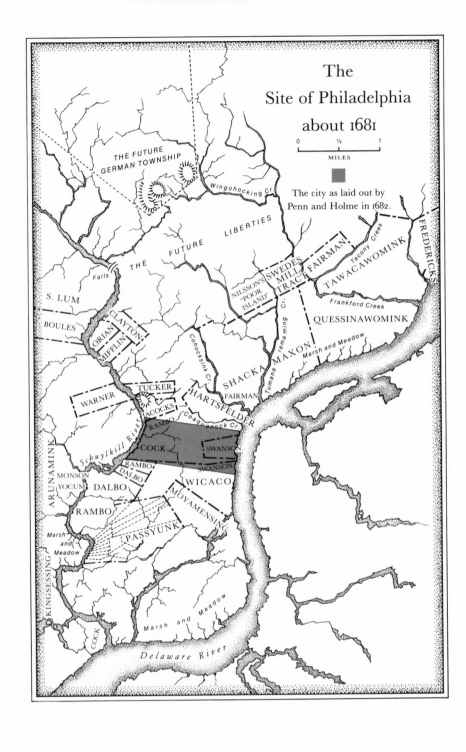

The
Site of Philadelphia
about 1681

0    ½    1
MILES

The city as laid out by
Penn and Holme in 1682.

THE FUTURE
GERMAN TOWNSHIP

Wingohocking Cr.

THE    FUTURE    LIBERTIES

Falls

S. LUM

BOULES

CLAYTON

ORIAN

MIFFLIN

WARNER

TUCKER

PACOCKS

HARTSFELDER

RAMBO

COCK

FAIRMAN

SHACKA MAXON

Cohocksink Cr.

Tumana

ramaming Cr.

NILSSON'S "POOR ISLAND"

SWEDES MILL TRACT

FAIRMAN

TAWACAWOMINK

Tacony Creek

FREDERICKS

Frankford Creek

QUESSINAWOMINK

Marsh and Meadow

Coaquanock Cr.

SWANSON

SWANSON

RAMBO

DALBO

WICACO

MONSON

YOCUM

DALBO

RAMBO

MOYAMENSING

PASSYUNK

ARUNAMINK

Schuylkill River

Marsh
and
Meadow

KINGSESSING

COCK

Marsh and Meadow

Delaware River

| John Nilsson | 300 [acres] |
|---|---|
| William Clayton, Jr. | 100 [acres] |

Moyamensing:[7]

Lars Anderson
Andros Binkson
John Matson
John Stille
Axel Stille
Andrew Wheeler

John Cock's Return:[8]

John Cock, aged 27 years, has 300 acres of land whereof he has improved 8 acres.

Lasse Cock, aged 37 years, has 550 acres of land whereof he has improved 30 acres.

Lasse Cock has a Negro 20 years of age. And a [servant?] named Bartholomew Sprint, 21 years.

Widow Jacob has 100 acres of land whereof there is 12 acres improved. Francis Jacob, her son living with her, aged 26 years.

Peter Cock, Jr., the younger, aged 25 years, has 100 acres of land whereof he has improved 3 acres.

Matthias Holstein, aged 41 years, has 150 acres of land where there is 12 acres improved.

William Snowden, aged 22 years, has 100 acres whereof there is 12 acres improved.

Peter Rambo has 600 acres of land whereof he has improved 16 acres.
Andrew Rambo, aged 25 years.
John Rambo, aged 22 years.

Peter Dalbo, aged 36 years, he has 600 acres of land and has improved 12 acres.

John Moenson, aged 45 years, has 300 acres of land and has improved 10 acres.
John Moenson, the younger, aged 22 years.

Dennis Rochford, above 16 years, has 160 acres of land and one acre improved.
William Askill, his servant.
John Swanson, his servant.

Patrick Robinson, aged 30 years, has 100 acres of land, improved 12 acres.
Robert Neverbegood, his Negro servant.

D and Printed Transcript. APS and *PMHB*, 7:106-7. Not published in *PWP*, Vol. Two.

1. Benjamin Chambers (d. 1715), the sheriff of Phila. Co., was a Quaker tanner from Kent who purchased 5000 acres of Pennsylvania land and immigrated in 1682.

2. This description of boundaries generally coincides with present-day Southwest Philadelphia. It begins with Peter Cock's Island in the Schuylkill River (see the map on p. 214), and follows Darby Creek north to Carkoen's Hook, the land on the east side of Cobb's Creek and Darby Creek. Then from Carkoen's Hook it follows Cobb's Creek, on which the Swedes built a mill in 1643, to Kingsessing, which ended at the west bank of the Schuylkill River. Cinnaminson is not readily identifiable, but should not be confused with the present town of that name in New Jersey. Many of the families mentioned in this list can be located on Holme's 1687 map of Pennsylvania.

3. Lawrence Dalbo (c. 1658-1721), whose father immigrated from Sweden, was a tax assessor for Phila. Co. in 1684.

4. Deleted on the original, perhaps because Cock was over sixty.

5. Deleted on the original.

6. Deleted on the original, perhaps because Boon was over sixty.

7. This list of residents of Moyamensing, in eastern South Philadelphia, was deleted on the original, probably because Moyamensing was not part of Dalbo's district.

8. John Cock (c. 1656-1717), son of the Swedish immigrant Peter Cock, Sr., was constable for the lower part of Phila. Co. His list identifies the residents of Passyunk, along the east bank of the Schuylkill River in South Philadelphia.

# 60 ∫
## To John Blaykling and Others

IN this letter to four Quaker ministers in northern England, WP considers the state of his "holy experiment" six months after his arrival in Pennsylvania. In effect, he is answering the charge, leveled against him in one form or another by English Friends such as Jasper Batt (doc. 54) and James Claypoole (doc. 58), that he is too much the lord proprietor and too little the humble servant of God. WP does not indeed sound very humble in this letter, but he insists that the founding of Pennsylvania is the work of the Lord: Friends' meetings are large, non-Quakers "flock in" to worship, and Pennsylvania is already, in important respects, a better country than England. In painting this rosy picture, WP slides over the awkward fact that many of the colonists, particularly the non-Quakers, were opposed to his pet ideas. He must have been upset when in December 1682 the first Assembly refused to accept without modification the *Frame of Government* which he had worked on for so long in England. The next Assembly, held in March and early April 1683 (see doc. 62), approved a revised *Frame* but questioned WP's authority and pressed for the right to initiate legislation. The issue of individual rights versus corporate authority, which had played such an important role in WP's career, had thus arisen in yet another form. In England,

WP had asserted during the Wilkinson-Story controversy, a dispute within the Society of Friends concerning the establishment of meetings to oversee Friends' behavior, that a religious group had the right to define orthodoxy among its members. From the royal government he had demanded religious liberty for dissenters. Now in Pennsylvania, he was confronting this broad issue in still another way, for his own authority as governor and proprietor was being challenged by Quakers who believed that he was becoming corrupt, and by non-Quakers who were not members of his community.

To John Blaykling, Thomas Camm, Thomas Langhorne,
  and Robert Barrow

From Pennsylvania, 16 April 1683

My dear Friends[1]

You are often remembered of me because you are beloved of me in the Lord's everlasting Truth, which is truly precious; and because of the sweet and heavenly communion that is therein, do we dearly love one another; and this love no waters can quench,[2] nor time nor distance wear away. It is some of the sweet comfort and consolation of our pilgrimage, which is hid out of the sight of the world, whose kindred is from below. Dear friends, in this hidden and eternal relation do you feel me, who have blessed the day in my soul; that it was brought into the fellowship of it. Oh! What is there to be compared unto it, beloved friends, that in the daily and fresh enjoyment of this glorious fellowship of life does spring! That we all may be kept to run our way, serve up our day in time, and in the end lay down our heads in peace.

I bless the Lord it has been well with me in this solitary land. It is a land of springs — blessings flow amongst us from the ocean of them: heavenly are our assemblies[3] and large, and the people flock in that are not Friends. Truth's authority is raising, I hope, an example to the nations; and they that see not the service of this providence will finally confess that it is of the Lord. All do not (as well as some will not) equally see the mind of the Lord therein; but some will see it and rejoice, and I believe some shall see it and be ashamed for their hard speeches. Oh! That I may be kept in my place, for that end the Lord has called me, in this unexpected thing. His ways are unsearchable and past finding out; for He it is that in His own time reveals them. He has placed His name in some measure upon me. I pray that He may be glorified by me, that in the end I may reap an everlasting inheritance. I know my weakness, but I also know His strength, and He is able to glorify Himself, and serve His poor people by me, in which I would not that any should be offended, for that will not be for their good. This country abundantly answers in good land, air, water, and provision naturally, doubtless a better country than our own in some respects. The General Assembly, about a month since, passed 83 laws, and all but 3, and those trivial, without any nay. The Living Word, in testimony and prayer, opening and closing our Assemblies in a most heavenly manner, like to our general meetings.[4]

I have your city lots ready; for your country ones, you must hasten over some servant, together, or else the comers will thrust you backwards, though the back lands be the best, one in three.[5] And the fishing of the rivers I have made free,[6] as well to such as live back as those that are upon them. And here families get in many barrels [of fish ?] in a week for winter store, [and] very good they are. Here is enough both for poor and rich, not only for necessity, but pleasure.

I have little more to add but my love to you and yours, and the Lord's true people among you, hoping in His blessed time to see you here. Yet strange things are coming to pass; and Oh! Amen may I say in the vision of the Lord, glorious things are [determined?] of thee. Oh! Thou solitary land! The Lord keep us in all our stations, that His will may be done in us and by us, to His praise, so that we go home at last to the mansions of our Heavenly Father with everlasting rejoicing. Amen, Amen!

I am, my dear Friends in the blessed Truth, your faithful, tender friend and brother

William Penn

Copy. FLL. (*PWP*, 2:375-77).

1. John Blaykling (1625-1705) and Thomas Camm (1641-1708) were both Quaker ministers who purchased land in Pennsylvania but did not emigrate. Thomas Langhorne (d. 1687), also a Quaker minister, purchased 500 acres in 1681 and emigrated in 1686. Robert Barrow (d. 1697) was a mason and Quaker minister who purchased 300 acres in 1682 but did not emigrate until 1694, when he was shipwrecked en route to America and captured by unfriendly Indians. He died in Philadelphia in 1697.

2. Song of Solomon 8:7.

3. Quaker meetings.

4. The minutes of the second Pennsylvania Assembly, which met in Philadelphia from 10 Mar. to 4 Apr. 1683, are printed in doc. 62, below. This Assembly was not nearly as peaceable as WP's comment might suggest. The assemblymen demanded the right to initiate legislation, and they objected to the governor's veto. At least six bills were rejected in their original form.

5. WP seems to be claiming that the interior land in Pennsylvania is three times as good as the land first taken up by the colonists, close to the Delaware.

6. WP's comment on fishing illustrates his adaptability to the changing demands of his settlers. In his "Concessions to the First Purchasers" (doc. 17), he had granted land-owners the sole right of fishing in rivers and streams that adjoined their lands. On 21 Mar. 1683, however, members of the Assembly requested that the rivers and creeks be opened to everyone for fishing and hunting. This bill became part of the second *Frame*, and WP now sees it as his policy.

# 61 §

## *From Joseph Harris*

THE early settlers in Pennsylvania often found that there were draw-backs to buying land sight unseen. The following letter airs the complaints of one pioneer. Joseph Harris (d. 1688) was a young, single Welshman who had lived near London; he arrived in Pennsylvania only to discover that he could not get the land he had expected. He wanted a town lot, which after "7 weeks with daily promises" he did not get. And the competition for land along the Schuylkill River was so intense that Harris found, to his annoyance, he would get only half of the river frontage he had planned on. But Harris was obviously an aggressive young man. He asks WP for a job, offering to manage the ferry across the Schuylkill or to be his bookkeeper. Harris seems poorly qualified for the latter post, since his letter is barely literate. Further, Harris wants permission to marry; see doc. 52 for the procedures he had to follow in order to take a Quaker bride.

Schuylkill, 19 May 1683

Governor:

Since I had the happiness to speak with thee, who gave me to understand that I must lose half the land, which I am well satisfied in, leaving all to thee. Though it is true we came here through great danger and hardship, having our goods spoiled by reason of our long voyage, after which we stayed 7 weeks with daily promises of our town land. At last when we saw [that] it was in vain to wait any longer, I got orders from thy deputy for 500 acres and it was surveyed by C[harles] Ashcom,[1] and I would know who must pay for the surveying of that which is taken away; and when my cousin [William] Powel[2] comes he will expect half this land which is too little for us both. If we had meadow and a few [acres] on the Schuylkill, [it] is and will be worth a great many in the woods. So we shall be at a loss and some may think hard to be one of the first comers and had endured the blunt for to lose part of their land. But for my part I am well contented, being well satisfied therein that I shall not be a loser by it, leaving all (as thou did mention) to thee in that point.

I have received a letter lately (dated the 7th of January) from my father wherein he does advise me to come to thee for advice and counsel, likewise one from Richard Davies[3] which does signify that he has paid my £24 to Philip Ford and that R. writ to thee concerning me, for I did hint in one of my letters that I heard the money was not paid, all the business being left to R. Davies, which was the cause I had not my deeds. Dear and loving friend, I am a young man and [far] from all my natural friends and relations and am now in this wide world to shift, hoping that through my friends' help and my own industry [I] shall be able in time to provide for myself. And if thee has any employment for me whereby I may have a moderate way to live, or else I must go down the river to Blackbird Creek[4] where I have bought 225 [acres] of land which is a good place for stock and I do think to settle myself or servants so soon as I have supplies from England, which if I do light of[5] any employment will be helpful. I hear that the ferry[6] is to be kept near where I am settled, and I have and could make the most convenient place for it. Though at low water here is a marsh, but with a small charge a way may be made and could so come here and have supplies from below for the accommodating a house, though I believe it will not quit charge[7] at present; therefore there must be a consideration thereof. And if I do undertake this occupation, I must desire supplies from thee and pay it in England, expecting from there enough whereby a man with industry may live happily.

And my father does signify that my brother, which is 10 years of age, and a servant, will be over this summer with William Powel and his family. And though I am single at present, yet people is not always of the same mind, especially if on the contrary be to their convenience; for a man cannot well be without a wife in this part of the world, which I hope I shall not long be. And we do entreat thee to give thy consent therein. For though I have not a certificate,[8] yet I have sufficient witnesses which know my friends, namely John Southworth,[9] C. Owen, T[homas] Jones,[10] [and] Nathaniel Harding,[11] and am clear from any such thing in that particular, as I writ to my friends to acquaint them thereof, and did hint that it was the duty of a child to ask his parents' consent. Yet I shall be my own chooser. For if I fail in my expectation, the blame will fall to me which shall be most concerned therein. For it is good to consider matters well on both parties and not to be fiddling and make business of nothing [but] hearing themselves talk, which sometimes proves to both parties' hurt, not only for the present but also the future. And I suppose proposals thereof will be made in a small time.

I shall live convenient for business and near where thee intends to build, and if thee has any occasion for me in any particular that I am capable of for keeping accounts, I understand enough for an [ordinary position?] and hope [I] shall be found faithful in whatsoever I am intrusted withal to the utmost. It is true my grandmother Margaret Davies has bought me 1250 acres,[12] which is more than I shall know what to do withal, and it will be more a pullback than a helper. I do desire £20 for a 1000 acres of land which is not yet taken up[13] with what addition thee pleases to make for the use of the money and trouble, and I shall have land enough still: 125 here, 225 on Blackbird Creek, and 125 acres which I lost on Schuylkill, and shall take it up behind my land below only allowing the 25 acres in marsh. And whereas I must pay two bushels of wheat, I hope thee will let it be as land bought in England,[14] being but a small matter. So, desiring thee to consider my proposals and pass by the errors and plainness, I being one which am not complimental but express myself in homeliness and reality, I shall [remain?] with my kind love to thee, desiring thee to remember the helpless, from thy everloving and faithful subject

whilst Joseph Harris

ALS. HSP. (*PWP*, 2:385-88).

1. Charles Ashcom (d. 1727), a Marylander, was deputy-surveyor for Chester Co. In 1687, he disputed with Thomas Holme over the accuracy of his surveys in the Welsh Tract and the payments due him for them.
2. William Powel, of Southwark, Sur., was a First Purchaser of 1250 acres who settled in Phila. Co. His exact relationship to Joseph Harris has not been determined.
3. Richard Davies was a leading Welsh First Purchaser; see doc. 95, below.
4. Blackbird Creek, in New Castle Co., Del., flows into the Delaware River.

5. Meet with.

6. Ferry across the Schuylkill.

7. Earn a profit.

8. A certificate from his Quaker meeting in Wales or England establishing that Harris is free to marry and is not engaged to a woman at home. The editors have found no record of Harris's marriage in the early Quaker records of Pennsylvania, New Jersey, or Delaware, but he was married to a woman named Rebeccah when he died in 1688.

9. John Southworth was a First Purchaser of 500 acres who acquired a city lot on Second St., between Walnut and Chestnut, and 300 acres in Phila. Co.

10. Harris probably means Thomas Jones (d. 1723), a Welshman who in Apr. 1683 bought 156¼ acres of land from Charles Lloyd and Margaret Davies (see n. 12, below). In 1684, Jones's mother, Katharine Thomas, bought land on the west side of the Schuylkill adjacent to Joseph Harrison, possibly the author of this letter.

11. Nathaniel Harding (d. 1699), a Quaker basketmaker, was the constable for upper Phila. Co. in 1683.

12. Margaret Davies, a widowed Friend of Dolobran, Mont., Wales, teamed with a near relative, Charles Lloyd, and six other Welshmen to buy 10,000 acres from WP. Half of this land was held by Lloyd and Margaret Davies; they sold 1250 acres to Harris on 29 June 1683 for £25, and 156¼ acres to Thomas Jones (n. 10, above) on 24 Apr. 1683.

13. Since Harris has more land than he needs, he apparently wants to sell back 1000 acres to WP for £20.

14. Harris wants to have the privileges of a First Purchaser, including the right to a town lot. His grandmother Margaret Davies was a First Purchaser, but when she transferred part of the grant to Harris, she could not automatically transfer her First Purchaser privileges to him.

# Part VIII

THE PENNSYLVANIA
GENERAL ASSEMBLY §
10 MARCH 1683–4 APRIL 1683

*WP's signature and his Provincial Seal attached to the Philadelphia City Charter, 1701, Philadelphia City Archives.*

PENNSYLVANIA'S legislative session of 10 March–4 April was by far the most important in the early years of the colony. The previous Assembly held in December 1682 (see doc. 50, above) had been a hastily improvised session, in which some forty-two assemblymen met with WP for only four days. The General Assembly of March–April 1683 was a much more elaborate affair in every way. Two separately organized legislative chambers met twice daily for nearly a month. Still, this General Assembly was not as large as WP had originally intended. When the freemen of the three Pennsylvania counties and the three lower counties gathered in February 1683 to choose representatives for this session, they informed WP that they were unable to elect twelve councilors and over thirty assemblymen from every county, as called for in the *Frame of Government* (doc. 30, articles 2, 3, and 14). Instead, the freemen chose three councilors and nine assemblymen from each county. Thus WP's first two-house legislature consisted of eighteen councilors and fifty-four assemblymen. Though several of these legislators never showed up, and others were absent much of the time, an important feature of the March–April session was that the leading inhabitants from the six counties came to know each other, and to work closely together, over an extended period.

When the six county sheriffs presented the councilors and assemblymen to WP on 10 March, he told the members of the General Assembly that "they might amend, alter, or add" to the constitution that he had drawn up for Pennsylvania, and both houses quickly began to press for substantial changes. The assemblymen wanted a more active voice in making laws, the councilors wanted a simpler committee system, and everyone wanted a smaller legislature than was provided for in the *Frame of Government*. When WP saw these pressures building for change, he asked the legislators to sign a declaration of loyalty to him, and urged them to do nothing that might invalidate his royal charter. On 19 March, the governor, Council, and Assembly agreed upon the first major legislation of the session, an Act of Settlement. This act reduced the size of the Council and Assembly, moved the provincial elections and legislative sessions from late winter to early spring, gave the governor effective veto power over Council actions, and authorized the Council and Assembly to vote by voice rather than by secret ballot in all legislative matters.

The Council and Assembly were not yet satisfied, however, and on 20 March WP told both houses that he was willing to accept a revised or second *Frame of Government* in place of the constitution that he had prepared and published in England. Much of the rest of the session was devoted to the drafting of this second *Frame;* it was eventually approved by the governor, Council, and Assembly on 2 April. Meanwhile, the Council drafted and the Assembly approved a new code of laws to replace WP's published *Laws Agreed Upon in England* (doc. 30, above). Many of these laws were copied directly from WP's *Laws,* but others were newly devised. Altogether, the governor, Council, and Assembly passed eighty-one new laws in this session, and the Assembly ratified fifty-two laws that had been enacted in the December 1682 Assembly. The new code dealt with such issues as criminal justice, moral behavior, land development, the regulation of business and commerce, taxation, the regulation of the labor force, fees paid to provincial officials, and local court procedures. Finally, during the course of this legislative session the governor, Council, and Assembly adopted a set of parliamentary procedures, largely borrowed from English practice, that regulated the working relationships between the three branches of government. Thus when the assemblymen adjourned to their homes and farms on 3 April, and the councilors on the following day, they had established a functional constitutional system.

Doc. 62, below, combines the daily journal kept by the clerk of the Provincial Council with the daily journal kept by the clerk of the Assembly in order to show how Pennsylvania's pioneer legislators operated day by day, and how the councilors and assemblymen interacted with each other. Doc. 63 presents the chief legislative enactment of this session, the second *Frame of Government,* which served as Pennsylvania's operating constitution for about a decade, starting in 1683.

## 62 §

## *Minutes of the Provincial Council and Assembly of Pennsylvania*

THE following daily record of the proceedings of the Provincial Council and Assembly from 10 March through 4 April 1683 combines the journal kept by Richard Ingelo, clerk of the Council, with the journal kept by John Southworth, clerk of the Assembly. The two records frequently overlap, but since both of these clerks often neglected to mention matters of importance, one must read the proceedings of both houses, day by day, in order to reconstruct the events of this session. The Council and Assembly minutes are discreet and formal in character; they devote much space to parliamentary procedure and little space to substantive or controversial issues. Thus we learn that Speaker Thomas Wynne took the chair at a particular hour and called the roll, or that there was a debate over a given bill, but we do not discover who spoke for or against this measure, or what the arguments were, and so we cannot tell why some bills were passed unanimously, others by a majority vote, and still others were defeated. The role of the governor is particularly elusive. The minutes tell us that WP presided over every Council meeting and that he made a number of speeches to the Assembly, but they rarely indicate what he said or did.

Nevertheless, the clerks' attention to procedure helps us to understand the differing character of the two houses. The Provincial Council, presided over by the governor, was designed by WP to be much more powerful than the Assembly. It was a relatively small body, especially since several of the eighteen councilors were frequently absent. The Council initiated all legislation and allocated the drafting of bills to a series of subcommittees (see the Council entries for 16 March, 21 March, 26 March, and 30 March). It also heard petitions and advised the governor on his executive decisions. The Assembly was intended to play a much more limited role: to accept or reject the Council's bills. But a careful reading of the following minutes shows that the lower house was constantly trying to expand its influence through frequent conferences with the governor and Council. During the March–April session, the Assembly did effectually participate in the drafting and revision of legislation. Speaker Wynne seems to have been a forceful manager who steered the assemblymen away from direct confrontation with the governor and Council; he was also a stickler for regular attendance and orderly behavior.

If WP hoped that his legislature would operate in a Quakerly spirit of brotherhood and achieve a harmonious consensus, he was doomed to disappointment. In 1683 the governor, Council, and Assembly had differences that could not be fully resolved. Indeed, the experience of meeting together for three and a half weeks seems to have made each branch of government more conscious of its own particular constitutional powers and privileges. But the General Assembly did work out a series of compromises that preserved WP's plan of government in modified form. Although the formal record of events in doc. 62 cannot reveal the full passion and tension of this three-cornered contest, the Council and Assembly journals do tell us quite a bit about how the early Pennsylvania government worked. The reader is particularly directed to the following entries in the minutes:

10 March, Council: The temporary reduction of the Council from 72 to 18 members, and of the Assembly from 200 to 54 members.

12 March, Assembly: A proposal that the Assembly receive the right to initiate legislation, rather than simply react to bills sent down by the governor and Council. WP did not yield on this point until 1701.

13 March, Council: The alteration of the Council quorum from forty-eight (for a seventy-two member Council) to twelve (for an eighteen-member Council).

14 March, Assembly: Debate on reducing the size of the Council and the Assembly for the coming year.

15 March (a.m.), Assembly: Discussion of whether to grant WP veto power so that he could prevent the legislature from passing any law that might violate provisions of WP's royal charter for Pennsylvania, which could result in his losing his colony. The Assembly decides to allow WP a veto of his Council's votes, but not of the Assembly's.

15 March (p.m.), Assembly: The first reading of the bill which became the Act of Settlement; this act reduced the size of the Council and Assembly for one year and formed the core of the revisions that became incorporated in the second *Frame of Government*.

15 March, Council: The Council agrees to the Assembly's decision to give WP a veto over Council votes, but not over Assembly votes.

19 March, Assembly: The House approves the final version of the Act of Settlement.

20 March, Council: The Council and Assembly jointly resolve to replace WP's first *Frame of Government* (doc. 30, above), with a new *Frame of Government*.

27 March, Council: The Council enlarges WP's power to establish courts and appoint officers; this change is incorporated into the new *Frame of Government*.

21 March–2 April, Assembly and Council: The two legislative houses work out the details of the second *Frame of Government*.

3 April, Assembly: WP permits the Assembly to initiate further legislative proposals.

The text of the Council and Assembly journals printed below is nearly complete. The clerk of the Council began each daily entry with a roll call which has been omitted here except for the opening entry on 10 March. In the Assembly, each bill was read three times before final action was taken, following the practice of the English House of Commons, and since no new information is supplied to the reader by the reports of these second and third readings, they have been omitted here, except for an illustrative example on 16–17 March. Omitted passages have been indicated by ellipses ( . . . ).

*Provincial Council*

PRESENT:

William Penn, Proprietary and Governor of Pennsylvania and territories annexed.

| | | |
|---|---|---|
| Capt. William Markham | Ralph Withers | James Harrison |
| Christopher Taylor | John Simcock | William Clarke |
| Thomas Holme | Edmund Cantwell | Francis Whitwell |
| Lasse Cock | William Clayton | John Richardson |
| William Haige | William Biles | John Hillyard |
| John Moll | | |

Then the sheriffs of each county were called in, viz.:

For the County of Philadelphia . . . . . . . . . . . . . John Test
For the County of Chester . . . . . . . . . . . . . . Thomas Usher
For the County of Bucks . . . . . . . . . . . . . . . Richard Noble
For the County of New Castle . . . . . . Edmund Cantwell
For the County of Kent . . . . . . . . . . . . . . Peter Baucomb
For the County of Sussex . . . . . . . . . . . . . . . . John Vines

The Governor ordered that one speak at a time, standing up, with his face to the Chair.

A debate being about the balloting box, the question was put whether the ballot should be used in all cases? Passed in the negative.

The question being put whether they would have the ballot in all personal matters? Resolved in the affirmative.

The question being put whether all bills should be passed into the laws by vote?[1] Resolved in the affirmative.

The returns of the sheriffs being read, with the petitions and addresses of the freemen to the Governor, and finding therein that the people have amply vested their 12 delegates out of each county with power to act as the provincial councilors and General Assembly. And it being proposed to the elected members aforesaid, if they were chosen to serve in both those capacities, they answered they were: that is to say, three of each twelve for the Provincial Council, and the remaining nine of each twelve to constitute the General Assembly, according to the returns.

After the reading of the returns and petitions, the Charter of Liberties[2] was read. Which requiring a greater number than was chosen to serve in Provincial Council and General Assembly, yet left to be explained and confirmed by the Governor, his heirs, and assigns, and the freemen of this province and territories, in Provincial Council and Assembly met, the deputies of the freemen in Provincial Council and Assembly do think the reason alleged in the sheriffs' returns and petitions of the freemen for not choosing more than 12[3] to serve in Provincial Council and General Assembly are sufficient, and that the seventy-two now chosen and returned have in them the power of the whole freemen of this province and territories thereunto belonging, and so [are] capable of serving as a Provincial Council and General Assembly.

A member moving that the Governor may be desired that this alteration may not hinder the people from the benefit of this Charter [of Liberties], because it seems thereby to be returned to him again by not being accepted as largely as granted. The Governor answered, they might amend, alter, or add for the public good, and that he was ready to settle such foundations as might be for their happiness and the good of their posterities, according to the powers vested in him.

The numbers to be increased by the Governor and Council, freemen in Provincial Council and Assembly met.

Upon the whole matter the Assembly went to choose a Speaker.

Adjourned till 12th of 1st month 1683.

12 March 1683

*Assembly*

Members elected for each county, as follows,

| *Kent* | *Bucks* | *Chester* |
|---|---|---|
| John Briggs | William Yardley | John Haskins |
| Simon Irons | Samuel Dark | Robert Wade |
| Thomas Hassold | Robert Lucas | George Wood |
| John Curtis | Nicholas Waln | John Blunston |
| Robert Bedwell | John Wood | Dennis Rochford |
| William Windsmore | John Clowes | Thomas Brassey |
| John Brinkloe | Thomas Fitzwater | John Bezar |
| Daniel Brown | Robert Hall | John Harding |
| Benoni Bishop | James Boyden | Joseph Phipps |

| *Philadelphia* | *New Castle* | *Sussex* |
|---|---|---|
| John Songhurst | John Cann | Luke Watson |
| John Hart | John Darby | Alexander Draper |
| Walter King | Valentine Hollingsworth | William Futcher |
| Andros Binkson | Casparus Herrman | Henry Bowman |
| John Moon | John DeHaes | Alexander Molestine |
| Thomas Wynne, Speaker | James [Walliam] | John Hill |
| Griffith Jones | William Guest | Robert Brassey |
| William Warner | Peter Alricks | John Kipshaven |
| Swan Swanson | Henrick Williams | Cornelius Verhoofe |

By the king's authority and special command of William Penn, proprietary and Governor of the province of Pennsylvania and territories thereunto belonging, by his writs issued forth to the sheriffs of each respective county for the election of the members of Assembly of parliament, being the deputies of the freemen of the province, etc., met at Philadelphia at the time aforesaid; and the names of the several members of each county were read over, then proceeded to choose their Speaker; and by the assent of the whole House, Thomas Wynne[4] (one of the elected members) is chosen Speaker of the House, whom the members having presented to the Governor, as Speaker, the Governor being very well satisfied therewith, approved of their choice.

They return again, and the Speaker being seated in the Chair, adjourns the House to the fourth hour in the afternoon.

About the fifth hour in the afternoon, the House sat, the Speaker assumes the Chair, and puts the House in mind of the intent of their coming, gives them advice suitable to their present undertakings, and bids them be mindful of their duties towards one another.

The Speaker then reads the orders and decorum of the House, both towards him as Speaker, and one towards another;[5] he reads their method to be observed in debates, and that every matter ought to be debated in the House before it can be put to vote.

It was moved by the Speaker, whether the Charter [of Liberties] of the province should be read over? Voted for, and carried in the affirmative.

The Charter was accordingly read, and then by the clerk delivered into the Speaker's hand.

A debate arose touching the select numbers mentioned in the Charter for members of Provincial Council and General Assembly, but immediately ceased.

A debate [arose] whether the fourteenth article of the Charter[6] should first of all be taken into consideration of the House, but in the end, for the present, ceased.

A very good proposal was made by a member of the House that it might be requisite, by way of petition or otherwise, to move the Governor and Provincial Council that the House might be allowed the privilege of proposing to them such things as might tend to the benefit of the province, etc., which possibly the Governor and Council might not think of, nor of very long time remember, which might, in the interim, tend to the great detriment of the province, etc.

The Speaker calling it to remembrance, reproves several members of the House for neglecting to convene at the time appointed when the House last adjourned.

A bill was sent from the Governor and Provincial Council to the Assembly, touching their fidelity and allegiance to the Governor, requiring subscription of their names, etc., but at the present was suspended.

Proposed to the House, whether they are willing to move the Governor and Provincial Council that they might be invested with a privilege of conferring with them. Voted, and carried in the affirmative.

The Speaker, with William Yardley and Thomas Brassey, members, were by the general consent of the House appointed to entreat of the Governor the privilege of conference above mentioned. Voted for, and carried in the affirmative.

By consent, the Speaker adjourns the House to the ninth hour the next morning.

*Provincial Council*

[16 councilors in attendance].

It being reported to the Governor and Council by several members of it, that Nicholas More, president to the Society of Free Traders in this province, took occasion in company in a public house,[7] to utter these words against the proceedings of the Governor, Provincial Council, and Assembly, as that: "They have this day broken the Charter [of Liberties], and therefore all that you do will come to nothing, and that hundreds in England will curse you for what you have done, and their children after them, and that you may hereafter be impeached for treason for what you do." Whereupon the Governor and Council did order that Nicholas More should appear before them. He accordingly did appear, and being charged with such discourse, said that he spoke rather by query than assertion, and if he had said as it was represented, he had been to blame indeed, but he said that he spoke not with such an intent. However, his discourse being unreasonable and imprudent, he was exhorted to prevent the like for the future.

Adjourned till 13th of 1st month 1683.

13 March 1683

*Assembly*

About the tenth hour the House sat. The Speaker assumes the Chair. The names of the members were called over, and several being wanting in the Assembly, occasioned the Speaker to reprove them as they came for neglect of attendance.

Then the Speaker declares the Governor's answer, touching their request for conference with him and the Council, which answer was condescential[8] to their request.

A debate arose in the House, concerning sundry needful things as might require the aforesaid privilege of conference with the Governor, etc., concerning them.

Moved by a member of the House, touching that power which the member said the Assembly was invested with, to debate concerning bills to be sent into the House by the Governor and Provincial Council. And it was debated and further argued, that the House presuming to take that power aforesaid seemed too much to infringe upon the Governor's privileges and royalties, and to render him ingratitude for his goodness towards the people. Several of the members agree that (the Governor's goodwill and demeanor towards the people being considered) they are all in duty bound, rather to restore that privilege [which] in his too great bounty he has conferred upon them, viz., of having the power of giving a negative voice, etc., to the bills proposed unto them by himself and Provincial Council, than to endeavor to diminish his power.

The Governor, etc., sends to the Assembly for conference with them. Put to the vote, whether the Assembly should resort to the Governor, etc., according to his desire or not? The number of votes was decided by beans put into the balloting box; and by the major[ity of] votes, it was carried in the affirmative.

The Assembly removes to the Governor and Council and confers with them. Afterwards return, and the Speaker reassumes the Chair. He advises the Assembly to take into serious consideration the good counsel of the Governor, as touching that weighty matter of their establishing a government for future ages, etc.

A test[9] requiring fidelity and lawful obedience from the members of Assembly to the Governor was twice read, and after reading, it was concluded by general vote of the House, that Griffith Jones and John Cann, two members, should be employed to demand of the Governor, etc., whether that test had been signed by the Provincial Council.

They return and bring answer that it was signed by the Provincial Council; therefore the whole Assembly subscribed their names to the aforesaid test.

The Speaker adjourns the House till the fourth hour in the afternoon precisely.

About the time appointed, the House met again.

The Speaker having assumed the Chair, orders the members' names to be called over; some of them being wanting, the Speaker sends the doorkeeper for them.

The House waits in expectation of bills from the Governor and Provincial Council. In the interim, one of the members of the House moves that a way might be considered of by the House, how every member might defray his particular charges during his attendance in the House for the country's service; which motion the Speaker putting to vote, it was carried in the affirmative, viz., that the Governor and Provincial Council should be addressed unto by the House touching that matter.

A debate arose in the House concerning the absence of some members, where their neglect of due attendance is generally observed; and they therefore concluded by the present members of the House to merit some severe penalty for the same.

The Governor sends for one of the members of the House to come and speak with him; whereupon the Speaker orders William Yardley, one of the members, to wait upon him. He returns, and signifies that the Governor by him informed the House that what matters of moment himself and the Provincial Council did intend to present to the House were at present unprepared; and therefore desires the House to adjourn themselves until the next day; whereupon,

The Speaker adjourns the House till the ninth hour the next morning.

*Provincial Council*

[15 councilors in attendance].

William Haige desiring leave to be absent this day, it was granted him.

Thomas Wynne, Speaker, accompanied with Thomas Brassey and William Yardley, members of the Assembly, came in the name of the whole Assembly to desire a conference with the Governor, which the Governor and Council yields to.

The result was this:

That twelve makes a quorum in all business relating to the former part of the fifth and sixth articles of the Charter [of Liberties] relating to the latter part of the same article. That during the present infancy of things, that the business of four committees in the 13th article be performed by the Council for the time being, in such way and manner as their numbers will give leave. Whereas it is said in the 7th article of the Charter, that the Governor and Provincial Council shall prepare and propose to the General Assembly all bills that they shall at any time think fit to be passed into laws within the said province and territories, it be added: "provided they are not inconsistent with the powers granted by the king's letters patents."[10]

Adjourned till 14th of 1st month 1683.

14 March 1683

*Assembly*

About the time appointed the House sat, the Speaker assumes the Chair, and orders the clerk to call over the burgesses' names, which was accordingly done. And the Speaker orders the clerk to set down the names of such members as were absent yesterday and are now absent without leave of the House; which was done accordingly, and delivered to the Speaker.

The Speaker stands up and reproves the members that absent themselves as aforesaid for their neglect of attendance.

The Speaker proposes to the House to debate amongst themselves, whether or not it be requisite that any of the members of the House shall be tolerated to absent themselves from the House without license from the Speaker and all the other members of the House? Whereupon a debate arose in the House concerning that matter; the result whereof was that all members absenting themselves from the House without license shall, for the future, be very considerably fined according to the discretion of the present members. This was voted throughout the whole House.

The Speaker reads to the House the orderly method of Parliaments and the demeanor of the members thereof observed in England, which he recommended to them as civil and good: as also the method observed by the English in committees.[11]

One of the members moves that the Charter [of Liberties] may be read again; but another member moving for a general register as a thing more material to be taken into consideration, the first motion was at present excluded. A debate arose in the House touching the register.

The Speaker reads the twentieth article, touching enrollments and registers;[12] whereupon the debate touching registers still continued a while, but ceased at length without determination.

Proposed by the Speaker, that the House should be adjourned till the fourth hour in the afternoon, which was generally agreed unto.

The Speaker adjourned the House till the fourth hour in the afternoon.

About the time appointed the House sat. The Speaker having assumed the Chair, ordered the members' names to be called over, who were all present except two, who were disappointed through sickness.

Proposed, that two members be sent to the Governor and Council to be informed whether they had any present business for the Assembly or not;

put to the vote, and carried in the affirmative. Whereupon Griffith Jones and John Songhurst, two members, were elected for that purpose. They return and signify to the House that some business would immediately be sent them from the Governor and Provincial Council.

A debate arose in the House, touching the number of members of the Provincial Council, intimating their number to be too great; as also the same touching the number of members of Assembly, but nothing relating thereto determined.

The Governor sends for two members of the House, and ordered by the House that John Cann and William Yardley be sent unto him. They return, and signify that the Governor and Provincial Council desire the attendance of the whole House.

Whereupon the House withdraws to attend the Governor, etc., as was desired. The House after some time returns; the Speaker reassumes the Chair and refers to the House's consideration the good disposition and wisdom of the Governor [and] the excellency of his speech unto them before the Provincial Council.

Another member hints at the undeserving reflections and aspersions cast upon the Governor, which the Governor himself and all good members and subjects do, not without cause, resent as evil from any subject, but especially proceeding from any of the members of Assembly.

The Speaker adjourns the House till nine in the morning.

*Provincial Council*
   [16 councilors in attendance].
   The Provincial Council resolved into a grand committee, while the Governor retired upon urgent business. Capt. William Markham, chairman. They received and read several petitions, but referred their answer to the Council.

Adjourned till two of the clock in the afternoon.
                              Post Meridiem.
. . . The petition of Abraham Mann, John Test, and John Vines, sheriffs, about establishment for their fees was read, and ordered that a table of fees should be forthwith established.[13] . . .

The petition of the inhabitants of Duck Creek[14] about the cutting of the way through the marsh for vessels to pass was referred to the county court in which the same does lie.

Adjourned till 15th of 1st month 1683.


                                                          15 March 1683
*Assembly*
   About the time appointed the House sat. The Speaker assumes the Chair and declares to the House that notwithstanding so many cautions, several members still neglect attendance. Voted, that each absent member shall pay, for the future, twelve pence sterling for their neglect. Whereupon orders were writ concerning the same and set upon the House door.

A member of the Provincial Council acquaints the House that the Governor and Council desire the attendance of the whole House. Whereupon the burgesses'[15] names being called over, immediately withdrew to the Council house.

About half an hour afterwards the House returns, the Speaker having assumed the Chair, orders the members' names to be called over again, who were all present except two that were finable, and some few others that were sick.

The Speaker prudently states and refers to the consideration of the House the proposals of the Governor, made to them in the Council house, as touching a counter security from them to him, viz., the Governor, "in case they forfeit his patent by enacting such laws as are contrary to the grant and tenure thereof, more especially considering that he, out of his great love and kindness, has granted the people a Charter [of Liberties] whereby they have the privilege of establishing laws themselves and giving a negative voice to all bills preferred unto them by the Governor and Provincial Council, if they approve them not." Whereupon a debate arose in the House touching the matter.[16] In the interim of the debate, the clerk of the Provincial Council and some members thereof bring in a paper, touching which the Provincial Council desires conference with the House.

The Speaker reads the paper which related to the Governor's security, etc., from the people, or power given him from the people to secure himself. The Council and Assembly debate the matter contained in the said paper and touching security to the Governor, as aforesaid,

Proposed to the vote of the House, whether the Governor shall have the power of an over-ruling voice in the Provincial Council and in the Assembly? As to the Provincial Council, it was carried in the affirmative, N.C.D.[17] But as to the Assembly, it passed in the negative.

By order of the Speaker, the House adjourned till the third hour in the afternoon.

About the time appointed the House sat. The Speaker having assumed the Chair, orders the clerk to call over the names of the members; several being absent, are fined by order of the Speaker.

The Governor sends for a bill tendered to the House in the forenoon, but not read in the House, deeming it then improper to be exposed to the view of the House. The Speaker, with two other members, return the bill into the hands of the Governor and Council, then return and report it to the House.

A member proposes that the Governor and Council might be moved, that some means may be by them prescribed for the recording of the minutes and transactions of the court,[18] viz., some order for the providing of books, etc., for that purpose. This was put to vote, and resolved in the affirmative, viz., that such motion should be made.

The clerk of the Provincial Council brought a bill into the House touching a method to be observed in proceedings of the Provincial Council and General Assembly: the time of their sitting, the manner of their establishing of laws, with the title to be prefixed unto such laws as are by them enacted, etc.

This bill, by order of the Speaker, was read by the clerk. After some debate on the said bill, the clerk was ordered to read over again some part of it, which was accordingly done, and finding in the said bill some variations from the printed Charter [of Liberties], it was put to vote whether the fourteenth article of the printed Charter should stand firm, together with those variations thereof in the bill, and it was resolved in the affirmative. The clerk, by command of the Speaker, reads the latter part of the bill; then it was put to vote, whether the whole bill, together with the printed Charter (the explanation of the said Charter mentioned in the bill being also admitted) should stand firm or not, and it was resolved in the affirmative.

The clerk, by order of the Speaker, adjourns the House to the third hour in the afternoon the next day.

*Provincial Council*

[13 councilors in attendance].

Ordered that John Richardson[19] pay five shillings for being disordered in drink and be reproved.

The question being put whether the Governor should have power to secure himself, his heirs, and assigns? It was resolved in the affirmative.

The question being put whether two of the members of this Council should go to the House of Assembly to have a conference about it? Resolved in the affirmative.

A conference was held with the Assembly and they withdrew to consider of it, and returned this answer by the Speaker. And John Cann [reported] that the Assembly have *Nemine Contradicente* agreed that all laws should be prepared and proposed by the Governor and Council.

Adjourned till three of the clock in the afternoon.

Post Meridiem.

The Governor yet again offering that if they had any other expedient yet to offer or propose, they might, though they had agreed to it in the morning. And after some consideration it was put to the question whether another expedient could be found out more safe to the Governor and people? Passed in the negative. It was resolved (none dissenting) that the words "jointly assenting" should be added to that part of the bill relating to the [seventh] article of the Charter.[20]

Thomas Pearce's petition concerning a sloop he bought for the service of the [Free] Society [of Traders] was read, and his allegation not being proved, the matter fell.

Adjourned until 16th of 1st month 1683.

16 March 1683

*Assembly*

About the time appointed the House sat. The Speaker having assumed the Chair, orders the clerk to call over the names of the members; which done, he proposes to the House, that the bill read yesterday might be read over a second time, which the House assented to. The bill, by order of the

Speaker, was read in the House, whereupon a debate arose, touching the number of members of Assembly thought meet for election; this being a while debated, it was put to vote, whether six members in each county were by the House thought a competent number for the Assembly the next year? The question being put, it was resolved in the affirmative.

The bill having been read a second time, the question was put to the House, whether the said bill (the alteration of it at the second reading being admitted) should stand firm or not, and it was resolved in the affirmative.

James Boyden, a member of the House, desired the liberty of departing the House for three days, his occasions being urgent, which was accordingly granted him. Little more business presenting itself, the question was put to the House, whether they were willing to be adjourned till the third hour in the afternoon the day following, and it was resolved in the affirmative.

John Blunston and George Wood, two members of the House, desired that they may have liberty of the House to depart for two days, which was accordingly granted them.

The Speaker adjourned the House to the third hour in the afternoon the day following.

*Provincial Council*
[15 councilors in attendance].

A letter received from Nicholas More, president of the [Free] Society [of Traders], to the Governor, desiring that the law against fornication might be explained not to extend to servants, because the present penalty would be to the master and mistress, wherefore prayed some severe punishment may be enacted more consistent with the master's and mistress's interest. [21]

These bills were prepared and drawn up to pass into laws:
A bill for planting flax and hemp.
A bill for building a house of correction in each county, 24 foot by 16.
A bill to hinder the selling of servants into other provinces and to prevent runaways.
A bill about passes. [22]
A bill about burning woods and marshes.
A bill to have cattle marked and to erect bounds.
A bill about fencing.

Three committees appointed to prepare bills for the Council:

| [1] | Capt. William Markham | Francis Whitwell | William Clarke |
| | | John Simcock | John Hillyard |

The paper of proposals from Kent County committed to them to put into a bill or bills.

| [2] | James Harrison | John Moll | Edmund Cantwell |
| | | Christopher Taylor | Ralph Withers |

To whom it is referred to prepare bills about prisons, sowing of hemp and flax, runaways, passes, selling of servants into other provinces, for destroying wolves, to raise money, and a bill for hog stealers.

| [3] William Clayton | William Biles | Thomas Holme |
| William Haige | John Richardson | Lasse Cock |

To whom is referred the burning of woods and marshes, to have cattle marked, to erect bounds of fences.

Adjourned till 17th of 1st month 1683.

17 March 1683

*Assembly*

About the time appointed the House sat. The Speaker having assumed the Chair, ordered the clerk to call over the burgesses' names; being called, all the members were present, but those that had leave of the House.

The Speaker advises the members to observe good order in the House, then orders the clerk to read the bill a third time, which being read accordingly, the Speaker put the question to the House, whether the bill (with the foregoing day's variations, to stand only for one year next ensuing) should stand firm and unalterable, as a part of and appendix to the printed Charter [of Liberties], except [as] altered by assent of six parts of seven of the General Assembly, consisting of the whole Provincial Council and whole Assembly. This question being put, it was resolved in the affirmative, viz., that it should so stand as now hereby is expressed.

The whole House now withdraw to the Council house to consult touching the bill, and to be certified by the Governor and Provincial Council whether they will pass the said bill, admitting the variations made in it by the House.

The House returns. The variations in the bill having passed in the Council house were ordered by the Speaker to be read by the clerk; the clerk according to order read the said variations a first, second, and third time. This done, the Speaker put the question to the House, whether the variations aforesaid should be admitted in the bill, and so the bill accepted as part of and [as] an appendix to the printed Charter [of Liberties]? The question being thus put, it was resolved in the affirmative.

The House withdraws to the Council house to make report that the abovesaid variations, etc., had passed the House. The House immediately returns, and brings back the bill, etc. Some variations therein concluded on in the Council house were openly read in the House three times; then the Speaker put the question to the House, whether the said variations should stand firm with the bill and printed Charter?

The question being thus put, it was resolved in the affirmative.

The Speaker, by consent of the House, orders the clerk to bring in a fair copy of the bill, together with the variations therein, against the next day of sitting. This done, he adjourned the House till the eighth hour in the morning, being the 19th day of the 1st month.

*Provincial Council*

[13 councilors in attendance].

The committees presented several bills to the Council, and adjourned till three of the clock in the afternoon.

Post Meridiem.

The Speaker and the whole House of Assembly attended the Governor and Council with a Bill of Settlement, acquainting them that he was commanded by the whole House to let them know they had passed the bill with one consent.

Adjourned till 19th of 1st month 1683.

19 March 1683

*Assembly*

About the time appointed the House sat. The Speaker having assumed the Chair, calls for a copy of the bill, which is now called *A Bill of Settlement*.[23] The clerk delivers the aforesaid bill, together with its variations, into the Speaker's hand.

By the Speaker's order, the burgesses' names were called over, they being all present, except such who had license from the House for their absence.

The Speaker addresses himself, touching the bill and its last variations. After some debate arose in the House, the bill's variations were read thrice; then the Speaker put the question, whether the bill, together with those last variations, should be admitted? The question having been thus put, it was resolved, N.C.D., in the affirmative, viz., that it should be admitted.

The House withdraws to the Council house, and there reports to the Governor and Council that the whole House had admitted the aforesaid variations in the bill. This done, two members of the House, Griffith Jones and Robert Wade, were appointed to bring the bill fairly engrossed, with its variations, to the Governor and Council; which they did accordingly.

William Clarke and Francis Whitwell, Thomas Holme, and James Harrison, four members of the Provincial Council, exhibit a bill to the House, touching some material provisions tending to the good of the province. Upon reading this bill, a proposal therein occurred, relating to some means whereby wolves might be destroyed; whereupon a debate arose in the House touching that matter, but as yet left undetermined.

By order of the House, adjourned till the third hour in the afternoon.

About the time appointed the House sat; the Speaker having assumed the Chair, ordered the names of the members to be called over; several members not coming into the House at the time appointed, ordered by the Speaker to be fined. But at their coming [and] making a reasonable plea for their absence, by consent of the other members of the House their fines were remitted.

A debate arose in the House, touching an article in the new bill, last before mentioned, relating to the burning of woods and marshes. The Speaker after this debate put the question, whether the first day of the first month, every year, should be fixed on for that purpose? And by general consent, it was resolved in the affirmative, that that article should stand.

Another article in the bill was read to this effect, viz., that every person departing this province shall leave upon the court door of the county whereunto they belonged, a bill of their departure, with their names, etc. The question being put, it was resolved in the affirmative that that article should stand.

Another article relating to a penalty for taking away of boats or canoes was read, debated on, put to the question, [and] generally resolved in the affirmative that that article should stand.

Another article was read, that all freeholders and purchasers in the province, not living in the province, etc., shall pay suitable taxes for their non-service to the province, etc. The question being put, it was resolved in the affirmative.

Another article relating to some means to be used for the destruction of wolves was read, etc. Being long debated, it was in the end concluded, viz.; the question was put, and it was resolved in the affirmative, etc., that that article should stand.

Another article was read, touching every county's care for building houses of correction, etc., for offenders in their respective counties. This was debated on, and the question being put, it was resolved in the affirmative.

Another article was read touching the propagation of hemp and flax, with its use and price; after debatement, the question was put, and it was resolved in the affirmative.

Another article was read touching runagate[24] and absenting servants, their penalties, etc. After debatement, the question was put, and it was resolved in the affirmative.

Another article was read touching unknown persons and servants, their limits of traveling, and their passes, etc. After debatement, the question was put, and it was resolved in the affirmative.

Another article was read touching a fine to be levied on masters and mistresses that shall sell their hired servants before their time of service be expired. The question being put, it was resolved in the affirmative.

Another article touching the presentment of a wolf's head, etc.[25] The question being put, it passed in the negative.

Another article was read touching the marking of cattle, etc. After debatement, the question was put, and it was resolved in the affirmative, etc.

A fine of five shillings upon default of any member's absence for one whole sitting, by general vote of the House, concluded to be paid by every member so offending.

Night approaching, the Speaker adjourned the House until the eighth hour the next morning.

*Provincial Council*

[14 councilors in attendance].

The Speaker with divers members came with the Bill of Settlement and divers amendments, which were yielded to by the Governor and Council.

Several bills relating to, carried by order of Council to the Assembly by William Clarke and Francis Whitwell.

Several bills relating to, carried by order of Council to the Assembly by Thomas Holme and James Harrison.

The Bill of Settlement, being amended, was returned to this Council by two of the members of the Assembly, namely, Robert Wade and Griffith Jones.

The petition of the mariners belonging to the *Friend's Adventure*[26] concerning their wages was read, and ordered that they shall have a hearing tomorrow at three of the clock in the afternoon.

Adjourned till four of the clock [in the] afternoon.

Post Meridiem.

Ordered that William Clarke and John Moll compare the fees of New York and Delaware,[27] and make a report to this Council.

Ordered that Capt. Edmund Cantwell and John Moll turn over the Duke's Laws,[28] and give a report proper for them to consider on.

Adjourned till 20th of 1st month 1683.

20 March 1683

*Assembly*

About the time appointed the House sat, the Speaker assumed the Chair, ordered the members' names to be called over; then read the bill (article by article) that was read the day before.[29] . . .

All things, matters, and suits of £10 sum or above depending in any inferior court in this province, in case of appeals to the Provincial Council, etc., shall there be heard. This article (its contents being put to the question) it was resolved in the affirmative, viz., that this article should stand. . . .

This done, no more business presenting, the Speaker adjourned the House till the third hour in the afternoon.

About the time appointed the House sat; the Speaker having assumed the Chair, orders the clerk to call over the burgesses' names.

Walter King, one of the members (his occasions urging) had leave given him of the House to absent till next sitting.

The Speaker moving that two members of the House might be chosen to go and report that the bill had passed after the second reading (with its variations) to the Governor and Council. The House chose the Speaker himself, as also John Songhurst and William Yardley, two other members, to officiate in that undertaking. Whereupon they absent from the Assembly to the Council house. After the expiration of about half an hour, the Speaker and members aforesaid return and report to the House that the Governor and Council desire conference with the whole House, whereupon the whole Assembly withdraws to the Council house. After the expiration of about one hour, the House returned.

The Speaker reassumed the Chair, reiterated the Governor's kindness, and the increase thereof proposed by him, to be mentioned in the Charter [of Liberties] at the new engrossing[30] thereof.

In the interim, Thomas Holme, and Lasse Cock, John Moll and John Simcock, four members of the Provincial Council, bring in some bills into the House, to be taken into the consideration of the House.

These bills were read once, and confirmed by the House.

By general consent of the House, Thomas Hassold, Griffith Jones, John

Darby, John Blunston, Thomas Fitzwater, [and] Luke Watson, six members of the House, were elected out of the six counties to compose and present to the Governor a salutation, by way of the House's acknowledgment of his kindness, etc.

Night approaching, the Speaker adjourned the House till the ninth hour the next morning.

*Provincial Council*

[13 councilors in attendance].

Adjourned till three of the clock [in the] afternoon.

Post Meridiem.

The Speaker, with two of the members of the Assembly, attended the Governor and Council with several bills that were sent up to them, after which the Governor and Council desired a conference with the whole House and freemen about the Charter [of Liberties], and then the question being asked by the Governor whether they would have the old Charter or a new one, they unanimously desired there might be a new one, with the amendments put into a law, which is passed.

The petition of Nathaniel Allen was read, showing that he had sold a servant to Henry Bowman,[31] for six hundred weight of beef, with the hide and tallow, and £6 sterling, which the said Bowman delayed to pay the said petitioner, showing likewise that the said Henry Bowman and Walter Humphrey hired a boat of the said petitioner only for one month and kept the same boat 18 weeks from the petitioner, to his great prejudice; then it was ordered that William Clarke, John Simcock, and James Harrison should speak to Henry Bowman concerning this matter.

The petition of John James, Timothy Metcalf, and Thomas Lincey, mariners belonging to the *Friend's Adventure,* was read, showing that the master of said ship denied to pay them their wages being demanded according to contract made with them in England.

Ordered that John Test, high sheriff of this county, bring the said petitioners before the Governor and Council tomorrow at eight of the clock in the morning.

Adjourned till 21st of 1st month 1683.


21 March 1683

*Assembly*

About the time appointed the House sat. The Speaker assumed the Chair; ordered the names of the members to be called over, etc. This done, Casparus Herrman, one of the chosen burgesses, having absented himself from the beginning of the House's sitting to this present day, was examined by the Speaker touching his absence. His pleas being weak, the House first voted him finable, then ordered him to pay the fine of ten shillings.

The Speaker proposes to the House that the printed Charter [of Liberties], article by article, might be openly read in the House and seriously considered on; that so it might be more thoroughly understood, and the disadvantages (if any therein) to the freemen of the province, proposed to the Governor, etc., to be removed, and the privileges propagated in the new (to be engrossed) Charter.

The House assented to the Speaker's proposal; whereupon he read the aforesaid Charter, paraphrasing upon every material thing appearing in any article thereof.

An amendment of the thirteenth article appearing necessary,[32] the Speaker observed it, and interlined it.

The printed Charter of Liberties having been read, the Speaker put the question to the House, whether the printed Charter, together with the bill relating thereto,[33] the variations of the said bill with its appendices, should be all engrossed together, and made into one entire Charter. The question being thus put, it was resolved, (N.C.D.), in the affirmative, etc.

The bills that were [at the] last sitting brought in by the members of Provincial Council, last before mentioned,[34] were in part read a second time.

An article relating that an estate of lands granted by court and not seated, etc., within the term of that grant, should be forfeited, was read, long debated on, and after correction, resolved in the affirmative.

A request and desire of the members and freemen of the Assembly (being also an acknowledgment of the Governor's lately offered kindness to the said freemen) was read openly in the House, the contents whereof related to a general liberty of fishing, fowling, hawking, and hunting, etc., in any creek or part of the river Delaware, with other privileges, etc.[35] After some debatement, the question was put whether the aforesaid request, etc., should be presented to the Governor, etc., and it was resolved in the affirmative.

Griffith Jones and Thomas Fitzwater, two members, etc., were chosen by the House to make the aforesaid presentment. This done, the House adjourned till the third hour in the afternoon.

About the time appointed the House sat, the Speaker assumed the Chair, ordered the members' names to be called over.

The members appointed in the forenoon for that undertaking withdrew to the Council house in order to present the aforementioned request to the Governor. This done, and no business presenting, the Speaker adjourned the House for one hour.

After the expiration of about an hour, the House returned. The Speaker having reassumed the Chair, reports to the House that the Governor and Council were not sat and that therefore no business was at the present to be expected from the Council house.

Andros Binkson, one of the members of the House, solicited the Speaker and rest of the House that he might have leave to be absent for the space of one day. The House, upon consideration of the emergency of his occasions, permits his absence for the time required.

Then the Speaker adjourned the House till the eighth hour the next morning.

*Provincial Council*

[13 councilors in attendance].

The seamen belonging to the *Friend's Adventure,* viz., John James, Timothy Metcalf, and Thomas Lincey, were brought before the Governor and Council and were ordered for a trial before them.

The petition of John James for himself and in behalf of the rest of the said ship's company being read, requesting that they might be put in capacity to address to the Governor and Council, it was ordered they shall have a hearing, and upon the hearing, it was ordered by the Governor and Council that the seamen should bring up the goods left at Upland to Philadelphia, and that then the Governor and Council will take care to order that the said seamen be paid their wages.

Whereas, Edward Southrin is returned to serve in Provincial Council for Sussex County, and that he has not yet made his appearance to perform that service, it is ordered by the Governor and Council that he give his attendance forthwith in Council at Philadelphia.

Committees for proposing several bills:

[1]      John Simcock          William Haige
         William Clarke          Edmund Cantwell

To whom it is referred to propose bills concerning: rules of county courts; bills of exchange[36] protested; possessions; public affairs; sailors' wrecks; [an] act of oblivion;[37] [and] scolds.[38]

[2]      Capt. Thomas Holme   William Biles
         William Clayton          John Richardson

To whom it is referred to propose bills concerning: to arrest goods in case of danger; limits of courts in criminal causes; justices of the peace to marry people; how far executors and administrators are obliged to proceed, and how to pay; public houses to credit no nonresident for above 20s. or else to lose it; not to remove his neighbor's landmark; [and] punishment for those that shall presume to alter their neighbor's ear or brand mark.[39]

[3]      James Harrison          John Hillyard
         Francis Whitwell          John Moll
         Christopher Taylor

To whom is referred to propose bills for: hogs to be ringed;[40] coroners to be established in each county; servants without indentures to be judged what shall be allowed them at the expiration of their time; how to bind any over to the peace; [and] twice a year a grand jury.

Capt. Lasse Cock desiring leave of the Governor and Council to go about the [Free] Society [of Traders'] business, leave was granted him.

Adjourned till four of the clock in the afternoon.

Post Meridiem.

Griffith Jones and Thomas Fitzwater came with a written message from the House of Assembly, containing the thankful acknowledgment of the House to the Governor for his kind speech to them yesterday, gratefully embracing his offers, proposing what they desired might [be] inserted in the Charter.

The several committees appointed to meet at several places.
Adjourned till 22d of 1st month 1683.

22 March 1683

*Assembly*

About the time appointed the House sat. The Speaker assumed the Chair, ordered the burgesses' names to be called over. This done, a debate arose in the House touching an article formerly read in the House relating to lands granted in any county court, etc. As also touching an amendment and explanation of the said article. The question being put, whether the aforesaid explanation, etc., should stand; it passed in the negative. But resolved in the affirmative, that the said article should stand (as formerly) without the explanation.

The latter part of the bills (before left unread) were now read a second time; after reading, the question was put, whether the whole bills, with allowance of their amendments, should stand, and it was resolved in the affirmative.

John Moll and James Harrison, two members of the Council, bring into the House another bill to be taken into the consideration of the House.

The Speaker himself reads the said bill.

The first article whereof related to some considerable gift to be passed from the master to the servant at the expiration of his servitude, thereby to oblige him to continue his service with diligence. The question being put, it was resolved in the affirmative.

The second article related to persons menacing one another's life, or harm, etc. Resolved, (N.C.D.), in the affirmative.

The third article related to a grand inquest to act [on] several material things in courts twice a year, etc., resolved (N.C.D.) in the affirmative.

The fourth article relating to common barrators,[41] etc., was read, and resolved (N.C.D.) in the affirmative.

The fifth article relating to the election of a person for viewing pipe staves,[42] etc., was read, debated on, and concluded to be corrected.

The sixth article, and last, was read, relating to drunkenness, profane speaking, etc., resolved in the affirmative, N.C.D.

The bill being thus once read, the Speaker adjourned the House till the eighth hour the next morning.

*Provincial Council*

[14 councilors in attendance].

The several committees brought in their bills to the Council to be considered of. William Haige and Capt. Edmund Cantwell desired leave for some time to go about their business, which was granted them.

Several bills relating to several matters, carried by John Moll and James Harrison to the Assembly, by order of the Governor and Council.

Adjourned till 23d of 1st month 1683.

*Assembly*

About the time appointed the House sat. The Speaker having assumed the Chair, ordered the clerk to call over the members' names; . . .

[A] new bill was read in the House the first time.

The first article was read relating to exchange bills, their protestation, etc., debated on, resolved, by major[ity] votes, in the affirmative. . . .

The fourth article relating to the hasting away of letters directed to the Governor, etc., was read, debated on, varied, then the article with its variations admitted, and resolved in the affirmative, N.C.D. . . .

The Speaker adjourned the House till the third hour in the afternoon.

About the time appointed the House sat again. The Speaker having assumed the Chair, ordered the members' names to be called over. . . .

James Harrison and William Clarke, two members of the Council, came into the House and presented some bills for laws, etc.

The first reading.

Chap. 7 of the former laws relating to murder, etc., was read and resolved in the affirmative.

Chap. 8 relating to manslaughter, etc., was read and resolved in the affirmative.

Chap. 40 relating to keeping of ordinaries[43] without license, etc., was read, debated on, and resolved in the affirmative.

Chap. 42 relating to courts of justice and final appeals, etc., was read, etc. It passed in the negative.

Nicholas Waln, one of the members of the House (by concession of the House) withdrew for a certain time.

The Speaker adjourned the House till the ninth hour the next morning.

*Provincial Council*

[13 councilors in attendance].

Several bills relating to, carried by Thomas Holme to the Assembly, by order of the Governor and Council.

The law of weights referred.

The question was asked in Council, whether peacemakers should sit once a month?[44]

It was proposed, what should be the punishment of manslaughter?

Ordered that the seal of Philadelphia be the anchor;

> of the County of Bucks, a tree and vine;
> of the County of Chester, a plow;
> of the County of New Castle, a castle;
> of the County of Kent, three ears of Indian corn;
> of the County of Sussex, one wheat sheaf.

Adjourned till 4 [of the] clock in the afternoon.

Post Meridiem.

Several bills relating to, sent by order of the Governor and Council to the Assembly by Thomas Holme and William Clarke.

Bills relating to weights and measures sent by order of the Governor and Council to the Assembly by William Clayton and John Hillyard.

Adjourned till 24th of 1st month 1683.

24 March 1683

*Assembly*

About the time appointed the House sat. The Speaker assumed the Chair, ordered the members' names to be called over, etc.

William Clayton and John Hillyard, two members of the Council, bring new bills into the Assembly.

First reading.

The first article relating to persons dying intestate, etc., was read and debated on. After some debates, several members of the House were elected committeemen, viz., Griffith Jones, Casparus Herrman, Thomas Fitzwater, Thomas Brassey, Luke Watson, [and] Benoni Bishop, to inspect the aforesaid article.

The second article was read, relating to a suit in law and form of proceeding, etc., and resolved in the affirmative, N.C.D.

The third article was read, relating to fines, etc., not to be levied upon men's working instruments, etc., and resolved in the affirmative, N.C.D.

The fourth article was read, relating to fornication, etc., and debated on; after debate, resolved in the affirmative.

The fifth article relating to marriage, etc., was read and resolved in the affirmative.

The sixth article relating to weights and measures was read and resolved in the affirmative. . . .

Christopher Taylor and James Harrison, two members of the Council, bring bills into the House. . . .

New bill, first reading.

The first article touching references and arbitrations, etc., was read, debated on, and resolved in the affirmative.

The second article touching deeds of sale, and third article relating to deeds of conveyance, etc., were read and resolved in the affirmative.

The fourth article touching the estates of deceased, etc., was read and ordered to be returned to the Council for amendment, etc.

The [fifth?][45] article was read, relating to children's good education and learning, and resolved (after some debate) in the affirmative.

This done, the House adjourned till the third hour in the afternoon.

About the time appointed the House sat. The Speaker assumed the Chair, and ordered the names of the members to be called over.

The fifth article of the aforesaid bill was read, relating to the building of ferryboats to creeks, necessary for carrying over horse and man; after reading, it was debated on and carried in the affirmative.

John Richardson and William Biles, two members of Council, present to the House new bills.

First reading.

The first article relating to building of bridges over creeks; and second article relating to penalty for making of weirs[46] over creeks, were read and resolved in the affirmative.

The third article touching a seal (called a county seal) in each county, resolved in the affirmative.

The fourth article touching children's guardians was read and somewhat debated on, etc.; then resolved in the affirmative.

The fifth article, [in which the] Governor [is] empowered to call members of Provincial Council to his assistance in extraordinary cases, resolved in the affirmative.

The sixth article relating to the passage and value of gold and silver coin, resolved in the affirmative.

The seventh and last article, relating to juries upon life and death, etc., resolved in the affirmative.

The House adjourned till the ninth hour in the morning.

*Provincial Council*

[13 councilors in attendance].

A debate was held concerning marriage, and parents disposing of estates.

William Haige desiring leave to go about the [Free] Society [of Traders'] business, it was granted him.

Several bills relating to, carried by order of Governor and Council to the Assembly by James Harrison and Christopher Taylor.

A petition of John Test for the payment of £120 sterling due from Griffith Jones being read, ordered that James Harrison and William Clarke this afternoon take up and make an end of the business.

A petition of Charles Pickering[47] read; ordered he shall be heard the 26th instant in the afternoon.

Several bills ordered by the Governor and Council to be carried to the Assembly by William Biles and John Richardson.

Adjourned till 26th of 1st month 1683.

26 March 1683

*Assembly*

About the time appointed the House sat. The Speaker assumed the Chair, and counsels the House to observe good order and decorum in their proceedings.

This done, bills were read the second time . . . [and] the House adjourned till the second hour in the afternoon.

About the time appointed the House sat again. The Speaker assumed the Chair. . . .

An act of oblivion touching the former breach of penal laws (except treason, murder, etc.) was read and resolved in the affirmative.

An appendix to an article touching fishing, fowling, and hunting was read, etc., and resolved in the affirmative.

An act touching aliens, their privileges, etc., resolved in the affirmative.[48]

An act touching mines, etc., resolved in the affirmative.

No further business accruing at present, the House adjourned to the seventh hour the next morning.

*Provincial Council*
[13 councilors in attendance].

Ordered in Council that John Moll, William Haige, [and] William Clarke be a committee to bring their report tomorrow morning of the fees of officers belonging to the customhouse.

Ordered in Council that William Biles, Francis Whitwell, and James Harrison do consider of the duties and fees of coroners, and make their report tomorrow morning.

The Speaker, with three members, came to this house with several bills.

The Council ordered a conference to be had with the whole House of Assembly concerning some amendments this afternoon.

A conference held in Council concerning the petition from the Assembly relating to fishing, fowling, mines, quarries, and minerals.

Christopher Taylor and John Moll ordered by Governor and Council to carry the old laws to the Assembly for them to look over.

Adjourned till 27th of 1st month 1683.

27 March 1683

*Assembly*
About the time appointed the House sat. The Speaker having assumed the Chair, ordered the members' names to be called over, as usually; this done, Thomas Holme and John Moll, two members of the Council, intimate to the House, from the Governor and Council, that they desire conference with the House.

Whereupon the House withdrew to the Council house. After some conference touching bills not passed, the House returns; the Speaker reassumes the Chair, reports and commends to the consideration of the House the things treated of (in the aforesaid conference) betwixt them and the Council.

The Speaker reads two articles in the printed Charter [of Liberties] relating to the election of officers by the Governor, etc.[49] A debate arose in the House touching the aforesaid articles. In the interim, bills are brought into the House by William Biles and William Clayton, two members of the Council.

The House adjourned to the third hour in the afternoon.

About the third hour in the afternoon the House sat. The Speaker assumed the Chair; ordered the members' names to be called over, etc.

Then proceed to the reading of new bills.

First reading.

The first article was read, relating to the defraying of public charges due to the Provincial Council and Assembly during their time of sitting, etc. This, after debatement, was resolved in the affirmative, N.C.D.

The second article being read, relating to the fees due to the Governor's secretary, surveyor-general, master of the rolls, treasurer, provincial secretary, register, justice of peace, sheriff, coroner, clerk of the county, constable, etc.

This second article being read, after some debate, a committee was resolved on by the House to inspect the same, viz.: for Sussex County, Luke Watson; for Kent, Thomas Hassold; for New Castle, John Darby; for Chester, John Blunston; for Philadelphia, Walter King; for Bucks, Robert Lucas.

The aforesaid committee withdraw apart, out of the House.

The laws passed [by] the first Assembly[50] were read by the Speaker's order.

The preamble, touching naturalization, etc., was read and resolved in the affirmative, N.C.D.

First reading.

Chapter 1 of [the] laws read,[51] touching liberty of conscience and breach of the sabbath; then a penalty, in case of breach of the contents of this chapter, etc., was debated upon, and in the end it was resolved (N.C.D.) that every offender in this case should for every offense of neglect pay five shillings; but in case of gaming, drunkenness, or other extravagancy, ten shillings or ten days imprisonment; and so for every repeated offense double the penalty of the offense last aforegoing.

Chap. 2 was read, relating to the qualification of officers, etc.; resolved in the affirmative, N.C.D.

Chap. 3 was read, touching the offense of swearing; resolved in the affirmative, N.C.D.

Chap. 4 was read, etc., relating to swearing also; resolved in the affirmative, N.C.D.

Chap. 5 was read, etc., touching prophane speaking, etc.; resolved (N.C.D.) in the affirmative.

Chap. 6 touching the offense of cursing, was read, etc.; resolved (N.C.D.) in the affirmative.

Chap. 9 was read, touching the defiling the marriage bed, etc.; resolved in the affirmative, N.C.D.

Chap. 10 was read, touching incest; resolved (N.C.D.) in the affirmative.

Chap. 11 touching sodomy was read, etc.; resolved (N.C.D.) in the affirmative.

Chap. 12 was read, touching rape or ravishment, etc.; resolved in the affirmative, N.C.D.

Chaps. 13, 14, 17, 18, 19, 20, and 21 were read, touching bigamy or polygamy; drunkenness; drinking of healths; selling strong liquors, as rum, etc., to Indians; firing of houses; burglary, or breaking of houses; lands and goods of thieves and felons; [all] resolved in the affirmative, N.C.D.

Chap. 22 was read, touching forcible entry; resolved in the affirmative, N.C.D., these amendments being admitted, viz., "in the judgment of the county court."

Chaps. 23, 24, 25, 26, 27, 28, 29, 30, 31, 32, 33, 34, and 36 were read, touching seditious and riotous meetings; assaults, and menacing of parents; menacing of magistrates; servants, their menacing masters and mistresses; assault and battery; challenges to fight; prizes, stage plays, bull-baits, etc., gaming, etc.; seditious writings; the abuse of magistrates; slanderers and defamers of magistrates and other persons, etc.; clamorous persons; and provision for the poor, etc.; [all] resolved in the affirmative, N.C.D.

Chap. 41 was read, touching the names of months and weekdays; resolved in the affirmative.

Chaps. 44, 45, 47, 51, 53, 54, 58, 60, 61, and 62 were read, touching witnesses in case of law trials, etc.; records in court; suits between plaintiff and defendant, upon bill or bond, balancing allowed; arrests; bargains in buying and selling; wills of the deceased; wills of distracted persons; factorage and factors; corrupters of charters, records, conveyances, etc.; payment of debts, its manner and form; the bail of prisoners, etc.; [all] resolved in the affirmative, N.C.D.

The House adjourned till eight in the morning.

*Provincial Council*

[13 councilors in attendance].

John Moll and Thomas Holme ordered by the Governor and Council to go to the Assembly to have a conference about the amendments.

William Haige and [Francis] Whitwell ordered by the Governor and Council to carry several bills to the Assembly relating to mariners, and a bill to give every provincial councilman 3s. per day, and each assemblyman 2s. 6d. per day, etc.

Adjourned for two hours.
Post Meridiem.

The Governor and Council being sat, Capt. William Markham desired leave to be absent a small time, which was granted him.

It being put to the question whether the 19th article[52] should be inserted in the Charter? Was passed in the negative.

It being put to the question whether these words in the 17th article of the Charter, "That after the death of the present Governor, the Governor and Council," should begin the said article? It was resolved in the affirmative.[53]

It being proposed whether the Charter should be transcribed? It was resolved in the affirmative.

Ordered by the Governor and Council [that] Thomas Holme, William Clarke, John Moll, John Simcock, and Christopher Taylor do consider the amendments of the Charter [of Liberties] and give a report concerning the same tomorrow.

Adjourned till 28th of 1st month 1683.

*Assembly*

About the time appointed the House sat. The Speaker, after taking of the Chair, ordered the members' names to be called over, etc.

Then the rest of the laws[54] were read by the Speaker.

Chap. 63 touching prisons being made workhouses was read, etc.; resolved (N.C.D.) in the affirmative.

Chap. 64 was read, touching the behavior of jailers toward prisoners; resolved (N.C.D.) in the affirmative.

Chap. 65 was read, touching persons wrongfully imprisoned; resolved (N.C.D.) in the affirmative.

Chap. 66 was read, touching fines and penalties for offenses, etc.; resolved (N.C.D.), amendments being admitted, in the affirmative.

Chaps. 67, 68, 69, and 70 were read, touching such persons as are to be accounted freemen of this province, etc.; the manner of electing members of [the] Assembly, etc.; raising of money by tax or levy, etc.; and the publication of the laws of this province; [all] resolved (N.C.D.) in the affirmative.

Chap. 71 was read, touching such material things as were not specified in the chapter of laws beforegoing, viz., that such things should be left to the Governor, etc.; resolved (N.C.D.) in the affirmative.

This done, the Speaker proceeded to read the bills touching fees belonging to officers in the province a second time, being amended by the committee. . . .

Whereas the Speaker, with great labor and kind respect to the House, after signifying to the House those customs practiced in parliaments concerning the duty which each member owes to each other, and so to this House; several members having showed themselves disrespectful, having made contumacies[55] by absenting themselves and breaking other good customs agreed upon by this House. It is therefore by the major[ity] vote of this House concluded, and by the Speaker ordered, that whosoever shall hereafter be guilty of the like offenses, unless in case of sickness or some very urgent and extraordinary case which the House shall judge to be so, every such person shall pay twelve pence sterling forthwith, or the value of it.

Signed in the behalf of the members, by

Thomas Wynne, Speaker

William Markham and Christopher Taylor, two members of the Council, bring in bills.

The first, second, third, fourth, fifth, sixth, seventh, eighth, ninth, tenth, eleventh, and twelfth articles were read, touching declarations, and freedom of pleas, etc., the estate of an intestate; murder; manslaughter; the counterfeiting of any person's hand and seal, or county seal, or broad seal; the penalty upon abusive Indians, etc.; inhabitants of this province, their allegiance to the governor, etc., such as shall derogate[56] from the judgment of a court by scandalizing it; stealers of any person's cattle; such as shall presume to buy lands of the Indians not licensed by the Governor; actions in court under £5;

and such persons as refuse to pay their debts; resolved in the affirmative, N.C.D.

The bills and laws read at this sitting were by vote of the House confirmed and established; then recommended to the Speaker to be presented to the Governor. . . .

This done, the House adjourned till the third hour in the afternoon.

About the time appointed the House sat. The Speaker assumed the Chair, etc., then produced several bills and laws which had been formerly twice read in the House and resolved on, fairly engrossed by the clerk of the Provincial Council. The aforesaid bills and laws were by the Speaker's order read in the House by the clerk a third time and resolved in the affirmative, viz., that they should be passed into provincial laws. This done, the Speaker in the name and by consent of the whole House, subscribes them committed, etc., then returns them to the Governor and Council.

The House now adjourned till nine in the morning.

*Provincial Council*
[12 councilors in attendance].

The business of Charles Pickering and [Thomas] Wall's[57] seamen was this day heard before the Governor and Council, and it was their opinion that the seamen (excepting one of them, namely John James) had done their duty.

Capt. William Markham and Christopher Taylor ordered by Governor and Council to carry to the Assembly several bills relating to.

Timothy Metcalf ordered to pay 5s. for being disordered in drink.

The Speaker, with several other members, brought several bills to this board.

The Governor and Council were pleased to inspect the fees.

And adjourned till 29th of 1st month 1683.


29 March 1683

*Assembly*
About the time appointed the House sat.

Immediately, Christopher Taylor and James Harrison, two members of the Council, give intelligence to the House that the Governor and Council desire conference with the House; whereupon the House withdrew to the Council house.

After a considerable time of conference, the House returned, and adjourned till the eighth hour the next morning.

*Provincial Council*
[12 councilors in attendance].

James Harrison and Christopher Taylor ordered to go to the Assembly to have a conference concerning the bills of the fees of this province, etc. A conference is had, viz.: all ships and vessels under 10 tons, and those that belong to this river, to pay no fees.

The question was proposed by the Governor whether offices should continue for life which are named by the Governor? Carried in the negative.

Also whether the Governor, that now is, shall choose his officers during his life? Carried in the affirmative.

The question was put whether the justices of the peace, sheriffs, and constables should be appointed by the Governor during his life? Carried in the affirmative.

The question was put whether the Governor should choose officers during his life and afterwards according to [the] Charter [of Liberties]? Carried in the affirmative.

The question was whether there should be a committee to draw up the Charter [of Liberties] with amendments? Passed in the affirmative.

The Committee of the Council, out of each county, one:
John Moll, New Castle County
Francis Whitwell, Kent County
William Clarke, Sussex County
James Harrison, Bucks County
William Clayton, Chester County
Thomas Holme, Philadelphia County

The Committee of the Assembly:
James Walliam, New Castle County
Benoni Bishop, Kent County
Luke Watson, Sussex County
Thomas Fitzwater, Bucks County
Dennis Rochford, Chester County
Thomas Wynne, Speaker, Philadelphia County
Agreed to sit upon the Charter this afternoon, at 6 of the clock.

A meeting of the surveyor-general and purchasers appointed to be held tomorrow in the evening, about the fees of surveying; both to be held at the Council chamber.

Adjourned till 30th of 1st month 1683.

30 March 1683

*Assembly*
About the time appointed the House sat, the Speaker having assumed the Chair.

Immediately John Moll and James Harrison, two members of the Council, present the Speaker with new bills from the Governor and Council.

First reading.

The first article touching a penalty upon such persons as shall kill any cow-calves or ewe-lambs in this province before the expiration of three years, etc., resolved with amendments in the affirmative, N.C.D.

The second article touching illegal felling of other persons' trees, etc., resolved (N.C.D.) in the affirmative. . . .

This done, a petition to the Governor (already signed by several members of the Council) touching the city lots was read in order to be signed by such members of the House as were free thereto, etc. The petition was accordingly signed.[58]

The House adjourned till the third hour in the afternoon.

About the time appointed the House sat; but no business then occurring, though expected, the House adjourned till the seventh hour the next morning.

*Provincial Council*

[13 councilors in attendance].

John Moll and James Harrison ordered by the Governor and Council to carry several bills to the Assembly.

The question put by the Governor, whether or not the old Charter [of Liberties] shall serve with amendments or a new one drawn? Agreed it should be drawn again and the amendments put in.

The Speaker, with some other members, brought several bills to the Council.

Adjourned till 3 in the afternoon.

Post Meridiem.

A committee ordered to prepare the Charter[59] by 8 of the clock tomorrow morning, being John Moll, James Harrison, John Simcock, Thomas Holme, and William Clarke.

Put to the vote, as many as are of opinion that a public tax upon land ought to be raised to defray the public charge, say "Yea." Carried in the affirmative—none dissenting.

John Moll, William Clayton, John Hillyard, John Richardson, and Francis Whitwell appointed for a committee to bring in the charges[60] of the province.

Adjourned till 31st of 1st month 1683.

31 March 1683

*Assembly*

About the time appointed the House sat. The Speaker assumed the Chair, etc.

Then informs the House that the Governor and Council will require conference with the House, etc., and that the Charter[61] of the province will be openly read. . . .

First reading another bill.

The first article relating to the defraying of each county's charges by taxes, in case of public business, was read and resolved in the affirmative.
. . .

James Harrison and John Simcock, two members of the Council, present the House with bills.

First reading.

The first article touching members of Provincial Council and Assembly, their paying but half taxes, etc., resolved by major[ity of] votes in the affirmative. . . .

The Speaker and some other members withdraw to the Council house to return the bills now last read. After some time they return.

The Speaker reports to the House from the Council that the bill touching half taxes only to be paid by the Council and Assembly had, as it were, surreptitiously and unknown crept into the House. Whereupon, the Speaker putting the question to the House, whether the said bill should be allowed? It passed in the negative, N.C.D.

No more business at the present occurring, the House adjourned till the second hour in the afternoon.

About the time appointed the House sat.

James Harrison and John Simcock, two members of the Council, give notice to the House that the Governor and Council desire conference with the House. Whereupon the House immediately withdrew to the Council house, where the provincial clerk read over the laws (being fairly engrossed) by command of the Governor.

The Governor orders the clerk aforesaid to read the said laws, article by article, and, after reading, put the question to the General Assembly touching each respective article; and it was resolved, touching every of the above-said articles, in the affirmative, viz., that all and every of the articles so read should pass into laws.

This done, the Assembly adjourned in the Council house till the seventh hour on the second-day morning next following, being the second day of the second month.

*Provincial Council*

[13 councilors in attendance].

James Harrison and John Simcock ordered by the Governor and Council to carry several bills to the Assembly relating to.

William Haige desires leave to be absent for some time. Leave is granted him.

The Speaker attends this house with several bills.

Adjourned till 3 of the clock in the afternoon.

Post Meridiem.

The Speaker came down this afternoon with the whole House to hear the Charter read, which was so done.

The Governor proposed whether they would have the 500 members stand in this new Charter, or have it altered that only two hundred should be the greatest number. The last was passed in the negative.

The question was put whether they would [provide] the clerk with the Charter to enroll it? Agreed *Nemine Contradicente*.

| | | |
|---|---|---|
| Capt. William Markham | John Richardson | James Harrison |
| Christopher Taylor | Francis Whitwell | John Hillyard |
| John Simcock | William Haige | William Biles |
| John Moll | Thomas Holme | Lasse Cock |
| William Clayton | William Clarke | |

The Governor and these members of Council, with the whole Assembly being present, the bills were read and passed into laws, *Nemine Contradicente*.

Adjourned till 2d of 2d month.

2 April 1683

*Assembly*

About the time appointed the House sat. The Speaker assumed the Chair, etc.

William Biles, one of the members of Council, presents bills into the Speaker's hands.

The Speaker audibly reads in the House a petition to the Governor from the Council and Assembly that the Charter of Liberties of the province of Pennsylvania might bear date at Philadelphia, and not in London. The above-said petition had been signed by the Council, and was now signed by the House.

A committee was chosen of six members of the House, out of each of the six counties, one; viz., to conclude and determine a fine to be levied upon the members that had absented themselves during the whole sessions of the Assembly, etc. The names of the said members of committee were William Windsmore, Joseph Phipps, Robert Hall, John Darby, Walter King, Luke Watson.

Thomas Holme, John Moll, William Haige, and John Hillyard, four members of the Council, present bills into the Speaker's hands.

Third reading. . . .

William Clarke and William Biles, two members of the Council, present more bills to the Speaker's hands.

First and second reading: an article was read, touching speedy justice to be done to the poor, etc.; resolved (N.C.D.) in the affirmative.

First reading: an article touching trials of freemen, etc., resolved (N.C.D.) in the affirmative. This article was read again, and resolved (N.C.D.) in the affirmative.

John Simcock and John Richardson, two members of the Council, present bills into the Speaker's hands.

First reading: an article was read, touching several laws already resolved on by the House, viz., that they should stand firm and irrepealable except six parts of seven of Provincial Council and Assembly should consent thereto; resolved (N.C.D.) in the affirmative.[62]

First reading: an article was read, touching fees to be paid in coin or produce of the country; resolved (N.C.D.) in the affirmative.

The two articles last aforesaid were read a second time and resolved (N.C.D.) in the affirmative.

James Harrison and Christopher Taylor, two members of the Council, present the House with bills.

First reading: a bill touching the assize[63] of bread was read, etc.; resolved (N.C.D.) in the affirmative. The said bill was read a second time and resolved in the affirmative, N.C.D.

A bill touching ships, the due entry of their cargo, was read twice and resolved (both times) in the affirmative, N.C.D.

The committee appointed for constituting fines, etc., to be paid by absent members for their neglect of attendance, etc., deliver a bill of those fines, etc., into the Speaker's hands. The Speaker reads it, and the question being put, etc., it was resolved in the affirmative, N.C.D.

Francis Whitwell, John Simcock, and John Richardson, three members of the Council, bring bills into the House.

First reading: an article touching taxes to be levied upon rum and other liquors, etc., was read, debated on, and left undetermined.

William Haige and William Biles, two members of Council, present more bills to the House.

First reading: a bill touching careful cleaning of corn[64] by the seller, etc., was read and debated on, etc., then resolved (amendments being admitted) in the affirmative.

First reading: a bill touching railers,[65] etc., was read and resolved (N.C.D.) in the affirmative.

John Simcock and James Harrison, two members of the Council, present bills to the House.

First reading: a bill touching the publication of the laws, etc., was read and resolved (N.C.D.) in the affirmative.

The House adjourned till the third hour in the afternoon.

At the time appointed the House waited upon the Governor and Council in the Council house. The clerk of the Council, by order of the Governor, read the Charter of the province fairly engrossed in parchment; which done, the Governor solemnly testifies to the General Assembly that what was inserted in that Charter was solely by him intended for the good and benefit of the freemen of the province, and prosecuted with much earnestness in his spirit towards God at the time of its composition. This done, he sealed and signed the said Charter, and delivered it to the Speaker of the House and two other members, who received it in the name of all the freemen of the province by signifying an acknowledgment of the Governor's kindness in granting them that Charter of (more than was expected) Liberty.

This done, the said Charter was attested by indorsement of the members of Provincial Council and Assembly subscribing their names, as also the Governor's secretary, clerk of the Council, and clerk of the Assembly, with such of the inhabitants of Philadelphia as were then present.[66] This done, its keeping was recommended to such person, or persons, as were thought most fit to be intrusted with a matter of so great concernment.

The General Assembly adjourns till the seventh hour the next morning.

*Provincial Council*
[13 councilors in attendance].

The Speaker, with two of the members of the Assembly, brought down a petition to the Governor.

Thomas Holme, John Moll, John Hillyard, and William Haige were sent by the Governor and Council with several bills to the Assembly.

William Clarke sent with several bills to the Assembly.

James Harrison and Christopher Taylor sent by the Governor and Council with several bills to the Assembly.

John Simcock brought several bills from the House.

The Speaker, with two other members of the Assembly, waited on the Council with several bills.

Two of the members of the Assembly waited on the Council with a message concerning the bill of cleaning of corn, which being put to the vote, was carried in the affirmative.

John Simcock, John Richardson, Francis Whitwell, William Haige, and William Biles were sent by the Governor and Council with several bills to the Assembly. John Simcock and James Harrison sent likewise with several bills.

Adjourned till 3 of the clock [in the] afternoon.

Post Meridiem.

The Speaker with the whole House came to the Council to hear several bills read and passed into laws, which was accordingly done.

Consideration arising whether the Governor's three voices should stand in Provincial Council as by the old Charter [of Liberties], the question was put: "All ye that are willing that the last proposition should stand so as it is, say yea." The question being put twice, was carried in the affirmative.[67]

The great Charter of this province was this night read, signed, sealed, and delivered by the Governor to the inhabitants, and received by the hands of James Harrison and the Speaker, who were ordered to return the old one with the hearty thanks of the whole House, which accordingly they did.

Edmund Cantwell, Lasse Cock, Ralph Withers, John Rhoads, and Edward Southrin, these members of the Council were absent.

The question was put whether skins should be prohibited? Carried in the negative. Also, if they would have an imposition laid upon them? Passed in the affirmative.[68]

Adjourned till 3d of 2d month 1683.

3 April 1683

*Assembly*

About the time appointed the General Assembly sat in the Council house.

The clerk of the Provincial Council called over the names of the members of Council; the clerk of the Assembly called over the names of the members of Assembly.

The Governor and members being present, it pleased the Governor to give liberty to the House of making proposals of such things and matters as they thought might prevent such evils and grievances as were likely otherwise to fall upon the people of this province; that so such matters as aforesaid might be passed into laws, for the good of its inhabitants. Whereupon a debate arose touching the value and weight of coin Spanish, etc., but in the end was suspended.

A debate arose upon a bill touching the transportation of felons into this province, etc. The question being put, it passed in the negative.

But it was resolved in the affirmative that (upon consideration of felons under conviction of conscience being likely to become good men) felons should and might be admitted into this province, etc., by a law which for that end should be established.

A bill touching the value and weight of English coin was read and debated upon. After debatement, the question being put, it was resolved in the affirmative that the said bill should stand firm, together with its supplement, touching the value of pieces of eight called perues.[69]

This done, the Governor read an article in the king's letters patents granted him, touching the necessity of the laws to be passed under the great seal of the province, and his own, the Council's, and Assembly's indorsement.[70]

The question was put (after reading) whether all laws should be passed under the great seal of the province; and thus indorsed by the clerk of the Council, "passed in the Council," his name being subscribed thereto; as also by the Speaker of the House, "passed in the Assembly," the Speaker's name being subscribed; and then recommended to the great seal? Resolved (N.C.D.) in the affirmative.

The Governor adjourned the House for a time.

About the noon time of the day the House sat, by the Governor's order. The Speaker having assumed the Chair, a debate arose in the House touching members finable.

Peter Alricks and John DeHaes ordered to be fined in the sum of £5 for non-attendance during the whole sessions of Assembly, and John Cann in the sum of 40s., Alexander Draper in the sum of £5.

The House adjourned to their respective places of habitation by the Governor's order, the third day of the second month, 1683.

*Provincial Council*

[14 councilors in attendance].

It was proposed that no felons be brought into this country.

Another concerning money or pieces of eight.

Another concerning apprentices that run away from their masters without certificate, should not be entertained;[71] and being put to the vote, was carried in the affirmative, that they may be brought in.

The question was put whether the law that is passed shall stand without altering? Carried in the negative.

The question was put whether pieces of eight should go by weight? Carried in the negative.

A supplement to the bill of money was put to the vote, whether it should be added? Passed in the affirmative.

The question was put whether they would have a seal to the laws of the province made every sessions? Carried in the affirmative.

The question being put if the clerk of the Council should endorse the consent of the Council on the laws every session? Carried in the affirmative, *Nemine Contradicente.*

Also if the Speaker should endorse the consent of the whole House of Assembly? Carried in the affirmative, *Nemine Contradicente.*

The Governor adjourned the Assembly till such time as he and the Provincial Council shall have occasion for them.

Adjourned till 4th of 2d month 1683.

4 April 1683

*Provincial Council*

[8 councilors in attendance].

This day Charles Pickering's business was tried, and the seamen are ordered to have 6 months pay and £5 given them over and above.

The Governor orders that these members of the Council attend him:[72]

Thomas Holme and Christopher Taylor, three-year men.

Edmund Cantwell and Edward Southrin, two-year men.

William Clayton and John Richardson, one-year men.

Adjourned till 2d of 3d month 1683.

Provincial Council: MBE. Bureau of Archives and History, Harrisburg. Assembly: Printed transcript. *Votes and Proceedings of the House of Representatives of the Province of Pennsylvania* (Philadelphia, 1752). Not published in *PWP*, Vol. Two.

1. A voice, or roll-call, vote. This decision altered WP's provision for legislative voting in the *Frame of Government* (doc. 30, article 20).

2. That is, the first *Frame of Government*, which is called either the Charter of Liberties or simply the Charter in these legislative minutes.

3. Twelve from each county.

4. See doc. 52, n. 2, above.

5. These orders had been agreed upon by the first Assembly in Dec. 1682.

6. Article 14 of the first *Frame of Government* (doc. 30, above), sets out the size and powers of the lower legislative house.

7. A tavern.

8. Favorable.

9. A declaration.

10. See articles 5, 6, 7, and 13 of the first *Frame of Government* (doc. 30, above). The fifth article sets a two-thirds quorum of the full Council of seventy-two members for major Council business; article 6 gives the Council the power to adjourn its own sessions. When the legislature decided to reduce the Council to eighteen members, they had to alter these clauses to make twelve councilors the quorum for major business, and for adjournment. "The king's letters patents" is the royal charter to WP, doc. 11, above.

11. The committee system of England's House of Commons was closely imitated by most colonial legislatures in English America.

12. The register recorded all land sales, wills, and major business transactions. See law 20 of the *Laws Agreed Upon in England* (doc. 30, above).

13. Mann (who had replaced Edmund Cantwell when Cantwell was elected to the Council), Test, and Vines were the sheriffs of New Castle, Philadelphia, and Sussex counties (see under 10 Mar., above). The Council took up the matter of fees for official services on 19 Mar. 1683; see n. 27, below.

14. Duck Creek is the principal stream in northern Kent Co., Delaware.

15. Assemblymen's.

16. WP was concerned that because he had not given himself a veto power in the *Frame of Government*, his Council and Assembly might pass some law in violation of English law, especially the Navigation Acts. This could result in the loss of his "patent," or royal charter to Pennsylvania (see doc. 11, especially sections 11 and 14, above). WP and his legislature resolved the issue by allowing the governor the right to block any legislation proposed by the Council (see n. 20, below) so that no veto power would be necessary.

17. *Nemine contradicente,* Latin for "without any opposing voices," or unanimously.

18. Probably the Assembly.

19. A member of the Provincial Council from Kent Co.

20. The "bill" is the Act of Settlement, passed by the Council and House on 19 Mar. 1683; the section of that bill referred to here altered article 7 of the first *Frame of Government* (doc. 30, above) to make it clear that both the governor and the Council had to approve all legislation proposed to the Assembly for passage.

21. The Dec. 1682 legislative session set the punishment for fornication — sexual intercourse between unmarried persons — at three months of hard labor for both offenders, followed by forced marriage. In keeping with More's proposal, the Mar. 1683 session gave county courts the power to fine or whip offenders, and to compel marriage, as the justices of the peace saw fit; thus a master would lose no work time from his servant or slave.

22. A pass was a certificate, stamped with a county seal, that identified the slave or servant who carried it and authorized him or her to travel without supervision.

23. The Act of Settlement reduced the size of the Council and Assembly, and set new dates for elections and legislative sessions. It became the basis for the second *Frame of Government;* see doc. 63, below.

24. Runaway, fugitive.

25. Any settler who brought a wolf's head to a local justice of the peace received a bounty, or reward.

26. The *Friend's Adventure* of Liverpool, under the command of Thomas Wall, arrived in Pennsylvania in Sept. 1682 with settlers from Cheshire and Staffordshire, England. The sailors on this ship apparently unloaded the cargo at Chester rather than Philadelphia, and Captain Wall refused to pay them their wages. For the Council's handling of this case, see the Council entries below for 20 Mar. (p.m.), 21 Mar., 28 Mar., and 4 Apr.

27. The Mar. 1683 legislative session established a schedule of fees charged for all official services performed by provincial treasurers and secretaries, and local justices, clerks, sheriffs, constables, and coroners.

28. The duke of York's laws were enacted in 1665 by the duke's governor in New York; until 1682 the colonists on the west bank of the Delaware had been subject to these laws.

29. This is the "new bill," first introduced into the Assembly on 19 Mar.; it consisted of a series of articles that were eventually enacted as separate laws. Most of these articles had been read for the first time on 19 Mar. and were read for the second time on 20 Mar., but the article providing for appeals from the lower courts to the Provincial Council was read for the first time on 20 Mar.

30. The copying of a public document (in this case, a revised version of the *Frame of Government*) in large or handsome lettering.

31. Nathaniel Allen was the Bristol cooper who sailed to Pennsylvania in 1681 as one of WP's commissioners for laying out Philadelphia (see doc. 22, headnote, above); he became a cooper and merchant in Philadelphia. Henry Bowman, a member of the Assembly from Sussex Co., was a merchant, landowner, and mill owner.

32. This article divided the Provincial Council into four committees. On 13 Mar.

1683 (see above), the Council had already discussed amending this article, which was dropped from the second *Frame of Government*.

33. The Act of Settlement, passed on 19 Mar. 1683.

34. On the afternoon of 20 Mar. 1683; see above.

35. In doc. 17, above, WP had promised that all First Purchasers should enjoy exclusive use of the rivers, lakes, and woods within their properties. When the Assembly challenged this decision, WP changed his policy. See doc. 63, article 22, below.

36. Written orders to pay a specified sum to a specified person. Since there were no banks in early America, bills of exchange performed the function of modern checks.

37. An act of oblivion was an amnesty dismissing criminal charges brought before a certain date. The Mar. 1683 legislature passed an act dismissing all charges, except for treason and murder, brought against the inhabitants of Pennsylvania and Delaware up to the date of the act.

38. Persons who used abusive language toward others in public.

39. An ear mark or cut on a domestic animal was (like a brand) a means of identifying ownership.

40. Hogs were restrained from rooting for food, and from fighting, by rings inserted in their noses.

41. Persons who bring frivolous and harassing law suits.

42. Barrel staves. Since most liquids and perishables were stored and shipped in barrels, it was very important to establish quality controls for barrel production.

43. Taverns. See doc. 57, above, for Pennsylvania's first tavern regulations.

44. The Mar. 1683 legislative session established local boards of three "peacemakers" who would hear civil disputes and settle them by arbitration in order to avoid lawsuits. This manner of settling disputes was strongly favored by early Quakers.

45. The text reads "fourth" here, but the recording clerk must have lost count. The "fifth article . . . relating to the building of ferryboats," discussed the following afternoon (see immediately below), was apparently part of another bill.

46. Fences set across streams to catch fish.

47. Charles Pickering from Cheshire, England; he was a part owner of the *Friend's Adventure* and is protesting the Council decision of 21 Mar., above, that the seamen on this ship be paid their wages. See the Council entry for 4 Apr., below.

48. This act dealing with the rights of foreigners was incorporated into the second *Frame of Government* (doc. 63, article 21, below).

49. See articles 17 and 18 in the first *Frame of Government* (doc. 30, above).

50. The Assembly of 4-7 Dec. 1682, held at Chester, had passed seventy-one laws, most of them closely based on the *Laws Agreed Upon in England* (doc. 30).

51. The first of the seventy-one laws passed by the Dec. 1682 Assembly. Since this first legislature had met as a single body, the assemblymen of Mar. 1683 seem to have regarded it as a meeting of the Council; therefore they were now pursuing their constitutional right to accept or reject its laws as if they were bills which required approval by a distinct lower house. On 27 Mar. they ratified forty-three laws enacted by the Dec. Assembly, and on 28 Mar. they ratified nine others. Nineteen of the seventy-one laws passed by the Dec. Assembly were not confirmed, but several were replaced by new legislation.

52. Article 19 of the first *Frame of Government* (doc. 30, above) gave the governor and Council the power to dismiss the Assembly, which could only gather again on the invitation of the governor and Council.

53. This clause increased WP's executive independence. According to the first *Frame* (doc. 30, articles 17-18), WP was initially entitled to select judges, sheriffs, justices of the peace, and other local officials, but when these officers died or were removed, he had to accept nominations from the Council and Assembly for their successors. By the terms of the second *Frame* (doc. 63, article 16), however, the Council and Assembly could only begin to nominate local officers after WP's death. See the Council's discussion of this issue on 29 Mar., below.

54. The laws enacted by the Dec. 1682 Assembly.

55. Behaved disobediently.

56. Detract from, disparage.

57. See nn. 26 and 47, above.

58. See doc. 96, below.

59. The new second *Frame of Government* (doc. 63, below).

60. The expenses of government.

61. The second *Frame of Government.*

62. This article established that certain of the new laws had the same fundamental nature as the *Frame of Government,* and made them just as hard to amend or repeal. These laws thus became rather like the Bill of Rights added to the United States Constitution.

63. Regulation of the weight and price of bread.

64. Grain; not Indian corn.

65. Scolds; persons who make abusive complaints in public.

66. See the signatures at the end of doc. 63, below.

67. WP's treble vote was now more significant, since the membership of the Council was being reduced from seventy-two to eighteen. This provision was not incorporated into the second *Frame of Government* (doc. 63), however, as it had been in the first *Frame of Government* (doc. 30, article 6). Instead, in the second *Frame of Government* the governor relied on his right to give or withhold his assent to all bills that the Council prepared for the Assembly (see nn. 16 and 20, above).

68. The Mar. 1683 legislature discouraged the exportation of animal skins from Pennsylvania by imposing a tax upon all hides that were sent anywhere but England.

69. The Mar. session valued the Spanish peso, or piece of eight, at 6s. local currency, and the perue at 5s. 6d.

70. See the Pennsylvania charter, doc. 11, section 4, above.

71. Given no food or lodging by private citizens or by tavernkeepers.

72. WP is here establishing an executive committee of the Council to advise him in his daily administration, as provided for in article 11 of the second *Frame of Government.*

# 63 ⸹
# *The Second* Frame of Government

THE second *Frame of Government,* printed below, was Pennsylvania's first operating constitution. It preserved most of the features of WP's first *Frame,* but scaled down the size of the government. The balance of power among the three branches of government remained much as before: WP had somewhat fuller control over the appointment of local officeholders than in the first *Frame,* the Council had a somewhat stronger voice in day-to-day administrative matters, and the Assembly remained relatively restricted. The second *Frame* also offered two new and seemingly somewhat contradictory rights to the inhabitants of Pennsylvania and the lower counties. All property holders, including aliens, were guaranteed quiet possession of their lands; and all inhabitants were given the freedom to hunt on other people's unfenced property and to fish on privately owned banks of boatable rivers and streams.

As is shown in doc. 62, above, the second *Frame of Government* took shape in two stages. On 19 March 1683 the Council and Assembly passed an Act of Settlement that reduced the Council to eighteen members, and the Assembly to thirty-six members, for one year. They then informed WP that they wished to rewrite his *Frame of Government* completely, incorporating into their revision both the Act of Settlement and other changes. This second process extended from 20 March to 2 April 1683, when the second *Frame of Government* was formally approved by WP and all members present of the Council and Assembly.

The numbering of the articles in the first and second *Frames* differs markedly, and the reader is directed to the following articles of the second *Frame of Government* which show changes from the corresponding sections of the first *Frame of Government:*

Preamble: The new constitution applies to the inhabitants of the lower counties on the Delaware, called "the territories thereunto annexed," as well as to Pennsylvania.

Article 1 ("Imprimis"): The Council is reduced from 72 to 18 members; the Assembly from 200 to 36 members.

Article 2: The day of election is moved from 20 February to 10 March, probably to avoid bad winter weather.

Article 5: The period for which proposed Council bills must be posted for public inspection before the meeting of the Assembly is reduced from thirty to twenty days.

Article 11: The complex system of four Council committees is replaced with an executive committee of six councilors appointed to consult with WP on all routine administrative business.

Article 12: The governor is prohibited from performing "any public act of state" except "by and with the advice and consent of the Provincial Council."

Article 13: The convening of the Assembly is advanced from 20 April to 10 May, again probably for better weather.

Article 16: WP is given full power to choose all local officials; only after his death are local officials to be nominated by the Council and Assembly.

Article 18: The Council and Assembly decide legislative issues by voice vote, rather than by secret ballot.

Article 21: All foreigners who invest in Pennsylvania, and who do not become naturalized citizens of the English dominions, are given the property and inheritance rights of citizens.

Article 22: All inhabitants get the right to hunt on unenclosed lands, and to fish on all boatable streams.

Article 23: WP pledges security of land tenure to all inhabitants of Pennsylvania.

The
# FRAME
OF THE
# GOVERNMENT
Of the *Province* of
**Pennsylvania**
In *America*

To all persons to whom these presents[1] may come:

Whereas King Charles the Second, by his letters patents under the Great Seal of England, bearing date the fourth day of March, in the thirty-third year of the king, for divers considerations therein mentioned, has been graciously pleased to give and grant unto me, William Penn, by the name of William Penn, Esquire, son and heir of Sir William Penn, deceased, and to my heirs and assigns, forever, all that tract of land or province called Pennsylvania in America, with divers great powers, pre-eminences, royalties, jurisdictions, and authorities necessary for the well-being and government thereof. And whereas the king's dearest brother, James, Duke of York and Albany, etc., by deeds of feoffment,[2] under his hand and seal, duly perfected, bearing date the four and twentieth day of August, one thousand six hundred eighty and two, did grant unto me, my heirs and assigns, all that tract of land lying and being from twelve miles northward of New Castle upon Delaware River in America to Cape Henlopen upon the said River and Bay of Delaware, southward, together with all royalties, franchises, duties, jurisdictions, liberties, and privileges thereunto belonging.

Now know ye, that for the well-being and governing of the said province, and territories thereunto annexed, and for the encouragement of all freemen and planters that may be therein concerned, in pursuance of the rights and powers aforementioned, I, the said William Penn, have declared, granted, and confirmed, and by these presents, for me, my heirs and assigns, do declare, grant, and confirm, unto all freemen, planters, and adventurers of, in, and to the said province and territories thereof, these liberties, franchises, and properties, so far as in me lies, to be held, enjoyed, and kept by the freemen, planters, and adventurers of and in the said province of Pennsylvania, and territories thereunto annexed, forever.

*Imprimis.* That the government of this province and territories thereof shall from time to time, according to the powers of the patent and deeds of feoffment aforesaid, consist of the proprietary and Governor, and the freemen of the said province, and territory thereof, in the form of a Provincial Council and Assembly, which Provincial Council shall consist of eighteen persons, being three out of each county, and which Assembly shall consist of thirty-six persons, being six out of each county, men of most note for their virtue, wisdom, and ability, by whom all laws shall be made, and public affairs transacted, as is hereafter limited and declared.

*2d.* There being three persons already chosen for every respective county of this province, and territories thereof, to serve in the Provincial Council, one of them for three years, one for two years, and one for one year, and one of them being to go off yearly in every county: that on the tenth day of the first month yearly,[3] forever after, the freemen of the said province and territories thereof shall meet together in the most convenient place in every county of this province, and territories thereof, then and there to choose one person qualified as aforesaid in every county, being one-third of the number to serve in Provincial Council, for three years, it being intended that one-third of the whole Provincial Council, consisting and to consist of eighteen persons, falling off yearly, it shall be yearly supplied with such yearly elections as aforesaid, and that one person shall not continue longer than three years. And in case any member shall decease before the last election during his time, that then at the next election ensuing his decease, another shall be chosen to supply his place for the remaining time he was to have served, and no longer.

*3d.* That after the first seven years, every one of the said third parts that goes yearly off shall be incapable of being chosen again for one whole year following, that so all that are capable and qualified, as aforesaid, may be fitted for government and have a share of the care and burden of it.

*4th.* That the Provincial Council, in all cases and matters of moment, as their arguing upon bills to be passed into laws, or proceedings about erecting of courts of justice, sitting in judgment upon criminals impeached, and choice of officers in such manner as is hereinafter expressed, not less than two-thirds of the whole shall make a quorum; and that the consent and approbation of two-thirds of the quorum shall be had in all such cases or matters of moment. And that in all cases and matters of lesser moment, one-third of the whole shall make a quorum, the majority of which shall and may always determine in such cases and causes of lesser moment.

*5th.* That the Governor and Provincial Council shall have the power of preparing and proposing to the Assembly, hereafter mentioned, all bills which they shall see needful, and that shall at any time be passed into laws within the said province and territories thereof; which bills shall be published and affixed to the most noted place in every county of this province and territories thereof twenty days before the meeting of the Assembly, in order to passing them into laws.

*6th.* That the Governor and Provincial Council shall take care that all laws, statutes, and ordinances, which shall at any time be made within the province and territories, be duly and diligently executed.

*7th.* That the Governor and Provincial Council shall at all times have the care of the peace and safety of this province and territories thereof; and that nothing be by any person attempted to the subversion of this Frame of Government.

*8th.* That the Governor and Provincial Council shall at all times settle and order the situation of all cities and market towns in every county, modeling therein all public buildings, streets, and marketplaces; and shall appoint all necessary roads and highways in this province and territories thereof.

*9th.* That the Governor and Provincial Council shall at all times have power to inspect the management of the public treasury, and punish those who shall convert any part thereof to any other use than what has been agreed upon by the Governor, Provincial Council, and Assembly.

*10th.* That the Governor and Provincial Council shall erect and order all public schools, and encourage and reward the authors of useful sciences and laudable inventions in the said province and territories thereof.

*11th.* That one-third of the Provincial Council residing with the Governor, shall with the Governor from time to time have[4] the care of the management of all public affairs relating to the peace, justice, treasury, and improvement of the province and territories, and to the good education of youth, and sobriety of the manners of the inhabitants therein, as aforesaid.

*12th.* That the Governor or his deputy shall always preside in the Provincial Council, and that he shall at no time therein perform any public act of state whatsoever, that shall or may relate unto the justice, trade, treasury, or safety of the province, and territories as aforesaid, but by and with the advice and consent of the Provincial Council thereof.

*13th.* And to the end that all bills prepared and agreed [to] by the Governor and Provincial Council, as aforesaid, may yet have the more full concurrence of the freemen of the province and territories thereof; it is declared, granted, and confirmed, that at the time and place in every county, for the choice of one person to serve in Provincial Council, as aforesaid, the respective members thereof at their said meeting shall yearly choose out of themselves six persons of most note for their virtue, wisdom, and ability, to serve in Assembly as their representatives, who shall yearly meet on the tenth day of the third month, in the capital town or city of the said province, unless the Governor and Provincial Council shall think fit to appoint another place to meet in; where during eight days the several members may confer freely with one another, and if any of them see meet, with a committee of the Provincial Council which shall be at that time purposely appointed to receive, from any of them, proposals for the alteration or amendment of any of the said proposed and promulgated bills; and on the ninth day from their so meeting, the said Assembly, after their reading over of the proposed bills by the clerk of the Provincial Council, and the occasions and motives for them being opened by the Governor or his deputy, shall, upon the question by him put, give their affirmative or negative, which to them seems best, in such manner as hereafter is expressed. But not less than two-thirds shall make a quorum in the passing of all bills into laws, and [the] choice of such officers as are by them to be chosen.

*14th.* That the laws so prepared and proposed as aforesaid, that are assented to by the Assembly, shall be enrolled as laws of this province and territories thereof, with this style: *By the Governor, with the assent and approba-*

*tion of the freemen in Provincial Council and Assembly met.* And from henceforth the meetings, sessions, acts, and proceedings of the Governor, Provincial Council, and Assembly, shall be styled and called: *The meetings, sessions, and proceedings of the General Assembly of the province of Pennsylvania, and the territories thereunto belonging.*

*15th.* And that the representatives of the people in Provincial Council and Assembly may in after ages bear some proportion with the increase and multiplying of the people, the numbers of such representatives of the people may be from time to time increased and enlarged, so as at no time the number exceed seventy-two for the Provincial Council, and two hundred for the Assembly; the appointment and proportion of which number, as also the laying and methodizing of the choice of such representatives in future time most equally to the division of the country or number of the inhabitants, is left to the Governor and Provincial Council to propose, and the Assembly to resolve, so that the order of proportion be strictly observed, both in the choice of the Council and the respective committees thereof, viz., one-third to go off and come in yearly.

*16th.* That from and after the death of this present Governor, the Provincial Council shall, together with the succeeding Governor, erect from time to time standing courts of justice, in such places and number as they shall judge convenient for the good government of the said province and territories thereof; and that the Provincial Council shall, on the thirteenth day of the second month then next ensuing, elect and present to the Governor or his deputy a double number of persons to serve for judges, treasurer, and master of the rolls within the said province and territories, to continue so long as they shall well behave themselves in those capacities respectively; and the freemen of the said province in an Assembly met, on the thirteenth day of the third month yearly shall elect, and then present to the Governor or his deputy, a double number of persons to serve for sheriffs, justices of the peace, and coroners for the year next ensuing; out of which respective elections and presentments, the Governor or his deputy shall nominate and commission the proper numbers for each office, the third day after the said respective presentments, or else the first named in such presentment for each office, as aforesaid, shall stand and serve in that office, the time before respectively limited. And in cases of death or default, such vacancy shall be supplied by the Governor and Provincial Council in manner aforesaid.

*17th.* That the Assembly shall continue [in session] so long as may be needful, to impeach criminals fit to be there impeached, [and] to pass such bills into laws as are proposed to them which they shall think fit to pass into laws; and till such time as the Governor and Provincial Council shall declare that they have nothing further to propose unto them for their assent and approbation; and that declaration shall be a dismissal to the Assembly for that time; which Assembly shall be, notwithstanding, capable of assembling together upon the summons of the Governor and Provincial Council at any time during that year, if the Governor and Provincial Council shall see occasion for their so assembling.

*18th.* That all the elections of members or representatives of the people to serve in Provincial Council and Assembly, and all questions to be determined by both or either of them that relate to choice of officers, and all or any other personal matters, shall be resolved or determined by the ballot; and all things relating to the preparing and passing of bills into laws shall be openly declared and resolved by the vote.

*19th.* That at all times when the proprietary and Governor shall happen to be an infant, and under the age of one and twenty years, and no guardians or commissioners are appointed in writing by the father of the said infant, or that such guardian shall be deceased, that during such minority, the Provincial Council shall from time to time, as they shall see meet, constitute and appoint guardians and commissioners, not exceeding three, one of which shall preside as deputy and chief guardian, during such minority, and shall have and execute, with the consent of one of the other two, all the power of a Governor in all public affairs and concerns of the said province and territories thereof, according to charter; which said guardian, so appointed, shall also have the care and oversight of the estate of the said minor, and be yearly accountable and responsible for the same to the Provincial Council, and the Provincial Council to the minor, when of age, or to the next heir in case of the minor's death, for the trust before expressed.

*20th.* That as often as the days of the month mentioned in any article of this charter shall fall upon the first day of the week, commonly called the Lord's day, the business appointed for that day shall be deferred until the next day, unless in cases of emergency.

*21st.* And for the satisfaction and encouragement of all aliens, I do give and grant that if any alien, who is or shall be purchaser, or who does or shall inhabit in this province or territories thereof, shall decease at any time before he can well be naturalized, his right and interest therein shall notwithstanding descend to his wife and children, or other [of] his relations, be he testate or intestate, according to the laws of this province and territories thereof in such cases provided, in as free and ample manner, to all intents and purposes, as if the said alien had been naturalized.

*22d.* And that the inhabitants of this province and territories thereof may be accommodated with such food and sustenance as God in His providence has freely afforded, I do also further grant to the inhabitants of this province and territories thereof, liberty to fowl and hunt upon the lands they hold, or all other lands therein not enclosed; and to fish in all waters in the said lands, and in all rivers and rivulets in and belonging to this province and territories thereof, with liberty to draw his or their fish on shore on any man's lands, so as it be not to the detriment or annoyance of the owner thereof, except such lands as do lie upon inland rivulets that are not boatable, and which are or may be hereafter erected into manors.

*23d.* And that all the inhabitants of this province and territories thereof, whether purchasers or others, may have the last worldly pledge of my good and kind intentions to them and their heirs, I do give, grant, and confirm to all and every one of them full and quiet possession of their respective lands to which they have any lawful or equitable claim, saving only such rents and services for the same as are or customarily ought to be reserved to me, my heirs, and assigns.

*24th*. That no act, law, or ordinance, whatsoever, shall at any time here-after be made or done by the proprietary and Governor of this province and territories thereunto belonging, his heirs or assigns, or by the freemen in Provincial Council or Assembly, to alter, change, or diminish the form or effect of this Charter, or any part or clause thereof, contrary to the true intent and meaning thereof, without the consent of the proprietary and Governor, his heirs or assigns, and six parts of seven of the said freemen in Provincial Council and Assembly met.

*25th*. And lastly, I, the said William Penn, proprietary and Governor of the province of Pennsylvania and territories thereunto belonging, for me, my heirs and assigns, have solemnly declared, granted, and confirmed, and do hereby solemnly declare, grant, and confirm, that neither I, my heirs, nor assigns, shall procure or do any thing or things whereby the liberties in this Charter contained and expressed shall be infringed or broken. And if any-thing be procured by any person or persons contrary to these premises, it shall be held of no force or effect.

In witness whereof, I, the said William Penn, at Philadelphia in Penn-sylvania, have unto this present Charter of Liberties set my hand and broad seal, this second day of the second month, in the year of our Lord 1683, being the thirty-fifth year of the king, and the third year of my government.

William Penn

This within Charter, which we have distinctly heard read, and thank-fully received, shall be by us inviolably kept; at Philadelphia, the second day of the second month, one thousand six hundred eighty and three.

The members of the Provincial Council present:[5]

| | | |
|---|---|---|
| William Markham | William Clayton | James Harrison |
| John Moll | Francis Whitwell | John Richardson |
| William Haige | Thomas Holme | Philip T. Lehnmann, |
| Christopher Taylor | William Clarke | Secretary to the |
| John Simcock | William Biles | Governor |
| | | Richard Ingelo, |
| | | Clerk of the Council |

The members of the Assembly present:[6]

| | | |
|---|---|---|
| Casparus Herrman | John Kipshaven | James Williams |
| John Darby | Alexander Molestine | John Blunston |
| Benjamin Williams | Robert Brassey, Sr. | John Songhurst |
| William Guest | Thomas Brassey | John Hill |
| Valentine Hollingsworth | William Yardley | Nicholas Waln |
| James Boyden | John Hastings | Thomas Fitzwater |
| Benoni Bishop | Robert Wade | John Clows |

| | | |
|---|---|---|
| John Bezar | Thomas Hassold | Luke Watson |
| John Harding | John Hart | Joseph Phipps |
| Andrew Bringston | Robert Hall | Dennis Rochford |
| Simon Irons | Robert Bedwell | John Brinkloe |
| John Wood | William Simsmore | Henry Bowman |
| John Curtis | Samuel Dark | Cornelius Verhoofe |
| Daniel Brown | Robert Lucas | John Southworth, |
| William Futcher | | Clerk of the Synod[7] |

Some of the inhabitants of Philadelphia present:

| | | |
|---|---|---|
| William Howell | Henry Lewis | Samuel Miles |
| Edmund Warner | | |

Printed tract. *The Frame of the Government of the Province of Pennsylvania in America* (London, 1691). This text has been supplemented and corrected by the text in *Minutes of the Provincial Council of Pennsylvania* (Philadelphia, 1852), pp. 42-48. Not published in *PWP*, Vol. Two.

1. The present document.

2. The possession of lands with only nominal feudal obligations; the most desirable kind of land tenure under English law.

3. Every 10 Mar. This *Frame of Government,* like its predecessor (doc. 30, above), numbers all months in Quaker style, with March as the first month.

4. The *Minutes of the Provincial Council* text reads: "That one-third part of the Provincial Council residing with the Governor from time to time, shall with the Governor have. . . ."

5. Six of the eighteen councilors were apparently absent from the signing ceremony: Lasse Cock of Phila. Co., Edmund Cantwell and Ralph Withers of New Castle Co., John Hillyard of Kent Co., and John Rhoads and Edward Southrin of Sussex Co.

6. Twelve of the fifty-four assemblymen were absent from the signing, one each from Chester, Kent, and Sussex counties, three from New Castle Co., and five from Phila. Co. The names of four of the forty-two assemblymen given below vary widely from the roll call of 12 Mar. 1683 (see doc. 62, above). Benjamin Williams is certainly Henrick Williams of New Castle Co. in doc. 62. Andrew Bringston is Andros Binkson of Phila. Co. in doc. 62; Binkson was evidently his un-Anglicized name. John Hastings is John Haskins of Chester Co. in doc. 62, but other records suggest that his name was John Hastings. William Simsmore is William Windsmore of Kent Co. in doc. 62; Windsmore (or Winsmore) is his correct name. In addition, the "James Williams" of New Castle Co. who appears on original lists in both docs. 62 and 63 is James Walliam (as he signed his name) who appears in other records; and William Futcher of Sussex Co. appears as William Fletcher in some records.

7. The synod (gathering) here means the Assembly.

# Part IX

CONFLICT WITH LORD BALTIMORE §
JUNE 1683–AUGUST 1683

*Charles Calvert, 3d Lord Baltimore, by Sir Godfrey Kneller, Enoch Pratt Free Library, Baltimore, Maryland.*

DURING the spring and summer of 1683 WP watched his colony grow. By June, eighty houses had been built in Philadelphia and over three hundred families had started farms. In his letters to John Aubrey (doc. 66) and to Lord North (doc. 71), WP described his province in glowing terms: the natives and their customs, the climate, plants, animals, and mineral wealth. Nevertheless, several nagging problems remained. The most serious of these was the border dispute with Lord Baltimore. It had been clear to WP for some time that the true location of the 40th degree of latitude was north of Philadelphia (see the headnote to doc. 35 and the map on p. 279), and this fact threatened to undermine all of WP's plans for a flourishing province. If WP accepted the southern boundary defined in his charter, he could not hope to open the Susquehanna Valley for settlement in the near future, and he might well lose control of the lower counties, and of commerce on the Delaware, to the proprietor of Maryland.

WP followed a number of strategies to obtain an inlet to the Susquehanna and to secure his title to the lower Delaware. Before leaving England he asked the king to write a letter (dated 19 August 1682) to Lord Baltimore, advising him to settle the boundary by measuring two degrees north from Maryland's border with Virginia at Watkin's Point, sixty miles to a degree. This was the number of miles a degree was thought to contain when Lord Baltimore obtained his patent, and WP would have gained about twenty miles by fixing the boundary in this way. WP delivered the king's letter to Lord Baltimore at their conference of 11-13 December 1682. He did not press for this solution, however, because measuring from Watkin's Point would not give him the entrance to the Susquehanna River that he sought. Instead, WP wanted to start measuring farther south—at the mouth of the Chesapeake; this would give him land at the head of the bay. Lord Baltimore rejected the notion of measuring from either point. He wanted WP to join him in locating the 40th degree of latitude, but since WP already knew that this would place the boundary much too far north, he avoided making the joint observation. He did, however, offer to buy land from Lord Baltimore at the mouth of the Susquehanna. The Maryland proprietor said he might consider exchanging that area for Kent and Sussex counties; however, WP found this offer unacceptable. The two men met again on 29 May 1683 at New Castle, but their positions remained essentially unchanged.

WP tried to strengthen his title to Kent, Sussex, and New Castle counties by getting Charles II to grant a charter for the lower counties to the duke of York; the duke would then transfer his rights to WP. But Lord Baltimore claimed that the Maryland charter, which included the territory of Delaware, predated the duke's claims to the region by over thirty years. In June 1683 the Maryland proprietor took more direct action by announcing that he was selling land in Kent and Sussex counties at low rates; in effect, he was inciting the inhabitants of Delaware to rebel against WP's government (doc. 67). WP quickly protested (doc. 69), but he could not persuade Lord Baltimore to back off.

By this time WP had also discovered that Lord Baltimore had sent to the Lords of Trade what WP considered a one-sided narrative of their boundary negotiations (see doc. 75). He thus resolved to send his cousin William Markham to England to plead his case (see docs. 74, 79). All pretense of what WP called "good neighborhood" had disappeared by the summer of 1683. Each governor accused the other of deceit, hypocrisy, and fraud, and both exhibited a bad-tempered stubbornness that prevented any chance of a compromise settlement.

# 64 §

## To Lord Baltimore

Philadelphia, 6 June 1683

My Noble Friend,

If upon my arrival in this province, I did immediately dispatch my secretary[1] with two other gentlemen to salute the Lord Baltimore and assure him of my respects and friendship? If so soon as I had paid my duty to my royal patron the duke, I did incontinently take a long journey in a cold and unpleasant season,[2] that I might personally give him the further pledges of a friendly agreement and neighborhood? And if I did then therefore waive to press my own advantages, because I found it uneasy to him? And lastly, if in my after-correspondences, and especially at our last interview,[3] I have declined the rigor of my plea, and both proposed and pressed some of the mildest and most healing expedients, that if possible, we might be the last arbitrators of our own affairs without the need of another umpire? Then [with] the good will we ought to bear to a mutual and lasting union, the Lord Baltimore, I would think, will be so kind as to let me hope he will pardon me if I stop here, and shall hold myself acquitted by the endeavors I have used, with so much industry and submission, for a friendly issue. And if there were anything below what I have already offered, besides ruin to my

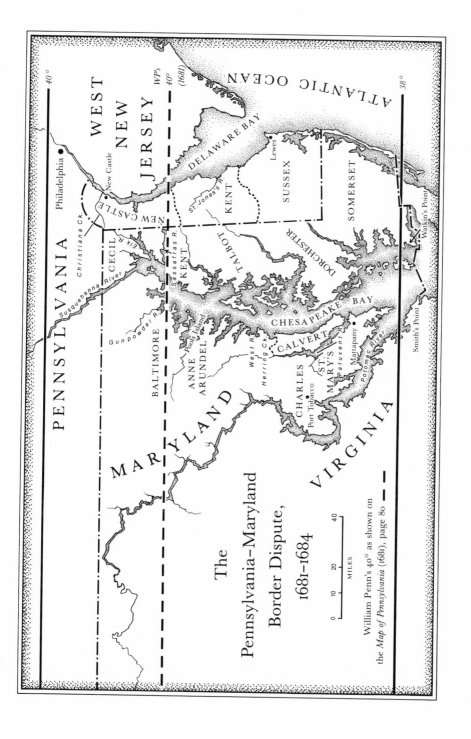

PENNSYLVANIA

WEST
NEW
JERSEY

WP's
40°
(1681)

ATLANTIC OCEAN

40°

38°

Philadelphia

New Castle

NEW CASTLE

Christiana Ck.

Susquehanna River

CECIL

Elk R.

Sassafras R.

KENT

DELAWARE BAY

St. Jones's R.

Lewes

SUSSEX

KENT

TALBOT

DORCHESTER

SOMERSET

Gunpowder R.

BALTIMORE

Pool's Island

ANNE
ARUNDEL

West R.

Herring Ck.

CHESAPEAKE BAY

CALVERT

ST.
MARY'S

Patuxent R.

Mattapany

Smith's Point

Watkin's Point

MARYLAND

CHARLES

Port Tobacco

Potomac River

VIRGINIA

The
Pennsylvania–Maryland
Border Dispute,
1681–1684

0    10    20    40
MILES

William Penn's 40° as shown on
the *Map of Pennsylvania* (1681), page 80

province, God is both my witness and my judge, I should be but too apt to incline.

My noble friend, I am not moved by the power of ambition or avarice. It is conveniency, yea, necessity that bids me stand. I deal freely; I have outrun all counsels, that I might purchase peace, though with loss; but with destruction, even nature and reason forbid. What I seek, be it my own and so my due, or the Lord Baltimore's and as such (if he pleases) my purchase, it is of that minute consequence to him and mighty moment to me, because to his country the tail or skirt, to my province the mouth or inlet,[4] that the disproportion of the value and conveniency that it bears to either of us, will defend, [or] at least indulge, my greater importunity. And yet while the advantage seems to be mine, it is most manifest it will be greatly [to] his profit to comply, since it will lay his province between two planted countries, and the people transporting themselves to Pennsylvania in ships consigned to Maryland, and those ships yearly bringing such English goods as we shall want, will naturally draw our people into his province to furnish themselves, and so make Maryland the mart of English trade, at least for many years.

What shall I say, my noble friend, if the powerful charms of interest, if the love of good neighborhood, if that which is always to be preferred with persons of the Lord Baltimore's loyalty—I mean duty to the king—prevail, I must yet promise myself an agreement in some fair and happy expedient, and lay by (which shall be with delight) the thoughts of an English voyage; that else the state of my affairs here and of my family there will of necessity oblige me to [go], and that speedily.[5]

I shall end with this assurance which I have often given, and shall most religiously observe, that I shall sincerely embrace all occasions by which I may prove myself, my noble friend,

Thy very firm and affectionate friend and neighbor,
Wm Penn

ALS. Maryland Historical Society, Baltimore. (*PWP,* 2:389-90).

1. Philip Theodore Lehnmann, who had been WP's secretary since about 1673 and who accompanied him to America on the *Welcome* in 1682.

2. In 1682 WP had traveled to New York in Nov., and then to Anne Arundel Co., Maryland, to meet Lord Baltimore on 11 Dec.

3. On 29 May 1683, at New Castle. See William Clarke's account of the two governors' hostile behavior at this meeting (doc. 67, below).

4. WP is talking here about the territory at the head of Chesapeake Bay and the mouth of the Susquehanna River that he has offered to buy from Lord Baltimore.

5. Both proprietors soon felt forced to return to England in order to appeal to the home government, but Lord Baltimore actually left three months before WP, in May 1684.

# 65 §

## William Kennerly to James Harrison

IN the following letter a prospective immigrant writes to WP's steward, James Harrison, who had come to Pennsylvania in 1682. He wants to know whether Harrison has staked out for him the land he has bought, and whether it is as fruitful as was advertised—two smart questions, considering the experience of Joseph Harris (doc. 61). His other practical questions must have been raised by every immigrant to Pennsylvania. There is no record that William Kennerly ever came to America, but James Kennerly, perhaps a relative, was a First Purchaser who moved from Cheshire County in England to Chester County, Pennsylvania.

Winslowe, 6 June 1683

Loving Friend James Harrison

These lines are to let thee understand that our desire and request is that thou would be pleased to let us understand whether the land of itself be as good soil and as fruitful as the reports were of it when thou was in England? And whether thou has taken up that parcel of land which I have bought of thee, so that it may be likely and suitable for us when we arrive there? We likewise desire to know of thee what thou thinks or knows to be the best commodities for us to bring over, and what time might be the best and [most] suitable for us to be there, and to what place might be the [most] convenient to bind our ship to land us there? And likewise if there be anything else that we are not acquainted with for the present that might be useful for us, that thou would not fail but let us know by the next and best opportunity, for our whole intent and purpose is to [go] over into Pennsylvania this next spring. Therefore my desire is that I might hear from thee that I might have time to furnish myself with conveniences for my journey. So having no more at present but my dear love, with my wife's, to thee.

I rest thy friend,<br>William Kennerly

ALS. HSP. Not published in *PWP*, Vol. Two.

# 66 §

## To John Aubrey

EVEN with all of his other activities, WP still found time for a favorite pursuit of the Restoration gentleman—the encouragement of science.

In November 1681 WP had joined the Royal Society of London, to which several of his friends already belonged, including the recipient of this letter, John Aubrey (1626-1697), who was a pioneer archeologist and folklorist. WP's letter to Aubrey shows his interest in the intellectual life of late-seventeenth-century England. But even in this letter, WP could not resist the opportunity to sell his colony. Always the real estate promoter, he gives his scholarly friend a glowing picture of Pennsylvania.

Philadelphia, 13 June 1683

Esteemed Friend

I value myself much upon the good opinion of those ingenious gentlemen I know of the Royal Society,[1] and their kind wishes for me and my poor province. All I can say is, that I and it are votaries to the prosperity of their harmless and useful inquiries. It is even one step to heaven to return to nature, and though I love that proportion should be observed in all things, yet a natural knowledge, or the science of things from sense and a careful observation and argumentation thereon, reinstates men, and gives them some possession of themselves again; a thing they have long wanted by an ill tradition, too closely followed, and the foolish credulity so incident to men. I am a Greshamist[2] throughout; I love inquiry not for inquiry's sake, but care not to trust my share in either world to other men's judgments, at least without having a finger in the pie for myself. Yet I love that inquiry should be modest and peaceable, virtues that have strong charms upon the wiser and honester part of the mistaken world. Pray give them my sincere respects, and in my behalf solicit the continuation of their friendship to my undertaking.

We are the wonder of our neighbors as in our coming and numbers, so to ourselves in our health, subsistence, and success. All goes well, blessed be God, and provisions we shall have to spare, considerably, in a year or two, unless very great quantities of people crowd upon us. The air, heat, and cold resemble the heart of France; the soil good, the springs many and delightful, the fruits, roots, corn, and flesh as good as I have commonly eaten in Europe, I may say of most of them better. Strawberries ripen in the woods in April, and in the last month, peas, beans, cherries, and mulberries. Much black walnut, chestnut, cypress or white cedar, and mulberry are here. The sorts of fish in these parts are excellent and numerous. Sturgeon leap day and night, [so] that we can hear them a bow shot from the rivers in our beds. We have roasted and pickled them, and they eat like veal one way, and sturgeon the other way. Mineral here is [in] great store; I shall send some suddenly[3] for trial. Vines are here in abundance everywhere; some may be as big in the body as a man's thigh. I have begun a vineyard by a Frenchman of Languedoc,[4] and another of Poitou, near Saintonge.[5] Several people from other colonies are retiring hither, as [from] Virginia, Maryland, New England, Rhode Island, New York, etc.

I make it my business to establish virtuous economy and therefore sit twice in Council every week[6] with good success, I thank God. My reception was with all the show of kindness the rude state of the country could yield; and after holding two General Assemblies,[7] I am not uneasy to the people. They, to express their love and gratitude, gave me an impost that might be worth £500 per annum, and I returned it to them with as much credit.[8] This is our present posture. I am debtor to thy kindness for two letters. Whether this be pay or no, or but wampum against sterling metal, pray miss not to continue to yield that content and liberality to

Thy very true friend,
Wm Penn

Particularly, pray give my respects to Sir William Petty, my friend [Robert] Hooke, [Robert] Wood, [Francis] Lodwick, and Dr. [Edward] Bernard, though unknown, whose skill is a great compliment.[9] Vale.[10]

LS. Bodleian Library, Oxford. (*PWP,* 2:394-97).

1. The Royal Society of London for Improving Natural Knowledge, chartered in 1662 by Charles II, became the leading center for scientific work in late-seventeenth-century England. Sir Isaac Newton, Robert Boyle, and the other important experimental scientists of the day were members, as were the philosopher John Locke, the architect Sir Christopher Wren, and the diarist Samuel Pepys. Many of the members of the Royal Society, such as WP, were gentlemen amateurs with no scientific expertise.

2. A natural philosopher or scientist, with a particular interest in practical knowledge and useful inventions. Gresham College in London offered instruction in science and technology, and the Royal Society held its meetings at the college from 1662 until 1710. Most members of the Royal Society shared WP's "Greshamist" interest in the practical application of scientific knowledge.

3. Soon.

4. In southern France. One of WP's viniculturists was Andrew Doz, a French Huguenot who came to Pennsylvania in 1682.

5. Two provinces in west central France.

6. In June 1683, at the time WP wrote this letter, the Pennsylvania Council was meeting twice a week, but in Apr.-May and July-Aug. it met much more irregularly than WP claimed.

7. The first Assembly met at Chester, 4-7 Dec. 1682; the second at Philadelphia, 10 Mar.-3 Apr. 1683.

8. See doc. 70, below.

9. All five of these men were members of the Royal Society. Sir William Petty (1623-1687) was a surveyor and political economist; Robert Hooke (1635-1703) was a wide-ranging experimentalist in chemistry, astronomy, and physics; Robert Wood (1622?-1685) was a physician and mathematician; Francis Lodwick had been elected to the Royal Society three weeks after WP in Nov. 1681; and Edward Bernard (1638-1696) was professor of astronomy at Oxford.

10. Farewell.

## 67 §
### From William Clarke

RELATIONS between WP and Lord Baltimore were rapidly growing worse. In the following letter, William Clarke, a provincial councilor and justice of the peace in Sussex County, reports several pages of bad news: Lord Baltimore has now openly laid claim to the lower counties, an action that has alarmed the local inhabitants, and stories are circulating about how poorly the two governors got along when they met at New Castle a month earlier. Clarke takes special pains in this letter to point out how helpful he has been to WP in calming the fears of the inhabitants. However, as a Quaker, Clarke is very concerned about the present and future status of Friends in the lower counties and in Maryland. Here he makes it pretty clear that he thinks WP's treatment of Lord Baltimore at their recent New Castle meeting was indeed arrogant, aggressive, and unwise.

Dover River,[1] 21 June 1683

Governor Penn:

These may serve to advise thee that I arrived at Lewes[2] the last first day.[3] Some [time] after, several of the neighborhood came to my house and told me that the Lord Baltimore did the last third day[4] cause a proclamation to be read publicly in Somerset County[5] Court, that all persons that would seat land in either the Whorekill or St. Jones's counties[6] that he would procure them rights at one hundred pounds of tobacco per right, and that they should pay but one shilling for every hundred acres of land yearly rent.[7] And if the inhabitants of both these counties would revolt from William Penn and own him to be their proprietary and governor, that they should have the same terms.[8] Reports were also given out that the Lord Baltimore did intend shortly to come with a troop of horse to take possession of these two lower counties, which caused great fear to arise in the people's minds, chiefly because most of the inhabited lands of the lower counties that are seated are claimed by some of the inhabitants of Maryland who had patents for it.

When the Lord Baltimore had the place,[9] he gave to any of his own province patents for what land here that they could desire although [they] never came to enjoy it. Which caused them[10] to be very earnest in their inquiry of me how things went at the meeting of Governor Penn and the Lord Baltimore.[11] And for the quieting of the people's minds, I saw a necessity lie upon me to let them know that the Lord Baltimore was so far from expecting to have these counties, that he had offered Governor Penn that if he would let him have these two lower counties, that he would give him as much at the head of Chesapeake Bay more than what would fall into our governor's line; and that I heard our governor say that at the same time that he parted with these two counties, he would part from Pennsylvania also.

And likewise I told them that these kinds of proceedings were no new things with the Lord Baltimore, he having declared the like overture to the people and inhabitants about two or three years since; which gave the inhabitants great satisfaction.

And the last third day, I coming here to Kent County Court, the like reports were here from Choptank, Dorchester, and Talbot counties.[12] And the like fears had seized upon the minds of the people, which caused them to be very desirous to know of me how things stood between the two proprietaries. I gave them the like answer as in the other counties; which caused them to banish all fears. And after that, I being willing to lay as strong obligations and ties upon the people as I could to bind them to be and continue faithful to thy interest, I put them upon petitioning to the governor for a charter to incorporate the town of Dover,[13] which they readily complied with and desired me to draw a petition for them, as also to take care to get the charter for them. Upon which I drew the enclosed petition which they readily voted to have sent to the governor and signed unto it, expressing that they feared not Baltimore or what he could do to them.

I hear that John Sharpe, whom thee were pleased to favor when here and passed by many offenses committed by him in thy government, has evilly rewarded thee in Maryland by running up and down, as it were, open-mouthed, telling the people that William Penn has forfeited his patent or charter by denying him an appeal.[14]

Our friend Richard Mitchell[15] was here at court, and tells me that the Lord Baltimore's party gives out in Maryland that he never saw any person carry himself so lofty and with so much majesty as Governor Penn did to him at New Castle. And that thee put as great a slight upon him as if he had been much thy inferior. And that after thee did come to New Castle, Governor Penn did take half an hour's time to repose himself, pretending the extremity of the heat, at his own lodging. And that instead thereof, [Governor Penn] stayed away three or four hours and in the meantime was advising with his Council. And although Governor Penn pretended to excuse himself by being asleep, he[16] had them there that informed him of his proceedings. And he cries out much against thee for breach of thy word to him.[17] And that thee came with about sixty horsemen better armed and accoutered[18] than his party, with a trumpet sounding before thee, and the great guns firing at thy going out and coming into the town. He said that thee offered to render unto him these two lower counties on condition that he would let thee have a landing at the head of his bay,[19] which is sounded up and down Maryland like a trumpet. And those Friends that were intending to come from thence to settle here and have purchased land for that purpose are much discouraged. This friend [Mitchell] also tells me that Baltimore begins to bring sufferings upon Friends in Maryland for refusing to train, and tells them that William Penn can come with a trumpet and armed men and fire great guns; and Friends have since been summoned or warned to train, and great fines laid upon them for refusing.[20]

To all these things I gave this friend [Mitchell] good satisfaction, telling him that thee ordered thy man to call thee when the Lord Baltimore was ready to go to dinner if within half an hour, which thy man neglected; at which I saw thee much troubled lest the Lord Baltimore should take an offense at it. And as to thy party being armed, there were several people that voluntarily went with thee — that went in their own way. And as for the firing of the great guns, I heard thee reprove Capt. [Peter] Alricks,[21] who was (as I thought) the occasion of it, for so doing. And that as for the trumpet, thee knew nothing of it; but I supposed it to be one that belonged to a ketch or ship that rode before the town that made use of it, without any order from thee. And that as to fighting, he knew Friends' principles so well that I should not need to say anything to that. The friend R[ichard] M[itchell] has [taken?] copies of two of the proclamations that I brought and set up here for the quickening and requiring of the ministers of justice to put the laws in execution against disorders and debaucheries;[22] which he says will be great satisfaction to Friends in Maryland and Virginia. Many intend for this place, he says, from Virginia.

Thus having, as in duty bound, communicated these things to thee, so that thee may know how ill thy pretended friend Baltimore makes use of thy friendship and respect for him, I shall take leave to subscribe myself thy true and faithful friend

Wm. Clarke

ALS. Hall of Records, Dover, Delaware. (*PWP*, 2:400-4).

1. St. Jones's River; see the map on p. 279.
2. In Sussex Co., Del.
3. 17 June 1683.
4. 12 June 1683.
5. The southernmost county on Maryland's Eastern Shore; see the map on p. 279.
6. Sussex and Kent counties in Delaware.
7. Actually, Lord Baltimore's terms were slightly different than Clarke reported. On 15 May 1683, he announced that he would issue rights, or grants of land, to settlers on the "seaboard side of the Whorekills" — that is, in southern Delaware — and charge fifty pounds of tobacco and one shilling annual quitrent for every fifty acres. This rate was half what he charged settlers in Maryland. When challenged later by WP, Baltimore explained that he and his father, Cecil Calvert, had often issued proclamations claiming title to the lower counties, and that the rents for the lower counties had always been set at half the rate of Maryland. WP's annual quitrent for lands in the lower counties was one penny per acre, over four times the amount Lord Baltimore set forth in this proclamation.
8. Lord Baltimore's proclamation of 15 May 1683 did not specifically mention WP or encourage the inhabitants of Delaware to revolt; however, anyone purchasing land in the lower counties from Lord Baltimore would by implication be rejecting WP's government.
9. Lord Baltimore had never really occupied the lower counties, although he claimed that the 1632 Maryland charter gave him title to the area. The lower counties were settled first by the Dutch and Swedes and then in 1664 were granted by Charles II to the duke of York. The closest Baltimore came to possession was in 1671-1672, when he sent troops into the lower counties.
10. The inhabitants of Sussex and Kent counties.
11. At New Castle, 29 May 1683. See the headnote to doc. 64, above.
12. The Choptank River, which flows into Chesapeake Bay, divides Dorchester and Talbot counties on the Eastern Shore of Maryland. See the map on p. 279.

13. WP responded to this petition by issuing orders to lay out the town of Dover and to survey lots for himself in the town, but the town was not in fact laid out until 1717.

14. John Sharpe, a Kent Co. landowner, had been ordered by the county court in Aug. 1682 to ask public forgiveness for slandering two local residents. Apparently he protested this order. There is no record that Sharpe appealed to WP and the Provincial Council, but he may have taken his case directly to the king, who reserved the right to receive, hear, and determine appeals.

15. Richard Mitchell (d. 1685) was appointed high sheriff and deputy-surveyor of Kent Co. in 1684.

16. Lord Baltimore.

17. Lord Baltimore claimed that in the mid-1670s, before he became proprietor of Pennsylvania, WP had recognized Baltimore's right to the lower counties.

18. Equipped.

19. Chesapeake Bay.

20. To train for the militia. Throughout the colonial period, Quakers in Maryland were liable to be punished for refusing to join the militia.

21. Peter Alricks (d. 1697?), a native of Holland, came to the Delaware Valley in 1656. Under WP's government, he was commissioned justice of the peace in 1682, and held many other offices. He was not a Quaker.

22. On 9 June 1683, WP and the Provincial Council issued a proclamation that ordered justices of the peace to execute the laws speedily and without prejudice, and another proclamation that ordered the justices to suppress disorders in taverns.

# 68 §

## Deed from the Delaware Indians

IN June and July 1683, WP concluded a series of treaties with the Delaware Indians for lands along the Delaware River, south of the purchase of 15 July 1682 (doc. 37) and west to and beyond the Schuylkill River. Doc. 68 is one of five extant deeds executed on 23 June 1683 for land in the vicinity of Neshaminy and Pennypack creeks in Bucks and Philadelphia counties. WP probably met with the Delaware sachems at Perkasie in late May, and the treaties were concluded in Philadelphia, where the Indian "kings" attended Quaker meeting and heard the traveling Quaker minister Roger Longworth preach.

23 June 1683

We, ESSEPENAIKE and SWANPISSE,[1] this 23rd day of the 4th month called June in the year according to the English account 1683, for us and our heirs and assigns, do grant and dispose of all our lands lying betwixt Pennypack and Neshaminy creeks[2] and all along upon Neshaminy Creek and backward of the same, and to run two days' journey with a horse up into the country as the said river does go, to WILLIAM PENN, proprietor and governor of the province of Pennsylvania, etc., his heirs and assigns forever, for the consideration of so much wampum and so many guns, shoes, stockings, looking glasses, blankets, and other goods, as he the said William Penn shall please to give unto us hereby for us, our heirs and assigns, renouncing all claims or demands of anything in or for the premises for the future from him, his heirs and assigns. IN WITNESS whereof we have hereunto set our hands and seals the day and year first above written.

Sealed and delivered
in the presence of
N[icholas] More
Lasse Cock   Thomas Holme
C[hristopher] Taylor   Thomas Wynne
      The mark of ⊗ Essepenaike   The mark of ⊗ Swanpisse

Indians present
Weanappe
Enshockhuppo[3]
Etpakeherah[4]
Alaenoh[5]

DS. HSP. (*PWP*, 2:404-5).

1. Essepenaike and Swanpisse both sold land to the English in 1681. See doc. 37.
2. Pennypack Creek flows into the Delaware River within the present city limits of Philadelphia, about seven miles southwest of Neshaminy Creek.
3. Indian names were spelled very inconsistently by the English clerks who prepared the early Pennsylvania Indian treaties. Enshockhuppo was probably the same Delaware sachem as Shakhuppo or Shakhoppah who, with other Delaware, sold WP land between Chester Creek and Pennypack Creek in 1685, and who met with the Provincial Council in 1694.
4. Perhaps the same as "Lare Packenah," who with Essepenaike and others sold WP land on the west bank of the Delaware between Duck Creek and Chester Creek in 1685.
5. Perhaps the same as "Alemeon," who with Shakhuppo and others met with the Provincial Council in 1694.


# 69 §

## To William Markham, James Harrison, and William Clarke

WHEN WP heard that Lord Baltimore was claiming title to the lower counties and that he was trying to entice the inhabitants of Kent and Sussex counties to rebel against WP (see doc. 67, above), he appointed three commissioners from the Provincial Council — William Markham, James Harrison, and William Clarke — to visit Lord Baltimore and protest these hostile actions. In doc. 69, WP instructs his commissioners on how to deal with the Maryland proprietor. Their visit to Maryland was a failure, for Lord Baltimore continued to claim the lower counties. For the next stage in this dispute, see doc. 75, below.

Philadelphia, 2 July 1683
Instructions to Captain William Markham and
James Harrison and William Clarke

1. As soon as you shall arrive at the Lord Baltimore's, present him with my first letter.

2. If he takes no notice to you of the contents, move [to] him the business of the proclamation.[1] If he confesses and owns it, show him the breach of friendship as well as of the treaty, and that no legal ejectment was served, and therefore an invasion upon the duke's long (and my late and present) quiet possession. Then give him my second letter, and stay two days for [an] answer.

3. If he says he resolves to proceed in disquieting the two lower counties,[2] protest against it in the king's name, and send letters to the presidents and sheriffs of those counties, informing them that the king has lately granted his letters patents under the Great Seal of England[3] and to warn them to suffer no surveyor or officer of the Lord Baltimore's to exercise any office therein; yet to keep within the compass of the civil magistrate and use no military power or force, being all subjects of one king who ought to decide the difference, and to whose judgment I do and will appeal.

4. If he waives to vindicate[4] his proclamation and inclines to my letters of the 6th and 9th last month,[5] the copies of which you have with you, proceed to appoint a time that we may meet to conclude matters between us, not before September.

5. Mention the indecent reflections of late made upon me and my late entertainment,[6] also upon my secretaries, by Major [Peter] Sayer[7] (both [Nicholas] More and [Philip] Lehnmann),[8] which you know of. These things, if by him suffered, will make all further correspondence impossible and impracticable between us.

6. But whatever is done, come away within 2 days after arrival, unless you go to Col. [Nicholas] Spencer,[9] in all which dispatch, for Singleton[10] must carry the result, who goes in 14 days at furthest. Be wise, be faithful, be cautious, and so God direct you.

Wm Penn

DS. HSP. (*PWP*, 2:410-11).

1. Lord Baltimore's proclamation of 15 May 1683 announced that he was selling land in the lower counties and that his rates were much lower than WP's. See doc. 67, n. 7.

2. Kent and Sussex counties in Delaware.

3. This is literally true, but is more complicated than WP admits. Charles II had indeed issued a patent, or charter, for the lower counties to the duke of York on 22 Mar. 1683, and the duke did plan to give his chartered rights to WP. But on 17 Apr., the Lords of Trade forbade the duke of York to transfer the title to WP until his dispute with Baltimore was settled.

4. Gives up trying to justify.

5. WP's letter of 6 June 1683 is doc. 64; his letter of 9 June has not been found.

6. Lord Baltimore complained that WP had insulted him at their second conference, which was held at New Castle on 29 May 1683. See doc. 67.

7. Peter Sayer (d. 1697) was a prominent Catholic of Talbot Co., Md., who had attended Lord Baltimore during the New Castle conference.

8. Sayer had accused More and Lehnmann of making hostile remarks at the time of the New Castle conference. Nicholas More was secretary of the Provincial Council, and Philip Lehnmann was WP's personal secretary.

9. Col. Nicholas Spencer (d. 1689) was president of the Virginia Council and the

chief executive in that colony after Gov. Thomas Culpeper left for England in May 1683. WP probably told his commissioners to visit Spencer in Virginia and appeal for his help if they judge it will put added pressure on Lord Baltimore.

10. Probably Thomas Singleton, the Quaker captain of the *Thomas and Anne,* who had arrived in Pennsylvania in Apr. 1683. See doc. 58, n. 1.


# 70 §

## Release of Customs Duty


**E**VEN though WP's expenses in governing his colony were considerable, he knew that the colonists in 1682-1683 had special initial expenses of their own; thus he collected no taxes or quitrents from First Purchasers during his first year in America. In April 1683, the General Assembly had enacted a duty on all imports, with a special tax on alcoholic beverages, to be paid to the proprietor. WP was eager to encourage trade and attract more settlers, and he probably underestimated his expenses, as he had so often done before (see doc. 41, above, for WP's financial problems); hence he issued the following proclamation announcing that he was surrendering this revenue for one year. He must have soon regretted this handsome gesture, for in November 1683 he was sufficiently short of funds that he sent out an agent to collect quitrents from his tenants; see doc. 83, below.

Philadelphia, 2 July 1683

By William Penn Proprietary and Governor of the Province<br>of Pennsylvania and Territories thereunto Belonging<br>A PROCLAMATION

Whereas the freemen of this province in Provincial Council and Assembly met did, as a testimony of their special respect to me to help to defray the divers charges incident to my public capacity, freely present me with a certain impost upon goods to be imported and exported to and from this province.[1] And though I have a deep sense of their kindness and good intent therein, yet that I may give them and all other persons coming and trading to this province a further pledge of my regard to their ease and prosperity, I do hereby freely remit the said impost or custom for one whole year, charging all collectors and their deputies within this province and territories to observe the same, as they will answer the contrary at their peril.

N[icholas] More, Secretary

DS. LCP, on deposit at HSP. (*PWP,* 2:411-12).

1. This act was passed on 2-3 Apr. 1683. It levied a two penny per gallon impost on all liquors, a one penny per gallon tax on cider, and a twenty shilling duty on every £100 of all other imports, except for molasses.

*The Blue Anchor Tavern and the Dock, by Isaac L. Williams, c. 1850-1860, HSP. The first tavern in Philadelphia, the Blue Anchor stood on the bank of the Delaware River at present Dock Street when WP arrived in 1682.*

# 71 §

## To Lord North

DURING July and August 1683, WP wrote letters to many of the king's chief ministers in England. These were "bread-and-butter" letters, in which WP thanked his patrons for past favors and pointed out that Pennsylvania deserved their support because it was in flourishing condition. The following letter to Lord North is a typical example. It seems ironic that WP should write a thank-you letter to a man who, in 1681, had advised the Lords of Trade to curb his chartered rights (see docs. 8-9, above). But WP realized that his boundary quarrel with Lord Baltimore would probably soon be arbitrated by the home authorities. If he could not recruit Lord North as an ally, perhaps he could at least prevent him from becoming an enemy.

Philadelphia, 24 July 1683

My Noble Friend

It has been sometimes a question with me, whether writing or silence were more excusable, for it is an unhappiness incident of[1] great men to be troubled with the respects of those their power and goodness oblige. But because I had rather want excuse for this freedom, than be wanting of gratitude to my benefactor, I determine to render my most humble thanks for the many favors I received at the Lord North's hand in the passing and great dispatch of my patent.[2]

I thank God I am safely arrived, and 22 sail more.[3] The air proves sweet and good, the land fertile, and the springs many and pleasant. We are 130 miles from the main sea and 40 miles up the freshes.[4] The town plat is a mile long and 2 miles deep. On each side of the town runs a navigable river, the least as broad as the Thames at Woolwich, the other above a mile.[5] About 80 houses are built, and I suppose above 300 farms settled as contiguously as may be. We have had since last summer about 60 sail of great and small shipping,[6] which we esteem a good beginning. A fair we have had, and weekly markets, to which the ancient lowly inhabitants come to sell their produce to their profit and our accommodation. I have also bought lands of the natives, treated them largely,[7] and settled a firm and advantageous correspondence with them, who are a careless, merry people; yet in property [they are] strict with us, though [they hold it in] a kind of community among themselves. In council, so deliberate; in speech, short, grave, and eloquent; young and old in their several classes; that I have never seen in Europe anything more wise, cautious, and dexterous. It is as admirable to me as it may look incredible on that side of the water. The weather often changes with notice and is constant almost in its inconstancy. Our trees are sassafras, cypress, cedar, black walnut, chestnut, and oak, black, white, red, Spanish and swamp, the most durable. Divers wild fruits as plum, peach, and grape, the sorts diverse. Mineral of copper and iron in diverse places.

I have only to add that it would please the Lord North to smile favorably upon us, a plantation so well regulated for the benefit of the crown, and so improving and hopeful by the industry of the people, that since rewards used to follow such enterprises in ancient times, at least encouragement and countenance might be yielded us, whose aims shall in everything be bounded with a just regard to the king's service. And we think we may reasonably hope that, England being the market both of our wants and industry in great measure, there is interest as well as goodness of our side. I have pardon to ask for a poor present I make by the hands of the bearer my agent and kinsman, Capt. [William] Markham. All I have to say is this: it is our country produce, and that of old time offerings were valued by the heart that made them.

I end with a congratulation of the honor the king has joined to thy great merit,[8] and my sincere and most affectionate wishes for thy future prosperity; being one of those many whom your goodness has obliged to own and approve, as really I am

Thy very sensible, thankful<br>
friend, and servant to my power,[9]<br>
Wm Penn

LS. Rosenbach Museum and Library of Philadelphia. (*PWP*, 2:414-15).

1. Liable to happen to.
2. For North's "favors" to WP in securing the charter, see docs. 8 and 9. As these documents show, North proposed that WP's chartered powers be severely restricted.
3. Twenty-three ships brought colonists to Pennsylvania in 1681-1682.
4. Above the ebb tide, where the Delaware River turns from salt to fresh water.
5. Woolwich, a borough of London, borders the Thames where the river widens east of the city. WP may be exaggerating here, for the Schuylkill and the Delaware are not now as broad as he describes them, but there has been much landfill along both riverfronts since 1683.
6. In another letter written the same month, WP reported only forty "great & small" trading ships since last summer.
7. Generously.
8. On 20 Dec. 1682 Charles II appointed North the Keeper of the Great Seal. In Sept. 1683 the king would make him Baron Guilford.
9. WP means: to the utmost of my power.

# 72 §

## Commission and Instructions
## to James Graham and William Haige

WHEN WP bought Indian title to the territory in southeastern Pennsylvania, he was able to deal directly with the local Delaware, or Lenni Lenape, Indians (see docs. 37 and 68, above, and the map on p. 159).

Buying Indian title to the territory further west along the Susquehanna River would be more difficult. This interior region of Pennsylvania was the home of the Susquehannock Indians, but in the late 1670s the Susquehannocks had been decimated and dispersed in a series of wars. Some of them were now living among the Iroquois Indians in northern New York. Since the English government of New York had a treaty system with the Iroquois, to whom the Susquehannocks were now subordinate, the New Yorkers could claim control over the Susquehanna River Valley and its fur trade. In handling this ticklish situation WP tried to deal directly with the Indians rather than with the New York government. As doc. 72 shows, he sent Provincial Councilor William Haige and a New York merchant named James Graham (d. 1701) to Albany and instructed them to negotiate with the Iroquois (as "conquerors" of the Susquehannocks) for the purchase of land along the Susquehanna River Valley. Not surprisingly, Governor Thomas Dongan of New York objected to this maneuver. For his response, see doc. 78, below.

Philadelphia, 2 August 1683
William Penn Proprietary and Governor of the Province of Pennsylvania and the Territories thereunto belonging
To My Trusty Friends James Graham and William Haige.

Reposing special confidence in your wisdom and integrity I do hereby constitute you my commissioners and impower you in my name to treat with the sachems of the Mohawk[1] and Seneca[2] Indians and their allies for the purchasing of the lands lying on both sides of Susquehanna River, and whatsoever you do therein I do hereby ratify and confirm. Given at Philadelphia the 2d of the 6th month 1683.

Instructions to James Graham and William Haige:

1. So soon as it shall please God that you are safely arrived where the Indians meet you, give them my letter (which get interpreted to them) and present them with such things as you shall see convenient, and that are to be had at [New] York.

2. Then read your commission that empowers you to treat in my name for purchasing of their lands, about which use your utmost skill and dispatch. Particularly insinuate that though this land lies so far from them, and nobody lives upon it, and consequently [it is] open to the next pretender, yet hearing they had some claim by conquest, or at least that the remainder of the Susquehannocks, who are right owners thereof, are amongst them, I was willing to send you to treat with them, that so I might lay a foundation for a friendly correspondence.

3. I would have you propose to them nothing less than what was the Susquehannock claim; but if that cannot be done, engage them as far as you can at the present and endeavor to oblige them to sell those lands to none else but me, whom our own Indians that often meet with them in the woods can

tell, I am not the worst man that have in my condition come into this part of the world.

4th. Whatever you buy, endeavor to get some time for the payment of it, especially if the quantity be great and the sum large.

5th. Lastly, know that if ever any of their Indians come our way, they should be received and entertained with kindness, and that which makes me the more to value their friendship is the account I have had that they are a wise and gallant people. And so I wish you a prosperous issue.

Copy. HSP. (*PWP*, 2:422-24).

1. The Mohawk Indians, one of the Five Nations of the Iroquois Confederacy and "keepers of the eastern door," lived along the Mohawk River in New York State. Being the tribe closest to Albany, they had considerable influence in the fur trade.

2. The Seneca Indians, westernmost of the Five Nations, lived south of Lake Ontario in western New York. As the Iroquois tribe farthest from Albany, they traveled in large groups while taking furs to Albany to guard against ambush by the Susquehannocks.


# 73 §

## From Margaret Lowther

THE following letter from WP's sister presents a somber picture of the English political scene during WP's absence. Margaret Penn Lowther (c. 1647-1718) was not a Quaker; she had married Anthony Lowther (c. 1640-1693) in 1667, and was expecting her fifth child at the time of this letter; she lived in Yorkshire, in northern England. The "melancholy" news she reports below concerns an unsuccessful plot, known as the Rye House Plot, against Charles II and his brother, the duke of York. It was alleged that several conspirators had planned to kill the royal brothers in April 1683, near a Hertfordshire building called the Rye House, as they returned to London from Newmarket. The king left Newmarket a week early, however, and the plan was foiled. As Margaret Lowther's letter shows, the alleged plotters paid dearly for being implicated in this scheme, and suspicions against all other leading critics of the Stuart monarchy produced a climate in England that was particularly dangerous for Protestant dissenters.

4 August 1683

My Dearest Brother

The bearer Joshua Hoopes[1] came just now in and tells me he is for Pennsylvania, and I was not willing to let slip any opportunity of writing to you and telling that, I bless the Lord, we are all well. Robin is now with us;[2]

we sent for him for a month this summer. So that now we are all together and I think I am in a way of increasing my stock, for I think I shall come in the latter end of November or the beginning of December.[3]

The times make my condition more melancholy. I suppose you'll hear the Lord Russell is beheaded[4] and others, and Mr. Algernon Sidney, [Aaron Smit?]h, [John] Hampden, [Sir John] Trenchard, [Sir John] Wildman, [Major John] Braman and 2 m[ore?] were tried either Thursday or Wednesday last. What their doom is I know not.[5] And Essex cut his throat in the Tower, though some won't believe it.[6] The times are so sad that Mr. Lowther wishes himself with you. He designs writing by this ship and I shall then do so too. We have yours to him and me.

The time will not permit of a long letter because the bearer is in some haste, who is a stranger to me but lived at Skelton.[7] I have showed him all the children that he may tell you we are all well. I am sorry I had no longer time that I might have thought of something to have sent you, though I don't find your place wants anything. I heard lately all at Warminghurst is well. I heartily wish this may do so too, who am, my dearest brother,

Your most cordially affectionate
sister and friend,
M. Lowther

Mr. Lowther's very affectionate love and says [he] is writ you. Peggy[8] and the other children do the same.

ALS. FLL. (*PWP*, 2:425–27).

1. Joshua Hoopes (c. 1640–c. 1723), a Quaker of Skelton, Yorks., immigrated to Pennsylvania in 1683 with his wife, Isabel, and three children. They arrived in Nov., and settled in Bucks Co.

2. Robert Lowther (1672–1695), the Lowther's eldest son, had probably come home from boarding school. The other Lowther children were Margaret (1668–1714), William (1675–1705), and a short-lived infant, John (b. c. 1682).

3. Anthony Lowther (1683–1703), the Lowther's last child, was in fact born on 30 Nov. 1683.

4. William, Lord Russell (1639–1683), was a leader among the Whigs who sought to exclude James, Duke of York, from inheriting the throne. He was tried for treason on 13 July 1683, sentenced to death on 14 July, and beheaded on 21 July.

5. The six men named here were all ardent opponents of the duke of York, and (like Lord Russell) were implicated in the Rye House Plot. All were arrested between 25 June and 15 July 1683, charged with treason, and imprisoned in the Tower of London. WP had been a personal friend of Algernon Sidney, who was executed in Dec. 1683; see doc. 28, above.

6. Arthur Capel (1631–1683), first Earl of Essex, another critic of the duke of York, was found dead in the Tower on 13 July. Authorities ruled that Essex had committed suicide, but speculation began at once that he had been murdered by order of the court.

7. Joshua Hoopes' village is three miles from Marske, the Lowthers' home.

8. Margaret Lowther, aged fifteen at the date of this letter.

# 74 §
## To Charles II

T HE following document is a rare example of a WP letter for which we
have a rough draft and a finished text, both in WP's hand. In composing a letter to the king, WP obviously chose his words with special care. The
rough draft (A) is an exceptionally messy scrawl, even by WP's standards,
and is full of deletions and insertions, especially in those passages where WP
is being most ingratiating. It is printed here in the original language and
spelling. WP's insertions are denoted by {braces}, and his deletions have
been ~~lined out.~~ The finished letter (B) is written very neatly and carefully, in
WP's best penmanship. It is printed here in modernized form.

A

[13 August 1683]

~~Great & Gracious Prince~~
It is a ~~sterrile~~ {barren} soyle that yeilds no returnes ~~for~~ {to} the dew ~~to~~ that
feeds it, & they are mean and ungratefull minds that are oblivious of the
favours ~~done~~ they receive. I would excuse ~~my~~ this freedom, if I were not
bound to use it, {for} ~~but~~ being destitute of better ways ~~to yeild my humble
thanks~~, Gratitude ~~desends~~ [make]s it necessary to me, {[and necessity is a
sollici]ter that takes no denial.} [torn deletion] [Le]t the [king in] goodness
be graciously please[d] {to} Accept ~~therefore Great & Gracious L^d the~~ {my}
most humble {thanks}, ~~sincere & Respectfull acknowledgem^ts~~ for the many
{Royal} favours {he has} Conferr'd upon me, {more especially this of
Pennsilvania: ~~w^th this assurance, that by Gods help, no man shall more stu-
diously endeaver to act suitable~~ Perticulerly this of Pennsylvania, ^X ~~& to
beleive, that among the Numerous subjects of his powr & Goodness, there
is none that w^th more truth zeal, & affection~~ {loves & honours hi^m} ~~wishes
his te[mporal?] & eternal glory~~ & ^X I {only} lament my own inability to
express {my selfe} ~~the sense I have~~ in a way suitable {to} the sense I have
of the obligations I lye under; But because the Alter ~~is for the poor as well as
rich~~ {was not ordain'd for the the {~~rich~~} great & rich only}, & that ~~all~~
Offerings are accepted by the hear[t] that makes them, I perswade my selfe
to hope that the King will pleas[e] to ~~accept~~ receive my dutifull acknowled-
ments by the integrety that sends them; & to beleive, that among the numerous subjects ~~of~~ {as well of his goodness as of} his powr ~~& goodness,~~ there is
none that w^th more truth zeal & affection loves & honours him. Give me
leave, next, to say tha[t] so soon as I was arrive[d and made any settle]ment
of the people & p[rovince] [torn out] ~~ned with.~~ I thought [it] my [du]ty to
[waite] upon the ~~Kinge~~ K. by {some [Per]son of the [Province]} ~~an extreordinary Agent~~ in {condition} ~~quality~~ of An Agent extreordinary, w^ch is the
Bearer my kinsman William Markham; And tho this {would not look}
~~were not~~ wholy free of vanity ({considering} my late private capaci[ty)]
~~cons~~ yet I take it to be the duty of thos Persons whom the Goodness of the

Kings of England hath {at any time} cloathed with extreordina[ry] powrs in thes parts of the world, to show their deferrance & {also} ~~dependency to the upon~~ to the emperial Magisty {& dependence upon it} by a perpetual attendance of ~~some~~ Agents in their Names. This, Great Prince, & Gracious Soveraign being the reason of my present presumption, I have only to ~~ask~~ pray pardon for it & a poor present of the country produce, & that it would please the King to ~~send~~ take me still into his favour & this Province into his protection, & God the Bountefull rewarder of all goods acts retalitate all temporal & ~~et~~ eternal glory. I am

B

Philadelphia, 13 August 1683

Great and Gracious Prince

It is a barren soil that yields no returns to the dew that feeds it, and they are mean and ungrateful minds that are oblivious of the favors they receive. I would fain excuse this freedom, if I were not bound to use it; for being destitute of better ways, gratitude makes it necessary to me, and necessity is a solicitor that takes no denial. Let the king then graciously please to accept my most humble thanks for his many royal favors conferred upon me, more especially, this of Pennsylvania. I only lament myself, that my own inability will not suffer me to express myself in a way suitable to the sense I have of the great obligations I lie under. But because the altar was not ordained for the rich and great only, and that offerings are to be accepted by the heart that makes them, I persuade myself to hope that the king will please to receive my dutiful acknowledgments by the integrity that humbly sends them. And to believe that among the numerous subjects, as well of his goodness as of his power, there is none that with more truth, zeal, and affection loves and honors him.

Give me leave next to say, so soon as I was arrived and made any settlement of this province, I thought it my duty to wait upon the king by some person of the province, in condition of an agent extraordinary, which is the bearer, my kinsman [William] Markham (formerly deputy in this government).[1] And though this would not look wholly free of vanity (considering my late private capacity), yet I take it to be the duty of those persons whom the goodness of the kings of England has at any time clothed with extraordinary powers in these parts of the world, to show their deference to the Imperial Majesty they are tributaries to, and their dependence upon it, by the mission and attendance of agents in their names at the court.

I have only now, Great Prince, to pray pardon and acceptance for a poor present of country produce,[2] and that it would graciously please the king to take me still into his favor, [and] his young province into his protection; and God, the bountiful rewarder of good and gracious acts, retaliate them both with temporal and eternal glory. I am with reverence and truth,

Great and Gracious Prince,<br>Thy most thankful, humble, and obedient<br>subject and servant in all I can,<br>Wm Penn

A: ADf. HSP. B: ALS. Tulane University Library, New Orleans. (*PWP*, 2:428-31).

1. William Markham, deputy-governor of Pennsylvania from June 1681 to Oct. 1682, and then WP's deputy in the lower counties, left for England about 1 Sept. 1683 to present WP's side of the Penn-Baltimore border controversy at court. See doc. 79, below.

2. WP's gifts to Charles II included snakeroot water, an early antitoxin. He sent the duke of York an otter skin, and had Markham give lumber from America to certain courtiers and officials who had been friendly to WP. See doc. 91, below.

# 75 §

## To the Committee of Trade

IN the following letter, WP takes his case against Lord Baltimore to the body that approved his original charter, the Lords of Trade. Since he had neglected to report to the Lords during his first ten months in America, WP begins with some lame excuses for not writing. Then he gives his side of the dispute in careful detail. In essence WP wanted to limit the north-south dimension of Maryland's territorial bounds to two degrees of latitude, with Lord Baltimore's southern boundary already established at Watkin's Point on the eastern shore of Chesapeake Bay (see map on p. 279). If a degree of latitude was measured at sixty miles, then Maryland's border with Pennsylvania would run 120 miles north of Watkin's Point—at approximately the line established when the boundary dispute between the two colonies was finally settled in the 1760s. If WP had his way, Pennsylvania's southern boundary line would run (as it does today) about twenty miles below the 40th degree of latitude.

But as WP reports, he could not persuade Lord Baltimore to accept this mode of calculation. Baltimore's boundary with Virginia at Watkin's Point had been fixed at slightly below the 38th degree of latitude, and he did not wish to be limited to two degrees in reckoning the latitude of his northern boundary line. Nor did he care to measure a degree at sixty miles when the true measurement was almost seventy. Instead, he wanted to run the Maryland-Pennsylvania boundary line at the 40th degree of latitude, as called for in the charters to both colonies. But if Baltimore had his way, WP's capital city of Philadelphia would lie within Maryland and the lower counties (to which Baltimore was now laying claim) would no longer be contiguous to Pennsylvania. Thus WP had every reason to be alarmed. As he told the Lords of Trade, "a province lies at stake" in the resolution of this boundary dispute.

Philadelphia, 14 August 1683

Though it be a duty I humbly own, to inform the Lords of the Committee of Plantations of what concern his Majesty's interest in the success of this province, I thought myself equally obliged to be discreet and cautious in doing it: to write when there was need, and not trouble persons of their honor and business with things trivial, at least raw and unfinished for their view. This hitherto put me by giving any account of the state of our affairs; to say nothing of the mighty difficulties I have labored under, in the settlement of six and twenty sail of people to content, within the space of one year.[1] Which makes my case singular and excusable above any other of the king's plantations.

But because my agent has informed me[2] that the proprietor of Maryland has been early in his account of our conference about the fixing of our bounds and made a narrative of my affairs, as well before as at that time, a little to my disadvantage,[3] and the rather because my silence might be interpreted [as] neglect, I am necessitated to make some defense for myself, which, as it will not be hard to make, so I hope it will be received as just.

I humbly say then first, that it seemed to me improper to trouble the Lords with my transactions with this proprietor till we were come to some result, which we were not, for we parted till spring and even then were but to meet about the methods of our proceeding. Next, this narrative was taken by this lord's order without my consent or knowledge, in a corner of a room, by one of his own attendants.[4] And lastly, when upon notice given of this usage I complained to him, he promised upon his word and honor it should go no further, and that it was for his own satisfaction he did it. I told him that mitigated the thing a little, but if he should divulge it before I saw and agreed [to] the copy, he must pardon me if I looked upon it as a most unfair practice. What that lord has done and what to call it, I leave to my betters; but the surprise and indigestion of the whole will, I hope, excuse me of neglect or disrespect. For though I am unceremonious, I would by no means act the rude or undutiful.

This said, I humbly beg that I may give a brief narrative of the matter as it then passed, since has been, and now stands, without the weakness and tautology[5] his relation makes me guilty of.

So soon as I arrived, which was on the 24th of October last, I immediately dispatched two persons[6] to the Lord Baltimore, proprietary of Maryland, with my respects, to ask of his health, offer kind neighborhood, and agree a time of meeting the better to establish it. While they were gone in this errand, I went to New York, that I might pay my duty to the duke in the visit of his government and colony. At my return, which was towards the end of November, I found the messengers I had sent to Maryland newly arrived, and the time fixed being the 19th of December, I prepared myself in a few days for that province. The 11th of that month I came to West River,[7] where I met the proprietor, attended suitable to his character, who took that occasion by his civilities to show me the greatness of his power. The next day we had a conference about our business of the bounds, both at the same table, with our respective members of Council.

The first thing I did was to present the king's letter,[8] which consisted of two parts: one that the Lord Baltimore had but two degrees, and the other that beginning at Watkin's Point he should admeasure his said degrees at 60 miles to a degree. This being read by him, first privately, then publicly, he told me that the king was greatly mistaken, and that he would not leave his patent to follow the king's letter, nor could a letter void his patent, and by that he would stand. This was the substance of what he said from first to last, during the whole conference. To this I answered, that the king might be misinformed, rather than mistaken, and that I was afraid the mistake would fall of his side; for though his patent begins at Watkin's Point, and goes to the fortieth degree of north latitude, yet it presumed that [southern boundary] to lie in thirty-eight, else Virginia would be wronged, that should extend to that degree. However, this I assured him, that when I petitioned the king for 5 degrees north latitude,[9] and that petition was referred to the Lords of the Committee of Plantations, at that time it was urged by some present that the Lord Baltimore had but two degrees, upon which the Lord President[10] turning his head to me, at whose chair I stood, said, Mr. Penn, will not three degrees serve your turn? I answered, I submit both the what and how to this honorable board.

To this his uncle and chancellor[11] returned, that to convince me his father's grant[12] was not by degrees, he had more of Virginia given him, but being planted and the grant intending only land not planted or possessed but of savage natives, he left it out, that it might not forfeit the rest.[13] Of which the Lord Baltimore takes no notice in his narrative, that I remember. But by that answer he can pretend nothing to Delaware, that was at and before the passing of that patent bought and planted by the Dutch, and so could not be given; but if it were, it was forfeited for not reducing it during twenty years, under the English sovereignty, of which he held it.[14] But [it] was at last reduced by the king, and therefore his to give as he pleases.[15]

Perceiving that my pressing the king's letter was uneasy, and that I had determined myself to dispose him with utmost softness to a good compliance, I waived that of the two degrees and pressed the admeasurement only, the next part of the letter. For though it were two degrees and a half from Watkin's Point to forty [degrees latitude],[16] yet let it be measured at sixty miles to a degree, and I would begin at forty, fall as it would. My design was that every degree, being seventy miles, I should get all that was over sixty, the proportion intended the Lord Baltimore, by the grant and the computation of a degree at that time of the day. Thus he had enjoyed the full favor intended him, and I had gained a door of great importance to the peopling and improving of this, his Majesty's province.

But this he also rejected. I told him it was not the love or need of the land, but the water; that he abounded in what I wanted, and had access and harborage even to excess. That I would not be thus importunate but for the importance of the thing, to save a province; and because there was no proportion in the concern. If I were a hundred times more urgent and tenacious, the case would excuse it, because the thing I insisted on was more than ninety-nine times more valuable to me than to him: to me the head, to him the tail. I added, that if it were his and he gave it [to] me, planting it would recompense the favor, not only by laying his country between two thriving provinces, but the ships that come yearly to Maryland for tobacco would have the bringing of both our people and merchandise, because they can afford it cheaper. Whereby Maryland would for one age or two be the mart of trade. But this also had no other entertainment but hopes that I would not insist on these things at our next meeting. After three days time we parted, and I returned to this province.

When the spring came, I sent an express[17] to pray the time and place when and where I should meet him to effect the business we [had] adjourned to that time. I followed close upon the messenger, that no time might be lost; but the expectation he twice had of the Lord Culpeper's visit,[18] disappointed any meeting in our affair till the month called May. He then sent three gentlemen to let me know he would meet me at the head of the Bay of Chesapeake. I was then in treaty with the kings of the natives for land;[19] but three days after, we met ten miles from New Castle (which is 30 from the bay). I invited him to the town, where having entertained him as well as the town could afford on so little notice, and finding him only desirous of speaking with me privately, I pressed that we might at our distinct lodgings sit severally with our Councils, and treat by way of written memorials, which would prevent the mistakes or abuses that may follow from ill designs or ill memory. But he avoided it, saying he was not well, the weather sultry, and would return with what speed he could, reserving any other treaty to another season. Thus we parted at that time.

I had been before told by divers [people] that the Lord Baltimore had issued forth a proclamation to invite people by lower prices and greater quantities of land to plant in the lower counties, in which the duke's goodness had interested me as an inseparable benefit to this whole province. I was not willing to believe it, and he being in haste, I omitted to ask him. But I had not been long returned before two letters came from two judges of two of the county courts[20] that such a proclamation was abroad, [and] that the people abhorred to hearken to it, but yet prayed my directions. I bid them keep their ground, and not fear, for the king would be judge.

Upon this, I dispatched to the Lord Baltimore three of my Council, with the clerk of it.[21] As they went, they got an authentic copy under the hand of one of his sheriffs,[22] to whom an original had been directed. But as the last civility I could yield him, I forbade them to seem to believe anything but what they had from his own mouth. Thus they delivered my letter. At first he denied any such proclamation — turning to two gentlemen of his Council that stood by, asked them if they remembered any such thing, they also denied it. Upon which the persons I sent produced the attested copy, which refreshing their memories, they confessed there was such a proclamation, but the Lord Baltimore told them that it was his ancient form and he only did it to renew his claim, not that he would encourage any to plant there. They then prayed him to call it in lest any trouble should ensue, but he refused it. This was during a civil treaty, without any demand made, and after the place had been many years in the quiet possession of the duke. What to call this I still humbly refer to my superiors. For his pretensions to those parts, I have thoroughly instructed my agent, who I hope will be able to detect them as of weakness and inconsistency. This is a true, though brief, narrative of the entertainment I have had from that lord in the business between us.

And because I have, as in duty bound, sent an agent extraordinary[23] to wait upon the king and his ministers in the affairs of this province (so soon as I could make any settlement in it), I shall only humbly pray leave to hint at two or three things relating to the business depending between this lord and myself about finding the fortieth degree of north latitude.

1st. That I have common fame on my side, grounded upon an ancient and constant judgment, that the fortieth degree of north latitude lies about Pools Isle.[24] This the Lord Baltimore himself has not denied, the country confesses, and I shall, when required, prove by some able masters of ships.

2dly. If this were an error, it is grounded upon such skill and instruments as gave measure to the times in which his patent was granted, and if he has got upon[25] Virginia by that error, he should not get upon me by an exacter knowledge, considering that Carolina, which ends by degrees, would as much advance upon Virginia if the reputed latitude of imprejudiced times should take no place. For by advancing her bounds twenty miles by a new instrument beyond the place which has generally been taken for 36 and a half, and Virginia not being equally able to advance upon Maryland (because of its beginning at a place certain), she will be greatly narrowed between both.[26]

3dly. I therefore most humbly pray that the judgment of ancient times, by which persons at the distance of England from America have governed themselves, may conclude that lord's bounds. Or that he may measure his two degrees according to the scale and computation of those times, which was sixty miles to a degree. Or if it be allowed that he had not his grant by degrees, that at least I might not lose the benefit of admeasurement, as before mentioned, from Watkin's Point (in whatsoever degree of latitude that shall be found) to the fortieth degree of north latitude, which I humbly take the more courage to press because a province lies at stake in the success of it.

I have only humbly to add that the province has a prospect of an extraordinary improvement as well by divers sorts of strangers as [by] English subjects. That in all acts of justice we name and venerate the king's authority. That I have exactly followed the Bishop of London's[27] counsel by buying and not taking away the natives' land, with whom I have settled a very kind correspondence. I return my most humble thanks for your former favors in the passing of my patent, and pray God reward you. I am most ready to obey all your commands according to the obligations of it; and beseech you to take this province into your protection, under his Majesty, and him, whom his goodness has made governor of it, into your favor, for that I am with most sincere devotion,

Noble Lords,
Your thankful, faithful
friend and servant to my power,
Wm Penn

LS. PRO. (*PWP*, 2:431-37).

1. WP's statement here is a bit misleading. Between Dec. 1681 and Dec. 1682, twenty-three passenger ships arrived in Pennsylvania; between Jan. 1683 and July 1683, another six arrived.

2. WP probably means Philip Ford.

3. Lord Baltimore sent an account of his conference of 11-13 Dec. 1682 with WP to the marquis of Halifax in Feb. 1683. Halifax, the lord privy seal, presented Baltimore's description of his problems with WP to the Committee of Trade in Apr. 1683. Baltimore's complaints persuaded the Committee to tell the duke of York not to transfer the title to the lower counties to WP until the differences between WP and Baltimore were settled. See doc. 69, n. 3.

4. John Llewellin, the clerk of the Maryland Assembly.

5. Tedious repetition.

6. In doc. 64, WP says he sent three persons (including his secretary, Philip Lehnmann) to visit Baltimore.

7. In Anne Arundel Co., on the west side of Chesapeake Bay.

8. Charles II to Lord Baltimore, 19 Aug. 1682; see the headnote to doc. 64, above.

9. The fragment that survives of WP's petition for a colony in America (doc. 1, above) does not mention five degrees. WP probably made this request orally when he attended the Committee of Trade on 14 June 1680 (doc. 2, above).

10. John Robartes, Earl of Radnor; see doc. 2.

11. Philip Calvert (1626-c. 1682), the third lord Baltimore's uncle, had come to Maryland in 1656 and had served as governor of the colony as well as chancellor.

12. George Calvert (c. 1580-1632), the first lord Baltimore and the father of Philip Calvert, died before his patent for Maryland passed the seals. The charter of 20 June 1632 was conferred to his son Cecil (1606-1675), the second lord Baltimore.

13. When the first lord Baltimore applied for a Chesapeake colony, royal officials changed its location several times as a result of objections raised by representatives of Virginia. The first proposal was for lands south of the James River, and a second was for the entire Eastern Shore peninsula. See doc. 3, n. 2, for the boundaries stipulated in the Maryland charter of 1632.

14. The Dutch had established a short-lived colony near Cape Henlopen in 1631, one year before the Calverts received the Maryland charter. The preamble to the Maryland charter granted only those lands "hitherto uncultivated" by Europeans. Lord Baltimore apparently ignored the presence of the Swedes or Dutch on the Delaware until 1654, when he demanded the territory from the Swedes. In 1659, after the Dutch had taken control of the area, Lord Baltimore claimed the lower counties once again. The Dutch refused to yield, asserting that their settlement predated Baltimore's charter.

15. A squadron sent by Charles II conquered New Netherlands — including the Dutch settlements on the Delaware—in 1664.

16. The true location of Watkin's Point is approximately 37 degrees and 57 minutes of latitude.

17. A letter by messenger.

18. Thomas, Lord Culpeper, the royal governor of Virginia, visited Lord Baltimore in Maryland on 20 May 1683.

19. See doc. 68.

20. See doc. 67 for one of these letters, from William Clarke.

21. The three members of the council were William Markham, James Harrison, and William Clarke. See doc. 69. The clerk was Richard Ingelo.

22. WP's commissioners obtained a copy of the proclamation from Stephen Gary, the Quaker sheriff of Dorchester Co., Md.

23. William Markham.

24. Pools Island, in Chesapeake Bay near the mouth of the Gunpowder River; see the map on p. 279. WP placed the 40th degree of latitude at approximately that location on his *Map of Pennsylvania* (p. 80), but earlier maps had situated the 40th degree farther north.

25. Encroached upon.

26. See doc. 79, below, for WP's extended discussion of changes in the boundaries of other colonies.

27. Henry Compton; see doc. 2.

# Part X

## NEGOTIATING WITH THE INDIANS §
## AUGUST 1683–DECEMBER 1683

The leopard with the harmless kid laid down
And not one savage beast was seen to frown

The wolf did with the lambkin dwell in peace
His grim carnivorous nature there did cease

The lion with the fading on did move
A little child was leading them in love;

When the great PENN his famous treaty made
With indian chiefs beneath the Elm-tree's shade.

*Peaceable Kingdom, by Edward Hicks, 1826, Philadelphia Museum of Art: Bequest of Charles C. Willis. Hicks painted about sixty versions of this scene. In many of these paintings, the Christ child makes peace between the lion and the lamb, while in the background WP makes peace with the Indians.*

ONE of the most distinctive features of WP's design for Pennsylvania was his Indian policy. Just a few years after the bloody King Philip's War in New England and Nathaniel Bacon's massacre of Indians in Virginia, WP was pursuing a policy of unarmed friendship with the native Americans in the Delaware Valley. By July 1683, as shown on the map on p. 159, WP had bought Indian title to most of the land bordering the west bank of the Delaware River. Delighted with this accomplishment, WP devoted nearly half of his long promotional letter of 16 August 1683 to the Free Society of Traders (doc. 76, below) to a lively description of the "persons, language, manners, religion, and government" of the local Delaware Indians. In recounting his treaty negotiations with the Delaware, WP could justly boast that "great promises passed between us of kindness and good neighborhood, and that the Indians and English must live in love, as long as the sun gave light."

But WP was also keenly interested in making money from the interior fur trade. When he discovered that the local Delaware could give him no access to that trade, he endeavored in 1683 to expand his treaty network northward and to negotiate with the Iroquois in New York in order to open up a trade along the Susquehanna River (see the headnotes to docs. 36 and 72, above). Inevitably, WP's expansionist policy brought him into conflict with the Albany fur traders and with the governor of New York. From WP's arrival in America until July 1683, he had dealt with a weak interim administration in New York, but Governor Thomas Dongan reached his colony in August and quickly moved to cut off WP's plans. The resulting Pennsylvania-New York conflict is discussed in the headnote to doc. 78.

In the fall of 1683 WP had another aggressive neighbor to worry about — Lord Baltimore. By this point WP and Baltimore had reached a total impasse over the Pennsylvania-Maryland boundary line. The new developments in their quarrel are discussed in the headnotes to docs. 79 and 86.

In other respects WP's colony was continuing to prosper. During the closing months of 1683, WP had the pleasure of welcoming a large new wave of immigrants to Pennsylvania. About as many ships and passengers arrived in 1683 as in 1682, and most of them reached Philadelphia between

August and November. The newcomers were conspicuous for their many talents as well as for their ethnic and geographic diversity. Francis Daniel Pastorius arrived and, with settlers from Krefeld, staked out Germantown (see docs. 81 and 89); Thomas Lloyd, who became the chief executive in Pennsylvania when WP returned to England, was one of many new Welshmen; and the incoming merchants included James Claypoole from London (doc. 85) and Samuel Carpenter from Barbados (doc. 92). To provide for these immigrants, WP's surveyors laid out new farms and city lots (doc. 84). With reason, WP could brag about the material prosperity and spiritual vitality of his fast-growing colony.

# 76 ∫
# Letter to the Free Society of Traders

IN many of WP's letters to his friends and patrons in England, he described his colony in glowing terms (for example, in docs. 66 and 71, above). Doc. 76 is the longest and most informative of WP's descriptions. He sent it to the London managers of the Free Society of Traders, and they published it in London in late 1683. This piece was immediately recognized as WP's most effective promotional tract. It was reprinted twice in 1683 and again in 1687 and was translated into Dutch, German, and French. We know that WP took considerable pains with this letter because we have a draft of it, mainly in his handwriting. This *Letter* is especially notable for its lengthy description of the Indians of Pennsylvania. In comparing the Indians to Europeans, WP betrays some of the common prejudices that Englishmen held against other groups—Jews and Italians, in this case. Despite this, and despite WP's willingness to stereotype the Delaware in many ways, his account is probably the best contemporary description we have of the Delaware Indians and their culture.

At the close of his *Letter,* WP also presents considerable useful information about his capital city of Philadelphia. He sent home what he called a "plat-form," or map, of the city, prepared by his surveyor Thomas Holme, and this map (which is reproduced on pp. 320-21) was printed as an illustration to his *Letter.* It shows the rectangular plan of the new city, and the grid network of streets that WP and Holme laid out; WP even supplied a key to the map so that the First Purchasers in England could locate their town lots. Today, Center City Philadelphia still retains WP's grid plan. Broad Street and High (now Market) Street are still one hundred feet wide, as he designed them—far wider, incidentally, than any street in seventeenth-century London. And the other principal streets and open squares on WP's grid still have the dimensions, and many of them have the names, that he assigned three centuries ago.

A
LETTER
FROM
William Penn
Proprietary and Governor of
PENNSYLVANIA
In America,
TO THE
COMMITTEE
OF THE
Free Society of Traders
of that Province, residing in *London.*
CONTAINING

A General Description of the said *Province,* its *Soil, Air, Water, Seasons,* and *Produce,* both Natural and Artificial, and the good Increase thereof.

Of the *Natives or Aborigines,* their *Language, Customs* and *Manners, Diet, Houses* or *Wigwams, Liberality, Easy Way* of *Living, Physic, Burial, Religion, Sacrifices* and *Cantico,*[1] *Festivals, Government,* and their order in *Council* upon Treaties for Land, etc., their *Justice* upon *Evildoers.*

Of the *first Planters,* the *Dutch,* etc., and the *present Condition* and *Settlement* of the said *Province,* and *Courts of Justice, etc.*

To which is added, an Account of the CITY of
PHILADELPHIA
Newly laid out.

Its Situation between two Navigable Rivers, *Delaware* and *Schuylkill*
WITH A
Portraiture or Plat-form thereof,
Wherein the Purchasers' Lots are distinguished by certain Numbers inserted,
directing to a Catalogue of the said Purchasers' Names
And the Prosperous and Advantageous Settlements of the *Society* aforesaid within the said City and Country, *etc.*

---

*Printed and Sold by* Andrew Sowle, *at the Crooked-Billet in* Holloway-Lane in Shoreditch, *and at several Stationers in* London, 1683.

My Kind Friends;

The kindness of yours by the ship *Thomas and Anne,*[2] does much oblige me; for by it I perceive the interest you take in my health and reputation, and the prosperous beginnings of this province, which you are so kind as to think may much depend upon them. In return of which, I have sent you a long letter, and yet containing as brief an account of myself and the affairs of this province as I have been able to make.

In the first place, I take notice of the news you sent me, whereby I find some persons have had so little wit and so much malice as to report my death, and to mend the matter, dead a Jesuit too.[3] One might have reasonably hoped that this distance, like death, would have been a protection against spite and envy; and indeed absence being a kind of death, ought alike to secure the name of the absent as the dead; because they are equally unable as such to defend themselves. But they that intend mischief do not use to follow good rules to effect it. However, to the great sorrow and shame of the inventors, I am still alive, and no Jesuit; and, I thank God, very well. And without injustice to the authors of this, I may venture to infer that they that willfully and falsely report, would have been glad it had been so. But I perceive many frivolous and idle stories have been invented since my departure from England, which perhaps at this time are no more alive than I am dead.

But if I have been unkindly used by some I left behind me, I found love and respect enough where I came; a universal kind welcome, every sort in their way. For here are some of several nations, as well as divers judgments; nor were the natives wanting in this, for their kings, queens, and great men both visited and presented me, to whom I made suitable returns, etc.

For the PROVINCE, the general condition of it, take as follows:

I. The country itself in its soil, air, water, seasons, and produce, both natural and artificial, is not to be despised. The land contains divers sorts of earth, as sand, yellow and black, poor and rich; also gravel, both loamy and dusty; and in some places a fast fat earth, like to our best vales in England, especially by inland brooks and rivers. God in His wisdom having ordered it so, that the advantages of the country are divided, the back lands being generally three to one richer than those that lie by navigable waters. We have much of another soil, and that is a black hazel mold upon a stony or rocky bottom.

II. The *air* is sweet and clear, the heavens serene, like the south parts of France, rarely overcast; and as the woods come by numbers of people to be more cleared, that itself will refine.

III. The *waters* are generally good, for the rivers and brooks have mostly gravel and stony bottoms, and in number hardly credible. We have also mineral waters that operate in the same manner with Chipping Barnet and Northhaw,[4] not two miles from Philadelphia.

IV. For the *seasons* of the year, having by God's goodness now lived over the coldest and hottest that the oldest liver in the province can remember, I can say something to an English understanding.

1st, of the fall, for then I came in. I found it from the 24th of October to the beginning of December, as we have it usually in England in September, or rather like an English mild spring. From December to the beginning of the month called March, we had sharp frosty weather; not foul, thick, black weather, as our northeast winds bring with them in England, but a sky as clear as in summer, and the air dry, cold, piercing, and hungry; yet I remember not that I wore more clothes than in England. The reason of this cold is given from the great lakes that are fed by the fountains of Canada. The winter before was as mild, scarce any ice at all, while this for a few days froze up our great river Delaware. From that month to the month called June, we enjoyed a sweet spring, no gusts, but gentle showers and a fine sky. Yet this I observe, that the winds here, as there, are more inconstant, spring and fall, upon that turn of nature, than in summer or winter. From thence to this present month, which ends the summer (commonly speaking), we have had extraordinary heats, yet mitigated sometimes by cool breezes. The wind that rules the summer season is the southwest; but spring, fall, and winter, it is rare to want the wholesome northwesterly seven days together. And whatever mists, fogs, or vapors foul the heavens by easterly or southerly winds, in two hours time are blown away, the one is always followed by the other, a remedy that seems to have a peculiar providence in it to the inhabitants, the multitude of trees yet standing being liable to retain mists and vapors, and yet not one-quarter so thick as I expected.

V. The *natural produce* of the country, of vegetables, is trees, fruits, plants, flowers. The trees of most note are the black walnut, cedar, cypress, chestnut, poplar, gumwood, hickory, sassafras, ash, beech; and oak of divers sorts, as red, white, and black, Spanish, chestnut, and swamp, the most durable of all; of all which there is plenty for the use of man.

The *fruits* that I find in the woods are the white and black mulberry, chestnut, walnut, plums, strawberries, cranberries, huckleberries, and grapes of divers sorts. The great red grape (now ripe) called by ignorance the fox grape (because of the relish it has with unskillful palates), is in itself an extraordinary grape, and by art doubtless may be cultivated to an excellent wine; if not so sweet, yet little inferior to the Frontignac,[5] as it is not much unlike [it] in taste, ruddiness set aside, which in such things, as well as mankind, differs the case much. There is a white kind of muscatel, and a little black grape like the cluster grape of England, not yet so ripe as the other; but, they tell me, when ripe, sweeter, and that they only want skillful *vignerons*[6] to make good use of them. I intend to venture on it with my Frenchman[7] this season, who shows some knowledge in those things. Here are also peaches, and very good, and in great quantities, not an Indian plantation without them; but whether naturally here at first I know not. However, one may have them by bushels for little; they make a pleasant drink and I think not inferior to any peach you have in England, except the true Newington.[8] It is disputable with me, whether it be best to fall to refining the fruits of the country, especially the grape, by the care and skill of art, or send for foreign stems and sets, already good and approved.[9] It seems most reasonable to believe, that not only a thing grows best where it naturally grows, but will hardly be equaled by another species of the same kind that does not naturally grow there. But to solve the doubt, I intend, if God give me life, to try both, and hope the consequence will be as good wine as any European countries of the same latitude do yield.

VI. The *artificial produce* of the country is wheat, barley, oats, rye, peas, beans, squashes, pumpkins, watermelons, muskmelons, and all herbs and roots that our gardens in England usually bring forth. Note, that Edward Jones, son-in-law to Thomas Wynne, living on the Schuylkill, had with ordinary cultivation, for one grain of English barley, seventy stalks and ears of barley; and it is common in this country from one bushel sown, to reap forty, often fifty, and sometimes sixty. And three pecks of wheat sow an acre here.

VII. Of living creatures, *fish, fowl,* and the beasts of the woods, here are divers sorts, some for food and profit, and some for profit only. For food as well as profit, the elk, as big as a small ox, deer bigger than ours, beaver, raccoon, rabbits [and] squirrels, and some eat young bear, and commend it. Of fowl of the land, there is the turkey (forty and fifty pound weight), which is very great, pheasants, heath-birds,[10] pigeons, and partridges in abundance. Of the water, the swan, goose, white and gray, brants, ducks, teal, also the snipe and curlew, and that in great numbers; but the duck and teal excel, nor so good have I ever eaten in other countries. Of fish, there is the sturgeon, herring, rock, shad, catshead, sheepshead, eel, smelt, perch, roach; and in inland rivers, trout, some say salmon, above the Falls. Of shellfish, we have oysters, crabs, cockles, conches and mussels; some oysters six inches long, and one sort of cockles as big as the stewing oysters; they make a rich broth. The creatures for profit only by skin or fur, and that are natural to these parts, are the wildcat, panther, otter, wolf, fox, fisher,[11] mink, muskrat; and of the water, the whale for oil, of which we have good store; and two companies of whalers, whose boats are built, will soon begin their work, which has the appearance of a considerable improvement; to say nothing of our reasonable hopes of good cod in the bay.

VIII. We have no want of *horses,* and some are very good and shapely enough. Two ships have been freighted to Barbados, with horses and pipe-staves, since my coming in. Here is also plenty of cow-cattle and some sheep; the people plow mostly with oxen.

IX. There are divers *plants* that not only the Indians tell us, but we have had occasion to prove by swellings, burnings, cuts, etc., that they are of great virtue, suddenly curing the patient. And for smell, I have observed several, especially one, the wild myrtle; the other I know not what to call, but are most fragrant.

X. The woods are adorned with lovely *flowers,* for color, greatness, figure, and variety. I have seen the gardens of London best stored with that sort of beauty, but think they may be improved by our woods. I have sent a few to a person of quality this year for a trial.

Thus much of the country, next of the natives or aborigines.

XI. The NATIVES I shall consider in their persons, language, manners, religion, and government, with my sense of their original. For their persons, they are generally tall, straight, well built, and of singular proportion; they tread strong and clever, and mostly walk with a lofty chin. Of complexion black, but by design, as the gypsies in England. They grease themselves with bear's fat clarified, and using no defense against sun or weather, their skins must needs be swarthy. Their eye is little and black, not unlike a straight-looked Jew. The thick lip and flat nose, so frequent with the East Indians and blacks, are not common to them; for I have seen as comely European-like faces among them, of both, as on your side [of] the sea; and truly an Italian complexion has not much more of the white, and the noses of several of them have as much of the Roman.

XII. Their *language* is lofty, yet narrow, but like the Hebrew; in signification full, like shorthand in writing; one word serves in the place of three, and the rest are supplied by the understanding of the hearer; imperfect in their tenses, wanting in their moods, participles, adverbs, conjunctions, interjections. I have made it my business to understand it, that I might not want an interpreter on any occasion; and I must say that I know not a language spoken in Europe that has words of more sweetness or greatness, in accent and emphasis, than theirs; for instance, Octoraro, Rancocas, Oreckton,[12] Shackamaxon, Poquessing,[13] all which are names of places, and have grandeur in them. Of words of sweetness, anna is mother; issimus, a brother; netap, friend; usque oret, very good; pone, bread; metse, eat; matta, no; hatta, to have; payo, to come; Sepassincks, Passyunk,[14] the names of places; Tammany, Secane, Menangy, Secetareus,[15] are the names of persons. If one asks them for anything they have not, they will answer, matta ne hatta, which to translate is "not I have," instead of, "I have not."

XIII. Of their *customs* and *manners* there is much to be said. I will begin with children. So soon as they are born they wash them in water, and while very young, and in cold weather to choose, they plunge them in the rivers to harden and embolden them. Having wrapped them in a clout, they lay them on a straight thin board, a little more than the length and breadth of the child, and swaddle it fast upon the board to make it straight; wherefore all Indians have flat heads; and thus they carry them at their backs. The children will go very young, at nine months commonly; they wear only a small clout round their waist, till they are big; if boys, they go a-fishing till ripe for the woods, which is about fifteen; then they hunt; and after having given some proofs of their manhood by a good return of skins, they may marry, else it is a shame to think of a wife. The girls stay with their mothers, and help to hoe the ground, plant corn, and carry burdens; and they do well to use them to[16] that [work] young [which] they must do when they are old; for the wives are the true servants of their husbands. Otherwise the men are very affectionate to them.

XIV. When the *young women* are fit for marriage, they wear something upon their heads for an advertisement, but so as their faces are hardly to be seen but when they please. The age they marry at, if women, is about thirteen and fourteen; if men, seventeen and eighteen. They are rarely older.

XV. Their *houses* are mats, or barks of trees set on poles, in the fashion of an English barn, but out of the power of the winds, for they are hardly higher than a man. They lie on reeds or grass. In travel they lodge in the woods about a great fire, with a mantle of duffels they wear by day wrapped about them, and a few boughs stuck round them.

XVI. Their *diet* is maize, or Indian corn, [in] divers ways prepared; sometimes roasted in the ashes, sometimes beaten and boiled with water, which they call hominy; they also make cakes, not unpleasant to eat. They have likewise several sorts of beans and peas that are good nourishment; and the woods and rivers are their larder.

XVII. If a European comes to see them, or calls for lodging at their house or wigwam, they give him the best place and first cut. If they come to visit us, they salute us with an *Itah,* which is as much as to say "Good be to you," and set them down, which is mostly on the ground, close to their heels, their legs upright. [It] may be they speak not a word more, but observe all passages. If you give them anything to eat or drink, [that is] well, for they will not ask; and, be it little or much, if it be with kindness, they are well pleased, else they go away sullen, but say nothing.

XVIII. They are great concealers of their own resentments, brought to it, I believe, by the revenge that has been practiced among them; in either of these they are not exceeded by the Italians. A tragical instance fell out since I came into the country. A king's daughter, thinking herself slighted by her husband in suffering another woman to lie down between them, rose up, went out, plucked a root out of the ground, and ate it, upon which she immediately died; and for which, last week, he made an offering to her kindred for atonement and liberty of marriage; as two others did to the kindred of their wives that died a natural death. For till widowers have done so, they must not marry again. Some of the young women are said to take undue liberty before marriage for a portion; but when married, chaste; when with child, they know their husbands no more, till delivered; and during their month[ly period], they touch no meat they eat but with a stick, lest they should defile it; nor do their husbands frequent them until that time be expired.

XIX. But in liberality they excel; nothing is too good for their friend. Give them a fine gun, coat, or other thing, it may pass twenty hands before it sticks; light of heart, strong affections, but soon spent, the most merry creatures that live, [they] feast and dance perpetually; they never have much, nor want much. Wealth circulates like the blood, all parts partake; and though none shall want what another has, yet [they are] exact observers of property. Some kings have sold, others presented me with several parcels of land;[17] the pay or presents I made them were not hoarded by the particular owners; but the neighboring kings and their clans being present when the goods were brought out, the parties chiefly concerned consulted, what and to whom they should give them? To every king then, by the hands of a person for that work appointed, is a proportion sent, so sorted and folded, and with that gravity that is admirable. Then that king subdivides it in like manner among his dependents, they hardly leaving themselves an equal share with one of their subjects; and be it on such occasions, at festivals or at their common meals, the kings distribute, and to themselves last. They care for little because they want but little; and the reason is, a little contents them. In this they are sufficiently revenged on us; if they are ignorant of our pleasures, they are also free from our pains. They are not disquieted with bills of lading and exchange, nor perplexed with chancery suits and exchequer reckonings. We sweat and toil to live; their pleasure feeds them, I mean, their hunting, fishing, and fowling, and this table is spread everywhere. They eat twice a day, morning and evening; their seats and table are the ground. Since the Europeans came into these parts, they are grown great lovers of strong liquors, rum especially, and for it exchange the richest of their skins and furs. If they are heated with liquors, they are restless till they have enough to sleep. That is their cry, "Some more, and I will go to sleep." But when drunk, one of the most wretchedest spectacles in the world.

XX. In *sickness,* impatient to be cured, and for it give anything, especially for their children, to whom they are extremely natural. They drink at those times a *teran* or decoction of some roots in spring water; and if they eat any flesh, it must be of the female of any creature. If they die, they bury them with their apparel, be they men or women, and the nearest of kin fling in something precious with them, as a token of their love. Their mourning is blacking of their faces, which they continue for a year. They are choice of the graves of their dead; for lest they should be lost by time and fall to common use, they pick off the grass that grows upon them, and heap up the fallen earth with great care and exactness.

XXI. These poor people are under a dark night in things relating to *religion,* to be sure, the tradition of it; yet they believe [in] a God and immortality, without the help of metaphysics;[18] for they say, there is a great king that made them, who dwells in a glorious country to the southward of them, and that the souls of the good shall go thither, where they shall live again. Their worship consists of two parts, sacrifice and cantico. Their sacrifice is their first fruits; the first and fattest buck they kill goes to the fire, where he is all burnt with a mournful ditty of him that performs the ceremony, but with such marvelous fervency and labor of body that he will even sweat to a foam. The other part is their cantico, performed by round-dances, sometimes words, sometimes songs, then shouts, two being in the middle that begin, and by singing and drumming on a board direct the chorus. Their postures in the dance are very antic[19] and differing, but all keep measure. This is done with equal earnestness and labor, but great appearance of joy. In the fall, when the corn comes in, they begin to feast one another. There have been two great festivals already, to which all come that will. I was at one myself; their entertainment was a great seat by a spring, under some shade trees, and twenty bucks, with hot cakes of new corn, both wheat and beans, which they make up in a square form in the leaves of the stem, and bake them in the ashes; and after that they fell to dance. But they that go must carry a small present in their money (it may be six pence) which is made of the bone of a fish; the black is with them as gold, the white, silver; they call it all *wampum.*

XXII. Their government is by *kings,* which they call *sachema,* and those by succession, but always of the mother's side. For instance, the children of him that is now king will not succeed, but his brother by [his] mother, or the children of his sister, whose sons (and after them the children of her daughters) will reign, for no woman inherits. The reason they render for this way of descent is that their issue may not be spurious.

XXIII. Every king has his *council,* and that consists of all the old and wise men of his nation, which perhaps is two hundred people. Nothing of moment is undertaken, be it war, peace, selling of land, or traffic, without advising with them; and, which is more, with the young men too. It is admirable to consider how powerful the kings are, and yet how they move by the breath of their people. I have had occasion to be in council with them upon treaties for land, and to adjust the terms of trade. Their order is thus: the king sits in the middle of a half moon, and has his council, the old and wise on each hand; behind them, or at a little distance, sit the younger fry, in the same figure. Having consulted and resolved their business, the king ordered one of them to speak to me. He stood up, came to me, and in the name of his king saluted me, then took me by the hand, and told me that he was ordered by his king to speak to me, and that now it was not he, but the king that spoke, because what he should say was the king's mind. He first prayed me to excuse them that they had not complied with me the last time; he feared there might be some fault in the interpreter, being neither Indian nor English.[20] Besides, it was the Indian custom to deliberate, and take up much time in council, before they resolve; and that if the young people and owners of the land had been as ready as he, I had not met with so much delay. Having thus introduced his matter, he fell to the bounds of the land they had agreed to dispose of, and the price (which now is little and dear, that which would have bought twenty miles not buying now two). During the time that this person spoke, not a man of them was observed to whisper or smile; the old, grave, the young, reverent, in their deportment. They do speak little, but fervently, and with elegance. I have never seen more natural sagacity, considering them without the help (I was a going to say, the spoil) of tradition; and he will deserve the name of wise that outwits them in any treaty about a thing they understand. When the purchase was agreed, great promises passed between us of kindness and good neighborhood, and that the Indians and English must live in love, as long as the sun gave light. Which done, another made a speech to the Indians, in the name of all the sachemakers or kings, first to tell them what was done; next, to charge and command them to love the Christians and particularly [to] live in peace with me and the people under my government; that many governors had been in the river, but that no governor had come himself to live and stay here before; and having now such a one that had treated them well, they should never do him or his any wrong. At every sentence of which they shouted, and said "Amen" in their way.

XXIV. The *justice* they have is pecuniary. In case of any wrong or evil fact, be it murder itself, they atone by feasts and presents of their *wampum,* which is proportioned to the quality of the offense or person injured, or of the sex they are of. For in case they kill a woman, they pay double; and the reason they render, is that she breeds children, which men cannot do. It is rare that they fall out, if sober; and if drunk they forgive it, saying, it was the drink, and not the man, that abused them.

XXV. We have agreed that in all differences between us, six of each side shall end the matter. Don't abuse them, but let them have justice, and you win them. The worst is, that they are the worse for the Christians, who have propagated their vices and yielded them tradition for ill, and not for good things. But as low an ebb as they are at, and as glorious as their own condition looks, the Christians have not outlived their sight[21] with all their pretensions to a higher manifestation. What good then might not a good people graft, where there is so distinct a knowledge left between good and evil? I beseech God to incline the hearts of all that come into these parts to outlive the knowledge of the natives, by a fixed obedience to their greater knowledge of the will of God. For it were miserable indeed for us to fall under the just censure of the poor Indian conscience, while we make profession of things so far transcending.

XXVI. For their *original,* I am ready to believe them of the Jewish race, I mean of the stock of the ten tribes, and that for the following reasons. First, they were to go to a land not planted or known, which to be sure Asia and Africa were, if not Europe; and He that intended that extraordinary judgment upon them might make the passage not uneasy to them, as it is not impossible in itself from the easternmost parts of Asia to the westernmost of America. In the next place, I find them of like countenance, and their children of so lively resemblance, that a man would think himself in Duke's Place or Berry Street[22] in London when he sees them. But this is not all: they agree in rites; they reckon by moons; they offer their first fruits; they have a kind of Feast of Tabernacles; they are said to lay their altar upon twelve stones; their mourning a year, customs of women, with many other things that do not now occur.

So much for the natives, next the old planters will be considered in this relation, before I come to our colony and the concerns of it.

XXVII. The *first planters* in these parts were the Dutch, and soon after them the Swedes and Finns. The Dutch applied themselves to traffic, the Swedes and Finns to husbandry. There were some disputes between them [for] some years; the Dutch looking upon them as intruders upon their purchase and possession, which was finally ended in the surrender made by John Rising, the Swedes' governor, to Peter Stuyvesant, governor for the States of Holland, anno 1655.

XXVIII. The Dutch inhabit mostly those parts of the province that lie upon or near to the bay, and the Swedes the freshes of the river Delaware. There is no need of giving any description of them, who are better known there than here; but they are a plain, strong, industrious people, yet have made no great progress in culture, or propagation of fruit trees, as if they desired rather to have [just] enough than plenty or traffic. But I presume the Indians made them the more careless by furnishing them with the means of profit, to wit, skins and furs, for rum and such strong liquors. They kindly received me, as well as the English, who were few before the people concerned with me came among them. I must needs commend their respect to authority and kind behavior to the English; they do not degenerate from the old friendship between both kingdoms. As they are people proper and strong of body, so they have fine children, and almost every house full; rare to find one of them without three or four boys, and as many girls; some, six, seven, and eight sons. And I must do them that right, I see few young men more sober and laborious.

XXIX. The Dutch have a meeting place for religious worship at New Castle, and the Swedes, three: one at Christiana, one at Tinicum, and one at Wicaco,[23] within half a mile of this town.

XXX. There rests that I speak of the condition we are in, and what *settlement* we have made, in which I will be as short as I can; for I fear, and not without reason, that I have tried your patience with this long story. The country lies bounded on the east by the river and bay of Delaware and eastern sea; it has the advantage of many creeks, or rivers rather, that run into the main river or bay, some navigable for great ships, some for small craft. Those of most eminence are Christiana, Brandywine, Shelpott,[24] and Schuylkill; any one of which has room to lay up the Royal Navy of England, there being from four to eight fathoms [of] water.

XXXI. The lesser creeks or rivers, yet convenient for sloops and ketches of good burden, are Lewes, Mispillion, Cedar, Dover, Crane Hook, Feversham, and St. George's, below; and Chichester, Chester, Tacony, Pennypack, Poquessing, Neshaminy, and Pennsbury in the freshes;[25] many lesser, that admit boats and shallops. Our people are mostly settled upon the upper rivers which are pleasant and sweet, and generally bounded with good land. The planted part of the province and territories is cast into six counties, Philadelphia, Buckingham, Chester, New Castle, Kent, and Sussex, containing about four thousand souls. Two General Assemblies have been held, and with such concord and dispatch that they sat but three weeks, and at least seventy laws were passed without one dissent in any material thing.[26] But of this more hereafter, being yet raw and new in our gear. However, I cannot forget their singular respect to me in this infancy of things, who, by their own private expenses so early considered mine for the public, as to present me with an impost upon certain goods imported and exported, which, after my acknowledgments of their affection, I did as freely remit to the province and the traders to it.[27] And for the well government of the said counties, courts of justice are established in every county, with proper officers, as justices, sheriffs, clerks, constables, etc.; which courts are held every two months. But, to prevent lawsuits, there are three peacemakers chosen by every county court, in the nature of common arbitrators, to hear and end differences betwixt man and man. And spring and fall there is an orphan's court in each county, to inspect and regulate the affairs of orphans and widows.

XXXII. Philadelphia, the expectation of those that are concerned in this province, is at last laid out to the great content of those here that are anyways interested therein. The situation is a neck of land, and lies between two navigable rivers, Delaware and Schuylkill, whereby it has two fronts upon the water, each a mile, and two from river to river. Delaware is a glorious river; but the Schuylkill being a hundred miles boatable above the falls, and its course northeast toward the fountain of Susquehanna (that tends to the heart of the province, and both sides our own), it is like to be a great part of the settlement of this age. I say little of the town itself, because a PLATFORM will be shown you by my agent, in which those who are purchasers of me will find their names and interests.[28] But this I will say, for the good providence of God, that of all the many places I have seen in the world, I remember not one better seated. So that it seems to me to have been appointed for a town, whether we regard the rivers or the conveniency of the coves, docks, springs, the loftiness and soundness of the land and the air, held by the people of these parts to be very good. It is advanced within less than a year to about four score houses and cottages, such as they are, where merchants and handicrafts [men] are following their vocations as fast as they can, while the country men are close at their farms. Some of them got a little winter corn[29] in the ground last season; and the generality have had a handsome summer crop, and are preparing for their winter corn. They reaped their barley this year in the month called May; the wheat in the month following; so that there is time in these parts for another crop of divers things before the winter season. We are daily in hopes of shipping to add to our number; for, blessed be God, here is both room and accommodation for them; the stories of our necessity being either the fear of our friends, or the scarecrows of our enemies; for the greatest hardship we have suffered has been salt meat, which, by fowl in winter and fish in summer, together with some poultry, lamb, mutton, veal, and plenty of venison, the best part of the year, has been made very passable. I bless God I am fully satisfied with the country and entertainment I can get in it; for I find that particular content which has always attended me, where God in His providence has made it my place and service to reside. You cannot imagine my station can be at present free of more than ordinary business, and, as such, I may say it is a troublesome work. But the method things are putting in will facilitate the charge, and give an easier motion to the administration of affairs. However, as it is some men's duty to plow, some to sow, some to water, and some to reap, so it is the wisdom as well as [the] duty of a man to yield to the mind of providence, and cheerfully as well as carefully embrace and follow the guidance of it.

XXXIII. For your particular concern, I might entirely refer you to the letters of the president of the Society.[30] But this I will venture to say, your provincial settlements both within and without the town, for situation and soil, are without exception. Your city lot is a whole street and one side of a street, from river to river, containing near one hundred acres, not easily valued;[31] which is, besides your four hundred acres in the city liberties, part of your twenty thousand acres in the country. Your tannery has such plenty of bark, the sawmill for timber, the place of the glass house [is] so conveniently posted for water carriage, the city lot for a dock, and the whalery for a sound and fruitful bank, and the town [of] Lewes by it to help your people, that by God's blessing the affairs of the Society will naturally grow in their reputation and profit. I am sure I have not turned my back upon any offer that tended to its prosperity; and though I am ill at projects, I have sometimes put in for a share with her officers to countenance and advance her interest. You are already informed what is fit for you further to do. Whatsoever tends to the promotion of wine, and to the manufacture of linen in these parts, I cannot but wish you to promote it; and the French people are most likely in both respects to answer that design. To that end I would advise you to send for some thousands of plants out of France, with some able *vignerons,* and people of the other vocation. But because I believe you have been entertained with this and some other profitable subjects by your president, I shall add no more, but to assure you that I am heartily inclined to advance your just interest, and that you will always find me

Your kind cordial friend,<br>William Penn

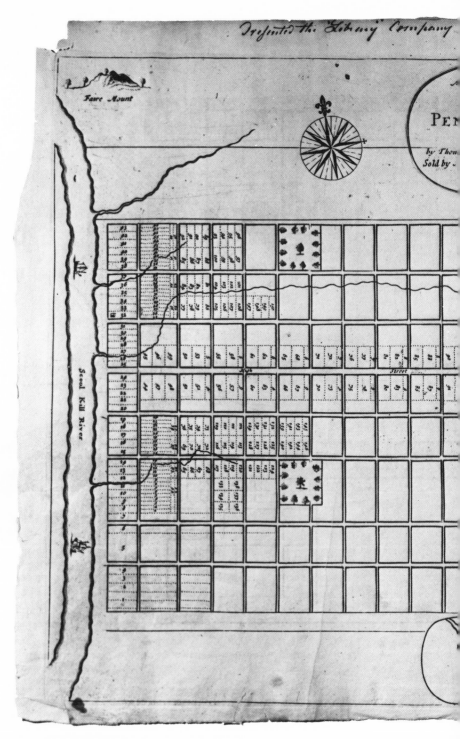

A Portraiture of the City of Philadelphia, *by Thomas Holme, 1683, Library Company of Philadelphia.*

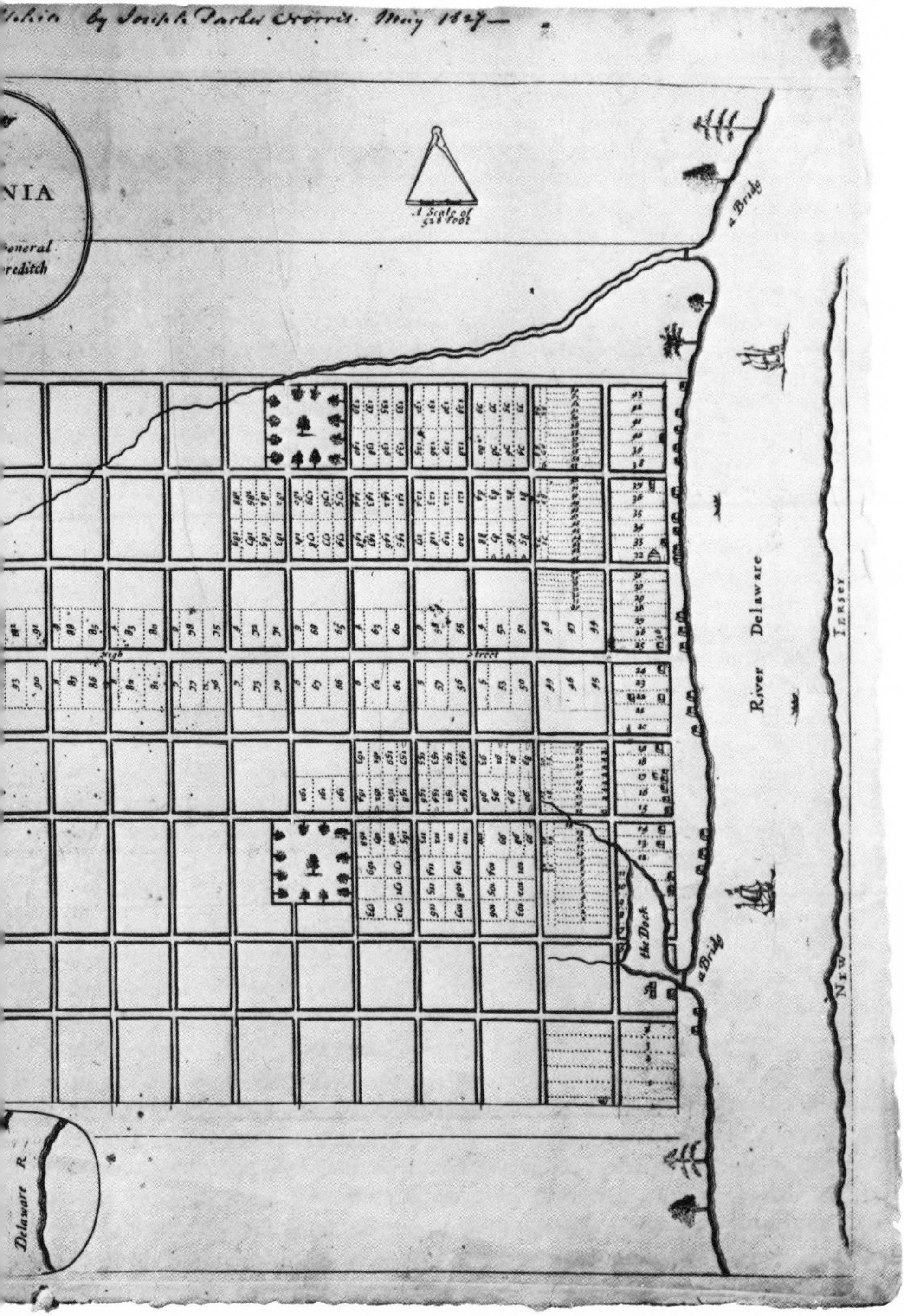

by Joseph Parker Norris May 1827 —

NIA

eneral
reditch

A Scale of
528 feet

a Bridg

a Bridg

the Dock

a Bridg

River Delaware

Iersey

New

Delaware R.

*A Short Advertisement upon the Situation and Extent of the City of Philadelphia and the Ensuing Plat-form thereof, by the Surveyor-General.*[32]

The City of Philadelphia now extends in length, from river to river, two miles, and in breadth near a mile; and the governor, as a further manifestation of his kindness to the purchasers, has freely given them their respective lots in the city without defalcation[33] of any [of] their quantities of purchased lands. And as it is now placed and modeled between two navigable rivers upon a neck of land and that ships may ride in good anchorage in six or eight fathom water in both rivers, close to the city, and the land of the city level, dry, and wholesome: such a situation is scarce to be paralleled.

The model of the city appears by a small draft now made, and may hereafter, when time permits, be augmented; and because there is not room to express the purchasers' names in the draft, I have therefore drawn directions of reference, by way of numbers, whereby may be known each man's lot and place in the city.

The city is so ordered now, by the governor's care and prudence, that it has a front to each river, one-half at Delaware, the other at Schuylkill; and though all this cannot make way for small purchasers to be in the fronts, yet they are placed in the next streets, contiguous to each front, viz., all purchasers of one thousand acres and upwards have the fronts (and the High Street), and to every five thousand acres purchase in the front about an acre, and the smaller purchasers about half an acre in the backward streets; by which means the least has room enough for house, garden, and small orchard, to the great content and satisfaction of all here concerned.

The city (as the model shows) consists of a large Front Street to each river, and a High Street (near the middle) from front (or river) to front, of one hundred foot broad, and a Broad Street in the middle of the city, from side to side, of the like breadth. In the center of the city is a square of ten acres;[34] at each angle are to be houses for public affairs, as a meeting house, assembly or state house, market house, school house, and several other buildings for public concerns. There are also in each quarter of the city a square of eight acres,[35] to be for the like uses, as the Moorfields in London;[36] and eight streets (besides the High Street) that run from front to front, and twenty streets (besides the Broad Street) that run across the city, from side to side; all these streets are of fifty foot breadth.

In each number in the draft, in the fronts and High Street, are placed the purchasers of one thousand acres and upwards, to make up five thousand acres lot (both in the said fronts and High Street), and the numbers direct to each lot, and where in the city; so that thereby they may know where their concerns are therein.

The front lots begin at the south ends of the fronts, by the numbers, and so reach to the north ends, and end at Number 43.

The High Street lots begin towards the fronts, at Number 44, and so reach to the center.

The lesser purchasers begin at Number 1, in the Second Streets, and so proceed by the numbers, as in the draft; the biggest of them being first placed, nearest to the fronts.

Printed tract. (See *PWP,* 2:442-60 for WP's draft of this letter).

1. Songs.
2. The *Thomas and Anne,* Thomas Singleton, master, had sailed from London in mid-January 1683 for New York and Pennsylvania.
3. Thomas Hicks, an Anabaptist controversialist who had quarreled with WP in the 1670s, made these charges. WP's steward answered them in a broadside printed in London, *A Vindication of William Penn.* See *PWP,* 2:443-45, for a fuller commentary by WP on Hicks' charges.
4. Chipping Barnet and Northaw, Herts., both have mineral springs that were considered healthful in the seventeenth century.
5. Frontignac was a muscatel wine, made at Frontignon, Languedoc, France.
6. Winemakers.
7. WP's French viniculturist was Andrew Doz, a Huguenot exile who came to Pennsylvania in 1682 and tended WP's vineyard in the manor of Springettsbury on the east bank of the Schuylkill.
8. Probably named for the town of Newington, Kent, in the English orchard district.
9. On WP's instructions, James Claypoole ordered grape vines from Bordeaux in 1682.
10. Black grouse.
11. Marten.
12. Octoraro Creek flows into the Susquehanna from the east. Rancocas Creek flows into the Delaware River opposite Philadelphia. See the maps on pp. 159 and 175. For Oreckton, see doc. 37, n. 12.
13. Shackamaxon, in the present Kensington section of Philadelphia, was the site of WP's legendary treaty of friendship with the Indians. Poquessing Creek forms the northern boundary of the present City of Philadelphia.
14. For Sepassincks, see doc. 37, n. 12, and the map on p. 159. Passyunk is in present South Philadelphia.
15. Tammany, a Delaware sachem, sold lands between Neshaminy and Pennypack creeks, on 23 June 1683. Secane sold WP land between the Schuylkill and Chester Creek on 14 July 1683. Menangy, or Menanget, met with Tammany, WP, and others at Perkasie Indian Town about 24 and 25 May 1683. Secetareus, sachem of Queonemysing Indian Town, with other Delaware sold the land between Christiana and Chester creeks to WP on 19 Dec. 1683. See doc. 68 and the map on p. 159.
16. Get them used to.
17. By 16 Aug. 1683, WP had bought five parcels of land from the Indians. See docs. 37 and 68, above, and the map on p. 159.
18. The branch of philosophy which treats of first principles, including the origins of life.
19. Fantastic.
20. The Indian seems to be referring here to WP's Swedish interpreter, Lasse Cock. See doc. 32.
21. Have not excelled the Indians' understanding of virtue.
22. Duke's Place and Berry Street were centers of the Jewish ghetto in London.
23. Christiana was a Swedish settlement at the site of present Wilmington, Del.; Tinicum was a Swedish settlement on the Delaware between Chester and Philadelphia; Wicaco was just south of the original boundary of Philadelphia. The church there is now known as Gloria Dei, or Old Swedes'.
24. Shelpott Creek flows into the Brandywine.
25. That is, beyond the salt water forced up the river by the tides.
26. See doc. 62, above.
27. See doc. 70, above.
28. At the end of the *Letter* WP appended Thomas Holme's plan of the City of

Philadelphia (reproduced on pp. 320–21) and a list locating the town lots of the First Purchasers (which the editors have not reproduced here).

29. Wheat.

30. Nicholas More.

31. The Free Society's lot was between Spruce and Pine streets.

32. Thomas Holme.

33. Reduction by taking away a part.

34. Center Square, the present site of Philadelphia's City Hall.

35. These squares are now Washington, Franklin, and Rittenhouse squares, and Logan Circle.

36. Moorfields was a marshy area to the north of the walls of the old city of London. It was first drained in 1527, laid out into walks in 1606, and first built upon c. early 1680s.

# 77 §

## Gulielma Penn to Margaret Fox

WHILE WP was in Pennsylvania, his wife Gulielma had a very difficult time in England. She had stayed behind to nurse her dying mother and to bear a child (see doc. 39). In this letter she reports the birth and death of her newborn daughter and her subsequent illness to Margaret Fox, wife of the founder of Quakerism, George Fox. She does not yet know whether WP wants her to bring their other children to Pennsylvania, but the sailing season for 1683 will soon be past, and Gulielma is clearly in poor shape for an ocean voyage.

Warminghurst, 21 August 1683

Dear M. F.

My dear and truly honored friend in the sense of that which has made thee so among the Lord's faithful chosen people, I most dearly salute thee; and I can truly say it is often brought before me how amiable thou has been and are in the eyes of those that truly have kept their first love. And the Lord has and will crown thee with blessings for thy faithful service all along to Him and His Truth, even when there were very few that stood for His name and thought. It is forgotten by many that are wandering abroad from their habitations, yet it may be brought to their remembrance, to their confusion, and they that abide therein see and know thee.

Dear M. F., I received thy dear and tender lines long since when I lay in. Several things prevented me from writing to thee again which I hope thou will pass by. I was very weak a long time after my lying in and it pleased the Lord to take away my little one when it was about 3 weeks old.[1] It was a mighty great child and it was near dead when it was born, which I think it never got over. Dear G[eorge] F[ox] came a purpose to see me,[2] which I took very kindly and was truly refreshed in his company. I have since had a sore fit of illness, that they call St. Anthony's fire,[3] in my face and a fever. I could not see [but] very little several days and nights, my face and eyes were so swelled but it pleased the Lord to raise me up again. I am not wholly come to my strength yet; my eyes are very weak. Thy son and daughter Rous have been here since to see me. Bethia has been here a pretty [long] while.[4] I think she will write.

I have had several letters from my husband. He was then very well and Friends [also]. They have large meetings at Philadelphia which is the city, 300 at a meeting. I lately received this epistle from him and Friends,[5] which I was desirous thou should see it. I know not whether thou has had it from any other. I expect to hear shortly what my husband will have me to do, whether I shall go this year or no, but fear if he does send I shall scarce be well enough yet to go. I am truly glad when I hear of you or from you. Here was Thomas Langhorne that gave me an account of your welfare. Our meetings here are quiet at present. I desire my very dear love to Thomas Lower and Mary, and to Daniel Abraham and Rachel, and to Isabell,[6] which is again to thyself beyond expression.

> Thy truly affectionate friend that truly
> loves and honors thee in the Lord,
> Gulielma Maria Penn

ALS. Chester County Historical Society. (*PWP*, 2:460-61).

1. Gulielma gave birth to her seventh child, a daughter, in early Mar. 1683. The infant was apparently "in good health" when James Claypoole visited Warminghurst on 20-26 Mar. (see doc. 58, above) but died soon after. Her name and exact birth and death dates are not known.

2. George Fox had visited Gulielma with the Claypooles; see doc. 58, above.

3. A disease that causes fever and intense local inflammation, particularly on the face or legs.

4. Margaret Fox's eldest child, Margaret, was married to John Rous, a Barbados Friend who had moved to London. Bethia Rous (b. 1666) was their daughter.

5. Only one letter written by WP to Gulielma from Pennsylvania now survives (doc. 100, below). The letter that Gulielma passed on to Margaret Fox was probably a circular letter from a Friends' meeting in Pennsylvania to Friends in England.

6. Mary, Rachel, and Isabell were Margaret's daughters. Mary was married to Thomas Lower and Rachel to Daniel Abraham; Isabell Fell Yeamans was a widow, and was probably living with her mother at Swarthmore Hall, Lancs.


# 78 §
## From William Haige

IN August 1683 WP sent commissioners James Graham and William Haige to Albany, New York, to purchase land along the Susquehanna River from the Indians (see doc. 72, above). On 27 August, Haige arrived in New

York City, where he met with the governor of New York, Thomas Dongan. Haige and Dongan had very different ideas about WP's proposed purchase. Haige intended to buy the land for WP, but Dongan thought that it should be bought for his master, the duke of York. Although Haige reports in the following excerpted letter that he had finally persuaded Dongan to let him buy from the Indians, in fact the governor of New York continued to block WP's plans. In September 1683 Haige went to Albany and opened negotiations with the Iroquois, who told him that they were ready to sell the Susquehanna River lands to Pennsylvania. But Dongan ordered these proceedings stopped, and shortly afterward he conducted his own negotiations with the Iroquois — the result of which was that Dongan himself acquired Indian title to the trading territory on the Susquehanna. For WP's response to this unwelcome development, see doc. 82, below.

New York, 29 August 1683

I arrived here a 2d[1] day and immediately went with Col. [Lewis] Morris[2] to wait upon the governor [Thomas Dongan], whom I found to be prepossessed with a slight opinion of thy affairs. He told me that we refused to suffer the people of this place to bring their effects from our river; both James [Graham] and I told him that thou were bound to see the king's interest secured in concerting the 1d. per pound on tobacco, and that it was never refused to any man to export tobacco that would give in bond that they should import it into England.[3] With which answer after a long scanning he was satisfied, but told me as he was vice admiral of all America under his master, the duke [of York], he must send to establish an admiralty in our parts.[4] What he meant by it I know not. He proclaims himself the Lord Baltimore's friend and I understand at second hand that he says thou has wronged him. And that there is a stop put to thy patent at home by reason of a caveat put in against the obtaining of it by the Lord Baltimore.[5] He has sent an express to the Lord Baltimore and gives it out that if the lord cannot come to him he will go to wait upon him, having encouragement for him concerning the lower counties as the people are made to believe. I intimate these things because I presume thou will see it needful to be here in thy own person either before or when the said lord comes hither.

We go to Albany 2 days hence along with the governor which will facilitate our matters with the Indians, the governor having sent for them to be all together, so that I came in good time. And he has promised his assistance; only there arose a strong debate betwixt him and I in whose name I should treat. He urged with a passionate deportment that no man should buy land of their Indians but in his master's name, and that if I should take any other means to accomplish my ends, that now the French were seeking means to destroy the Indians[6] he would protect them. I told him he misconceived my affair, for I came to buy land for Governor Penn and not for the duke of York, and that the duke had already sold all his interest of the land I sought to buy to my master, and that he had not reserved to himself any Indian interest, and that he was a person of that honor not to claim any part in that which he had already parted from, and that the governor himself was a person so just that he would not desire us to treat in any man's name but in his whose was the property. If otherwise I must then take my leave of him, for I dared not.

John West[7] and some others that were by (for it was before all the magistrates in this town) said to him that it was but reason I should treat in Governor Penn's name, seeing the interest was his. At last he condescended and we agreed; I told him I doubted some ill-minded person had misrepresented thee and thy affairs to him. He said he had heard strange things, but thou were a wise man and he was resolved to keep a good correspondence with all his neighbors. T[homas] R[udyard] is a great man with him. He is much governed by him, and it is here said that the governor was recommended by the duke's counsel to him for advice. Though this may seem strange to thee, it is most certainly true; he carries him to Albany along with him.[8] . . .

There are some idle stories here about your patent, that you have not privilege to send a ship to Barbados or any other place but England.[9] . . .

Pray write frequently to Albany, directing to J[ames] Graham's house who will always send it. So soon as we return [we] shall send word. In the meantime [we] shall give account of passages as we go. Is all from thy affectionate

William Haige

ALS. HSP. (*PWP*, 2:466-71).

1. Monday, 27 Aug. 1683.
2. Morris was a Barbados Quaker who lived in the Bronx, N. Y.
3. Tobacco shipped from the British colonies was subject to an export tax. Apparently Dongan was complaining that WP would not allow his colonists (especially those in the lower counties, who had once been subject to the duke of York's government at New York) to ship their tobacco through New York, where the duty would be collected. Haige answered that WP required bond to be posted to insure that the tax would be paid in England; hence no tax was due on this tobacco in America. Obviously, Dongan would prefer to collect the duty himself in New York.
4. Dongan was claiming the right to inspect the commerce of the Delaware River for violations of the English Navigation Acts.
5. Caveat: a legal order of suspension. This refers to the order by the Lords of Trade that WP could not get a royal patent to the lower counties until his dispute with Lord Baltimore was settled; see doc. 69, n. 3.
6. The French in Canada planned to attack the Seneca, westernmost of the Iroquois, in the summer of 1684; however, the invasion never took place.
7. John West, an attorney, was city clerk and clerk of the Council in New York.
8. Rudyard was the deputy-governor of East New Jersey at this time, and he may have helped to give Gov. Dongan a poor opinion of WP. Although Rudyard had worked in close partnership with WP in 1681-1682 in England (see doc. 29, above), the two men became estranged in 1683-1684 in America; see doc. 96, n. 29, below.
9. WP's charter (doc. 11, article 11, above) stipulated that Pennsylvania's exports must be shipped to England only, but the charter also required WP to observe the Navigation Acts, which permitted English colonists in North America to ship such products as lumber, meat, and fish to the English colonies in the West Indies.

## 79 §

## To William Markham

BY August 1683, it was clear that WP and Lord Baltimore could not settle their dispute themselves. Both men turned to the Lords of Trade for help. As early as February 1683, Baltimore had sent a narrative of his case to the Lords; on 31 May, the Lords heard agents from both sides and directed WP to prove that the Dutch had held Delaware before Lord Baltimore received his patent. WP sent his cousin William Markham to England as his agent and gave him the following instructions on how to argue his case. To begin with, WP claims that the Dutch held Delaware before Lord Baltimore received his patent and that the Maryland proprietor had never conquered the Dutch (this was not quite true, since Baltimore's troops burned Whorekill during the Dutch War of 1672-1674). WP also points out that the king had the right to grant land acquired by conquest and that he could, and did repeatedly, take away land from previous grants in issuing new ones. WP then tells Markham to insist on a strict interpretation of Maryland's territorial limits. His instructions here repeat the arguments he advanced in doc. 75, above. His arguments sound complex, but his purpose is simple—to avoid by every possible stratagem running the Pennsylvania-Maryland line at the true 40th degree latitude. WP still hopes to obtain land at the entrance to the Susquehanna River at the head of Chesapeake Bay, and he is also determined to block Lord Baltimore's pretensions to the lower counties and the Delaware River.

[c. 1 September 1683][1]

Instructions to Capt. Markham about the matter and arguments of the lower counties.

When the Lord Baltimore's patent comes to be pleaded, be it before the duke's commissioners[2] in relating matters, or the king and [Privy] Council, these following heads of argument are those chiefly to be insisted upon:

1. That King Charles the First gave him a country in America bounded southward by Watkin's and Wighcomico Point,[3] eastward by the main ocean, northward by the 40th degree of latitude to be found upon Delaware Bay, and westward by the first fountain of Potomac, being all of it uncultivated and unplanted, saving by a few savage natives, which was a misinformation to the king. And query whether that will not vacate the very grant, for part of the eastern shore and Delaware Bay was before, and at the passing of his patent, claimed and planted and purchased of the natives by the Dutch, a Christian and European state in peace with the crown of England.[4]

2dly. If he objects that he has the king's right of what the Dutch wrongfully settled, it may be said, first, that supposing the Dutch were invaders, yet his patent gives him only land in the possession of the savages, and not planted by Christians.

3dly. If he had a right to it, yet his plainly suffering invaders to live above 30 years there *and not under the English sovereignty* while he had it as part thereof, is a treachery to the crown and so a forfeiture of his patent.

4thly. If he says he did take the Whorekills, tell them it was in the king and duke's wrong, for it was so late as the end of the second Dutch War since the king's restoration,[5] which was about 7 years after it had been first in the duke's possession.[6] And then show the people's affidavits [of] how he took it: Halmanius Wiltbanks', John Rhoads's, Harmon [Cornelison]'s and another Englishman's,[7] and desire satisfaction for their wrongs; then let their acknowledgments of me be read, too.[8]

5thly. But the Dutch had the title of the civil law, by which the crown of England holds these parts of the world, to wit, *quæ nullius sunt, in bonis, dantur occupanti,* "that which is nobody's is the right of him that occupies and enjoys it;" for there was no Christian body there at the time the Dutch seated it to prevent them by a prior claim.

6thly. The Dutch had the natives' right, of whom they fairly purchased it; who, if allowed to be natural lords of the soil (that are as exact preservers of property as we are), it does indeed overthrow the Dutch claim by that maxim of the civil law. But then it establishes it by another, which is also the law of all nations, that whosoever buys anything of the true owner becomes rightful owner of that which he bought. And that the Indians are true lords of the soil, there are 2 reasons: 1st, because the place was never conquered; 2dly, that the kings of England have always commanded the English to purchase the land of the natives, as appears by many letters sent to governors and colonies to that effect, which, it is supposed, they would never have done to the prejudice of their own title, if the right of the soil had been in them and not in the natives.

7thly. If in this debate the right of discovery should be alleged, query how far that discovery goes? If no farther than the discoverers see with their own eyes, not only the Dutch would have the better of it in all these parts, formerly their colony, but the king's territories in America would be very small; the hundredth part of the English claim having not yet been seen. If by discovery is understood, coming to any part of the whole and taking possession of that part for the whole, the king of Spain will easily defeat our whole pretense to America, who by Columbus 14 October anno 1492, did not only take a part of the whole, but [also took] Florida, a part of the northern America in which we have reason chiefly to hold ourselves interested.[9] Emanuel, King of Portugal, did the same by Amerigo Vespucci anno 1501,[10] and then comes in Henry the VII of England by John and Sebastian Cabot, Venetians.[11] This I mention to show how slight and yet dangerous such pleas may be; and yet if discoveries will do, the Dutch will not be without pretense, for they bought [Henry] Hudson's charts and maps and paid him for his voyage, who was the most exact discoverer of that which was formerly the Dutch colony in this part of America.[12]

8thly. If it be objected, he was an Englishman (as Sir Samuel Argall[13] once did) and so no foreign state ought to be benefited by his discoveries, then we are at as ill a pass as we were before; for our pretensions are grounded upon 2 Venetians, and consequently, we shall have no right at all.

9thly. The Lord Baltimore neither claimed nor marked his eastern bounds for 26 years, nor [his] northern [bounds] to this day. It has been the practice of America, as well as the reason of the thing itself, even among Indians and Christians, to account not taking up, marking, and (in some degree) planting, [as] a reversion of right; for the Indians do make people buy over again that land the people have not seated in some years after purchased, which is the practice also of all these governments towards the people inhabiting under them.

10thly. But granting the Lord Baltimore had an unquestionable right to it by his patent from the king, yet since the king's right under which he claims is grounded upon the law of nations, and that *jure belli*[14] the Dutch possessed themselves of it and that it was retaken by the king, it becomes the king's right again, and the Lord Baltimore having neglected a new patent for the said place, and the king having granted it to his Royal Highness, it must necessarily follow [that] the title is in his R. H. or his assigns.

11thly. The Lord Baltimore has rescinded and cut off Delaware from his pretensions by divers laws which he has made to exclude Delaware from being any part of the province of Maryland, in right of which he pretends to it, forbidding correspondence with the inhabitants thereof in divers matters of trade.[15]

But there is one reason more, very cogent in this affair, which shall be the last I will urge at this time, that New York was as much given to Connecticut by patent as any part of Delaware could be given to the Lord Baltimore, as the bounds do manifest.[16] Yet it having been the king's conquest, according to the law of nations, he has since granted it to his Royal Highness, and by the same rule that the Lord Baltimore can claim the one, the New Englanders may claim the other; to say nothing of prior patents for Carolina and Long Island, etc.[17] I shall conclude this argument with the Lord Baltimore's [patent], which was granted out of and directly against the patent of Virginia, which was called in only, as the order of [the Privy] Council expresses, *for the better suiting the government of it to the monarchy of England;* but by no means to deprive them either of the government or a foot of the soil thereof, whose northern bounds was the 40th degree of northern latitude, now the northern bounds of the Lord Baltimore's patent; the very mention of which ought to terrify him, as being the most surreptitious patent that ever yet abused the Great Seal.[18] Press this on all occasions when he alleges the king's not being able to grant that to another which he had granted to him before.

Instructions about the other business of finding the fortieth degree of northern latitude, which is the northern[19] bounds of my patent.

First, get the Virginia patents, examine all the bounds most diligently, and if the first goes to forty, get the reasons of calling it in; and if possible, [get] a printed book against the Lord Baltimore's patent, as injurious to Virginia, which Philip Ford may procure of Colonel Lloyd's father, or directions where to have one; and that will enlighten you all how to fall on his plea against surreptitious patents.

Secondly, if there were a second patent that went to thirty-eight,[20] that spoils Lord Baltimore though it doesn't help me, and if there be no such a patent, yet get a good understanding which way the Lord Baltimore came to have but two degrees.[21] So Secretary [William] Blathwayt told Philip Ford, and he sent me word of it, and so Blathwayt and others said at the passing of my patent in [the Privy] Council, and upon what thou can learn or find of that, thou may draw some strength to my plea upon the king's letter[22] for two degrees only. The records of the Secretary's office or Council may show the rise of the business.

Thirdly, but if that should fail, as I hope it will not, then fall to work with the admeasurement, which, though it were but two degrees, I should get by measure more than by the exactest observation twenty miles, there being seventy miles to a degree. This the king may do, sixty miles being the computed length of a degree when that patent was passed,[23] especially when the improvement of a province is at stake, and the Lord Baltimore is not the worse, but he and his interest much the better for my being so accommodated. Importune the king to stick to that way of finding out forty, by taking the old ascertained latitude of the capes[24] or finding that of a Watkin's Point at least, and so measure. This makes good the king's grant, and makes another province that is otherways spoiled.

Fourthly, if the king and Council should go about to conclude us to take an observation at the head of the [Chesapeake] Bay, and not according to the king's last letter in my favor, press that the latitudes may go according to the opinion of ancient artists, by instruments in use at the date of the Lord Baltimore's patent. For if by later instruments [that are] more exact, it should appear they have given the latitude of forty [degrees], twenty minutes (or miles) more southerly than should be. If I am not considered according to the old instruments, the Lord Baltimore will get upon[25] Virginia by the old instruments at the beginning of his country, and upon me at the end of it by these new ones. Nor is this all, for that which reduces the old forty degrees to thirty-nine degrees and forty minutes will make thirty-seven degrees (which is the latitude of the capes) thirty-six degrees and forty minutes, whereby Carolina, that begins by degree, to wit, at thirty-six and a half, will by an advance of twenty minutes come within ten miles of Cape Henry, which will lose Virginia a great country to Carolina.[26] So that Virginia, not advancing upon Maryland (because that province begins certain) as Carolina advances upon Virginia, and the Lord Baltimore upon me, it will follow that Virginia will be a reduced and spoiled country. This press earnestly, especially upon the Lord Culpeper.[27]

Fifthly, but if this prevails not, observe the Lord Baltimore's bounds, which says that his north latitude shall be *that part of Delaware Bay which lies under the fortieth degree of north latitude.* Now in the first place, there is no such latitude in the bay, and a new patent must pass before that will give him to forty degrees up the narrows of the river.

Lastly, what I desire will be in a good measure wrapped up in the success of the Dutch conquest, for if that be carried, take out a new patent for all bought by the Dutch of the natives and by them claimed in pursuance thereof according to the last bounds sent by me to Philip Ford and to the duke.[28] For remember this, that from Bombay Hook to Christiana Creek the country was bought by the Dutch of the natives to the Minquas or Susquehannocks country; as from Cape Henlopen to Bombay Hook, they bought three days' journey into the woods, as the papers with thee do show;[29] which get Ephraim Herrman and John Moll to translate here, or some Dutchman in England.

Sixthly, remember that it is not Cape Lopen, nor Cape Inlopen, but Cape Henlopen, which is eight leagues to the southward of the cape by the Whorekills (which is called of the Dutch in their maps, Cape Cornelis), for it was at the most southern cape the Dutch set up their arms in brass fifty years ago, which I now call, in respect to the duke, Cape James.

D. HSP. (*PWP*, 2:471-79).

1. These instructions are undated, but WP probably wrote them about the first of Sept. 1683. By late July, WP had decided to send Markham as his agent (see doc. 71), but Markham did not leave for England until after 31 Aug. 1683.

2. The duke of York's Commission of Revenue, which supervised the duke's territory in America.

3. Watkin's Point marks the Maryland-Virginia boundary on the eastern shore of Chesapeake Bay. Wighcomico Point is Smith's Point, which marks the Maryland-Virginia boundary on the western shore of Chesapeake Bay. See the map on p. 279.

4. See doc. 75, n. 14.

5. The third Anglo-Dutch War (the second since Charles II's restoration in 1660) lasted from 1672 to 1674.

6. WP is not quite correct here. The duke of York first took possession of what is now Delaware in 1664; the governor of Maryland sent surveyors into the duke of York's territory in 1669, and in 1671 directed an armed band led by Capt. Thomas Jones to take control of Whorekill. These soldiers withdrew in 1672 when the New York government asserted the rights of the duke. In Dec. 1673, after the Dutch seized New York and the Delaware colony during the third Anglo-Dutch War, another Maryland troop burned all the buildings in Whorekill except one barn and left the residents, who numbered about fifty-two persons, with little food or shelter.

7. The Englishman was named Richard Patte. WP had secured statements from Wiltbanks, Rhoads, Cornelison, and Patte, who were all residents of southern Delaware and testified that Lord Baltimore's troops had burned the town of Lewes in 1673.

8. Soon after WP arrived at New Castle in Oct. 1682, John Moll, Ephraim Herrman, and Edmund Cantwell visited Sussex Co. (then called Deal) and obtained from the justices an acknowledgment of their allegiance to WP.

9. Columbus never discovered the North American mainland, but shortly after he claimed San Salvador in the Bahama Islands for Spain (note that WP has the date wrong), Pope Alexander VI in 1493 issued bulls of demarcation—not recognized by England and some other European nations—which confirmed Portugal's rights to Africa and Spain's rights to the New World and India.

10. Vespucci had sailed to America in the service of Emanuel I of Portugal in 1501. Four years before, in 1497, Vespucci claimed to be the first European to sight the American mainland.

11. John Cabot and his son Sebastian reached Cape Breton Island in 1497 and took possession for Henry VII of England.

12. Henry Hudson (d. 1611), English navigator and explorer, was hired by the Dutch East India Company in 1608; the next year he looked into the Chesapeake and Delaware bays, and entered the Hudson River, exploring as far north as the site of Albany.

13. Sir Samuel Argall (d. 1626) was an early governor of Virginia and explored the Chesapeake Bay in 1609-1613.

14. By the law of war.

15. Lord Baltimore and the Maryland Assembly recognized on a number of occasions that Delaware was a separate colony under the government of New York.

16. The Connecticut patent of 19 Mar. 1632 from Robert, Earl of Warwick, to William, Viscount Say and Seal, and others, granted lands westward from Narragansett Bay to the Pacific Ocean; it therefore included the southwestern section of what was later New York.

17. WP is making the point here that overlapping patents were commonly granted. Much of the territory later known as Carolina was included in the Virginia charters of 1606, 1609, and 1612, and Long Island was first included in the Virginia charter of 1606, and then granted to the Council of New England in 1620, before the duke of York received it in 1664.

18. WP is referring here to the first lord Baltimore's highhanded tactics in negotiating his territorial limits in 1632. Baltimore first obtained a warrant for a colony south of the James River; when the Virginians protested that such a colony would encroach upon their Southside settlements, he obtained a second warrant for a colony occupying the entire Chesapeake Eastern Shore; when the Virginians again protested that Baltimore was encroaching upon their Eastern Shore settlements, the Privy Council authorized a third warrant for a colony north of Watkin's Point.

19. WP means "southern."

20. WP wonders whether there is a Virginia patent, granted sometime between 1623 and 1632, which established that colony's northern boundary at the 38th degree of latitude. No such charter was issued.

21. The Maryland charter of 1632 fixed Lord Baltimore's southern boundary at Watkin's Point and his northern boundary at the 40th degree of latitude. This was commonly believed to be two degrees of latitude, although in fact Watkin's Point was several miles below the 38th degree, and thus Baltimore was granted slightly more than two degrees. WP is telling Markham to downplay Baltimore's claim to the 40th degree, and to stress instead his restriction to two degrees of latitude; he hopes by this tactic to fix Maryland's northern boundary below the 40th degree.

22. In his letter of 19 Aug. 1682, Charles II told Baltimore that the dispute should be settled by measuring two degrees from Watkin's Point. See the headnote to doc. 64, above.

23. When Lord Baltimore received his charter in 1632, English geographers believed that each degree of latitude equaled sixty miles. In 1671, a more exact measurement was taken, showing a degree to be 69.1 miles.

24. WP wanted to measure north from the latitude of the mouth of Chesapeake Bay between Capes Charles and Henry (37 degrees 5 minutes), at sixty miles per degree. This measurement would have given him land at the head of Chesapeake Bay; measuring from Watkin's Point would not.

25. Encroach upon.

26. WP is incorrect. The northern border of Carolina specified in the second charter of 30 June 1665 was 36 degrees 30 minutes north latitude; this line is about twenty-five miles south of Cape Henry.

27. Gov. Thomas Culpeper of Virginia could not be of much help to WP as he was now in disfavor with the Lords of Trade. He had returned to England in May 1683 and was replaced as governor by Francis Howard, Lord Effingham, on 28 Sept.

28. I.e., the revised boundaries requested by WP for a charter for Delaware from Charles II to the duke of York.

29. WP is claiming here that the Dutch bought Indian title to the territory encompassing Sussex and Kent counties, from Bombay Hook in the Delaware River to what he called Cape Henlopen at the present Delaware-Maryland line. It was important for WP to try to establish that the "most southern cape" in Dutch possession, twenty miles below the entrance to Delaware Bay, was called Cape Henlopen, and that the promontory now known as Cape Henlopen was called Cape Cornelis by the Dutch. See the map on p.175.

# 80 ∫

## From James Walliam and John White

FROM the following letter WP learned the unwelcome news that Lord Baltimore—galled by WP's refusal to join him in fixing the Maryland-Pennsylvania line—was finding the 40th degree of latitude for himself and running his own northern boundary line.

New Castle, 8 September 1683

Most Excellent Sir

There is a report that the Lord Baltimore is arrived at the head of the [Chesapeake] Bay and that he has run a line piercing into part of your lands, having particularly surveyed John Darby's[1] plantation, and cut his [coat of] arms on several remarkable trees. Those messengers who are gone to compliment the new governor of [New] York[2] pretend their lord will suddenly assert his pretensions to your seigniories in these parts. Likewise common fame reports the said lord designs to visit your town of New Castle.

Sir, we could wish we knew your pleasure and our duty in the manner of his reception, who, if he comes [as] your friend and ally, I suppose may be as honorable as his quality and our ability can make. But if uninvited he comes to advance his pretensions, or to draw the minds of the people from their due obedience, how those that love and honor your service may act in those circumstances we would gladly know. For there be some among us who think your just and happy government does reproach their former evil administration, and for fear of rendering an account for the oppressions and wrongs they have done would I suppose betray all and do new and greater mischiefs to secure the old.

Sir, our zeal to your service has made us bold to trouble you with these lines: but the least intimation of your pleasure shall be the rule of our actions in this and all other public services. But if these slender remarks may [in] any way advance your service, we have our desire which is always to serve, honor, and obey you while we are,

James Walliam and John White[3]

Postscript

As this was ready to seal: Ephraim Herrman is just now arrived, who says Baltimore is gone up Elk River[4] with thirty persons, or thereabout, well equipped, intending to see the utmost bounds of his line which the said lord is informed is fourteen miles above Esquire Talbot's.[5] Ephraim says the Lord Baltimore is tender[6] how he touches the reserved twelve miles around New Castle.

ALS. HSP. (*PWP,* 2:485-86).

1. John Darby was a landowner and innkeeper in New Castle Co. who had represented his county in WP's first two assemblies. See doc. 50, and doc. 62 (entry for 12 Mar. 1683).
2. Thomas Dongan.
3. Walliam and White were both justices of the peace in New Castle Co.
4. The Elk River flows south from Chester Co., Pa., through Cecil Co., Md., into Chesapeake Bay.
5. George Talbot was a first cousin of Lord Baltimore. According to depositions given in the 1730s by residents who witnessed these events or heard about them, Talbot ran a line of marked trees from the mouth of Octoraro Creek to a point just south of Naaman's Creek on the Delaware. This line was quite close to the present boundaries dividing Maryland, Delaware, and Pennsylvania.
6. Cautious. Baltimore was avoiding the arc around New Castle claimed by the duke of York and WP.

# 81 §
## The Surveying of Germantown

ONE of the most distinctive features of early Pennsylvania was its remarkable ethnic and cultural diversity. Dutch, Swedish, and Finnish settlers were already established before 1681, and English, Irish, Welsh, and German immigrants came over with WP. The settlement of Germantown, a few miles northwest of Philadelphia, was founded in 1683 by an alliance of German-speaking investors, whose Frankfort Company had bought 15,000 acres from WP, and Dutch-speaking emigrants from Krefeld in the Rhine Valley. Francis Daniel Pastorius (1651-c. 1720) acted as the spokesman for both groups. These Germantown settlers shared WP's Quaker principles, but they were separated from the English-speaking majority by language and custom. Pastorius envisioned a "German colony" in Pennsylvania and negotiated for a single tract. WP respected this wish, and in the warrant below he directed Thomas Holme to survey a block of 6000 acres for their town. The land was accordingly surveyed on 24 October, and the following day the immigrants gathered at the cave on the Philadelphia riverfront in which Pastorius was living and drew for the location of their lots. Immediately they began building homes for their first winter in Germantown.

Philadelphia, 12 October 1683

William Penn, Proprietary and Governor of the province of Pennsylvania and the territories thereunto belonging.

At the request of Daniel Pastorius[1] in behalf of the German and Dutch purchasers, that I would grant them six thousand acres to settle upon, these are to will and require thee forthwith to survey, or cause to be surveyed, unto him for them the said number of acres on the east side of Schuylkill River, and make returns thereof into my secretary's office.

Wm Penn

For Thomas Holme, Surveyor-General

DS. HSP. (*PWP,* 2:490).

1. Pastorius, a Quaker, was a lawyer from Frankfurt am Main who purchased land from WP for the Frankfort Company. He reached Philadelphia on 20 Aug. 1683 and later served as a teacher in Germantown, a member of the Pennsylvania Assembly, and Germantown's first bailiff (mayor) upon its incorporation in 1691. He signed America's first anti-slavery petition in 1688. For Pastorius' commentary on pioneer life in Pennsylvania, see doc. 89, below.

# 82 §

## Purchase of the Mouth of the Susquehanna River

ALTHOUGH Gov. Thomas Dongan of New York prevented him from securing his territory on the upper Susquehanna River, WP moved in the fall of 1683 to purchase the Indian rights for the lands along the lower Susquehanna which bordered on Chesapeake Bay. In September 1683 he bought land on the eastern bank of the Susquehanna from the Indian Kekerappan, and in October he purchased the rights of the Indian Machaloha to the mouth of the Susquehanna. As a way of strengthening his claim, WP sent the following declaration to the Lords of Trade. In fact, ownership of this tract was uncertain. Lord Baltimore did not have an Indian deed to this area, and WP may have thought that his own deed would help his case against Baltimore.

New Castle, 18 October 1683

William Penn, Proprietary and Governor of the province of Pennsylvania and the territories thereunto belonging.

I do hereby declare that I have bought of Machaloha[1] all his land lying between Delaware River, the bay of Chesapeake, and Susquehanna River. And do warn all persons that they presume not to settle thereon without my leave, and that those that are already, or shall hereafter, settle upon any part of the same do behave themselves justly and lovingly towards him and his fellow Indians.

Wm Penn

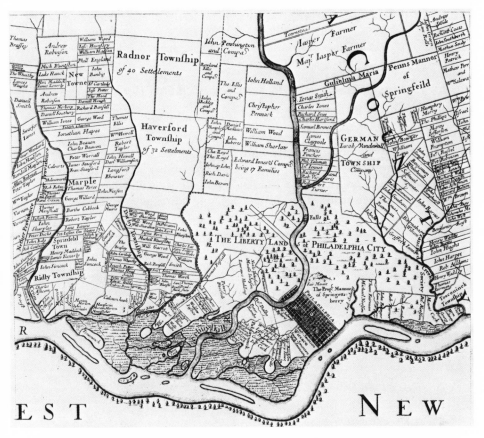

A Map of the Improved Part of Pennsylvania in America, *by Thomas Holme,*
*1687, HSP. This detail of Holme's famous map includes the City of Philadelphia,*
*Germantown, and the Welsh Tract. The entire map, containing seven sheets of paper*
*and measuring five by three and one-half feet, shows all of Bucks, Philadelphia, and*
*Chester counties.*

DS. PRO. (*PWP*, 2:492).

1. Machaloha was perhaps a Susquehannock who had assumed a Delaware name. His claim to the ownership of this land is very questionable.

# 83 §

## To Tenants in New Castle, Chester, Philadelphia, and Bucks Counties

ALTHOUGH in July 1683 WP had released his subjects from paying an import duty (see doc. 70, above), by November he was in great need of money. In the following circular letter, he informs the landholders in four of his six counties that he must begin collecting quitrents on their lands.

Philadelphia, 9 November 1683

Loving Friends and Tenants

I kindly salute you and wish you heartily well. I have sent the bearer, James Atkinson,[1] to gather in my quitrents among you,[2] and you must not take it hard that I press you in this matter, for you know that I receive neither custom nor taxes, but maintain my table and government at my own cost and charges, which is what no governor does besides myself. This makes me endeavor to get in my own dues for my winter supply. I expect you will all strive to answer me herein, and so engage the kindness of

Your friend and landlord
Wm Penn.

Transcript. HSP. (*PWP*, 2:500-1).

1. James Atkinson (d. 1711) arrived in Pennsylvania in Dec. 1682 from Belfast, Ireland. A member of the Philadelphia Monthly Meeting of Friends, he was appointed by WP to Philadelphia's first Common Council in 1701.
2. The quitrent for land in Bucks, Chester, and Philadelphia counties, as announced in *Some Account of the Province of Pennsylvania* (doc. 15), was one shilling per 100 acres, starting in 1684. Thus WP was trying to collect his rents early. The quitrent for the lower counties was set at a considerably higher rate: one penny per acre or 8s. 4d. per 100 acres.

# 84 §

## From Thomas Holme

BY November 1683, WP's surveyors had laid out about 170 town lots in Philadelphia according to Thomas Holme's grid plan (see docs. 56 and

76). Holme was now concerned that the best lots would soon be gone, and so he asked WP to reduce them in size. Holme's other worry — that the Philadelphians were cutting down all the timber near the town — would soon be alleviated, because the townspeople quickly learned to build their houses out of brick.

[Philadelphia, c. 9 November 1683]

Governor

Please to excuse my further attendance on thee today, 3 o'clock (an hour hence) this afternoon being appointed for the burial of my son's corpse.[1]

These few things I offer to thy consideration:

The necessity of ascertaining the bounds of the counties of Chester and this, as also betwixt this and Bucks, lest hereafter I may err in placing people.[2]

I find it may be requisite for thy affair in the concerns of this city, where many people may (probably) come, more than formerly expected[3] — to reduce the breadth of the High Street lots, and also to reduce the Second Streets and other backward streets from both the river fronts,[4] and yet leave sufficient room to make way for new purchasers amongst them to some content, to prevent being all placed backward, of which many are unwilling. Yet I intend not the altering or removal of any in these back streets that have already built or in the least improved.

The orders for cutting trees in the swamps for building is not observed; but havoc made on dry lands, which John Songhurst[5] and I cannot avoid, for it may not be expected that we can go and see our orders executed. Therefore, there is need for a certain man to be appointed for that service, and to be paid by those that have warrants to cut trees, that he may see it done in the swamps, according to orders. And thy proclamation (finally) to forbid any to cut any trees, not only out[6] of swamps, but also not without that said certain person be present, may be serviceable, in the opinion of thine to serve thee

Thos Holme

ALS. FLL. (*PWP*, 2:501-2).

1. William Holme (b. 1665), the tenth and youngest child of Thomas and Sarah Holme, died in Philadelphia on 8 Nov. 1683.
2. The boundaries between Bucks, Philadelphia, and Chester counties were not fixed by the Provincial Council until 1 Apr. 1685.
3. Thirteen ships brought passengers to Pennsylvania in Sept.-Nov. 1683, and many of these newcomers wanted city lots. By Nov., according to WP, one-fifth of the 3000 settlers in Pennsylvania lived in the city.
4. High Street lots were 132 feet wide; Second Street lots, like those on Front Street, were 102 feet wide. Despite Holme's recommendation, WP did not change these dimensions.
5. John Songhurst was a carpenter who helped Holme to survey the woods and regulate the cutting of timber.
6. Outside.

# 85 §

## James Claypoole to Edward Claypoole

THE following excerpted letter illustrates how an immigrant merchant set up his new business in Philadelphia. It shows the mixed results of the plans James Claypoole had laid a year before (see doc. 44) for arranging his move from London. Claypoole lives in a house "like a barn, without a chimney"; the black slaves he ordered from his brother Edward in Barbados have not arrived; and he spends too much time working for the Free Society of Traders and not enough on his own mercantile business. Yet Claypoole is buoyant about Philadelphia's commercial prospects, and his letter evokes the dynamic character of Pennsylvania's economy in the 1680s.

Philadelphia, 2 December 1683

Dear Brother Edward Claypoole

My last to thee was the 10th, 5th month,[1] which I sent from Gravesend[2] by Captain [James] Manbey, with 6 agate knives,[3] which I hope are come safe to hand. If I can, I will upon this sheet send thee [a] copy of the said letter.

As to our voyage from England to this place, we went on board the *Concord* at Gravesend the 24th, 5th month, and after we lost sight of England, which was in about 3 weeks' time, we were 49 days before we saw land in America; and the 1st, 8th month,[4] some of us went ashore in Pennsylvania. The blessing of the Lord did attend us so that we had a very comfortable passage and had our health all the way.

We came to this city the 8th or 10th, 8th month, where I found my servant had built me a house like a barn, without a chimney, 40 foot long and 20 broad with a good dry cellar under it, which proved an extraordinary convenience for securing our goods and lodging my family, although it stood me in very dear. For he had run me up for diet and work near £60 sterling, which I am paying as money comes in for goods. To this I built a kitchen of 20 foot square where I am to have a double chimney, which I hope will be up in 8 or 12 days.

I wrote to thee to send me 4 blacks, viz., a man, a woman, a boy, a girl,[5] but being I was so disappointed in England as not to send thee those goods thou wrote for, I could not expect thou would send them. If they had been sent, I should have taken it very kindly and have balanced [the] account with thee in some reasonable time. Now my desire is that if thou does not send them all, however, to send me a boy between 12 and 20 years, and, if thou will, send some rum and molasses which are now in great demand, 5s. per gallon and 2s. per gallon. I will dispose of it for thee and send the produce either in bills [of exchange] for England or silver or oil,[6] or some other way which yet we know not. Thou must send also a ton of sugar, 2 hogsheads thirds and 2 hogsheads fourths,[7] and ½ ton of ginger, 500 lbs. scraped, and 500 lbs. scalded,[8] and I shall, if thou will, be ½ concerned.

My lot in this place proves to be especially [good] for trade, one of the [best] in the city,[9] and though I employ my time in serving the [Free] Society [of Traders], being treasurer, for which I have £100 sterling, yet my wife and children with my direction shall manage the business as well as if I did it myself, and I will be accountable for all. So I desire thee, let us have a little trade together, and as I writ formerly, if thou will take for thyself, or for any other, 1000 or 2000 acres of land in this country, the sooner the better. For people come in so fast that it is like to be much dearer in a little time. It's judged about 1000 people came in 6 weeks, so that it is already worth double what it was, 1000 acres being now at £40 sterling.[10]

Samuel Carpenter[11] is next but one to me and is likely to get a great estate quickly. William Frampton[12] is on the other side of me, building a great brewhouse. If I had time and could write, for [it is] cold, having no chimney, I would have filled some sheets of paper in giving thee account of the country and our settlement, trade, and laws, etc. But now I must be excused till another time, only this in short, I do believe it will prove a very healthy country, and that great improvements may be made in a few years by industry and skill. . . .

Advise what commodity whale oil may be with you, for we have 24 men fishing in the [Delaware] Bay[13] that are like to make a good voyage. Here is a great deal of silver in our river that was taken at the wreck, which may be purchased at reasonable rate with goods, as rum, molasses, and sugar. I have a great deal more to write, but time fails, for the boat is going quickly, so must conclude.

Thy assured loving brother.

LBC. HSP. Not published in *PWP,* Vol. Two.

1. 10 July 1683.
2. A seaport on the Thames, below London.
3. Probably knives with agate handles.
4. 1 Oct. 1683.
5. See doc. 44, above.
6. Whale oil; see n. 13, below.
7. Sugar harvested from the third or fourth growth of cane. It was of poor quality, and cheaper than sugar from the first growth.
8. Ginger was exported from the West Indies in two forms: the young shoots were peeled or scraped for use in ginger preserves or sweetmeats, or the plants were scalded and dried, ready to be ground up for use in food or medicine.
9. The lot, 100 feet wide along the Delaware, stretched back to Second St. Claypoole's house was at the southwest corner of Front and Walnut streets.
10. WP sold 1000 acres to a First Purchaser in England for £20.
11. Samuel Carpenter (1649-1714), a Quaker from Barbados (where Edward Claypoole lived), was the most energetic merchant in early Pennsylvania. An active participant in the colony's government, he owned large tracts of land in Pennsylvania and West New Jersey and invested in milling and lumbering. Carpenter built the first wharf in Philadelphia; see doc. 92, below.

12. William Frampton (d. 1686), a wealthy Quaker merchant, had lived in New York before moving to Pennsylvania. Besides the brewery, he also built a bakery in Philadelphia.

13. This whale fishery was operated by the Free Society of Traders. Claypoole obviously anticipates — quite incorrectly — that whale oil will become a chief Pennsylvania export.


# 86 §

## Lord Baltimore to Richard Burke

THE boundary dispute between WP and Lord Baltimore has been presented in this volume mainly from WP's point of view. Doc. 86 gives Lord Baltimore's side of the case. The proprietor of Maryland is writing to his agent in London, Richard Burke, who has been representing him at preliminary hearings before the Lords of Trade. By late 1683, Baltimore has decided to go to England himself, but it will be some months before he will arrive, and so he instructs Burke on how to handle WP's agent, "that idle fellow" William Markham, at Whitehall. It is evident from this letter that Baltimore is pursuing many of the same tactics as WP. He asks Burke to solicit help from as many government officials and privy councilors as possible, and he sends over letters and papers to document his case before the Lords of Trade. Baltimore also has some interesting—and probably inaccurate—gossip about "Prince Penn." Like WP, he clearly believed that he was the aggrieved party. As it turned out, his comments were all too frank, for this letter was intercepted by WP's friends (see the note at the close of the letter), and WP himself was able to read Baltimore's insulting reflections when he reached England in 1684. The letter is printed here in abbreviated form; sections dealing with Baltimore's family and financial matters have been omitted.

Mattapany,[1] 7 December 1683

Dick Burke

There being a small vessel now ready to sail for Scilly,[2] I take this opportunity of sending you a duplicate of my letter of the 7th of November, the original of which I sent you per [Captain] Bowman.[3] I will now give you my answer to such letters as I have received from you since my sending you my letter above mentioned.

Yours of the 10th of September makes mention that Mr. [William] Blathwayt told you Mr. Penn was upon selling his patent for Pennsylvania, being not able to make good to the Quakers such proportions of land as he stands obliged to furnish them with. You may be assured, that if he has occasion to buy of me, my land shall not want a price; but as yet, it is not my resolution to spare him any; for I like not his neighborhood[4] and therefore shall not encourage his stay in these parts. I do believe that he may have got above £15,000 of his friends,[5] some of which are very plain in telling him that he has not done well by them; others a little more plain in saying that truly William Penn has cheated them. So that now I understand he has an uneasy life amongst them; and (as I suppose) is not so fond of his principality as he has been in the business of Delaware. He has dealt underhand, falsely, and treacherously with me; for while he was endeavoring to get a grant of my interest there, he made the greatest protestations of kindness and friendship imaginable. And now his false dealings and treacherous proceedings begin to render him odious amongst such persons as afore had much esteem for him. I am glad to hear the patent[6] will not pass until William Penn or his agents have cleared and answered the objections put to them at the Council board; which I am sure they cannot answer. For put the case, [that] there were Dutch seated on Delaware before my patent was granted (which will them give some difficulty to prove), yet that will not serve their turn; for if any such were seated, they were but usurpers and disowned by the states of Holland, as I can sufficiently prove. And that William Penn is sensible I am provided for; it is for this and other reasons that I have pressed so much to be heard in person afore I be concluded; which you must take care to mind[7] [to] these lords of the Council that you know are my friends, assuring such that I am provided to clear all matters in relation to my interest at Delaware.

. . .

I am now come to that [letter] of the 25 of September being the last that as yet I have received from you. Therein you signify that there was a report of Mr. Penn's being come for England, and that Mr. St. Leger had raised it; who possibly might think that Penn was arrived because it had been reported here before St. Leger went, that William Penn was fully resolved for England, which he had certainly done, but that the Quakers would not suffer him to quit Pennsylvania by reason that he had not, nor, as I think, will ever be able to comply with his engagement to them, he having received money for lands which he is not able to find for them on the water, which is expected by them.[8] When Penn found that the Friends would not suffer him to quit Pennsylvania, he then resolved to send that idle fellow, his cousin Capt. William Markham,[9] of whom I made mention in the first long narrative I sent you. The said Markham went from Delaware in a small vessel the latter end of August last, his errand and chief business being the complaint of me for a proclamation I caused to be issued forth the 15th of May last, in which I caused my new conditions of plantation to be published.[10] And there being in the said proclamation mention made of the lands on the seaboard side and at the Whorekills, where the conditions of plantation were in my father's time (as now they are in mine) easier than in other parts of my province, this gave offense to Prince Penn, upon which he sends commissioners to me,[11] as by my letters and papers sent you in the box designed by Eaton; as also by their duplicates sent by the way of Westchester will fully appear.

And I hope that the original or duplicates may arrive at your hands by that time Markham gets to London, and when you find he is come, you may do well to acquaint my Lord Bishop of London, the Earl of Craven, the Earl of Bath, the Earl of Chesterfield, Sir Leoline Jenkins, and if you can, my Lord Marquis of Halifax, and as many more as you can of the Council,[12] that Capt. Markham is the person mentioned in the long narrative to have refused complying with his Majesty's positive commands in the letter of the 2d of April in the 33rd year of the king's reign,[13] being the king's first letter commanding the setting forth our bounds. And the said Markham slighting and in contempt refusing to comply with the same has been the occasion of all the difference between Penn and me.[14] And what was set down in that long narrative in relation to the proceedings betwixt Markham and me will be made out by me to his face; from letters under his own hand, which let him know from me I will suddenly do, as also when I see him in England, know his reasons for his dirty and rude carriage to me in that business. This is all at present I shall say in that business; by the first ship bound for London, I will enlarge further. In the meantime watch the motions of the said Markham, though I do not fear his interest will be able to do me any mischief. Besides he has owned to my two secretaries[15] that both Penn and his Council do expect I shall recover my right to Delaware and that all Penn's proceedings hitherto were but only to make a better bargain with me; this much he owned to Secretary Sewall and Secretary Darnall when he came the last summer [as] one of the commissioners from his master Penn. . . .

Your loyal friend,
C. Baltimore

Copy. HSP. (*PWP*, 2:628-30). This letter was sent on a ship that was wrecked off the coast of Cornwall, in southwestern England. A quick-witted Quaker minister, John Ellis, intercepted it and sent a copy to WP's friends in London.

1. Lord Baltimore's manor in St. Mary's Co., Md.
2. The Scilly Islands, off the southwest coast of England.
3. In this earlier letter (which was also intercepted by WP's friends), Baltimore had thanked Burke for representing him at a series of meetings of the Lords of Trade between Apr. and Aug. 1683.
4. Nearness.
5. Actually, according to WP's business records, he had received £6700 in Pennsylvania land sales by the time he left England in Aug. 1682, and an additional £2400 by Mar. 1685. But Blathwayt and Baltimore are correct in stating that the First Purchasers were dissatisfied with WP's land distribution policy; see doc. 96, below.
6. The duke of York had applied to Charles II for a patent, or charter, granting him title to the whole west bank of the Delaware from the Schuylkill River to Cape Henlopen; he planned to convey the rights he received from the king to WP. But in Apr. 1683 Burke had persuaded the Lords of Trade to stop this patent until the Maryland-Pennsylvania boundary was settled.
7. Remind.
8. Baltimore is probably correct in stating that some of the First Purchasers were unhappy with the land they were given and, in particular, with not having received enough land along the Delaware or Schuylkill rivers. But there is no evidence that the First Purchasers tried to stop WP from returning to England in 1683-1684.
9. See WP's instructions to Markham, doc. 79.

10. See doc. 67, n. 7.

11. See doc. 69.

12. All these men were members of the Privy Council. In previous letters Burke had told Baltimore that they appeared to be friendly to his cause, and hostile to WP.

13. Charles II wrote Baltimore on 2 Apr. 1681, describing the chartered boundaries of Pennsylvania and asking Baltimore to meet with WP's agent in running the Maryland-Pennsylvania boundary. Markham delivered this letter to Baltimore in Aug. 1681.

14. For an example of Baltimore's dealings with Markham before WP reached America, see doc. 35, above.

15. Nicholas Sewall and John Darnall (who was not the lawyer John Darnall who composed doc. 5, above) were Baltimore's personal secretaries.

# Part XI

## FRICTION WITH THE COLONISTS §
## JANUARY 1684–JULY 1684

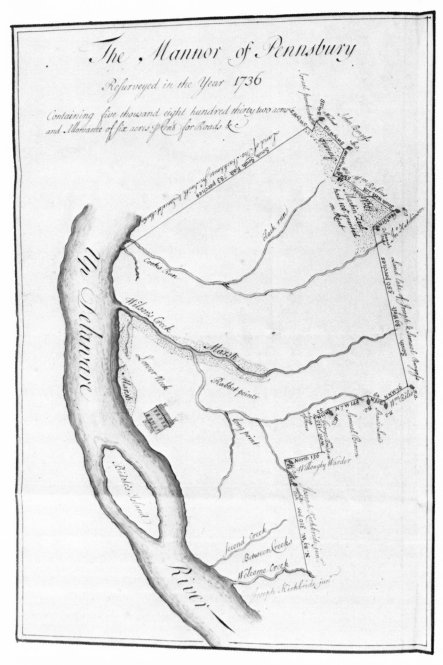

*Map of Pennsbury Manor, 1736, HSP. WP acquired his estate at Pennsbury by July 1683. It is located in present Falls Township, Bucks County, about twenty-five miles north of Philadelphia.*

DURING his first year and a half in America, WP had played the role of kindly father to his colonists with much success. During 1682-1683, while his relations with neighboring governments were frequently stressful, he kept in harmony with the settlers in Pennsylvania and the lower counties. In these early days WP could take advantage of his proprietary control over land grants and administrative offices, and since he obligingly paid for all governmental expenses out of his own pocket, he freed the colonists from burdensome taxes. Many of the early immigrants to Pennsylvania were humble folk, unused to sharing political power, and since they frequently arrived as strangers to one another, they required time to become aware of their common interests and needs. WP's only real internal defeats in 1682 and 1683 had been the Assembly's insistence upon revising his *Frame of Government* (see docs. 62 and 63, above) and their refusal to endorse his commercial corporation, the Free Society of Traders. Overall, the Quaker colonists saw their leader as a blessed instrument of the Lord. Francis Daniel Pastorius saw him as a "very worthy man and famous ruler" (see doc. 89). Elizabeth Gretton in Barbados, who had never met WP, rejoiced at God's heavenly appearance in Pennsylvania (doc. 90). Richard Davies in Wales, on hearing of WP's loving care for the incoming settlers, quaintly told him: "Thou are no bubble nor mushroom" (doc. 95).

However, WP's boundary quarrel with Lord Baltimore became ever more serious during the spring and summer of 1684, and began to damage his holy experiment. When the Maryland proprietor sent agents into the lower counties to claim the area, some of the inhabitants switched their allegiance from WP to Baltimore. The rebellion in the lower counties is discussed in the headnotes to docs. 87 and 93. Most of the settlers along the lower Delaware were non-Quakers without strong personal commitment to WP or his policies, and they could be tempted by Maryland's offer of lower quitrents. Lord Baltimore could never have stirred a similar rebellion among the Quakers in Pennsylvania. But Baltimore's armed invasion convinced WP that he had to return to England in order to protect his colony. Once the Pennsylvanians knew of his impending departure, they saw him less as a father figure and more as a landlord, and criticized him openly for the first time. The leading Philadelphia merchants, with whom WP had heretofore worked in close partnership, blocked his efforts to establish a colonial revenue in May, and then in July presented him with their "Remonstrance and Address" (doc. 96) which attacked his policy on land grants and city lots.

## 87 §
# From William Welch

IN early 1684 the competing claims of WP and Lord Baltimore led to the realization of one of WP's worst fears: a number of Delaware residents rejected his government and sided with Lord Baltimore. The trouble started in Kent County, where Baltimore had announced in May 1683 that colonists who seceded from WP's colony need pay only one-fourth the quitrents WP required (see doc. 67, above). By October 1683, Kent County residents were demanding better terms from WP. Then in February 1684, Lord Baltimore sent agents who renewed his offer of reduced quitrents in return for oaths of allegiance. In the following letter, Provincial Councilor William Welch (d. 1684), a London Quaker merchant who had recently moved to New Castle County, reports to WP about Baltimore's latest maneuver. As WP's loyal supporter, Welch was ready to arrest Baltimore's agent George Talbot if he should again venture into the lower counties and try to "withdraw the people from their obedience" to WP. But he suspected that some of WP's other officials in Delaware were ready to join Talbot and Baltimore.

New Castle, 18 February 1684

My Honored Friend

Through the mercy of the Lord I came well to this place the last 4th day,[1] where I found all things reasonably well. But soon after I received some information as if all things were not so well about Appoquinimink[2] and those parts, with reference to [Lord] Baltimore, which beginnings of his stirring in that place may probably have its influence upon this in a short time if not prevented. I understand one J. G.[3] is gone up to wait upon thee to communicate the matter more plainly by word of mouth to thee, whom I perceive knows much more of that matter than I can tell thee, and so to his relation I refer thee, and do entreat a few lines from thee, for my better government in that affair. I do humbly offer with submission to thy better judgment, whether if [George] Talbot or any other should come hither upon such like errand as to withdraw the people from their obedience to thee, the legal proprietary and governor, we might not seize them and convey them to Philadelphia. Or if he does not come, yet whether we might not send warrants for all who appear disaffected to thee, and who have been tampering with him, to come and take the engagement of fidelity to thee or forfeit their land according to the law in that case provided.[4]

And if in case Talbot should come hither in a hostile manner, how shall we govern ourselves in that case? I am of opinion that if thou does not think fit to put 5 or 6 men into the fort here to keep it from a surprise, it were better demolished, or at least the guns and arms removed to some remote parts, and not suffer them to fall into their hands. Griffith Jones (the bearer hereof) will relate to thee the baseness of some men about St. Jones's where Baltimore has been tampering, and I will assure thee here does not want some in this place that may be perfidious. I broke the business to Peter Alricks whether he had any orders from thee or Capt. [William] Markham about the fort. I gave him a hint of what intelligence I had of Baltimore's underhand dealing and asked him whether it were not fit to put a few men in it, that it might not be surprised. He gave me a kind of a cold answer that I did not like, and I had a real sense upon me that he is not right to thy interest. I say no more, it is thy own concern to provide remedy in such matters, and I may with humility say it does deserve a consideration to do somewhat by way of prevention not inconsistent with the Truth. I leave it with thee and remain

Thy sincere friend to serve thee,
Wm Welch

Whether were it not fit at the next election to cause all electors [to] take the engagement of fidelity as the law in that case directs?

ALS. Library of Congress. (*PWP*, 2:522-23).

1. Wednesday, 13 Feb. 1684.
2. In southern New Castle Co., adjacent to Kent Co.
3. Possibly John Glover (d. 1684), of Kent Co., who was a member of the Assembly.
4. A law to this effect was passed at the Assembly of 12 Mar.-3 Apr. 1683.

# 88 §

## From James Harrison

BETWEEN 1683 and 1684 WP began to stake out his country seat and to build his large brick manor house at Pennsbury in Bucks County. Very little is known about the beginnings of Pennsbury. Doc. 88 indicates that WP bought the place from a troublesome character named Thomas King. We know that WP had acquired the property by 21 July 1683 when he issued a commission from Pennsbury, and he hosted a Bucks County court session there on 11 March 1684. James Harrison, who became the steward of Pennsbury when WP returned to England, was evidently already looking after the place in February 1684. According to Harrison's letter (which is torn in several places and hard to read), WP did not start his country estate from scratch: there were already on the premises a corn crib, fenced fields, a peach orchard, and a house or barn with a lockable door—to which King had kept the key.

Bucks [County], 23 February 1684

Will: Penn

My much esteemed friend and renowned governor, after true love with reverence unto thee presented, these are to let thee know of divers great and unsufferable trespasses and abuses committed here by Thomas King, since thou bought the plantation of him.[1] First, he, with some to assist him, pulled down 14 panels of rails in fence. 2dly, he has pulled down and burned and otherwise disposed [of] a place that was for securing of Indian corn in the ear and husk, and has impaired the fence in divers places, so that beasts[2] and swine come in where I had sown a[nd planted ?] some thousands [of] wheat, clover, and other seeds, even when I had made good 14 panels with new rails gotten in the wood. Likewise, he has cut in pieces some cleft[3] that was to be palisades, and has carried away divers of the palisades belonging to the building (he never sweat for) bought of Samuel Field,[4] not yet paid for. And worst of all he is gone and keeps the key of the door to my prejudice, although he has been here since he had brought his beasts to the new place. Likewise, there is in the neck[5] about 2[00] or 300 lb. [of] clapboards in the rough.

Now my request is that thou would command him to bring again those pieces of the building he has taken away, set up [and make ?] good the place as it was in, provide so many rails to those that [he and ?] G[eorge] B[rown][6] carried away out of their place and set [them] well up where I shall appoint him on the plantation, and make another place to lay Indian corn in, give satisfaction for treading the corn and causing the peach trees to be eaten and broken, to carry away no more timber nor clapboard, and withal[7] to bring me the key forthwith, because I was never in legal possession. Therefore I thus trouble thee, but humbly desire thee to use thy power, for I and mine are kept at a distance from our business, and besides that he does it in contempt and to provoke. Thou has been long looked for up [here], and I hope will be well, when come, to most, which is all but love and good respects from thy real friend in Truth.

Ja: Harrison

ALS. HSP. (*PWP*, 2:524-26).

1. Little is known about the man who sold Pennsbury to WP. Probably he was the Thomas King of Bucks Co. who accused a local woman of being a witch—and was then tried and convicted of slandering her. He died in 1693.
2. Probably cattle.
3. Split pieces of wood.
4. Field had lived in the Pennsbury area since at least 1680.
5. Perhaps the neck of land between Welcome Creek and the Delaware River, on which the Pennsbury manor house was built.
6. George Brown (c. 1644-1726) emigrated from Leicestershire to New Castle in 1679, and then to the Pennsbury area, where he became a justice of the peace in 1680.
7. Also.

## 89 §

# Positive Information from America,
# *by Francis Daniel Pastorius*

FRANCIS Daniel Pastorius arrived in Philadelphia in August 1683 as the agent of the Frankfort Company, a German corporation that had bought 15,000 acres of Pennsylvania land (see doc. 81, above). After spending his first winter in Pennsylvania, he reported home to his friends in Germany. His report was later published as a promotional tract, aimed at encouraging other Germans to immigrate to Pennsylvania, under the title *Sichere Nachricht aus America, wegen der Landschaft Pennsylvania.* A translation of this tract, somewhat abridged, is printed below.

Pastorius' account should be compared with WP's *Letter to the Free Society of Traders* (doc. 76). Both men wrote about some of the same subjects, including the Indians, the Swedish and Dutch inhabitants, and the pattern of settlement in the colony. Pastorius' letter, however, adds many valuable new details to our knowledge about life in early Pennsylvania and provides the unique perspective of a German immigrant. Like the Welshman Edward Jones (see doc. 42, above), Pastorius found the voyage over to be difficult and he encountered major delays before his purchased land was laid out. But Pastorius, again like Jones, was not discouraged by these obstacles. He praised the provincial government and characterized WP as a true Christian and a good governor who expressed genuine fondness for the German people. In spite of his praise, most stockholders of the Frankfort Company took Pastorius' advice to delay their immigration until the province was more settled, and as a result the Germans in Pennsylvania in the 1680s found themselves to be a small group "wedged in among the English"—contrary to Pastorius' wish for a small separate German province.

Philadelphia, 7 March 1684

### POSITIVE INFORMATION FROM *AMERICA* CONCERNING THE COUNTRY OF PENNSYLVANIA
### BY A GERMAN WHO TRAVELED THERE.

To fulfill my duty as well as my promise made at my departure I will somewhat more fully state what I have found and noted of these lands; and since I am not unaware that by imperfect relations many of you have been misinformed, I give my assurance beforehand that I with impartial pen and without deceptive additions will set forth faithfully both the inconveniences of the journey and the defects of this province, as well as that plentifulness of the same which has been praised by others almost to excess. For I desire nothing more in my little corner of the earth than to walk in the footsteps of Him who is the way, and to follow His holy teachings, because He is the Truth, in order that I may forever enjoy with Him eternal life.

I. Accordingly I will begin with the voyage, which is certainly on the one hand dangerous on account of the terror of shipwreck, and on the other hand very unpleasant on account of the bad and hard fare; so that I now from my own experience understand in a measure what David says in the 107th Psalm, that on the sea one may observe and perceive not only the wonderful works of God, but also the spirit of the storm. As to my voyage hither, I sailed from Deal[1] on the tenth of June with four menservants, two maidservants, two children, and one young boy. We had the whole way over, for the most part, contrary winds, and never favorable for twelve hours together; many tempests and thunderstorms. Also the foremast broke twice, so that it was ten weeks before we arrived here; yet *sat cito, si sat bene,*[2] considering that it seldom happens that any persons arrive here much more quickly. The Krefelders, who arrived here on October 6, were also ten weeks upon the ocean, and the ship that set out with ours from Deal was fourteen days longer on the voyage, and several people died in it. The Krefelders lost a grown girl between Rotterdam and England, whose loss however was replaced between England and Pennsylvania by the birth of two children. On our ship, on the other hand, no one died and no one was born.

Almost all the passengers were seasick for some days, I however for not more than four hours. On the other hand I underwent other accidents, namely, that the two carved lugs over the ship's bell fell right upon my back, and on the 9th of July during a storm in the night I fell so severely upon my left side that for some days I had to keep to my bed. These two falls reminded me forcibly of the first fall of our original parents in Paradise, which has come down upon all their posterity, and also of many of those falls which I have undergone in this vale of misery of my exile *Per varios casus, etc.*[3] But praised be the fatherly hand of the divine mercy which lifts us up again so many times and holds us back that we fall not entirely into the abyss of the evil one. George Wertmüller also fell down extremely hard, Thomas Gasper had an eruption of the body, the English maid had the erysipelas, and Isaac Dilbeck, who according to outward appearance was the strongest, succumbed for the greatest length of time.[4] So I had a small ship hospital, although I alone of the Germans had taken my berth among the English. That one of the boatmen became insane and that our ship was shaken by the repeated assaults of a whale, I set forth at length in my last letter.

The rations upon the ship were very bad. We lived *medice ac modice.*[5] Every ten persons received three pounds of butter a week, four cans of beer and two cans of water a day, two platters full of peas every noon, meat four dinners in the week and fish three, and these we were obliged to prepare with our own butter. Also we must every noon save up enough so that we might get our supper from it. The worst of all was that both the meat and the fish were salted to such an extent and had become so rancid that we could hardly eat half of them. And had I not by the advice of good friends in England provided myself with various kinds of refreshment, it might perhaps have gone very badly for me. Therefore all those who hereafter intend to make the voyage hither should take good heed that they either, if there are many of them, procure their own provisions, or else agree distinctly with the captain as to both quantity and quality, how much food and of what sort they are to receive each day; and to hold him down the more completely to this agreement, one should reserve some small part of the passage money, to be paid on this side. Also when possible one should arrange with a ship which sails up to this city of Philadelphia, since in the case of the others which end their voyage at Upland, one is subjected to many inconveniences.

My company on board consisted of many sorts of people. There was a doctor of medicine[6] with his wife and eight children, a French captain, a Dutch cake baker,[7] an apothecary, a glassblower,[8] a mason, a smith, a wheelwright, a cabinetmaker, a cooper, a hatmaker, a cobbler, a tailor, a gardener, farmers, seamstresses, etc.; in all about eighty persons besides the crew. They were not only different in respect to age (for our oldest woman was sixty years of age and the youngest child only twelve weeks) and in respect to their occupations, as I have mentioned, but were also of such different religions and behaviors that I might not unfittingly compare the ship that bore them hither with Noah's Ark, but that there were more unclean than clean (rational) animals to be found therein. In my household I have those who hold to the Roman, to the Lutheran, to the Calvinist, to the Anabaptist, and to the Anglican church, and only one Quaker.

On the 11th of August, we cast the lead[9] for the first time and found that we were close to the great sand bank, and so had to sail back and around and consequently to run more than a hundred leagues[10] out of our course. On the 16th, we came with joy in sight of America and on the morning of the 18th arrived in Delaware Bay, which is thirty English miles long and fifteen wide, and is of such unequal depth that since our ship drew thirteen feet of water we sometimes stuck upon the sand. On the 20th, we sailed past New Castle, Upland, and Tinicum, and arrived at evening, praise God, safely at Philadelphia; where I on the following day delivered to William Penn the letters that I had, and was received by him with amiable friendliness; of that very worthy man and famous ruler I might properly write many things.

II. But my pen (though it is from an eagle, which a so-called savage lately brought to my house) is much too weak to express the high virtues of this Christian — for such he is indeed. He often invites me to his table and has me walk and ride in his always edifying company; and when I lately was absent from here a week, in order to fetch provisions from New Castle, and he had not seen me for that length of time, he came himself to my little house and requested that I should at least once or twice a week be his guest. He heartily loves the Germans, and once said openly in my presence to his councilors and those who were about him, I love the Germans and desire that you also should love them. Yet in any other matter I have never heard such a command from him. This however pleased me so much the better because it entirely conforms with the command of God (see I John 3:23).[11] I can at present say no more than that William Penn is a man who honors God and is honored by Him, who loves what is good and is rightly beloved by all good men. I doubt not that others will come here and by their own experience learn that my pen has in this case not written enough. . . .

IV. Philadelphia daily increases in houses and inhabitants, and presently a house of correction will be built in order that those who are not willing to live in a Philadelphian manner may be disciplined, for some such are to be found to whom fittingly applies what our dear friend[12] mentions in his letter, that we have here more distress from the spoiled Christians than from the Indians. Furthermore, here and there other towns are laid out; for the [Free] Society [of Traders] is beginning to build about an hour and a half from here[13] one [town] bearing the name of Frankfort, where they have erected a mill and a glass factory. Not far from there, namely two hours from here, lies our Germantown, where already forty-two people are living in twelve dwellings. They are mostly linen weavers and not any too skilled in agriculture. These good people laid out all their substance upon the journey, so that if William Penn had not advanced provisions to them, they must have become servants to others. The way from here to Germantown they have now, by frequent going to and fro, trodden out into good shape. Of that town I can say no more at present than that it lies on black rich soil and is half surrounded with pleasant streams like a natural defense. The chief street therein[14] is sixty feet wide, and the cross street, forty. Every family has a house lot of three acres.

V. As to the inhabitants, I cannot better classify them than into the native and the implanted. For if I were to call the former savages and the latter Christians, I should do great injustice to many of both varieties. Of the latter sort, I have already mentioned above that [my] sailing ship was not to be compared to anything but Noah's Ark. The Lutheran preacher, who, like a statue of Mercury, ought to show the Swedes the way to heaven, is, to say it in one word, a drunkard.[15] Also there are coiners of false money and other vicious persons here, whom nevertheless, it may be hoped, the breath of God's wrath will in His own time drive away like chaff. . . .

The first [Indians] who came before my eyes were those two who at Upland came in a canoe to our ship. I presented them with a dram of brandy. They attempted to pay me for it with a sixpence, and when I refused the money they gave me their hands, and said, "thank you, brother." They are strong of limb, swarthy of body, and paint their faces red, blue, etc., in various ways. In the summer they go quite naked, except that they cover their private parts with a piece of cloth; and now in winter they hang duffels upon themselves. They have coal-black hair, while the Swedish children born here have hair snow-white.

I was once dining with William Penn where one of their kings sat at table with us. William Penn, who can speak their language fairly fluently, said to him that I was a German, etc. He came accordingly on the third of October, and on the twelfth of December another king and queen came to my house. Also many of the [Indian] common people come over to me very often, to whom however I almost always show my love with a piece of bread and a drink of beer, whereby an answering affection is awakened in them and they commonly call me "German," also "Carissimo" (that is, brother). Particularly, their language is manly and in my opinion is little inferior to the Italian in gravity, etc. As to their manners and nature, one must, so to speak, distinguish between those who have associated for some time with the so-called Christians and those who are just beginning to come forth out of their burrows. For the former are crafty and deceitful, which they owe to the above-mentioned nominal Christians. *Semper enim aliquid haeret.*[16] Such a one lately offered me his belt as security that he would bring me a turkey, but in its place he brought an eagle and wished to persuade me that it was a turkey. When, however, I assured him that I had seen many eagles, he acknowledged to a Swede who stood by that he had done it out of deception, in the belief that because we had lately come into the land I should not be well acquainted with such birds. Another at my fireside tested my brandy thus: he stuck his finger into it and then put the latter into the fire to see whether water had been mingled with the liquor. Those of the second class, on the contrary, are of an honest spirit, injure nobody, and we have nothing whatever to fear from them. . . .

Of those persons who came hither with me, a half dozen are already dead. I and mine, however, have throughout the whole time found ourselves in good condition and good appetite, except that Isaac Dilbeck has for a week been somewhat indisposed, and Jacob Shoemaker on the first of October cut his foot severely with an ax and was for a week unable to labor.[17] Of the Krefelders, no one has died thus far, except Herman op den Graef's[18] decrepit mother, who, soon after her arrival, wearied of the vanities of the world and departed to enjoy the delights of heaven. The wife of Abraham Tunes,[19] our farm tenant, has now lain very weak for more than two months in my cottage, and was for some time quite unconscious, but now bids fair to get well.

Now as to the purchased land. It is divided into three kinds. First, 15,000 acres lying together in one piece, on a navigable stream. Secondly, 300 acres within the city liberties, which is the stretch of land between the Delaware and the Schuylkill. Thirdly, three lots in the town, on which to build houses. When after my arrival I applied to William Penn for warrants to measure off these three kinds, and to obtain possession of them, his first answer respecting this was:

1. The three lots in the city, and the three hundred acres in its liberties, could not rightly go to the Frankfurters because they were bought after he, William Penn, had already left England and the books at London had been closed. After I had represented to him, however, that you were the forerunners of all Germans and therefore to be regarded with more consideration, he caused three lots to be measured off for me at the beginning of the town, one after another, out of his younger son's share.[20] . . .

Upon the front lot I have, with our man-servant, built already a small house, half under the ground and half above; which indeed is only thirty feet long and fifteen feet broad, yet when the Krefelders were lodging here with me, could harbor twenty persons. On the oilpaper window[21] over the door I wrote: *Parva domus sed amica bonis, procul este prophani.*[22] This William Penn lately read and was pleased. Also I have a cellar seven feet deep and twelve broad and twenty long, dug in the banks of the Delaware,[23] and am now occupied with building a stable. All three lots are cleared of the trees, and I shall immediately fence them and plant them with Indian corn. Note well, it is especially difficult and expensive to fence all the land, yet on account of the horses, cattle, and swine running at large we cannot dispense with doing it. Also one cannot, the first year, plant either rye or wheat in such new land, but only Indian (or as you call it, Turkish) corn, which however does not taste nor satisfy so well.

2. As to the three hundred acres in the city liberties, I have made various applications to William Penn in respect to them, and have especially urged that B[enjamin] Furly had promised them in the sale to us, etc. He however for a long time would not agree to this, the reason being that not more had been reserved for city liberties than that for which buyers of five thousand acres had been found while he was yet in England; and among these the Frankfurters were not included. Finally a few days ago, when I again delivered to him a memorial, he gave me the pleasing answer that he out of particular regard for you would allow me the said three hundred acres additional, but would give no more to any man who had bought after the closing of the books, no matter who he might be. So I intend as soon as possible to start Indian corn here on these three hundred acres (which are not more than half an hour's distance from this town), in order that I may better keep the cows and swine, may raise more produce, and thereby help those who come after me.

3. Concerning the fifteen thousand acres, two chief difficulties arose, namely, that William Penn did not wish to give them all together in one piece in order that so very large a space in the land might not lie uncultivated and empty, nor would he give them on the Delaware River, where indeed everything had already been taken up by others. But after I had repeatedly represented to him both orally and in writing that it would be very prejudicial to us and our German successors to be so completely wedged in among the English,[24] and likewise that B. Furly had communicated to the Frankfurters his (William Penn's) letter in which he had promised otherwise to our nation, etc., he finally gave me a warrant to have our land in one tract,[25] provided that we within a year would settle thirty families upon the fifteen thousand acres, namely, three townships, each of ten households, among which might be reckoned the three which are already here (but in case thirty families do not come he will not be bound to give the land in one piece). I for my small part could indeed wish that we might have a small separate province, and so might the better protect ourselves against all oppression.
. . .

In regard to my household, I very much wished to arrange it in the good German style and Jacob Shoemaker and the old Swiss[26] are very serviceable to me toward this purpose. But the Hollanders whom I have with me adapt themselves but ill to this, especially the maid, who cannot get on well with the English one,[27] so that I, to preserve the peace, must send the latter away because the former with her two children cannot so easily remove or attach herself to another master. I greatly desire to obtain as soon as possible a German maid whom I can trust better than, I am sorry to say, I now can do. . . .

One cannot yet obtain from this land any return goods to send to England. William Penn, to be sure, intends to establish weaving and wine making; and for this reason, when you have a good opportunity, send us good vines on whose prospering one can count. Also send all sorts of field and garden seeds, especially of lentils, millet,[28] etc. Also, in particular, some great iron cooking pots and some double boilers. Also an iron stove, because the winter here is usually as cold as with you and the rough north winds much harsher. Also some coverlets or mattresses, because I did not bring more with me than just what I needed, yet have already got an additional manservant. Finally, if you would also send me some pieces of fustian and Osnaburg linen cloth, it can be sold to good advantage.

A tanner can undertake his work with great profit, since we can obtain enough skins in the country around us, exchanging one dressed for two undressed, and also keep the very best for a pair of shoes. A certain amount of capital must be employed for this, but since these sums of money thus expended would in a short time bring a rich revenue, I leave the matter to your due consideration. The two most necessary things are: (1) to build upon the lots in this town comfortable houses, which may be leased for a good deal of money and from which twelve per cent per annum can be obtained; (2) to establish a brick kiln, for which William Penn has promised to give us a suitable place, for as long as we make no bricks our housebuilding is only of wood. Other artisans may well wait at home a few years yet.

To the four questions I give these brief answers: (1) William Penn has laid a good foundation for a righteous government and from time to time he publishes useful laws. (2) He maintains neighborly friendship with all the adjoining governors and hopes that the still-continuing contest with [Lord] Baltimore may soon be settled and removed by royal decree. (3) William Penn is much loved and praised by all people, insomuch that even the old vicious inhabitants have to acknowledge that they have never before seen so wise a ruler. Ah, what impressive and penetrating sighs this dear man sent forth on the first day of the New Year to the heavenly heights and to the throne of our Emmanuel, because the true "Philadelphia" and brotherly love is not yet so abundantly to be found in this our Philadelphia as he on his part desires, and for whose advancement he has so earnestly busied himself as a true father of his country. (4) The Indians, of whose nature a little something has been stated in a previous passage, grow less numerous here daily, retiring some hundred miles farther into the country.

Now you might perhaps ask whether I with a pure and undisturbed conscience could advise one and another of you to come over to this place. I answer with good deliberation that I would be heartily glad of your dear presence; yet unless you (1) find in yourselves freedom of conscience to go, (2) can submit to the difficulties and dangers of the long journey, and (3) can resolve to go without most of the comforts to which you have been accustomed in Germany, such as stone houses, luxurious food and drink, etc., for a year or two, then follow my advice and stay where you are for some time yet. But if the things I have mentioned do not come too hard for you, depart the sooner the better from the European Sodom, and remember Lot's wife, who indeed went forth with her feet but left her heart and inclinations there.[29] . . .

Herewith I send a sample of the Indian money used here, of which six of the white and three of the black make an English farthing; and these Indians will not sell anything more for silver money, but will be paid with their own money, since for the most part they wish to quit this land and to withdraw some hundred miles farther into the woods. For they have a superstition, that as many Indians must die each year as the number of Europeans that newly arrive.

Thus much I have to inform you, in order to comply with my bounden duty, and I take the greatest care to be truthful, of which William Penn and other reasonable people, as well as my own conscience (which I value more than thousands), can give an irreproachable witness. That it falls quite hard upon me in this expensive and unprotected land to care for so many menservants and married couples, you can easily judge. But trust in our Heavenly Father overcomes all. Give all other acquaintances hearty greetings from me.

I remain ever your true and devoted servant,

[Francis Daniel Pastorius]

Translation of printed tract, by J. Franklin Jameson, in Albert Cook Myers, ed., *Narratives of Early Pennsylvania, West New Jersey, and Delaware, 1630-1707* (New York, 1912), pp. 392-411. Not published in *PWP,* Vol. Two.

1. Deal, Kent, a port on the English Channel.
2. Quickly enough, if well enough.
3. This is the opening of a quotation from the *Aeneid,* I, 204: "Through various accidents, through so many hazards, we go on to Latium."
4. These four persons were servants of the Frankfort Co. brought over by Pastorius. The English maid was Frances Simpson, who suffered from erysipelas, a skin disease.
5. In a healthy and ordinary way.
6. This was Thomas Lloyd (d. 1694), a Welsh Quaker who became a major figure in early Pennsylvania. WP appointed him keeper of the seal and master of the rolls, and when he left for England in Aug. 1684, WP nominated Lloyd to be president of the Provincial Council and hence the chief executive in the colony (see doc. 97, below). His wife, Mary, died shortly after they reached Pennsylvania, and Lloyd then married a New York widow, Patience Story.
7. This was Cornelius Bom (d. 1688), who set up a bake shop on the southeast corner of Third and Chestnut streets.
8. This was Joshua Tittery, from Newcastle-upon-Tyne, who came as a servant to the Free Society of Traders.
9. Took a sounding, to see if they could touch bottom.
10. About 300 English miles. They had probably touched the treacherous Georges Bank, east of Cape Cod, and were thus much too far north.
11. "And this is his commandment, that we should believe in the name of his Son Jesus Christ, and love one another, as he gave us commandment."
12. Jacob Vandewalle, a Frankfurt pottery merchant, who was one of the original stockholders of the Frankfort Co.
13. I.e., from Philadelphia.

14. Now Germantown Avenue.

15. In Greek mythology, Mercury was the guide of souls. The preacher, Rev. Jacob Fabritius (d. 1693), came to New York in 1669 from Holland, and to the Delaware in 1671; he was pastor of the Swedish church at Wicaco.

16. For always something sticks.

17. These men are servants of the Frankfort Co.

18. Herman op den Graef (d. c. 1704), a linen weaver from Krefeld, was one of the first four burgesses of Germantown.

19. Abraham Tunes, another weaver from Krefeld, was a member of the Quaker meeting and a burgess in Germantown in 1694.

20. The lots given to the Germans were on Front St., between South and Pine streets. WP's younger son, William Penn, Jr., was left with a lot on the corner of Front and South.

21. Pastorius used oilpaper for his windows because glass was so scarce.

22. A reference to Virgil's *Aeneid,* VI, 258, meaning: "A little house, but a friend to the good; the profane, stay away."

23. Probably the cave where the Krefelders gathered to draw the lots for the Germantown settlement (see doc. 81, above).

24. Compare with doc. 42, above.

25. Pastorius did not, however, have enough money to pay WP's surveyors their fee of £28 to survey 15,000 acres, and so he settled for 6000 acres; see doc. 81, above.

26. His servant George Wertmüller.

27. The Dutch maid was Marieke, wife of Isaac Dilbeck; the English maid was Frances Simpson.

28. A grass, cultivated for its seed or hay.

29. Sodom, a city in ancient Palestine, was destroyed by fire as God's punishment for the sinful ways of her inhabitants. The wife of Abraham's nephew Lot turned into a pillar of stone when she looked back on Sodom in her flight from the burning city.


# 90 §

## From Elizabeth Gretton


W P'S work in Pennsylvania gained fame among Quakers outside the colony. There was a Quaker community on the sugar island of Barbados, one of whose members was Elizabeth Gretton (d. 1687), a widowed planter who owned twenty-six black slaves. When Gretton's son sailed to Pennsylvania, she wrote the following letter (printed here in abbreviated form) to tell WP how she admired his work; the "wholesome laws and statutes" of Pennsylvania were "as marrow to my bones." She offered WP a small token of her esteem, an awe-inspiring pill that purges wind and urine, but never hurts the body.


Barbados, 20 March 1684

Dear and Honored Friend Wm Penn

My true and unfeigned love is to thee in that measure of the blessed Truth, which through the mercy of God I am made partaker of. A full stream of which the Lord has made to pass through thee, to the refreshing of the hearts of many that never saw thy face outwardly, of which I am one of the least of God's people, yet can truly say I have been refreshed by the blessed measure in thee. And has made me bless God on thy behalf, who has made thee a good instrument in His hand and has endued thee with wisdom from above to execute justice and judgment for God. . . . My prayer to God is for thy preservation and [that] God's power and heavenly wisdom may assist you all to the amazement of all evildoers and to the refreshment of all the upright-hearted to God. For my heart rejoiced and melted before the Lord in thankfulness for God's heavenly appearance amongst you. When I read the wholesome laws and statutes [passed?],[1] it was as marrow to my bones. The Lord raise more, that a manifest of His heavenly power may sound more and more through the faithful and that it may cause the unacquainted with God to wonder and be amazed. . . .

Dear friend, I have sent thee a small token of my love to thee, a pot of very good pill that I make myself; it is very good in many distempers and is very serviceable to very many here. With some directions here inclosed and one small barrel of suckets,[2] it is the widow's mite[3] which I desire thee to accept of. It comes in my son's[4] chest whom I have ordered to deliver it to thee, or some for thee. So with my dear love and true desire to God for thy prosperity and well-being here and hereafter, I take leave and I hope shall remain thy friend in my measure of the truth,

Eliz. Gretton

The pill is very good in fevers, in fluxes,[5] for worms, in agues,[6] headaches, a very great purger of wind and urine. A child may take one pill as big as a gray pea. It never hurts the body, but rather provokes an appetite. The Lord has made it very serviceable in this island to many for many distempers, blessed be His holy name.

Eliz. Gretton

ALS. HSP. (*PWP*, 2:533–34).

1. Gretton has probably seen a copy of WP's *Frame of Government* and *Laws Agreed upon in England* (doc. 30).
2. Fruits preserved in sugar, or sweetmeats.
3. A small contribution from one who has little to give.
4. Probably Robert Gretton; her other two sons were not yet of age.
5. Heavy discharges of liquids from the body; an early name for dysentery.
6. Fevers accompanied by chills and shivering.

# 91 §

## From William Markham

WP had sent his cousin William Markham to England in September 1683 to plead his case against Lord Baltimore (see doc. 79, above).

In the newsy letter that follows, Markham intended to report to WP on his progress. Unfortunately, the ship carrying this letter had such a difficult crossing that it arrived in Pennsylvania only after WP had departed for England. In amusing detail, Markham recounts his dealings with his enemies in London—the duke of York's secretary, Sir John Werden, and Lord Baltimore's agent, Richard Burke—as well as his audience with Charles II and his labors in delivering WP's gifts to the Lords of Trade. Markham judges that Lord Baltimore's standing at Whitehall is not particularly strong, but he warns WP that the Rye House Plot has greatly changed the political climate in England. The government is now openly favoring Catholics and is pursuing authoritarian policies. Thus Markham urges WP to return to England and resume the personal lobbying at court that had been so successful in 1680-1681.

27 March 1684

Honored Sir

Being very desirous you should have a full copy of the two letters sent by my Lord Baltimore to his agent, the one bearing date the 7th of November, the other of December 1683,[1] may I fear force me to a conclusion of this too soon. But Mr. [Philip] Ford gives me hopes that I may reasonably expect you in England by that time this may arrive in Pennsylvania, not believing you will stay in those parts after the Lord Baltimore had left them,[2] that you may be upon equal terms with him here, well knowing the humor of courtiers. Though all that you directed me to are seemingly your fast friends, especially my Lord Rochester, Lord Keeper [North], Lord President [Radnor], [and] Lord Marquis [of] Halifax, but find a great want of my Lord Dartmouth to oppose Sir John Werden,[3] who seeks all occasions to oppose your interest, though the duke [of York] told Sir John himself he was resolved to maintain his interest and title to Delaware.

When I gave Sir J. Werden your letter, he (as usually) betrayed a great deal of folly in his strange gestures while reading of it, sometimes shrugging up his shoulders, sometimes laughing to himself. And then at a passage [that] was in it that you thought somebody did reflect upon you, his report upon it was that he knew none (laughing) that was not reflected on. I told him I had a letter for the duke but desired I might give it myself, desiring he would introduce me. He made answer he would if he were there at that time; but finding him so indifferent, [I] made Col. Graham[4] my friend, who upon the receipt of your letter was mighty kind and would not only introduce me to the duke but also minded him upon all opportunities of your affair, which I did perceive gave occasion of snuff to Sir J. Werden.

I doubt not but Mr. Ford has given you an account of the proceeding of your business, there being a stop put to it till my Lord Baltimore's coming over (if he arrive by April or May next) before I came into England.[5] But if I have time before Capt. East[6] sails [I] will draw a narrative of it to the best of my knowledge. The last minutes were (before that caveat[7] was entered) that Mr. Penn's agents should prove that Delaware Bay and River or any part of them was cultivated before the date of my Lord Baltimore's patent. The which minutes I got out of the office attested by Mr. Blathwayt and gave it to Mr. Ford and (if the caveat had not been entered) was intended to [have] got an order from the Council Board for the examining of the records of [New] York and such people as could not conveniently be brought into England, and thought that it would be convenient to have it directed to Colonel [Thomas] Dongan[8] as the most proper person. And yet [I] still do believe it the best way (that if you should not be here at the trial and the Lord Baltimore be) to petition the Lords it may not proceed to your disadvantage in your absence and with all for such an order, and bring it with me unless it goes on our side. But I doubt not but if you come not yourself you will send us further instructions and order how to proceed and how far. You find in my Lord Baltimore's letter to Mr. Burke that he thinks it best for him to let you complain first. I know not what he means by that he calls his long narrative if it be not a complaint, which was with the Lords before I arrived in England.[9] But I think what you have in your possession you need not make complaint of first, but keep it till he makes one. I intend to do nothing without advice of Mr. [John] Darnall, your counsel, who I doubt not is very cordial on your part and most exactly sensible of the whole affair.

There came a draft[10] to England by the last shipping of Maryland. I heard it was at Mr. Blathwayt's office and went to see it, but Mr. Burke had taken it away again. I not knowing Mr. Burke, got Mr. [John] Tucker[11] to go with me to Mr. Burke's house, that by his acquaintance with him I might get a sight of it. Which we did, Mr. Burke not knowing me all the time, for wherever he hears I am he will not be. The map is drawn by one Richard Jones, an under-surveyor. He makes the line of 40 [degrees of north latitude] to run as near as I can guess over Philadelphia, and on the map in writing has an abstract of that he calls the long narrative relating how often I had promised to meet him but deceived him; and while I was perusing the map, Mr. Burke could not forbear speaking hard of W. M., not thinking I was the man. Mr. Burke says my Lord Baltimore will stand by that, but as my Lord Baltimore says in one of his letters that he does not believe my interest will do him any harm, so I may say by what observation I made on Mr. Burke that all his sense can do you as little.

I was introduced to the king by Mr. [Francis] Gwyn who was mighty pleasant when I delivered him your letter,[12] asking me several questions about the country. The one was whether they were all Quakers. I made answer: "Your Majesty had many subjects there that were not Quakers." Major Oglethorpe,[13] standing behind me, replied that they were all fanatics though. I said "No, for I am not one." The king then bending said, "What you are building of a great city, let me see" (says he pausing for the name); "what do you call it?" I replied, "Philadelphia." "Aye, Philadelphia," said he; then asked me how big it might be. I told him as near as I could. Then he asked me how many houses there were built. I told him about 100. He asked me if they were built close to one another. I said that at present they stood a little straggling. The king laughed heartily and lifted up his leg as high as he could, asking me if I thought he could straggle from house to house; then asked me of your health and how you agreed with the country. Then he broke open the letter and gave the outside to one about him, and went away with the rest in his hand.

When I delivered the duke your letter, he inquired mightily after your welfare and expressed a great satisfaction in hearing of it. At another time, waiting on him with the otter skin you sent him, he asked very kindly how you did and took the otter skin and showed it to the duke of Beaufort and marquis [of] Halifax (both which I had waited on before and, though before the duke, they gave me a bow and asked how you did), saying it was a very fine skin and did believe it would make a brave muff. Then turned to me and bade me remember him to you and to let you know he received your present very kindly. I forgot to mention above that the king esteemed of the snake root water[14] very much. The duke of Beaufort expressed a great kindness for your presents. And as to the disposing of the plank,[15] Mr. Ford, I suppose, has given you a particular account, who was at the charge of all, only I went with the carts to deliver them to the particular lords here mentioned, viz., my Lord Keeper [North], who ordered me to give you many thanks. The Lord President [Radnor], he told me he did not expect any present, but what service he could do you he should be very ready. My Lord Halifax took it mighty kindly and said it was the more acceptable as it was the growth of your country. My Lord Sunderland was not in town when I delivered his at his house but always seems very kind.

My Lord Culpeper and I had a long discourse about proprieties.[16] [The] New England patent is almost gone and he says [he] is confident [it] will be canceled in Westminster Hall by Michaelmas term come twelve month.[17] They have sent over a fresh letter of attorney with some presents to a friend of mine to follow their business, who is in the same mind that in few terms their patent will be canceled. And my lord says the king and Council will endeavor to bring back the governments to the king. My Lord Baltimore, he says, has lost most of his royalties and is forced to truckle very much for fear they should *quo warrant* his patent.[18] He says you stand the fairest of any, and the fewer by-laws you make, the safer you'll be. My lord told me that the duke says he is weary of his propriety[19] and that if the king would take it he would deliver it up. But says my lord he would fain[20] have somebody give him £16,[000] or £20,000 for his surrender. I have desired Mr. Tucker to send you all the news at court, which I hope he has.

I know not what to think of the times. The last plot, which they call a Presbyterian one,[21] has made a strange alteration. I am loathe to pass my judgment upon it, but if this had not been found they could not have had a pretense to have taken bail for the papists in the Tower and elsewhere as they have.[22] For all are bailed out that were papists throughout the kingdom, and St. James's[23] is fuller of papists than I ever yet saw it. Here are daily addresses made to the king from all parts of England to congratulate his and his brother's safe deliverance from the horrid Presbyterian Plot, and that corporation, society, or grand jury that has not is looked upon almost as bad as those that were in it. I am very well satisfied that if you come not yourself, if you'll be pleased to compliment the king (pray pardon the expression) and duke in a letter on that subject, it will be mighty kindly received.

We have had a mighty hard winter all over Europe. The coaches plied upon the river of Thames more frequently than upon the land. It has made all sort of provisions very dear, and killed most of the fish in the ponds. On the 20th of this month after it was high water in the river of Thames according to the true course of the tides and it had ebbed again about a foot, the tide of flood came in again and ran strong for two hours longer; it was occasioned by a violent storm at northeast, but several believe it presages some ill event.

About 3 weeks after my arrival in England I was taken with a violent fit of sickness as I was in the king's presence chamber talking with Colonel [John] Ashton, who presents his service to you. I got home in a coach, but it was a month before I could get out again; since which time I am mightily broke out in my body, and though I have taken physic for it several times and have been let blood 4 times, yet cannot get clear of it. And although it does not prevent my going abroad about business, yet it does from dining where I have been often invited, and is the only reason I have not been to wait on my cousin[24] for fear of bringing such an ill distemper into a family I so much honor and respect, well knowing besides how tender my cousin is of her children.

About two months since it was my fortune to marry one, who though but of a small fortune, [I] am confident her birth and education will bring no disparagement to my relations.[25] I shall forbear speaking anything in her praise but am well satisfied in my choice. She being a woman of a very agreeable temper and will well suit the humor of the people of your country, whom I as much endeavored to please, or to get one [who] should as much please them, as myself. She was the widow of one Capt. Ewen Johnson that used[26] the East Indies.

Sir, I intended this but as a rough draft but find [I] shall not have time to make a fair one; therefore beg excuse and that you'll be pleased to accept my wife's love and service to you though unknown, and his who is unfeignedly,

Sir,
Your affectionate kinsman
and humble servant,
Wm Markham

ALS. The first part of this letter is in the Darlington Memorial Library, University of Pittsburgh; the last section is in HSP. (PWP, 2:534-39).

1. Doc. 86, above.
2. Lord Baltimore left for England in late May 1684; WP did not leave Pennsylvania until mid-Aug., much later than Markham expected.
3. George Legge (1648-1691), created Baron Dartmouth in 1682, was a favorite of the duke of York. The duke's secretary, Werden, had long been opposed to WP's plans; see docs. 4 and 7, above.
4. Col. James Graham (1649-1730) was keeper of privy purse to the duke of York.
5. On 17 Apr. 1683, the Lords of Trade put a stop on the patent granting Delaware to the duke of York (who would then transfer it to WP). During the summer of 1683 the

Lords agreed to delay the hearings until the following April, by which time Lord Baltimore was expected to arrive in England.

6. Benjamin East, a Quaker sugar baker of London, undertook a voyage in which WP owned seven-eighths share; he arrived in the Delaware River in late Aug., about a week after WP had departed.

7. Lord Baltimore's request for a postponement; see n. 5, above.

8. The governor of New York.

9. Lord Baltimore had sent a narrative of his negotiations with WP to the Lords of Trade in Feb. 1683.

10. A map of the Maryland-Pennsylvania boundary line, prepared by Lord Baltimore's surveyor, Richard Jones.

11. John Tucker, the London secretary for the Bermuda Co., was one of WP's agents.

12. Doc. 74.

13. Col. Theophilus Oglethorpe (1650-1702) served in Charles II's lifeguards and the duke of York's troop.

14. An antidote for snake poison. This was one of WP's presents to the king.

15. WP had shipped over some lumber from Pennsylvania as presents to his English patrons.

16. Proprietary colonies, such as Pennsylvania and Maryland, which were viewed suspiciously by the Lords of Trade. Lord Culpeper had himself been the governor of the royal colony of Virginia, but he had been replaced in Sept. 1683; see doc. 55, above.

17. That is, by the fall of 1684 (Michaelmas term being the autumn term of the High Court of England). The Lords of Trade considered Massachusetts to be the most objectionable of the colonies in America because it refused to obey the Navigation Acts. Therefore the English government sought, and obtained on 23 Oct. 1684 in the Court of Chancery, the invalidation of the Massachusetts Bay Company charter.

18. In Oct. 1683 the officers of the Massachusetts Bay Company had been served with a writ of *quo warranto,* a writ demanding to know by what right or warrant they exercised their chartered powers. Lord Baltimore was vulnerable to a similar prosecution because in 1682 the king had reprimanded him for obstructing the collection of tobacco duties and had warned that his charter would be revoked if he did not cooperate with the king's collector.

19. The colony of New York.

20. Gladly.

21. The Rye House Plot, which the government crushed in 1683; see doc. 73.

22. Of the five Catholic lords who had been arrested in 1678 for complicity in the Popish Plot, three survived and were freed in Feb. 1684.

23. St. James's Palace, London, the residence of the duke of York.

24. WP's wife, Gulielma.

25. Nothing is known about Markham's wife except that her name was Joanna.

26. Plied the trade route to.

# 92 §

## From Samuel Carpenter

IN laying out Philadelphia, WP had reserved to his own use the river frontage on the Delaware side of the city. However, the merchants who settled in Philadelphia needed riverfront wharves and warehouses to facilitate the unloading and loading of ships. Samuel Carpenter was a leading figure among these merchants, and in doc. 92 he petitions WP for the right to build the first wharf on the Delaware River bank, equipped with cranes and storehouses. Carpenter said that he needed 162 feet of river frontage; WP granted him 204 feet on a fifty-year lease. When Carpenter constructed his wharf, he evidently modified the elaborate design for twin piers he proposes here, because WP reported in 1685 that Carpenter's wharf was "about three hundred feet square," and built so that a 500 ton ship could berth broadside.

[c. April 1684]

To Wm. Penn, proprietary and governor of Pennsylvania and the territories thereunto belonging; the submissive request of Samuel Carpenter.

1st. I desire that the governor would be pleased to grant me leave to build a wharf against my lot upon Delaware River,[1] to the use of me, my heirs and assigns forever, for and upon such considerations and conditions as the governor in his wisdom shall see meet.

2d. That I may have the like grant to build out on each side of my front bounds about 30 foot, with consent of those upon whose lots it bounds, viz., Christopher Taylor or Thomas Hooton, above, and Robert Greenway,[2] below, because 102 foot will be too narrow to contain a convenient dock within the wharf, a dock being most requisite and needful for accommodation of vessels and boats, etc.

3d. That I may run out into the river so far as I may now or hereafter think fit, purposing very speedily to go so far as goods may be safely and commodiously landed or shipped at the lowest ebb, and hope to make it so far out that a ship of 100 tons or upwards may come and unload or load at it.

4th. That I may have liberty to build in the bank, flat roofed not ascending above the top of the bank, and to erect chimneys that may be ornamental and not prejudicial, and also to dig cellars or vaults between the edge of the bank and my own land, provided it be done and kept without prejudice to the road above.

5th. That I may build low buildings, below, upon the wharf for storehouses if it be not found prejudicial and if there be convenient room for it.

6. That I may build a crane or cranes upon the wharf or bank, or both, for the landing and shipping of goods, and getting them up and down the bank.

7. That if hereafter the governor should see meet to permit building houses upon the edge of the bank, I desire I may have the same privilege to build upon that part fronting my lot.

8. That I may have leave to contract and bargain with and receive of all persons whatsoever shipping or landing any goods, or masters of ships and small vessels, etc., as the governor shall see meet.

9. The governor and his heirs (and assigns as governors of this province) excepted, who may land and ship their own goods freely forever.[3]

10. I am willing to make and maintain forever, 2 pair of stairs, viz., 1 pair from the water up to the wharf and the other from the wharf to the top

of the bank, for the commodious passing and repassing of all persons to and from the water, free forever.[4]

AD. HSP. (*PWP*, 2:541-43).

1. Samuel Carpenter's lot was 102 feet wide, fronting on Front and Second streets, between Chestnut and Walnut. To his north, Thomas Hooten (d. 1694), a dealer in ship stores from London, held a lot 51 feet wide which he had bought from Christopher Taylor. To Carpenter's south, Robert Greenway held a 30½ foot wide strip. The area between Front Street and the Delaware River had not been granted in Holme's original plan; Carpenter was petitioning to build a wharf on this strip, directly in front of his 102 foot lot, but also extending in front of Hooten and Greenway's adjacent lots.

2. Robert Greenway (d. 1685) was the Quaker master of the ship *Welcome,* which brought WP to Pennsylvania in 1682.

3. Apparently Carpenter means to give WP and his heirs free use of the wharf.

4. Carpenter did build a flight of stairs, known as Carpenter's Stairs, that led from his wharf up to Front Street. By 1685 he also had a limekiln on his wharf.


IN March 1684 Lord Baltimore made his most belligerent move in the boundary dispute with WP. He authorized George Talbot to claim the area south of the 40th degree of latitude in his name, and he directed Talbot to build a fort near Christiana Bridge in central New Castle County (see doc. 94, below). These steps created havoc in the lower counties. On 2 April the Pennsylvania Provincial Council heard that many residents of Kent, including three provincial councilors (John Hillyard, John Richardson, and Francis Whitwell), were on the brink of revolt. In response, WP and the Council dispatched four emissaries to calm the inhabitants. Doc. 93 gives instructions on how to win back the defecting councilors if possible, and to arrest Lord Baltimore's agents and any Delaware residents joining with them. Doc. 94 shows that WP's emissaries were unable to arrest Talbot, and that they had difficulty in stemming the revolt. By May 1684, however, two of the dissident councilors, Hillyard and Whitwell, had returned to WP's side. With other residents from the lower counties, they signed an acknowledgment of WP's authority as governor. Nevertheless, Talbot's men remained at their small Christiana fort for at least several months more.


# 93 §
## To John Simcock and Others


Philadelphia, 2 April 1684

William Penn, proprietary and governor of the province of Pennsylvania and the territories thereunto belonging, to my trusty and loving friends, John Simcock, William Welch, James Harrison, and John Cann: Greeting.
Instructions for your observance upon your expedition.

1st. You are first to go to Duck Creek,[1] where if it shall please God that you are safely arrived, go to John Hillyard's. Take notice who is in, near, or about the house, and let your company be strictly careful to watch that no one goes away to carry intelligence elsewhere.

2dly. While some of you stay to talk with him, first about his not coming up to [Provincial] Council and next about the late disaffection in the country, let the others proceed immediately unless you see cause to apprehend him and take him into the boat or carry him with you, and go to Francis Whitwell's with a part of your company and apprehend him with the same watch and care that no person goes from his house to carry intelligence elsewhere.

3dly. If they will discover[2] the whole business on foot in the county, and you can trust what they say, take them with you in your apprehension of any other person you shall think fit to seize; which done, let the people have summons to meet you at the [torn] court which is to be held for that county, at which court let your commission be read; and in the first place call upon the magistrates and lay hard upon them their treachery and cowardice in suffering Baltimore's emissaries to run up and down the country to seduce people from their obedience, and dismiss such of them as you shall have cause to believe have been unfaithful and are not fit for that trust for the future with that brand upon them, and to put in the names of such persons in my blank commission as you shall judge most honest and true to our just interest. And if you find any former magistrate so guilty as to deserve to be brought upon his trial, either try him there or let him be brought up to be tried here; but be assured that one judgment of the jury of that county were worth two of any jury of this place. And therefore, I charge you to be industrious to try the people upon some of the charges against the proprietary, showing the mischiefs they are allowing [to happen ?] upon the whole, as arraigning particulars in the colony and the county, and branding the inhabitants with treachery and rebellion. And if this succeeds in inflaming them against the men who are most guilty, be[fore?] the multitude, immediately try those two and make them pay the reckoning for the whole, unless you think fit to have such brought hither.

4thly. In the next place, let the sheriff be apprehended and brought up with the rest. Do you put in the name of such a person in my blank commission, as you shall be advised upon the spot, but be sure he be honest and bold, that at such a time as this will try the strength of his authority; for such a one in an emergency may keep or drive a county before him.[3]

5thly. Endeavor all you can to know the motives inducing to disaffections, and in your conversations [try to con?]fute them as dangerous, foolish, and ungrateful on their side. Cherish them that you find well affected and offer to them all redress of their grievances when they shall make them known in a humble and dutiful manner.

6thly. Open to them the inconveniencies of their being divided from us, of the cheat of the pretended better terms between his government and mine.[4] Let the planters give me credit for being willing to take my quitrent in tobacco at 2d. per pound; as also for this, that I being a governor upon my

own costs hitherto, and separated from the greatest comforts of my life —
my wife and children — for the good of all, I hope my half of my quitrents
to supply me with bread will not be made a reason of rebellion by men in
their wits, that love their own lives and estates.

7thly. When you have settled your temporal business the best you can,
which to your truth and wisdom I refer, I should be glad [if] you had a good
meeting or two amongst them; and if even serious rebukes, with Truth
mixed with sorrow for and authority to them, were the preface and beginning (as I would have it the end) of the whole expedition, I could hope a
good issue. And I beseech God to strengthen your hearts and give you wisdom in the commission [and] in the transacting of these weighty matters,
that the name of the Lord may be glorified and exalted, and we all comforted
and established, to His praise, who is our Rock forever.

WM PENN

DS. Historical Society of Delaware, Wilmington. (*PWP,* 2:543-45).

1. Duck Creek marked the boundary between New Castle and Kent counties.
2. Disclose.
3. Apparently WP's commissioners removed Peter Baucomb as sheriff and appointed Richard Mitchell in his place pursuant to this order. On 13 May 1684, Baucomb
petitioned the Provincial Council for fees due him as sheriff and attempted to justify his
failure to arrest Baltimore's agent by explaining that the local justice of the peace had
denied him a warrant.
4. For Baltimore's offer of cheap land and low quitrents to settlers in Delaware, see
doc. 67, above.


# 94 §

## From William Welch


New Castle, 5 April 1684

My Dear Friend

I wrote to thee the last night by thy own pinnace,[1] which I hope is long
before this arrived thy hands. I therein gave thee an account of what intelligence I had of George Talbot's being come with a number of men to Christiana Bridge[2] where he was erecting of a fort, to which I refer thee. Since
which I raised the *posse comitatis,*[3] but a very few appeared. Some of this
town, I am of opinion, knew of his being there and on purpose absented
themselves, some one way and some another. And as for the country, no
one, neither Abraham Mann, [William] Guest, [Thomas] Wollaston[4] nor
none else on that side appeared, so that the appearance was small, insomuch
that I then resolved to take no more with me than 5 or 6 as attendants, and
left John Williams behind to take care of the town. James Walliam accompanied me, so did our new sheriff [Samuel] Land, John White, George More,
John Hendrickson (the late constable), Gerrardus Wessels (the new con-

stable), with his staff, and James Graham[5]—who was very serviceable to me upon thy account and we jumped so exactly in opinion for taking our measures that he was a great comfort to me, who being the messenger of this, is capable to inform thee passages too large to repeat here, considering I want time and for want of sleep [am] somewhat unfit to write much. I therefore refer thee pretty much to his relation, and because I know it would be acceptable to thee to hear frequently from hence, I was obliged to let thy shallop[6] carry him up, there being no other boat here at this time to be had, and I conceived it unsafe to send it by land, lest the enemy at the bridge should intercept it.

The sum in brief is this. We being in all about ten persons, all on horseback, we went first to the widow Ogle's[7] house, where 4 or 5 ordinary men that were her acquaintance met us on foot. There we took her and another's evidence of George Talbot and many other persons (to the jury unknown) having made a forcible entry upon her land, and had cut down her timber, and was making a log house thereon. This we recorded, and thereupon went to the place, and in very good order rode up to him where I found only 3 men beside himself with any arms in their hands. The rest, being about the number of 14 or 15, were without arms, some near thereabouts and others of them a stone's throw off.

When I came up to him, I asked him what it meant for him to hold that unlawful riotous assembly in terror of the people and against the peace of the king and proprietor. He told me it was by orders from the Lord Baltimore. I demanded if he had any grant or order from the king. He said the Lord Baltimore had. Said I, "Thou means his old patent?" and demanded of him if he had any new one. He said no. I then asserted thy right against his, and told him and the people I could produce thy title of a very late date from the king and his royal brother,[8] which had put thee in the actual possession thereof, and that it was a great invasion thereof for which he and those there present might ere long be accountable. So I proceeded to the forcible entry, and made proclamation for him and them all present to depart upon pain of rebellion and imprisonment, and then demanded of him again if he would leave the place, disperse that riotous assembly, and quit the widow's land to her again. He said no. Whereupon I insinuated to the people the danger they were in and how severe the laws were against such offenses, and made record thereof and so left them.

James Graham will inform thee more particularly, who has manifested great respect and kindness to thy interest in this business, and may be of use to thee in representing the whole truth of the business, as he was an eye and ear witness, to the governor of [New] York,[9] and I hope therefore that will excuse my brevity. I being weary and sleepy can scarce tell what, or whether I write sense or not. I am

Thy faithful friend to serve thee,<br>Wm Welch

ALS. HSP. (*PWP*, 2:547–49).

1. WP's pinnace was a small sailing vessel suitable for passage up and down the Delaware.

2. The bridge across Christiana Creek, near present-day Christiana, about five miles west of New Castle.

3. Force of the county: the body of men that a peace officer can call together to maintain order.

4. Mann was a justice, Guest an assemblyman, and Wollaston an undersheriff in New Castle Co.

5. From New York; see doc. 72, above.

6. A boat smaller than WP's pinnace (see n. 1 above), propelled by oars or sails.

7. Elizabeth Ogle, the widow of John Ogle (d. 1684), who had come to the Delaware in 1664 and acquired large tracts of land in New Castle Co.

8. This was not quite true. WP had received deeds for the lower counties from the duke of York, but had not yet obtained the patent from Charles II to the duke of York that was needed to bolster his title. See doc. 91, n. 5.

9. Thomas Dongan.

# 95 §

## From Richard Davies

A large number of the early Quaker immigrants to Pennsylvania came from northern Wales and the English counties on the Welsh border. Collectively, First Purchasers from Wales and the border counties bought 100,000 acres of Pennsylvania land from WP. The author of the following letter, Richard Davies, a leading Quaker from Welshpool, was one of the earliest and largest investors in WP's colony. In July 1681 he signed WP's Concessions to the First Purchasers (doc. 17, above); he bought 5000 acres from WP which he distributed in small parcels to twenty-seven fellow Welshmen, and then bought another 1250 acres for his son David Davies, who came over to Pennsylvania in 1683.

Richard Davies' letter (printed below in slightly abbreviated form) conveys the author's spiritual brotherhood with WP as well as his vital family and community ties with the relatives and neighbors who had migrated to America. It should be compared with the letter from Edward Jones to John ap Thomas (doc. 42, above). Welsh Quakers were a doubly oppressed people in the 1680s: they were persecuted for their religion and handicapped by extreme poverty. The move to Pennsylvania appeared as a heaven-sent opportunity for freedom and prosperity. But Davies is obviously a bit worried that his immigrant son has become overly intoxicated with this New World opportunity, and he asks WP to give him guidance. As for Davies himself, despite his talk of bringing the rest of his family over, he remained in Wales.

My cordial friend and brother W: Penn

Thine of the 6th 10th month 1683[2] from New Castle came to my hand at [Welsh]pool[3] the 12th of the second month 1684. It was not a little to me and many more. The receipt of it came to hand upon a first day[4] after meeting, where Charles Lloyd[5] with many Friends were at my house. First thy true and constant love to me and mine in the Truth cannot be forgotten, because it is felt in that which neither seas nor land can separate, [and] in that eternal unchangeable love do I dearly salute and embrace thee. . . . Dear Will, it rejoices my heart to hear and see, by several letters that come to me, of thy care and love thou has for the people and how honorably they speak of thee. One writes of their good governor; for all their tossings at sea, yet they rejoice they be with thee and the people there. As for the grumbling dissatisfied spirits, they be not to be regarded.

Thine was the first that gave me to understand of my son's arrival,[6] which did much affect our hearts though he was in a diseased ship.[7] As for my part, I was [for] some time under great exercise by visions that I had seen that many of them were cast into the sea, but could see or know little of my son. But my wife was all along well satisfied of the well-being of her son, which was great comfort to me, and now it is more than all the losses I had. And dear William, I had it much under consideration, and I can but tell thee that I think it strange that there should be more dead out of thy ship[8] and this that I was so deeply concerned in, for anything I know, than in all the rest that came in.

My son writes me word that there were 22 dead at sea and 5 or 6 since. Some of them were as leading men in that concern. The names of them he did not send me, but what I hear by others; but I hope that Hugh Roberts and the widow Thomas are alive.[9] If thou has opportunity, remember me to them and the rest.

It [was] long before I had a letter from him though there to me from others yet mine was not come.[10] The first that came was dated the 27th 9th month; it came to hand the 29th 3d month 1684. This last the 18th 4th month was dated 29th 1st month, whereby [I] understand of thy care, love, and kindness to him which cannot be forgotten by me. I hope that he will behave himself so that thou will continue thy respects to him not only for my sake but for his truth and faithfulness in that he shall be trusted withal. I thought to write to him to accept no office or place that he might put off his [business?], but mind his plantation and servants, but finding by this thou upon good consideration does bestow something of profit upon him to be among his servants. He writes to me that the inhabitants about there were in agitation to choose him assemblyman for that county and some other office, he hears.[11] Which I desire that it may be put off for the present till he has his plantation in better order, and withal I desire thee to advise [him] not to be too eager in that neither. For we know his temp[er?] so well that when he takes a thing in hand, he never spares himself to get through with it, that so we are afraid lest he will [have?] a surfeit by his overdoing. I am glad that his servants write so well of him and that they serve him in love and that he is careful of them. . . .

Dear Will, it's not neither seas nor storms, neither danger of shipwreck [that] keeps me from thee: for I am often with thee in spirit and glad would I be if I in Truth be serviceable to thee or any as belongs to thy country. I have freely left myself to the disposing of my God in whose fear I stand, by whose counsel I desire to be guided. Dear William, keep no place or places for me to the prejudice of the people, for if I come thou shall see, if it pleases God so to be that we shall embrace one another in that country, that it shall not be for honor or profit. For if those things had been in my eye, I might have snapped at them when thy love extended so largely to me, as I see it does continue; the feeling and seeing by letters of thy cordial continued kindness to me and mine still oblige me more and more to love thee. Thou are no bubble nor mushroom. Thou are born of that stock and seeds that the blessing is unto, that we with thee and all the families that believe in Him come to be blessed.

Dear William, though the beginning and the middle of thy letter was comfortable, yet the close of it was very sorrowful to me to hear of the departure of so near a friend and relation.[12] Though her life was not to be expected long, almost spent out with us here, yet when it came to us my soul much lamented the loss of her. She was near me in that which is beyond flesh and blood. I mourn still; my eyelids can hardly contain at this present in remembrance of her. . . . In all her weakness here, when I thought that she would not live many hours, she was for her husband and children going to that country, and when she had counseled her children in much fear and tenderness of spirit, and had also told me on what side of our burying place she would have her body laid if she departed before her husband came from London. My soul travailed[13] much for her, and my cries were to the God of my life that He would prolong her days; which He did that she with the rest of them came to see that country that she desired her husband and children to be in; which is an evident token to me that the hand of the Lord was in it.

Dear Will, the foremost of this was written before, and now Charles Lloyd, John ap John,[14] and myself being together in Merionethshire, taking our leave of Friends that are bound for thy country, seeing many letters that came from thence to their Friends here speak well of thee, the country, and government, and also that thou has granted us 40,000 acres of land together which is great content to them.[15] They be hastening to it as fast as they can, that I think this country will be shortly with but [few?] Friends in. Some grumble that so many should go away, but it is to little purpose. The God of my life continue thy health and life among them.

I cannot otherwise but take notice of thy kindness to me as well as to thyself in granting them their 40,000 acres which [I] was intrusted by them at first to purchase for them. I had many discontented spirits [to] deal with, but now their mouths be shut. I think it strange that John ap John's agent should be so slack that he had not [gathered subscribers?] together amongst the Britains, his neighbors.[16] He is much dissatisfied and so am I at them. I, knowing that John was one of the first subscribers and constant to thee, should go with 2500 acres, if thou be pleased to speak to Thomas Wynne about it that it may be rectified if possible.

My son writes to me that he has a mind to sell that plantation he is upon and so to build among the rest of them. I have written to him to do nothing without thy advice. I desire thee to take that trouble upon thee as to do so. Upon consideration I think it not best to sell it, for I think to order a family upon that, and he to begin upon the other, and I find that my daughter has a mind to come over but her mother cannot spare her. But I think that another letter from her son will invite his mother to come. Then I think I shall not stay behind. Dear Will, I have not much to enlarge save the remembrance of my unfeigned love to thee and Friends that inquire for thy true friend and brother in that which changes not,

R. Davies

My dear love to Thomas Lloyd. I am heartily glad that my son writes so cordially of him. Things are very well here in love, peace, and unity as in days of old. I know not if we come for Pennsylvania, but we may come both together. I am informed by one that came from Liverpool that Samuel Jennings landed safely there and that he is gone for London.[17] As for the sufferings and persecutions in England, I shall leave it [for an]other to give thee account of. Charles Lloyd and John ap John's dear love is to thee. Charles Lloyd thinks to write to thee shortly, he being now straitened for time.

ALS. HSP. (*PWP*, 2:561-66).

1. On Cardigan Bay, in western Wales.
2. 6 Dec. 1683.
3. Davies' hometown, in Mont., Wales.
4. Sunday.
5. Charles Lloyd (1637-1698) of Dolobran, Mont., was, like Davies, a First Purchaser who did not come to Pennsylvania. In June 1683 he conveyed his 2500 acres of Pennsylvania land to his brother Thomas Lloyd.
6. David Davies (d. 1686), son of Richard, was a surgeon who arrived in Pennsylvania in Nov. 1683. He staked out a farm at Neshaminy in Bucks Co., separate from the other Welsh settlers.
7. The *Morning Star* of Liverpool left the Welsh port of Mostyn, Flint, in Sept. 1683 and picked up more passengers in Dublin. About half of her 100 passengers were from Merionethshire. This was the only ship to arrive in Pennsylvania in 1683 with heavy losses, caused by the "bloody flux," which was probably dysentery.
8. The *Welcome* lost thirty-one passengers in a smallpox epidemic during WP's voyage in 1682.
9. Roberts and Thomas, both from Merionethshire, survived the ocean voyage and became founding members of the Welsh settlement of Merion, Pa. Katherine Thomas was the widow of John ap Thomas (see doc. 42, above); like Hugh Roberts, she became a leading member of the new Merion Friends Meeting.
10. Davies seems to be saying that the first letter he received from his son David arrived later than letters which his son wrote to others.
11. There is no evidence that David Davies was elected to public office in Pennsylvania.
12. Probably Mary Jones Lloyd, who was born in Welshpool, married Thomas Lloyd in 1665, bore him ten children, and came with him to Pennsylvania in 1683. She died in Nov. 1683 and is said to have been the first person buried in Friends Burial Ground, Fourth and Mulberry streets, Philadelphia.
13. Struggled.
14. John ap John (c. 1625-1697) of Ruabon, Denbigh, was the principal organizer of

the Welsh Quaker migration to Pennsylvania. He bought 2500 acres from WP, but did not himself emigrate.

15. The Welsh immigrants to Pennsylvania asked WP to let them establish a barony of 40,000 acres with their own local government, and in Mar. 1684 WP agreed to lay out a Welsh Tract west of the Schuylkill River. However, WP's surveyors did not lay out the boundaries of this tract until 1687, and the Welsh were never able to secure exclusive political or economic control over this sprawling territory.

16. Davies is concerned that since neither John ap John nor his agent had yet found buyers for his 2500 acres of Pennsylvania land, his First Purchaser privileges were endangered. Eventually John ap John sold all but 200 acres.

17. Samuel Jennings (d. c. 1708), the Quaker deputy-governor of West New Jersey, had come to England to try to persuade the colony's chief proprietor, Edward Byllynge, to abandon his claim to control the government of West New Jersey.


# 96 §
## Remonstrance from the Inhabitants of Philadelphia

ON New Year's Day in 1684, according to the German settler Francis Daniel Pastorius, WP protested in Quaker meeting that "brotherly love is not yet so abundantly to be found in this our Philadelphia as he on his part desires" (doc. 89, above). Six months later, the leading inhabitants of Philadelphia gave WP further cause for lamentation. The "Remonstrance and Address" printed below was presented to him in July 1684 by a number of First Purchasers of extensive acreage who held large city lots on Front Street, facing the Delaware River. They charged that WP, in making changes in the design of Philadelphia in 1682-1683, had given them less land than he had contracted to do in 1681. They also complained that he withheld hunting, fishing, and mineral rights from them; that he levied quitrents on their city lots to which they had never agreed; and that he denied them the exclusive use of the river bank fronting their properties. They further protested that WP had given many of the best lots in the city to First Purchasers of smaller country plots, and to other settlers who were not First Purchasers at all.

WP made an irritated reply to this Remonstrance. Although he accepted a few of the First Purchasers' complaints, he refused to alter the major features of his land distribution policy in Philadelphia or in Pennsylvania. Since WP was very proud of his Indian land purchase policy, he was particularly angered by the remonstrants' insinuation (in section 11) that their land was not yet cleared from Indian claims. Furthermore, it vexed him to find that Thomas Rudyard, who had collaborated closely with him two years before in drafting the *Frame of Government* (see doc. 29, above), was now the ringleader of the remonstrants. Rudyard's chief grievance was that WP was forcing the First Purchasers to take out new patents in Pennsylvania that granted fewer privileges than the original deeds they had received from him in England. WP denied this charge in a sharp exchange with Rudyard. The issues at stake in this dispute could not be settled by appeals to brotherly love because aggressive colonists like Rudyard were interested primarily in their individual property rights, while WP was interested in the overall development of his colony and in proprietary profits. Thus the dispute of 1684 introduced a division of interests that would separate WP from his settlers for the rest of his life.

The text below is in three parts. "The Remonstrance" (A) was written and then passed among Front Street lot owners for their signatures in July; "The Proprietor's Reply" (B) was probably written in mid- or late July; and WP's "Exchange with Thomas Rudyard" over the new patents (C) was probably written in early August.

A
The Remonstrance

[c. July 1684]
To William Penn, Esquire, proprietary and governor of the province of Pennsylvania and the territories thereunto belonging.

The humble Remonstrance and Address of several [of] the adventurers, freeholders, and inhabitants within the city of Philadelphia in the said province, whose names are hereunto subscribed,[1] in the behalf of themselves and others therein concerned.

Showeth, that being encouraged (while in the kingdom of England) by the printed proposals there published by the proprietary,[2] and the tender respects and real affections they bore towards him, [they] became adventurers and purchasers of land from him within the said province upon the then proposed terms. And each purchaser (for the security of his purchased lands) has deeds of conveyance made to him from the proprietary to assure the purchased lands to the respective purchasers, their heirs and assigns; and to hold the same as of the Manor of Windsor in the county of Berks.[3] Which said lands (by a clause in every of their deeds of conveyance expressed) were to be laid out to the respective purchasers in such parts and portions and in such manner and wise as was mentioned and contained in an indenture of concessions made (or mentioned to be made) between the proprietary and respective purchasers.[4] But so it is, that the said purchasers, what through the confidence they had in the proprietary and stress in their own affairs to remove themselves and families out of their native country into these parts, were omissive to procure those indentures of concessions which should assure, prescribe, and direct the [lay?]ing out of the lands to the respective purchasers, their heirs and assigns; and without which they account themselves very uncertain and insecure not only in their lot of land already laid out, but more especially for such portions thereof as are not yet laid out unto them.

And the said adventurers and purchasers further show that, being not only encouraged as abovesaid but more especially by a certain deed or grant made by the proprietary in England and sent to his late deputy-governor, Captain Markham, and other his commissioners here,[5] the purport whereof was not only to give the adventurers and purchasers some assurance and certainty in relation to the laying out of lands in general, but also to the laying out and ascertaining [for] each adventurer and purchaser respective lots and proportions in the city of Philadelphia, [they] have at their own charge transported themselves and families into this city and province; and by their own expense in building and improvements [have] made the city [and] have turned a wilderness into a town of value; and by this have not only improved their own lots, but also the interest of others therein concerned. Yet notwithstanding their cheerful concurrence in person and purse to encourage the [place?], [they] have hitherto had but weak assurance of privileges or properties answerable to their expectations, not only while in England, but also since their arrival in these parts.

And they further show, that upon some particular discourses with the proprietary on the subject matter before related or somewhat relating thereunto, he was pleased to express himself desirous to hear of any grievance, and ready to redress the same, before his intended voyage for England. And being thereby encouraged, do present with all dutiful respect these particulars following as our present grievances, viz.,

1. That although we have our deeds of purchase from the proprietary in England, which with the survey of lands to us and recorded (as we conceive) is a sufficient title, yet we are obliged to take out new patents for every respective parcel or lot of land, to our great charge and needless expense.[6]

2. These patents neither refer to our deeds nor express our purchase money paid, nor are of the same hold as our first deed, which is of the Manor of Windsor in the county of Berks, but of new erected manor here whose privileges and powers we know not.[7]

3. Although in the printed proposals the proprietary assured all persons that all royalties as fishing, fowling, hunting, [mines?], minerals, etc., should be annexed to our lands, yet in all patents these properties and privileges [are] wholly omitted;[8] so that the royalties, etc., must remain in the proprietary and his heirs, successors, and assigns, and his and their new erected manors, which may and will be a sore grievance to us and our heirs forever.

4. That many persons and families, being purchasers of 5000 acres in England, are denied to take up more land than 500 acres at one place and are bound to settle it within six or 12 months, so that a purchaser of 500 acres for £10 is equal to a purchaser of 5000 acres for £100, which we conceive is not only contrary to all proposals in England, but great injury to the most considerable purchasers, as if every purchaser of 5000 acres should be bound to bring over ten families or not have the land he paid for in England laid out for him and his children here.[9]

5. That there being no indenture of concessions under the hand and seal of the proprietary (such as is mentioned in our purchase deeds) in the custody and power of the respective purchasers, there lies no obligation upon the heirs and successors or assigns of the proprietary to lay out to us or our heirs what the present proprietary or his assigns refuse or omit to lay out to us.

6. That by the deed of directions sent to Capt. Markham,[10] and now in the proprietary's hands, every purchaser of 5000 acres was to have a hundred acres in the new intended city and bounds thereof as part of his purchased lands, and other purchasers (*pro rata*) proportionably.

7. That at the time of the making the same deed, the then purchasers were not so numerous but that every [one] of us might have a hundred acres that was a purchaser of 5000 acres, and other purchasers according to that rate proportionably; but by reason of after purchasers, and persons admitted into this city of favor, the first adventurers and purchasers are wronged in their rights, and abridged of their due—viz., smaller lots in the city, and 20 acres abated in the town bounds.[11]

8. Although the first adventurers and purchasers are thus abridged of their due, yet several of them reposing confidence in the justice of the proprietary, and presuming on his equal ascertaining the town lots to each purchaser and that no person should be wronged of his just lot, gave by some writing under their hands the trust thereof to him.[12] Whence it is argued against such subscribers — yea, and against all others — that those persons gave up and surrendered all our rights in the city to the governor and his heirs, and that from thence the city lots are no part of our purchase but the proprietary's gift, and thereupon 5s. per acre [is] imposed on them for a yearly rent forever.[13] Which writing and trust we presume can bear no such construction in general, nor can extend in anywise to affect the rights of them especially who never subscribed the same.

9. That although the present inhabitants have, with their own great costs and large expense, within this city built upon their front lots on Delaware River, always accounting that each builder (especially where the bank is too high for common wharfage) should have the privilege to build vaults or stores[14] in the bank against his lot, and enjoy them as his right, yet in each patent this [is] not only omitted to be granted to the builders, but alleged that it's not theirs, nor [owned by] the people in general, which is a great discouragement to the builders and adventurers here.

10. That although the present inhabitants of this city have not been wanting in laying out their estates in building the same, and their industry therein and willingness thereunto has effected that in two years time, that many years has not produced in the neighboring colonies and provinces; yet to this day they are only a nominal city, having no charter to incorporate them, or grant of the least privileges of a corporation.[15]

11. As we bought our land in England to be free from Indian title and encumbrances, and must settle thereon our persons, families, and estates, we cannot but be concerned that of such title the land be cleared by plain and regular purchases: Indian gifts of land, and their permits to us to sit down thereon, will continue so long as the proprietary's reciprocal kindness continues to them in his daily gifts and presents to the Indians. These present acts of civility and courtesy between the proprietary and the Indians, being no regular purchase nor clearing of Indian title, as often experience has evidenced in America,[16] we cannot but express our fears and apprehensions of future insecurity, desiring that due care and effectual provision be made for the regular purchasing of the lands from the natives laid out, and to be laid

out to us, and that persons may be commissioned to see the same effected, by taking the Indians' deeds of sale, paying the purchase value, marking out the land, and giving livery of seisin,[17] which has been found the only way to prevent future quarrels and to preserve a firm correspondence with the natives.

These things lying with some weight upon our thoughts we could not but with all due respect to our proprietary, and tender regard to the future peace, safety, and prosperity of this city and province, unburden our minds unto him, hoping that with the same favor and tenderness he has ever expressed to us, he will take the premises into his serious consideration and favorably redress the same as he in wisdom shall see meet.

B

The Proprietor's Reply

[c. July 1684]

Answer to the Address

1. I impose no patents, but shall be glad that vexation end, [and] have told all they may have them if they will or stand on their survey recorded. One man that proves he was compelled shall have all for nothing, aye, as desired.

2. If the patents refer to the deed, it is enough, and that I long since ordered.

3. I think that [the grant] of royalties is in the general charter; if not, never refused, nor will I refuse them.[18]

4. For settlements of proportion I say I answer [no?] self end, but preserve the country from a desolation by laying out land at 500 acres to a family. Yet this has been by persuasion, not injunction, though the concessions nor deeds oblige me not to the contrary.

5. For the concessions, the commissioners had them as W[illiam] Haige, N[athaniel] Allen, and J[ohn] Bezar,[19] but I have a counterpart, by which I learn that the executing them in whole, as must be, or not at all, will pinch the people more than me far; however I have not broken them, for the 100 acres to 5000 is "if the place allows of it,"[20] and it is a mistake to think that any besides the first 100 shares have a foot but what they buy of the First Purchasers. This to the 5th, 6th, and 7th [clauses above] [which?] make no distinction but make all to pay 5s. yearly for every lot.

To the 8th, let them give me back the land I bought and added to the city, and they shall have the [city?] as of right of purchase.[21]

To the 9th, the bank is a top common from end to end, the rest next [to] the water belongs to front lot men no more than back lot men. The way bounds them. They may build stairs, and [on] the top of the bank a common exchange or walk, and against the streets, common wharf may be built freely; but into the water and the shore is no purchaser's.[22]

To the 10th, it is the people's fault, not mine. I was not to wait on them with drafts, I am still ready if time permits, and shall leave a security by a promise under my hand and a charge on my heirs to do it.[23]

To the 11th, I say it is disingenuous. For I have made the most purchases and been at the greatest charge of any proprietor and governor in America. This is not thought enough, but I must let others have the buying and paying with my estate for greater security; this is beyond modesty and justice. The land is both bought, the bounds either marked or natural; and if the Indians are unjust, we shall all partake enough where I see no hand but one and he a stranger in our business.[24]

W. Penn

C

Exchange with Thomas Rudyard

Philadelphia, 3 August 1684

[THOMAS RUDYARD]

As to the patents.
The title (by the providence of God).
1. *might well* be omitted.
2. [is] of *dangerous consequence.*

[WILLIAM PENN]

1. Not by a Christian.
2. I know none.

3. The term to be *of the Manor of Windsor* and no other ought to be inserted.

3. My patent holds of Windsor and the purchasers of me as of that manor, or as I hold of that Manor of Windsor.

4. To pay to the *successors*[25] —dangerous— government and propriety being frequently different in 2 hands. The proprietary's heirs shall have no quitrents.

4. That [is] my wrong. I shall observe it; the clerk copied too much.

5. *Letters made patents and teste me ipso.*[26] Too large[27] for a proprietary of Pennsylvania —exceptions may be taken, etc.

*Verbum sat sapienti*[28]

T. Rudyard[29]

5. The same fault in the clerk, but I see no harm in it; only it is regal language, ceremoniously; I own the king as my duty leads me.

The heads of this within written by persons considerate[30] in this city were drawn up — by me digested into this method.[31] When the persons aggrieved had so eased themselves, they were quiet. I have endeavored and desired they might be so kept and continued. My only request is that due care may be taken that this with more may not arise in the governor's absence. But that provision may be made to take away all just occasions of offense which in sincere good will is the desire of,

Tho. Rudyard

ALS. HSP. (*PWP*, 2:569-78).

1. The signers' names are not affixed to this document. The resident First Purchasers who had lots on Delaware Front Street in 1684 were Nathaniel Allen, Elizabeth Barber, Thomas Bowman, Samuel Carpenter, James Claypoole, Silas Crispin, Joseph Fisher, Enoch Flower, Thomas Holme, Griffith Jones, Humphrey Morrey, Elizabeth Palmer, William Stanley, Christopher Taylor, Robert Turner, William Wood, and Thomas Wynne. Most of these purchasers had bought full 5000-acre shares in Pennsylvania. The signers of the "Remonstrance" could have included any or all of these men and women.

2. See the terms of purchase that WP announced in *Some Account* (doc. 15, above).

3. The "Manor of Windsor" clause appears in the royal charter granted to WP, doc. 11, p. 42, above. This clause insured that the grantee of land owed no quasi-feudal obligations to the grantor beyond a quitrent, or small annual tax.

4. Doc. 17, above.

5. Doc. 22, above.

6. WP signed over fifty of these patents, most of them in June and July 1684, at the request of purchasers who were concerned about their property rights during the proprietor's absence in England.

7. The "new erected manor" inserted in the patents was Springettsbury, at Fairmount, just northwest of the city (now the site of the Philadelphia Museum of Art), where WP planned to build a country residence for himself and his son and heir, Springett Penn.

8. See doc. 17, p. 73; and doc. 63, p. 271, above.

9. In his July 1681 "Concessions" (doc. 17, above), WP had stipulated that each First Purchaser must take up his land in plots of no more than 1000 acres and must seat a family on each plot within three years, before he could seat more of the land he had purchased. As he admits in sect. 4 of his reply (B) to the "Remonstrance," WP subsequently decided to reduce the maximum size of rural plots to 500 acres and to demand that they be immediately settled, before the purchasers could receive more of their land.

10. Doc. 22, above.

11. Between July 1681 and Apr. 1682, WP sold the 500,000 acres of land to which he had attached First Purchaser rights and made plans to set out 10,000 acres in Philadelphia for these purchasers, as he had pledged to do. In 1682-1683, when he was unable to secure this much land along the Delaware River, he devised a new plan. He assigned only about two-thirds of the lots in Philadelphia to First Purchasers; he awarded choice lots to a number of "after purchasers" who had bought land after Apr. 1682 (for example, to Pastorius and the Frankfort Company; see doc. 89, above); and he rented other well-placed city lots. This meant that First Purchasers received less than 1000 acres in what became the City of Philadelphia (now Center City), plus something over 7000 acres in liberty lands north of the city.

12. The remonstrants are referring here to a lost agreement between WP and his settlers, made about 1 Nov. 1682, that revised WP's initial plan for the city along the lines given in n. 11, above.

13. This quitrent was not mentioned in WP's "Instructions" of 30 Sept. 1681 (doc. 22). WP may have declared his intention to collect this quitrent in the lost Nov. 1682 agreement (see n. 12, above).

14. Storage spaces.

15. On 26 July 1684, WP appointed three of his councilors to draw up such a charter, but the first known city charter was drawn up only in 1691.

16. Indians in the Delaware Valley often sold the same tract of land several times to different European purchasers. WP, who had designed his own land policies to encourage rapid settlement and discourage land speculators, thought this Indian policy was proper as long as the earlier purchasers had not settled the land before the Indians again sold it to other purchasers. Moreover, he was confident that his Indian purchase policy offered

better security of land tenure to Pennsylvania settlers than the policies of any other colony offered to settlers. Thus he indignantly rejected sect. 11 of the Remonstrance.

17. The legal transfer of property by handing over some object from that property. For an example of such a transfer, see doc. 45, above.

18. Doc. 17 clearly shows WP's intention of granting royalties from minerals to his purchasers; however, a provision for this in a rough draft of the laws accompanying the Frame of Government did not become part of the published *Laws Agreed Upon in England* ("the general charter"). See doc. 30, above.

19. WP probably means his "Instructions" of Sept. 1681 (doc. 22); he gave one copy to Nathaniel Allen and John Bezar in Sept. 1681 at Bristol, and a second to William Crispin and William Haige in London a few weeks later. WP, of course, also had his own copy, to which he refers here.

20. See doc. 17, p. 73, above.

21. WP is apparently referring to additional land he bought from the Swedes in 1682-1683 to increase the size of Philadelphia to 1200 acres; if the First Purchasers return this land to WP, then he will stop charging quitrents on their city lots.

22. This disagreement between WP and his First Purchasers over the ownership of the Philadelphia waterfront dragged on for years and became quite bitter. WP's original plan for Philadelphia, set out in doc. 22, above, offered all purchasers river frontage, with no back lots. Although WP abandoned this plan, those purchasers who were awarded Front Street lots apparently thought they still had waterfront rights. Their jealousy was probably incited by WP's award of a fifty-year lease to 204 feet of waterfront to Samuel Carpenter in Apr. 1684 (see doc. 92, above), which gave that merchant a great commercial advantage over his neighbors.

23. See n. 15, above.

24. A probable reference to Thomas Rudyard; see n. 29, below.

25. In the new patents, grantees were to pay their quitrents "to me, my heirs and successors." "Successor" was the traditional term for a political heir, while a legal heir of property was usually designated as an "heir or assign."

26. WP closed each new patent with the sentence: "In witness whereof I have caused these my letters to be made patents." Rudyard's Latin reads "Witnessed by myself."

27. Pretentious.

28. "A word to the wise is sufficient."

29. Thomas Rudyard, who had been WP's lawyer and constitutional advisor in England, served as governor of the Quaker colony of East New Jersey from Nov. 1682 to Feb. 1684. He then came over to Pennsylvania, where he tried to get back the post as master of the rolls to which WP had appointed him two years before. WP, however, sharply rebuffed this attempt in June 1684 and criticized Rudyard's un-Quakerly lifestyle. The Front Street purchasers probably chose Rudyard to help compose their "Remonstrance" because of his legal training.

30. Considerable.

31. Rudyard may mean that he composed the "Remonstrance," although it is not in his hand; but he may mean only that he reduced the petitioners' complaints about the new patents (see nn. 6-7, above) to the concise objections in his exchange with WP (C).

# Part XII

RETURN TO ENGLAND §
AUGUST 1684

*William Penn, by Francis Place, c. 1698, HSP.*

ON 18 August 1684 WP sailed for England on the *Endeavour* to defend his colony against Lord Baltimore. Before leaving, he made arrangements for the management of his colony and of his proprietary estate. Writing on board ship, WP drafted several last-minute documents that show signs of haste and confusion. His instructions to President Thomas Lloyd and the Provincial Council (doc. 97) are sketchy, to say the least; and his will (doc. 99) and his letter to his wife (doc. 100) are similarly rushed and informal. But in the midst of his hurried departure, WP managed to issue detailed directions to his gardener at Pennsbury Manor (doc. 98), and to write an emotional, deeply religious farewell address to the inhabitants of his colony (doc. 101).

WP's plan for the administration of Pennsylvania in his absence was a highly original one: instead of appointing a deputy-governor, he distributed responsibility and power as evenly as possible among eleven colonists. Thomas Lloyd, James Claypoole, and Robert Turner were his Commissioners of Propriety who allocated and sold land in Pennsylvania; Thomas Holme, Samuel Carpenter, James Harrison, Philip Theodore Lehnmann, and Turner were his Commissioners of Estate and Revenue who collected proprietary revenues; Nicholas More, William Welch, William Wood, John Eckley, and Turner were the judges of the Provincial Court; Holme was WP's surveyor; Harrison was the steward of Pennsbury, his Bucks County manor; Lehnmann was his personal secretary; and Lloyd became president of the elected Provincial Council. In naming Lloyd to the presidency of the Council, WP chose a quite recent immigrant in preference to several veteran advisors, especially James Harrison, Thomas Holme, and Christopher Taylor. In the year that Lloyd had been in America, however, he had performed several tasks effectively for WP, and had been an exemplary councilor. He seems also to have had no close connection with the Philadelphia merchants on Front Street who caused WP so much irritation in late July (see doc. 96, above).

WP probably decided against appointing a deputy-governor because he wished to retain as much personal control of his colony as possible. He may also have believed that the colonists would be jealous of any one man to whom he delegated executive authority. By distributing power among a number of colonial leaders, he could hope to foster the Quaker spirit of consensual harmony that he had aimed for in drafting the *Frame of Government*. But this plan could work only if WP quickly returned to Pennsylvania. And he did not return quickly, for once WP reached England he found that the Lords of Trade were in no hurry to settle the Pennsylvania-Maryland boundary dispute, and when his patron, the duke of York, became King James II in 1685, WP decided that he could accomplish more by working with the royal government in England than by going back to America. As it turned out, WP stayed away from Pennsylvania for fifteen years, until 1699. This prolonged absence greatly weakened his control over the colony. Economically, Pennsylvania continued to develop along the lines that he had hoped for, but in politics the colonists were leaderless and divided, and they adopted an unruly, quarrelsome style of government that was far removed from WP's original goals. Thus WP's return to England marked a major turning point, both in his career and in the development of his colony. From September 1684 onward, for better or worse, the settlers of Pennsylvania were mainly on their own.

## 97 §

### Commission to President Thomas Lloyd and the Provincial Council

Philadelphia, 6 August 1684
William Penn, Proprietary and Governor of the Province
of Pennsylvania and the Territories thereunto belonging,
To the Members of the Provincial Council of the Province of Pennsylvania
and the Territories thereunto belonging.

Since it has pleased God so to dispose of me as to call me by His providence into England, and that it is requisite that the power I have should be left to maintain and exercise government for the good of the province and territories, to the end that the people may be sensible of the entire confidence I have in them which I hope will beget the like in them to me and mine, I do hereby commit the power vested in me to you, their chosen Provincial Council; and do hereby nominate and appoint my trusty and loving friend, Thomas Lloyd, president of the same; he and you to act and do all things that by law and charter you may do for the good of the province and not to the detriment of me, my heirs and assigns, which power shall remain as granted till further order. Given at Philadelphia, the sixth day of the sixth month, one thousand six hundred eighty-four, being the thirty-sixth year of the king's reign and the fourth of my government.

Wm Penn

Memorandum

By the power within expressed and mentioned I understand the use of the executive power chiefly as choosing officers, etc., intending that all laws that shall or may be made should receive and have my further determination, confirmation, and consent—or else to be void in themselves.[1] Given the day of the within date, on board the ketch *Endeavour*.[2]

Wm Penn

DS. HSP. (*PWP*, 2:583-84).

1. WP is here surrendering to the Council appointive powers that were reserved to him in the second *Frame of Government* (doc. 63, article 16), but he is also demanding the power to veto legislation after it had passed both the Council and Assembly. This was a right that WP did not have under the second *Frame of Government*.

2. Probably the *Endeavour* of Liverpool, George Thorpe, master, which had sailed from England to Pennsylvania in 1683, proceeded to Barbados, and apparently sailed back to Pennsylvania before returning to England. A ketch is a two-masted sailing vessel.

# 98 §

## Gardening Directions for Ralph Smyth

[August? 1684]

Directions to Ralph Smyth:[1]

1. Get the courtyards paled[2] and gates like Philadelphia[3] in the places I have appointed before, behind and on each side [of] the house, more than which need not be, save one against the gate that goes across the waterside court into the garden.

2. Let the land in the water court be levied,[4] and steps be made of brick covered with stone, or stone such as by [the] waterside, covered with quarry stone.

3. Set out the garden by the house; plant sweet herbs, asparagus, carrots, parsnips, artichokes, salatin,[5] and all flowers and kitchen herbs there.

4. Let a peach be planted between every apple tree.

5. Let all the peaches about the grounds in Indian fields be saved, make a barrel of wine or two, and dry the rest, save that a few be preserved when almost ripe.

6. Get more quicksets[6] to set about the pales, at least in the orchard.

7. Get the walks to the house in the courts graveled, 20 [feet] broad.

8. Let handsome steps be made at the waterside; the present gate is not right[7] against the house.

9. Get what good seeds thou can get here, lay out for.[8]

10. Remember to make both wine and vinegar.

WP.

ADS. HSP. (*PWP*, 2:584-85).

1. Ralph Smyth (d. 1685) was WP's gardener at Pennsbury. Apparently he was a New Englander who settled at Upland as early as June 1681.

2. Fenced.

3. Probably like the fencing and gates at WP's house in Philadelphia.

4. Embanked to prevent flooding.

5. Herbs and vegetables used for salad.

6. Slips or cuttings of plants, especially those used for hedges.

7. Straight.

8. WP probably means "spend money for."


# 99 §

## Last Will and Testament

IN drawing up his will, WP observes the standard seventeenth-century English practice of primogeniture. That is, he bequeaths almost all of his Pennsylvania property to Springett Penn, his eldest son and proprietary successor (though Springett would actually die before WP, in 1696), and he reserves comparatively small grants to his other two children and to his wife. WP also observes the seventeenth-century custom of *noblesse oblige* (high rank requires generous conduct) by making donations of land to help poor families, to support schools and hospitals, and to take care of his numerous servants in England and America.

6 August 1684

My last will and testament made this 6th day of the 6th month 1684.

Not knowing how the Lord may please to deal with me, lest the sea be my grave and the deeps my sepulcher,[1] I have made this my last will and testament.

1. I confirm and ratify all the matter of my last will made in England.[2]

2. I give this lot I live at in Philadelphia to my dear wife for her life, and then to Laetitia Penn, my dear daughter.[3]

3. I give to my dear wife the enjoyment of Pennsbury, till my son, Springett, is of age; then to him and his, for a manor.[4]

4. I bequeath to my son, William Penn, a lot running through from Delaware to Schuylkill on the south side of the city called commonly my son's lot,[5] with 100 acres of the overplus land of Passyunk,[6] and ten thousand acres on Schuylkill, and four hundred acres on Delaware by Poquessing[7] according to warrant, and I further give him five thousand acres in each county, and twenty thousand acres on the Susquehanna River with the second best island in it.[8]

5. I do give to my daughter, Laetitia, another town lot on Schuylkill and two in the High Street, as set down in the city plat, and all the land from the creek where the bridge is north of Pennsbury toward the Falls, to the

land of James Harrison on the main river called Sepassinck,[9] and five thousand acres on the Schuylkill,[10] and so in each county, and ten thousand on Susquehanna with an island as also that island in Delaware called Oreckton, which I call Laetitia's Isle, if that before Pennsbury comes to that seat; else the said Oreckton to belong to Pennsbury.[11]

6. I give to my son William and my daughter Laetitia £100 yearly forever, that is, to each of them one, out of my quitrents of the province to be paid by my heir or his receiver; the payment to begin from my decease, and by those I intrust, or rather their dear mother, to be kept or laid out in improving their plantations by labor and stock.

7. I give to my dear wife, the love of my youth and my crown and blessing from the Lord, the enjoyment of the rest of my rents till my son Springett, or my heir, comes to age, to enable her the better to educate the children and live comfortably, together with ten thousand acres of land where she pleases and for what use she pleases.

8. I give fifty thousand acres for poor families, as one or two hundred apiece, as my executors please, on the Susquehanna River or nearer, paying the shilling for each hundred,[12] which I understand all along.

9. I give ten thousand acres of land in the County of Philadelphia toward the support of a school, and as much for a hospital in that city,[13] and the like quantity on Susquehanna for the like uses in the first city there to be built.

10. I give all my servants I had before I came, and that came with me, two hundred acres each of them, my old servants that stayed with my wife the like proportion, and everyone that is with my concerns in America a hundred acres, as if they had bought the same.

The Lord bless my dear family and keep them and the people of this province and territories in His fear, that in love and concord they may live together while the sun and the moon endure. Amen, amen.

Say [torn]

Witnesses present
Thomas Lloyd
Thomas Holme
James Harrison
William Clarke

AD. Pierpont Morgan Library, New York City. (*PWP*, 2:585-87).

1. WP repeated this phrase in his letter to Gulielma, doc. 100, below.

2. Presumably WP made a will in England before he departed for Pennsylvania, but the editors have not found a copy of it. The will printed here was never probated, since it was superseded by WP's wills of 1701, 1705, and 1712.

3. WP's Philadelphia lot was between Second and Third, High and Chestnut streets. The house built for the proprietor in 1682 has not survived. A cottage built about twenty years later on this site, the so-called Letitia Cottage, still stands; it was moved to Fairmount Park in 1883.

4. WP's manor house at Pennsbury was nearly completed before the proprietor returned to England. WP inhabited it during his second visit to Pennsylvania in 1699-1701, but during the eighteenth century the house was abandoned, and it gradually fell into ruin.

The present restored manor house was built in the 1930s on the foundations of WP's original building.

5. On Holme's *Portraiture* (pp. 320-21, above), the lot of William Penn, Jr., is plotted out between Spruce and Cedar [South] streets, but only on the Schuylkill and Delaware River frontages; it is not marked as continuing through the city.

6. In present South Philadelphia.

7. At the boundary between Philadelphia and Bucks counties.

8. William Penn, Jr., had received 5000 acres from his father in 1682. In his map of 1687 Thomas Holme shows William Penn, Jr.'s manor of Williamstadt on the east bank of the Schuylkill and a corresponding tract on the west bank, in the neighborhood of the present town of Conshohocken.

9. Near the Falls of the Delaware. See doc. 37, n. 12.

10. Laetitia Penn had received 5000 acres from her father in 1682. In his map of 1687 Thomas Holme shows Laetitia Penn's manor of Mountjoy on the west bank of the Schuylkill, adjoining her brother's land, in the vicinity of Valley Forge.

11. Oreckton's Island is probably the modern Biles's Island, opposite Trenton, N. J. (see doc. 37, n. 12). Pennsylvania's claim to the islands in the Delaware was disputed by West New Jersey.

12. The poor families would receive their land free, but they were obligated to pay WP's standard annual quitrent of one shilling per hundred acres.

13. Enoch Flower opened the first school in Philadelphia, but he soon died. The first permanent school, now known as the William Penn Charter School, dates from 1689. No hospital was started in WP's era.

# 100 §

## To Gulielma Penn

Philadelphia, 6 August 1684

My most dear G. Penn.

Being now to leave this part of the world and ready to come to thee, not knowing how the Lord pleases to deal with me in my passage, lest the sea be my grave and the deeps my sepulcher, I write unto thee, as my beloved one, the true and great joy and crown of my life above all visible comforts, always valued by me, and honored above women. I do most dearly salute and embrace thee with thy dear children, praying the God of our many and rich blessings to be with you and that He would preserve you from the evil that is in the world, and among those that profess a faith that is above it, faithful to His blessed Truth and in constant communion with the faithful remnant that keep the testimony of Jesus with zeal and fidelity to the end. The Lord crown you with His life, love, and heavenly presence, lead you not into temptation, but deliver you from evil and bless you with the mercies of His chosen, both here and hereafter.

I have herein inclosed my will as to this place,[1] the rest being settled already.[2] Again does my soul embrace thee and thine, and forever shall our spirits live together where no tears nor troubles shall divide or separate or grieve us, which is our country and lasting dwelling place; and blessed will you be if here you be strangers and sojourners, as were our fathers Abraham,

*View of Philadelphia City Hall with Statue of William Penn by Alexander Milne Calder, photograph taken from Logan Circle by Lewis W. Meehan.*

Isaac, and Jacob. Dearly I bid thee farewell, and my children, whom breed in the fear of the Lord and in the strict way of His holy Truth, and the Lord God Almighty bless, keep, and be with you forever. I am

Theirs and thine in that which
is not of this dying world,
Wm Penn

Pay my debts, though thou sell anything to do it, that what thee and my dear children have may be clear.[3] I should think well of thy coming and living here, where a sweet place and retired[4] is provided for thee and thine, this being the place God by His providence has given to me and my off-spring, and where is a fine people. Farewell, farewell my dearest and my lambs.

Yours in the best of love as God would have it,
Wm Penn

Live sparing, have little cumber,[5] teach the children love and humility to the people, and that my promises to them be in all fulfilled. T[homas] Lloyd, T[homas] Holme, J[ames] Harrison, C[hristopher] Taylor, J[ohn] Simcock, J[ames] Claypoole, R[obert] Turner, Sa[muel] Carpenter, with others, are the friends of my family and interest; and know this, that it is for thy children's good thou come, and by thy sweet, grave, and upright carriage and life among them thou introduce the children before thy departure into those capacities they are like to have in the land; else am[bition?] and avarice in some may [hurt?] their just interest. I l[eave?] all with the Lord, and thee [to?] his will, to whom b[ehold?] with eternal praise . . . both here and fo[r ever?] again.

Thine in [the?] will of God,
Wm Penn

ALS. Pierpont Morgan Library, New York City. (*PWP*, 2:587-88). The last part of this letter is badly torn, and the editors have inserted WP's probable words in square brackets, and replaced one brief indecipherable passage with an ellipsis.

1. Doc. 99, above.
2. WP's will made in England, referred to in doc. 99, but now lost.
3. See doc. 39, n. 3, and the headnote to doc. 41, above.
4. Pennsbury Manor. See doc. 98, above.
5. Burdensome business.

# 101 §

## *Farewell to Pennsylvania*

WP'S farewell address may seem at first glance to be a piece of sentimental piety, but on closer inspection one finds that he is saying something important. In a few short paragraphs the Quaker proprietor sums up his highest hopes and his deepest fears. Quoting from a series of scriptural passages that his fellow Pennsylvanians knew by heart, WP reminds the colonists that they have been commissioned by God to build a very special society, and that with WP himself returning to England, they are now fully in charge and fully responsible. He also points out that hostile critics, who suppose the Quakers to be irreligious and ungovernable, are eager to see this experiment fail. Thus, like the Puritan John Winthrop in Massachusetts fifty years before, WP urges his fellow Quakers in Pennsylvania to carry on with the work of building their godly city on a hill, "many eyes being upon you." WP closes with a prayer of special fervency for the city of Philadelphia — and here he is not merely addressing the townspeople on the Delaware River; he is also evoking the ideal that inspired his whole American plan, the concept of a religious community joined in brotherly love. For as WP sailed away in 1684, he knew just how rare it was in human experience for men and women to sustain such a society and to live together (as WP puts it) in a state of "grace, mercy, and peace."

From on board the ketch *Endeavour,* 12 August 1684[1]

Dear Friends and people

My love and my life is to you and with you, and no waters can quench it nor distance wear it out or bring it to an end.[2] I have been with you, cared over you, and served you with unfeigned love, and you are beloved of me and near to me beyond utterance. I bless you in the name and power of the Lord, and may God bless you with His righteousness, peace, and plenty all the land over. Oh, that you would eye Him in all, through all, and above all the works of your hands, and let it be your first care how you may glorify God in your undertakings; for to a blessed end are you brought hither and if you see and keep but in the sense of that providence, your coming, staying, and improving will be sanctified. But if any forget God and call not upon His name in Truth, He will pour out His plagues upon them and they shall know who it is that judges the children of men.

Oh, now you are come to a quiet land, provoke not the Lord to trouble it. And now liberty and authority are with you and in your hands, let the government be on His shoulders, in all your spirits, that you may rule for Him, to whom the princes of this world will one day esteem it their honor to govern under and serve in their places. I cannot but say, when these things come weightily into my mind, as the apostle [Peter] did of old, what manner of persons ought we to be in all godly conversation.[3] Truly the name and glory of the Lord are deeply concerned in you as to the discharge of yourselves in your present stations, many eyes being upon you. And remember that as we have been belied[4] about disowning the true religion, so of all government. And that to behold us exemplary and Christian in the use of that, will not only stop our enemies, but minister conviction to many on that account prejudiced. Oh, that you may see and know that service and do it for the Lord in this your day.

And thou Philadelphia, the virgin settlement of this province, named before thou were born,[5] what love, what care, what service, and what travail have there been to bring thee forth and preserve thee from such as would abuse and defile thee. Oh, that thou may be kept from the evil that would overwhelm thee, that faithful to the God of thy mercies in the life of righteousness thou may be preserved to the end. My soul prays to God for thee that thou may stand in thy day of trial, that thy children may be blessed of the Lord and thy people saved by His power. My love to thee has been great and the remembrance of thee affects my heart and my eye. The God of eternal strength keep and preserve thee to His glory and thy peace.

So dear friends, my love again salutes you all, wishing that grace, mercy, and peace with all temporal blessings may abound richly among you. So says, so prays,

Your friend and lover in the Truth,
Wm Penn

ALS. HSP. (*PWP*, 2:590-91).

1. WP had boarded the *Endeavour* on or before 6 Aug. 1684 (see doc. 97, above), and the ship may have already started down the Delaware River by the date of this farewell, because WP sat in Council at Lewes, Del., on 14 Aug. 1684.

2. WP incorporates several biblical passages into this and the following paragraph, from the Song of Solomon (8:7), 1 Chronicles (4:40), Isaiah (9:6), 1 Corinthians (2:6,8), and 2 Peter (3:11).

3. "Conversation" commonly meant "conduct" or "behavior" in the seventeenth century.

4. Misrepresented.

5. WP named Philadelphia on 28 Oct. 1681, before the first commissioners whom he had appointed to establish the city had reached America. See doc. 24, above.

# Abbreviations

| | |
|---|---|
| AD | Autograph document, not signed. |
| ADf | Autograph draft. |
| ADS | Autograph document (deed, will, diary, etc.), signed. |
| ALS | Autograph letter, signed. |
| APS | American Philosophical Society, Philadelphia. |
| Copy | Contemporary (seventeenth-century) copy. |
| D | Document in the hand of a clerk, not signed by the author. |
| DS | Document in the hand of a clerk, signed by the author. |
| FLL | Library of the Religious Society of Friends, London. |
| HSP | Historical Society of Pennsylvania, Philadelphia. |
| LBC | Letterbook copy (as from James Claypoole's Letterbook, 1681-1684, HSP). |
| LCP | Library Company of Philadelphia. |
| LS | Letter in the hand of a clerk, signed by the author. |
| MBE | Minute book entry (as from the Privy Council Minute Book). |
| *PMHB* | *The Pennsylvania Magazine of History and Biography.* |
| PRO | Public Record Office, London. |
| *PWP* | Mary Maples Dunn and Richard S. Dunn, eds., *The Papers of William Penn* (Philadelphia, 1981-    ), multivolume series in progress. |
| Transcript | Modern (eighteenth-twentieth century) copy. |
| *WMQ* | *The William and Mary Quarterly.* |

# Glossary

*ague:* a fever, with chills and shivering.

*alienation:* the selling of land.

*almsman:* a person receiving poor relief.

*assign:* any person to whom one leaves land or other wealth; usually used to indicate non-family heirs.

*bailiff:* a local official who maintained the jail, brought prisoners into court, and kept order there. This official sometimes acted as a mayor, as in early Germantown.

*bill of exchange:* a written order to pay a specified sum of money to a specified person. Since there were no banks in early America, a bill of exchange performed the function of a modern check.

*borough:* an incorporated city or town, with its own officials and bylaws, and, in England, the right to send representatives to Parliament.

*burgess:* a representative in a legislative body.

*certificate of marriage:* a statement by a Quaker monthly meeting that a couple was free of any commitments or obligations that might prevent their marrying.

*certificate of removal:* a statement from a Quaker monthly meeting that one of its members was of good standing, and free to join a local Quaker meeting in another area.

*Charter of Liberties:* the common name for either the first or the second *Frame of Government.*

*Committee of Trade and Plantations* (also called the *Lords of Trade*): the advisory body which supervised trade between England and the colonies, reviewed colonial laws, and advised the king and Privy Council on colonial policy.

*copyholder:* an English tenant farmer who held a secure lease to a plot of land, with the right to pass the lease on to his heir, but without any right to sell the land.

*corn:* any edible grain, especially wheat, rye, or barley; Indian corn was generally called maize by seventeenth-century English settlers.

*court-baron:* a court held on a manor, presided over by the lord of the manor or his deputy, in which civil disputes, cases of small debts, misdemeanors, and trespasses involving the tenants of the manor were resolved.

*distraint,* or *distress:* the legal seizure of possessions, either for non-payment of rent, taxes, or tithes, or to cover a fine. Quakers frequently had their property distrained when they refused to pay tithes (see below) or attend Church of England services.

*divers:* a common seventeenth-century term meaning "several"; to be distinguished from *diverse,* meaning "various," or "different."

*duffel:* coarse woolen cloth.

*enfeoffment, feoffment:* a grant of a plot of land (a fief), to be held in fee simple (see below).

*entail, entailment:* the restriction of the ownership of land to a specified succession of heirs.

*exchequer:* the tax-collecting office in England, in charge of managing most of the accounts of the central government.

*factor:* an agent who conducts business for an employer, who is generally at a distance; for example, an English merchant would employ an American factor.

*fathom:* a unit of measure equal to six feet.

*fee simple:* a type of land tenure whereby the owner can lease or sell his land, or leave it to his heirs, without any feudal obligations. This was the most advantageous type of land ownership in England and the English colonies.

*feoffee:* a person to whom a plot of land (a fief) is granted in fee simple.

*feudal:* laws and customs, arising out of the medieval (c. A.D. 500-1500) property system, which governed the holding of land and the relations between the feudal lord and his tenant (or liegeman).

*First Purchaser:* one of the persons who bought the first half-million acres of Pennsylvania sold by William Penn between July 1681 and April 1682. The owners of this land had rights to city lots in Philadelphia which were not extended to later purchasers.

*flux* (or *bloody flux*): dysentery.

*frankpledge, view of:* the yearly assembly of freemen on a manor which evolved into a court to resolve certain disputes on the manor.

*free and common socage:* a form of land tenure in England that originally involved feudal service by the tenant to his lord. By the seventeenth century, however, the tenant's only obligation was a small annual quitrent, and this land tenure was virtually the same as tenure in *fee.*

*freeholder:* any owner of land in fee simple. In Pennsylvania, nearly all adult male freeholders could vote; in England, small freeholders could not.

*fustian:* coarse cloth made of cotton and flax.

*Great Seal:* a seal affixed by the king to royal charters and parliamentary laws in England. Governors in American colonies used similar seals.

*gulden:* a Dutch coin, worth about two shillings; it was often called a guilder, or gilder, by the English.

*headright:* a grant of land awarded to each master for every servant brought to Pennsylvania, and to each servant who came to Pennsylvania, at the termination of his service.

*hereditament:* land, whether urban or rural, which could be willed by its owner to heirs, or be sold.

*House of Commons:* the lower, elected house of Parliament in England. It was the model for all legislative assemblies in British North America.

*House of Lords:* the upper house of Parliament in England, consisting of hereditary noblemen and the appointed bishops of the Church of England.

*hundred:* a subdivision of a county. The three lower counties (Delaware) were divided into hundreds, but the counties of Pennsylvania were not.

*indenture:* a contract which transferred land from one party to another, or which obligated one party to pay another for some goods or services.

*indentured servant:* a man or woman in the British Isles or Europe who was obligated to serve a master for several years in America in return for passage to the colonies and room and board for the term of the contract.

*kersey:* woolen fabric, often ribbed.

*knight's service:* military or other service that a knight was bound to render as a condition for holding his land from a lord or the king. Freeholders did not have this obligation.

*lease and release:* a combined transaction whereby a seller first agreed to lease land to a buyer for a long term—usually several hundred years—and then to sell the land outright. The two documents were usually agreed to on consecutive days, with the lease meant to secure the buyer against any loss if the seller discovered he did not have the right to sell the land outright.

*letters patent* (or simply *patent*): a document issued by a person in authority which confers a right, or a title to property.

*liberty lands:* bonus grants by WP to the First Purchasers, in the area which is now North Philadelphia.

*liege:* bound to render feudal service to another person. The term was usually applied to the inferior landholder, a liegeman, who owed service or homage to a superior landholder, a liege lord.

*manor:* a tract of land whose owner, called the lord of the manor, could exercise certain feudal rights over his tenants, particularly the right to hold court to decide all civil disputes among the tenants.

*morris dances:* dances in costume, like mummers' dances.

*Navigation Acts:* acts of Parliament, passed in 1660, 1663, and 1673, that regulated all trade between the English colonies and the rest of the world, and forced most trade to be conducted directly between England and the colonies.

*osnaburg:* coarse linen cloth.

*penny* (abbreviated *d.*): the smallest regularly used unit of English money. Twelve pence made a shilling.

*pound sterling* (abbreviated £): the largest unit of English silver money. Its value, in the seventeenth century, was worth at least $100 in current purchasing power.

*Privy Council:* the king of England's supreme advisory and executive body.

*Privy Seal:* a seal affixed to official documents upon order of England's Privy Council. Certain documents needed only this seal to be valid; others, like WP's charter to Pennsylvania, also required the Great Seal.

*proprietary, the:* sometimes used for the proprietor of a colony.

*proprietary colony:* a colony owned by one man or family, or by a few men, who had the right to govern it and to hold, lease, or sell all land in it.

*Quaker meeting for worship:* the gathering of Friends on first day (Sunday) for the prayer, meditation, and informal sermons that made up the Quaker worship service.

*Quaker monthly meeting:* a business meeting of the Religious Society of Friends, with jurisdiction over a relatively small area, usually several towns or townships. These meetings settled controversies among Friends, disciplined wayward members, supervised Quaker charities, and managed the meeting's finances.

*Quaker yearly meeting:* a business meeting of prominent Friends from a large area—an entire colony or nation — to resolve major controversies between groups of Friends and to set out common policies for the coming year. The most important meetings for WP were the Philadelphia Yearly Meeting, which included all of Pennsylvania and New Jersey, and the London Yearly Meeting, which included all of England.

*quitrent:* a small feudal obligation, which all Pennsylvania landowners were required to pay WP, even though they owned their land in fee simple. It was intended as a land tax to help support the government.

*quorum:* the number of members that must be present in any law-making body to make its decisions valid and official.

*register:* a book for recording official transactions. Each county in Pennsylvania kept three sets of registers: for business and land transactions; for marriages; and for indentured servant contracts.

*remise:* to release from a legal obligation.

*replevin:* the return of goods seized by distrain or distress, upon the defendant's giving security that he will submit his case to a court for resolution.

*royalty:* a right to profits from minerals, fisheries, and other assets attached to land grants.

*sachems* (or *sachemakers*): leaders, or "kings," of Indian tribes.

*scot and lot:* a municipal tax levied on most free heads of families in English towns. Those paying the tax in England usually had the right to vote, as did all men who paid municipal taxes in Pennsylvania under the first and second *Frames of Government.*

*seigniory:* a manor; land on which a lord had special rights over his tenants.

*seisin* (also *livery of seisin*): the act of legally taking possession of a tract of land by physically taking some object from that land.

*serge:* ribbed woolen cloth.

*shallop:* a small boat propelled by oars or sails, used for river and coastal travel.

*shilling* (abbrevated *s.*): a unit of English money containing twelve pence; there were twenty shillings in a pound sterling (£). In the seventeenth century a shilling was worth about $5 in modern American currency.

*stroudwater:* blue and red woolen cloth made in England.

*tenement:* land occupied by a renter or leaseholder.

*tithe:* a tax, traditionally one-tenth of all income, levied on all persons for the support of the established church in England, and in European countries.

*viz.:* an abbreviated Latin word meaning "namely."

*wampum:* cylindrical beads of shell or fishbone, carried on strings or thongs, used as money by Delaware Valley Indians.

*watch and ward:* guard duty in towns, an obligation that was usually imposed on all adult white male inhabitants.

*writ:* a legal order directing an official to carry out a particular act.

# Suggestions for Further Reading

General

Dunn, Richard S., and Dunn, Mary Maples, eds. *The World of William Penn.* Philadelphia, forthcoming.

Hawke, David. *The Colonial Experience.* Indianapolis, 1966.

Myers, Albert Cook, ed. *Narratives of Early Pennsylvania, West New Jersey, and Delaware, 1630-1707.* New York, 1912.

Nash, Gary B. *Red, White, and Black: The Peoples of Early America.* Englewood Cliffs, N. J., 1974.

Zuckerman, Michael, ed. *Friends and Neighbors: Group Life in America's First Plural Society.* Philadelphia, 1982.

WP Biography

Dunn, Mary Maples. *William Penn: Politics and Conscience.* Princeton, 1967.

Jenkins, Howard M. *The Family of William Penn, Founder of Pennsylvania, Ancestry and Descendants.* Philadelphia, 1899.

Peare, Catherine Owens. *William Penn.* Philadelphia, 1956.

Trussell, John B., Jr. *William Penn, Architect of a Nation.* Harrisburg, Pa., 1980.

Development of Pennsylvania

Bronner, Edwin B. *William Penn's "Holy Experiment."* New York, 1962.

Browning, Charles H. *Welsh Settlement of Pennsylvania.* Philadelphia, 1912.

Illick, Joseph E. *Colonial Pennsylvania: A History.* New York, 1976.

Lemon, James T. *The Best Poor Man's Country.* Baltimore, 1972.

Levy, Barry John. "'Tender Plants': Quaker Farmers and Children in the Delaware Valley, 1681-1735," *Journal of Family History,* 3:116-35.

Nash, Gary B. "The Free Society of Traders and the Early Politics of Pennsylvania." *PMHB,* 89:147-73.

_____. *Quakers and Politics: Pennsylvania, Government in Pennsylvania.* New 1681-1726. Princeton, 1968.

Pennypacker, Samuel W. "The Settlement of Germantown, and the Causes Which Led to It." *PMHB,* 4:1-41.

Shepherd, William Robert. *History of Proprietary Government in Pennsylvania.* New York, 1896.

Sheppard, Walter Lee, Jr., ed. *Passengers and Ships Prior to 1684.* Baltimore, 1970.

Planning of Philadelphia

Dunn, Mary Maples, and Dunn, Richard S. "The Founding, 1681-1701." *Phil-*

404

*adelphia: A 300-Year History.* Ed. Russell F. Weigley *et al.*, pp. 1-32. New York, 1982.

Nash, Gary B. "City Planning and Political Tension in the Seventeenth Century: The Case of Philadelphia." *Proceedings of the American Philosophical Society,* 112:54-73.

Roach, Hannah Benner. "The Planting of Philadelphia: A Seventeenth-Century Real Estate Development." *PMHB,* 92:3-47, 143-94.

Ryerson, Richard Alan. "William Penn's Commissioners." *Pennsylvania Genealogical Magazine,* 32:95-117.

Scharf, J. Thomas, and Westcott, Thompson. *History of Philadelphia, 1609-1884.* Philadelphia, 1884, Vol. 1.

Quakers

Balderston, Marion, ed. *James Claypoole's Letter Book, London and Philadelphia, 1681-1684.* San Marino, 1967.

Braithwaite, William C. *The Beginnings of Quakerism.* London, 1912.

——————————. *The Second Period of Quakerism.* 2d ed., ed. Henry J. Cadbury. Cambridge, 1961.

Penney, Norman, ed. *The Journal of George Fox.* 2 vols. Cambridge, 1911.

——————————. *The Short Journal and Itinerary Journals of George Fox.* Cambridge, 1925.

Tolles, Frederick B. *Meeting House and Counting House: The Quaker Merchants of Colonial Philadelphia, 1682-1763.* Chapel Hill, 1948.

Vann, Richard T. *The Social Development of English Quakerism, 1655-1755.* Cambridge, Mass., 1969.

Delaware

Munroe, John A. *Colonial Delaware: A History.* Millwood, N.Y., 1978.

Scharf, J. Thomas. *History of Delaware, 1609-1888.* 2 vols. Philadelphia, 1888.

Baltimore Controversy

Browne, William Hand, ed. *Archives of Maryland.* Baltimore, 1887, 5:371-460.

Garrison, Hazel Shields. "Cartography of Pennsylvania Before 1800," *PMHB,* 59:255-83.

Scaife, Walter B. "The Boundary Dispute Between Maryland and Pennsylvania," *PMHB,* 9:241-71.

Wainwright, Nicholas B. "Tale of a Runaway Cape: The Penn-Baltimore Agreement of 1732," *PMHB,* 87:251-93.

Frame of Government

Landsman, Ned C., "'Of the Grand Assembly or Parliament': Thomas Rudyard's Critique of an Early Draft of *The Frame of the Government of Pennsylvania*," *PMHB,* 105:469-81.

Nash, Gary B. "The Framing of Government in Pennsylvania: Ideas in Conflict with Reality," *WMQ,* 3d ser., 23:183-209.

Indians

Jennings, Francis P. "Glory, Death, and Transfiguration: The Susquehannock Indians in the Seventeenth Century," *Proceedings of the American Philosophical Society,* 112:15-53.

————————. "Miquon's Passing: Indian-European Relations in Colonial Pennsylvania, 1674 to 1755." Ph.D. diss., University of Pennsylvania, 1965.

Kraft, Herbert C., ed. *A Delaware Indian Symposium*. Harrisburg, 1974.

Trelease, Allen W. *Indian Affairs in Colonial New York: The Seventeenth Century.* Ithaca, 1960.

Trigger, Bruce G., ed. *Handbook of the North American Indians, Volume 15: Northeast.* Washington, D.C., 1978.

Wallace, Paul A. W. *Indians in Pennsylvania*. Harrisburg, 1968.

Weslager, C. A. *The Delaware Indians: A History.* New Brunswick, N. J., 1972.

# Index

Page references to identifications are set in **bold face type.**

Briggs, John, 193, 230
Bringston, Andrew, 273; *see also* Binkson, Andros
Brinkloe, John, 230, 273
*Bristol Factor* (ship), 197n
Brockholls, Anthony, 56n, 81, 187, **188n,** 191n
Brookes, Edward, 148, **152n**
Brown, Daniel, 230, 273
Brown, George, **352n**
Bucks County, Pa., Assembly members for, 230; letter to tenants in, 338; seal of, 247
Burke, Richard, **25n;** letter from, 25; letter to, 342-44; and Penn-Baltimore dispute, 363, 364
Byllynge, Edward, **90**

Cabot, John, 329
Cabot, Sebastian, 329
Caleb (Biblical), 59, 65n
Callowhill, Thomas, 85, **86n**
Calvert, Cecil, second lord Baltimore, 286n
Calvert, Charles, third lord Baltimore, **21,** 326; letter to, 57; letters from, 154, 342-44; claims lower counties, 302; and tobacco duties, 367n; *see also* Penn-Baltimore boundary dispute
Calvert, George, first lord Baltimore, **304n,** 333n
Calvert, Jane, lady Baltimore, **57n**
Calvert, Philip, **304n**
Camm, Thomas, 216-18, **218n**
Canada, emperor of; letter to, 156
Cann, John, 193, 230, 233, 237, 261, 369-71
Cantwell, Edmund, 187, **188n,** 229, 238, 242, 245, 246, 260, 262, 273n, 332n
Cape Cornelis, Del., 188n
Cape Henlopen, Del., 187, 188n, 332
Capel, Arthur, first earl of Essex, **296n**
Carmarthenshire, Wales, 176
Carolina, colony of, 330; boundary with Virginia, 331
Carpenter, Samuel, 308, **341n,** 383n, 394; appointed commissioner, 387; requests river frontage in Phila., 367-69
Carteret, Elizabeth, 171n
Carteret, Sir George, 171n
Chamberlain, Hugh, 75
Chambers, Benjamin, 212, **216n**
Charles II, 372; WP's petition to, 22-26, 30-32; and Pa. charter, 20, 21; names Pa., 36, 55; writes to lord Baltimore, 57; letter to, 297-98; and Penn-Baltimore dispute, 289, 344; and Rye House Plot, 295, 365; converses with Markham, 364-65
Charter of Liberties; see *Frame of Government*
Chesapeake Bay, 66n, 153; importance to WP of, 277-80; in Penn-Baltimore dispute, 284, 285
Chester (Upland), Pa., 81, 83, **85n,** 174-75; Assembly at (Dec. 1682), 8-9, 188, 192; Assembly members for, 230; letter to ten-

ants in, 338; seal of, 247
Chesterfield, earl of, 344
Chicheley, Sir Thomas, 24
Choptank River, Md., 285
Christiana Bridge, fort at, 369, 371
Christiana, Del., 317
Church of England, 3
Clarendon, earl of; *see* Hyde, Henry
Claridge, Samuel, **205n**
Clark, Benjamin, 58, **65n,** 91
Clarke, William, 191, **192n,** 193, 304n, 391; and Penn-Baltimore dispute, 284-86; at Council, 229, 240-243, 247, 249, 256-58, 260; on Council committee, 238, 245, 250, 255; letter from, 284-86; letter to, 288-89; signs revised *Frame*, 272
Claypoole, Abigail, 181n
Claypoole, Edward, **179;** letters to, 179-181, 340-41
Claypoole, George, **181n**
Claypoole, Helena Mercer, **181n,** 209, 210, **211n**
Claypoole, James, 10, 144, **151n,** 201, 308, 323n, 383n, 394; appointed commissioner, 387; and Free Society, 148; letters from, 179-181, 208-11, 340-41
Claypoole, John, **181n,** 209, 210, **211n**
Claypoole, Joseph, **181n**
Claypoole, Nathaniel, **181n**
Claypoole, Wingfield, 180, 181n
Clayton, William, 229, 239, 245, 248, 250, 255, 256, 262, 272
Clayton, William, Jr., 215
Clowes (Clows), John, 230, 272
Clutterbuck, Sir Thomas, **211n**
Cock, Eric, 197
Cock, Gabriel, 213
Cock, John, 212, 215
Cock, Lasse, **144,** 188, 229, 239, 242, 260, 288
Cock, Mouns, 197
Cock, Peter, 204, 213
Cock, Peter, Jr., 197, 215
Cole, Edward, **181n,** 209
Columbus, Christopher, 329
Commission of Revenue, 332n
Committee of Trade; *see* Lords of Trade
Committee of Trade and Plantations; *see* Lords of Trade
Commons, House of, 228, 234
Commonwealthmen, 96
Compton, Henry, bishop of London, 24n, 33, 303, 344
Compton, John, **178n**
"Concessions to the First Purchasers," 218n
*Concord* (ship), 210, 340
Connecticut, colony of, 330
Cooke, John, 55n
Cornelison, Harmon, 329
Cox, Laurence; *see* Cock, Lasse
Coxe, Thomas, 76
Craven, William, earl of, 344

describes, 292, 308, 312-17; letters to, 88, 156; negotiations with, 155-61; sell venison to colonists, 176; Pastorius describes, 356-57, 360; *see also* Lenni Lenape Indians, Susquehannock Indians, Mohawk Indians, Iroquois Confederacy

Ingelo, Richard, 226, 272, 304n

Irish purchasers, 205

Irons, Simon, 230, 273

Iroquois Confederacy, 155, 294, 307; and Susquehanna Valley negotiations, 325-26

Jacob (Biblical), 167

Jacob, Francis, 215

Jacob, Widow, 215

Jamaica, 59, 65n

James, John, 243, 245, 254

Janottowe, 156, 158

*Jeffrey* (ship), 179n

Jeffries, William, 210

Jenkins, Sir Leoline, **24n,** 33, 55n, 344

Jennings, Samuel, 376, **377n**

Jethro (Biblical), 200

Jobson, Samuel, 75

John, John ap, 375, 376, **376-77n**

Johnson, Banke, 213

Johnson, Ewen, 366

Johnson, Neils, 213

Jones, Charles, Jr., 85, **86n**

Jones, Daniel, 193

Jones, Edward, 10, 144, **174,** 311; letter from, 174-77

Jones, Griffith, 75, 195, **196n,** 351, 383n; Assembly member, 230; at General Assembly, 233, 235, 240, 242, 244, 245, 248, 249

Jones, Jonathan, 174, 177

Jones, Martha, 174, 177

Jones, Mary, 86n

Jones, Mary Wynne, **174**

Jones, Richard, 364

Jones, Thomas, 220, **221n**

Joseph (Biblical), 167

Joshua (Biblical), 59, 65n, 169

Josiah (Biblical), 167

Judah, tribe of, 199

Justis, Charles, 213

Justis, Hance, 213

Justis, Mouns, 213

Justison, Justa, 213

Kekerappamand, 158, 160

Kekerappan, 336

Kennerly, James, 281

Kennerly, William; letter from, 281

Kent County, Del., 189; petitions for union with Pa., 192-93; Assembly members for, 230; seal of, 247

King, Thomas, 351, **352**

King, Walter, 230, 242, 251, 258

Kingsessing, Pa., 212

Kipshaven, John, 230, 272

Kowyockhicken, 158

Krefeld, Germany, 308, 335; emigrants from, 354

Kyn, Jören, **85n**

Lamb, Hugh, 75

Lamb, Patrick, **190-91n**

Land, Samuel, 371

Langhorne, Thomas, **218n,** 325; letter to, 216-18

*Laws Agreed Upon in England* (by WP, 1682), 139n, 140n, 192; summarized, 119-20; text of, 128-33; electoral system, 128-29; judicial system, 129-30, 131; religious toleration in, 132; moral standards in, 132; replaced by Pa. General Assembly (1683), 226

Laykan, Peter Nilsson, 197

Legge, George, baron Dartmouth, 363, **366n**

Lehnmann, Philip Theodore, 85, **86n,** 156, 280n; signs revised *Frame,* 272; and Penn-Baltimore dispute, 289; appointed commissioner, 387

Lenni Lenape Indians, **86,** 89n, 143; negotiations with, 144-45; deeds from, 156-60, 287-88; described by WP, 312-17; described by Pastorius, 356-57, 360; *see also* Indians

Lewger, William, 180

Lewis, Henry, 196, **197n,** 273

Lincey, Thomas, 243, 245

Llewellin, John, 304n

Lloyd, Charles, 221n, 374, 375, 376, **376n**

Lloyd, Mary Jones, 360n, **376n**

Lloyd, Thomas, 308, **360n,** 376, 391, 394; WP's commission to, 388-89; appointed commissioner, 387

Locke, John, 139n, 283n

Locket's eating house, London, 190, **191n**

Lodge, Esther, 212n

Lodge, Robert, **211-12**

Lodwick, Francis, **283n**

Loe, Thomas, 67n

London, bishop of; *see* Compton, Henry

London, England, 61, 66n

Long Island, N. Y., 330

Longworth, Roger, 287

Lords of Trade (Committee of Trade and Plantations), **21;** and WP's petition for Pa., 24, 26; and Pa. charter, 21, 29, 32-36; minutes of, 24, 33; and Penn-Baltimore dispute, 299-303, 328-32, 342-44, 363, 365, 366-67n; and lower counties, 289n

Love, Henry, 213

Lower, Mary Fell, 325

Lower, Thomas, 325

Lowestoft, battle of, 41, 49n

Lowther, Anthony (brother-in-law of WP), **295,** 296

Lowther, Margaret Penn (sister of WP), **295;**

Owen, C., 220
Owen, Robert, 177, **178n**
Oxford University, 67

P., Rich., 177
Palmer, Elizabeth, 383n
Parker, Alexander, 4, 201, **202n,** 208
Parliament (England), 116
Partridge, Susanna, 204n
Paschall, Thomas, 213
Paschall, William, 213
Passyunk, Pa., 212, 313
Pastorius, Francis Daniel, 10, 308, **335, 336n;**
    author of *Positive Information from America,*
    353-60
Patte, Richard, 332n
Paul, Porten, 173
Pearce, Thomas, 237
Peirce, Edward, 148, **151n**
Penington, Isaac, 165, **171n**
Penington, Mary Proude Springett, 143, 165,
    **171n**
Penmaenmawr, Wales, 54, **55n**
Penn, Bucks., 54, **55n**
Penn, Giles, 23n
Penn, Gulielma Maria Springett (first wife of
    WP), 19, 143, **170n,** 204, 366; letters to, 164-
    70, 392-94; letter from, 324-25; in WP's will,
    390-91; Claypoole visits, 209
Penn, Hannah Callowhill (second wife of WP),
    86n, 170n
Penn, Joan Gilbert, 23n
Penn, Laetitia (daughter of WP), 19, **170n;** in
    WP's will, 390-91; letter to, 172
Penn, Lady Margaret Jasper Vanderschuren
    (mother of WP), **23n;** death of, 143, 146
Penn, Springett (son of WP), 19, **170n;** in WP's
    will, 390-91; letter to, 171
Penn, William (identified in text as *WP*): CA-
    REER (topics listed in order of first appear-
    ance): hopes for Pa., 3, 5, 53, 54-55, 217-
    18; early career, 3-5; and Quakers, 4-5, 19;
    character of, 5; finances, 5, 19, 71, 143, 144-
    45, 164, 165-66, 167, 170-71n, 172-73, 290,
    338, 344n; chronology (1680-84), 14-15; and
    Pa. settlers, 55, 58, 218-20, 282-83, 349-50,
    374; prepares to go to Pa., 143-44; and wife
    and children, 164-72, 209, 324; report of
    departure for Pa., 178-79; arrives in Amer-
    ica, 185-88; property in Pa., 202n; rumors
    about, 208, 309-10, 343; and government
    of Pa., 216-18; and General Assembly
    (1683), 225-62 *passim;* signs second *Frame,*
    259; interest in science, 282; Pastorius de-
    scribes, 355; land policy, 357-58, 377-82; as
    governor, 359, 361-62, 374; returns to
    England, 387-88; will of, 390-91; farewell
    to Pennsylvania, 394-96
LETTERS, INSTRUCTIONS, AND COMMISSIONS

FROM WP: to John Aubrey, 282-83; to
Charles, lord Baltimore, 57, 278-80; to Jasper Batt, 199-202; to William Blathwayt and
Francis Gwyn, 190; to John Blaykling and
others, 216-18; to Charles II, 297-98; to
Committee of Trade (Lords of Trade), 299-
303; to William Crispin, John Bezar, and
Nathaniel Allen, 83-86; to Thomas, lord
Culpeper, 203-4; to Philip Ford, 188; to
James Graham and William Haige, 294-95;
to James Harrison, 77-78; to Thomas
Holme, 205; to the Indians, 88, 156; to the
inhabitants of Pa., 55; to justices of the
peace, 194; to Thomas Lloyd and Council,
388-89; to William Markham, 89, 328-32;
to William Markham, William Crispin, and
John Bezar, 89; to William Markham, James
Harrison, and William Clarke, 288-89; to
Maryland planters, 79-81; to Francis, lord
North, 292-93; to Gulielma Penn and chil-
dren, 164-72, 392-94; to Roger Roberts, 67;
to Anthony Sharp, 67; to Algernon Sidney, 111-12; to John Simcock and others,
369-71; to Ralph Smyth, 389; to tenants,
338; to Robert Turner, 54-55, 67; to John
Vines, 189; to Elizabeth Woodhouse, 146
LETTERS AND PETITIONS TO WP: from Robert
Barclay, 90-91; from Samuel Carpenter,
367-69; from William Clarke, 284-86; from
James Claypoole, 208-11; from Richard
Davies, 373-76; from Elizabeth Gretton,
361-62; from William Haige, 326-27; from
Joseph Harris, 218-20; from James Harri-
son, 351-52; from Thomas Holme, 205, 339;
from Margaret Lowther, 295-96; from
William Markham, 362-66; from Philadel-
phians and his reply, 377-82; from James
Walliam and John White, 334-35; from
William Welch, 350-51, 371-72
WP'S PUBLISHED WORKS: *Brief Account of the
Province of Pennsylvania,* 54, 78n; The *Frame
of Government and Laws Agreed Upon in
England,* 118-28; *Letter to the Free Society of
Traders,* 309-22; *No Cross, No Crown,* 143,
169; *Some Account of the Province of Pennsylvania,* 54, 58-65
WP'S UNPUBLISHED WORKS: "Certain Conditions or Concessions" to First Purchasers,
72-76, 218n; Frame of Government (draft),
109-110
Penn, Sir William (father of WP), 20, **23n,** 33n,
41, 49n; and WP, 3-4; crown's debt to, 21
Penn, William, Jr. (son of WP), 19, 76n, 86n,
**170n,** 357; in WP's will, 390-91; letter to,
172
Penn-Baltimore boundary dispute, 8-9, 21, 79,
81n, 152-54, 277-80, 307, 359, 388; Baltimore claims lower counties, 284-86, 334-
35, 342-44; WP sends commissioners to

negotiate with Baltimore, 288-89; WP and Lords of Trade, 299-303, 328-32; and Charles II, 344; Markham lobbies in London, 362-66; rebellion in lower counties, 349-51, 369-72

Penn-Mead trial, 113

Pennock, Christopher, **205n**

Pennsbury Manor, Pa., 77, 351-52, 387, 390, 394; WP's directions for, 389

Pennsylvania, charter of: 234; summarized, 39-41; text of, 41-49; negotiations for, 20-36; Darnall's outline for, 28-30; and Bishop of Durham clause, 28-29; WP's powers under, 28-30, 32-35; and *Frame*, 236; WP lists advantages of, 62

Pennsylvania, colony of: immigration to, 53-55, 63-65, 144, 163-64, 185, 281, 307-8, 339, 353-355; settlers in, 281, 317, 356, 373-76; ethnic make-up of, 335; WP's hopes for, 3, 5, 10, 19, 190; "a holy experiment," 77; Charles II names, 36, 55; land policy in, 62-63, 71-75, 77-78, 90, 357-58, 377-82; constitution of, 7, 95-97; government of, 9-10, 67, 169, 216-18, 318, 362; English law in, 74; judicial system in, 193-94; hunting and fishing rights in, 218, 244, 264n; tavern regulations in, 206-7, 286; customs duties in, 283, 290; boundaries of, 24, 30-32, 277-80, 299, 307, 334-35, 364; counties of, 318, 339; economic conditions in, 174, 176-77, 340-41; wages in, 174, 177; growth of, 277; WP describes, 203, 282, 292-93, 310-12; resources of, 62, 176-77, 217-18; creeks and rivers of, 318; Quaker meetings in, 217; lower counties petition for union with, 192-93; conflict with New York, 307; *see also* Penn-Baltimore boundary dispute, *Some Account . . .*

Pennsylvania Assembly: 7, 9, 200, 217, 218n; and *Frame of Government*, 118, 216; and Free Society of Traders, 147; at Upland (Chester), Pa. (Dec. 1682), 188, 189, 192; powers of, 227; members sign revised *Frame*, 272-73; *see also* Pennsylvania General Assembly

Pennsylvania General Assembly (March-April 1683): discussed and summarized, 225-28; text of minutes of, 229-62; declares loyalty to WP, 233; legislation ratified by, 250-54; grants WP impost, 283, 290

Pennsylvania Provincial Council: 200, 282, 387; and *Frame of Government*, 118; powers of, 227; members of, 229; members sign revised *Frame*, 272; defection in, 369; WP's commission to, 388-89; *see also* Pennsylvania General Assembly

Pennypack Creek, Pa., 287

Penrith, Cumberland, 54, **55n**

Pepys, Samuel, 4, 283n

Perth, earl of; *see* Drummond, James

Peterson, Andris, 213

Peterson, Hance, 213

Peterson, Renner, 213

Petition of Right, 106, **108n**

Petty, Sir William, **283n**

Philadelphia, 147, 174, 176, 177; WP names, 89; WP's plans for, 82-85, 204-5, 308, 318-22; Quaker meetings in, 194-96, 325; river frontage in, 219, 367-69, 381; lots in, 339, 357; merchants of, 350; Germans in, 357; Pastorius describes, 356; Charles II inquires about, 364-65; remonstrance from inhabitants of, 377-81; WP's prayer for, 396

Philadelphia County, Pa.; Assembly members for, 230; census of, 212-15; court of, 197; seal of, 247; letter to tenants in, 338

Philadelphia Monthly Meeting, **194;** minute of, 195-96

Philadelphia Yearly Meeting, 195

Phipps, Joseph, 230, 258, 273

Pickering, Charles, 249, 254, 262, **264n**

Pierce, Richard, 205n

Pigott, Sir Richard, **50n**

Playwicky, Pa., 157, **162n**

Pools Island, Md., 303, 304n

Poquessing Creek, Pa., 313

Powel, William, 75, 219, 220, **220n**

Pownall, Elinor, **164n**

Pownall, George, **164n**

Presbyterian Plot; *see* Rye House Plot

Privy Council (English), 21, 54, 344; and Pa. charter, 32-35

Pytechay, 158, 160

Quaker meetings in Pa., 194-96, 217, 325

Quakers; customs and beliefs of, 4, 89, 171n, 195-96, 206-8, 221n; persecution of, 208, 211n; WP's service to, 19; recruited to settle Pa., 53-55, 66-67; and government of Pa., 199-201, 202n; and slavery, 179, 180, 340; question WP's authority, 216-17; and Penn-Baltimore dispute, 284, 285; in Wales, 373

Rambo, Andrew, 215

Rambo, Gunnar, 197

Rambo, John, 215

Rambo, Peter, 197, 204, 215

Ramsey, Isle of Man, 163, **164n**

Rancocas, N. J., 313

Reese, Evan, 177, **178n**

Religious toleration, 19, 132, 217

Rhoads, John, 191, 193, 260, 273n, 329

Richardson, Francis, 209

Richardson, John; at General Assembly, 229, 237, 248-49, 256-60; on Council committee, 239, 245; on WP's executive committee, 262; signs revised *Frame*, 272; defection of, 369

Robartes, John, earl of Radnor, **24n, 304n**, 363, 365

68600

DATE DUE